Women's Ways of Leading

Dear Joyce -
You initiated this
book and have continued
enlightened leadership -

Linda Lambert & Mary E. Gardner

Linda   *Mary*

Cover
Public Statue by Mahmoud Mokhtar at Cairo University
The Awakening of Egypt
Photograph by Linda Lambert

First published by Dog Ear Publishing
4010 W. 86th Street, Ste H
Indianapolis, IN 46268
www.dogearpublishing.net

dog ear
PUBLISHING

ISBN: 978-160844-112-9

This book is printed on acid-free paper.

Printed in the United States of America

Dedication

p. 40 touching hearts, convincing minds, raising consciousness.

It is with great joy that we recognize and celebrate the lives of seven generations of women from our families, beginning with Mary Gardner's great grandmother, Ann Lydia and ending with Linda Lambert's great granddaughter, Emily. These are the women—great grandmother, grandmothers, mothers, ourselves, daughters, granddaughters and great-granddaughter—who have and will experience the profound tide of history ushering in women's rights and equality.

We wish to dedicate this book, *Women's Ways of Leading*, to all of our grandchildren and great grandchildren, young women and men alike, for it is they who will shape and enjoy the future envisioned herein. Linda's grandchildren are: Eric Morita, Jered Johnson, Jessica Fuller, Chloe Smock, Keely Lambert, Shannon Pintane, Ashley Lambert, Dylan Smock, Catherine Lambert, Madeline Lambert and John Lambert. Her great grandchildren are: Bradley and Emily Fuller. Mary's grandchildren are: Olivia DiNapoli, Claire Mulcahy, Henry DiNapoli, Ella Mulcahy, Grace DiNapoli, and Camille Mulcahy. The future is theirs.

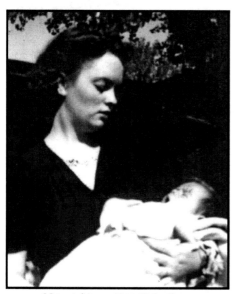

Mary and her mother, Eloise Jones

**Linda and her mother,
Lucretia Todd**

Linda's Mother

Linda's Grandmother

Mary's Daughters

*Linda's Daughter
and her Children*

*Linda's Step-Daughter
and Great-Grandson*

Linda's Step-Daughter

Contents

Acknowledgments

*I suppose there is one friend in the life of each of us who
seems not a separate person, however dear and beloved,
but an expansion, an interpretation of one's self, the very
meaning of one's soul.*
                    -Edith Wharton, writer, and the first woman to
                                    win the Pulitzer Prize, in 1921

First, we want to thank each other for continually deepening our understanding of reciprocity and friendship. During the last two decades, we have worked on two other books together, but it has been this study of women's leadership that has woven itself into the fabric of our relationship, as well as the fabric of our lives. We listen to each other, construct knowledge together and accept responsibility for mutual decisions. Within a landscape of laughter, we realize that a lightness of spirit is like a shared secret, a magnetic circle, sometimes blurring lines of separateness. We often laugh at ourselves as well, making fears and hesitations buoyant and fleeting. Our fervent wish for the reader is that sometime in her life such a working relationship will become possible.

We want to thank Linda's husband, Morgan Lambert, for his patience and editorial services, but especially for keeping the male perspective in the room. He was determined to save us from stereotypical thinking about men and women, and we hope that he succeeded most of the time. Morgan inspired us to believe that enlightened men were afoot in the world.

All of the women with whom we worked inspired us by telling us stories, asking provocative questions, modeling women's leadership. We thank you all. A few, like Emily Brizendine, Director of the Contra Costa Campus of California State University, East Bay and Ann Lieberman, a Fellow with the Carnegie Foundation, encouraged us by opening possibilities to work together and reading our initial findings; Jodi Servatius and Arthurlene Towner by bringing us together at Cal State Hayward in 1989.

The women in our interview study, from the San Francisco and Santa Cruz Bay Areas, Los Angeles, Seattle, and the province of Alberta, Canada, are too numerous to name. We trust these remarkable women will see their responses and stories reflected in this work.

A third group of women took the time to write their stories for us. In responding to the themes in this study, they were willing to be vulnerable, to generously and publicly share their struggles and achievements. These women include: Nancy Arnold, Sharifah Hadjarah Aziz, Julie Biddle, Bonita Calder, Martie Connor, Anne Conzemius, Sheila Jordon, Sumedha Mona Khannas, Kawsar Kouchok, Kristin Levine, Claire Mulcahy (Mary's granddaughter), Jan O'Neill, Cindy Ranii, Elizabeth Reilly, Barbara Ryan, April Smock (Linda's daughter), Barbara Storms, Janet Todd (Linda's sister-in-law), Judy Vandegrift, Katherine Wagner and Colleen Wilcox.

The outstanding women whose lives provided the cases that appear throughout this book deserve our appreciation as well. Their lives are open books, available to the hungry learner who would partake of their stories of struggles and achievements. Their stories lent a backdrop against which our themes and concepts could be made more vivid. We thank them for the places they occupy in history

And finally, we wish to thank editors Linda Jay Geldens and Linda and Dave Sibley for their insightful and responsive technical assistance in completing *Women's Ways of Leading*.

Women's Ways of Leading

An Introduction

*Empowering women today is perhaps the greatest legacy
we can bestow upon our children. Our daughters, watching in admiration, will be inspired to emulate our initiatives and excel in their chosen fields. Our sons, proud of
the positive changes they see not only in their families but
also in society, will recognize the value of empowering
women. Ultimately, we will all benefit from a more cohe-
sive and active global community renowned for respect-
ing each other and proud of the strong foundations we
have built together.*

-Queen Abdullah of Jordan

We were compelled to write this book. The voices of our mothers haunted us; our more than a century of lived experience informed
us; our research left open no other door. So here we are, two women
whose journeys have instilled us with passion, whose values have
defined us, whose evolution bound us to this question. The questions
before us are: What are women's ways of leading? And why does that
matter?

It has been a journey of discovery.

In our professions and in our writing, we have pursued leadership in all its forms. We have served in multiple leadership positions,
written several books on the topic and mentored the next generation
as role models and personal mentors. Our original mentors were our
mothers, separated by state, religion and experience...yet strikingly
similar. Both mothers were artists...artists from whom we learned to
appreciate beauty and understand imagination.   Linda's mother,
Lucretia Todd, would wake her in the early morning, wrap her in a
warm blanket and carry her out to a sacred, secret place in the dew-
soaked grass to watch the sunrise. Lucretia's paintings, poetry and
stories enriched life in her small Kansas town...a life that may have

otherwise been circumscribed by the ordinariness of women's lives in the 1950s. Among Lucretia's poems to Linda that signified the reciprocity of their relationship is the following:

> We've laughed together, cried together
> Had many good times too.
> I think I would be safe to say,
> I grew up with you.

As a child, Mary was enthralled by her mother's natural ability to write stories and plays, draw landscapes and flowers, recite poetry, and play the piano by ear. Although Eloise Jones, like Lucretia Todd, never finished high school, many rural women in Wyoming admired her wisdom and talents. Eloise was called upon to produce pageants for the Mormon Church, play the piano for congregational singing and paint scenery in windows for various celebrations.

Both of us have been educators who served in multiple roles: teacher, administrator, professor and consultant. As researchers, we have talked with hundreds of women throughout the United States, Canada, and around the world. During the last three decades, our writings set forth our changing notions of leadership that irretrievably and deeply connected leading and learning. Between us, we bring more than 80 years of experience to this endeavor. We have continually searched for a deeper understanding of women's ways of leading.

Yet leadership, especially women's leadership, remains both a provocative and an elusive idea to many. For generations, leadership referred to the person in power, the person in charge, the person in a particular authority role or designated position. Such roles included president and priest, chief executive officer and director, superintendent and principal, and, yes, father and brother. The insistence on attaching leadership to a specific person often excluded those who were not readily invited in, who were excluded by tradition, mythology, bigotry or fear. In the United States, those individuals were most often women and people of color.

As authors, we find it intriguing how definitions and assumptions can protect old kingdoms and generate a historical field littered with unfulfilled lives. For many women, dreams remained dreams and memories lay unformed. All but the most extraordinary of women notoriously stopped short of becoming their full selves. This arrested development effectively occurred in co-conspiracy with men who held an even more limited view of what the selves of women could be. Women permitted themselves to believe these limitations as well; they hesitated to open the gates.

This co-dependency or "social contract" imprisoned women by shaping the patterns of relationships within which they learned. These patterns—-the conventional entanglements of men and women—-limited learnings by parsing language, experience and opportunities. These limitations, argued Simone de Beauvoir inhibited the formation of fraternity between men and women. Without the reciprocity inherent in fraternity, she argued, ascendancy into a full intellectual and activist life could not occur.[1] Reciprocity, as we shall argue, is an essential dynamic in co-constructing leadership.

Once conform, once do what other people do because they do it, and lethargy steals over all the fine nerves and faculties of the soul.

–Virginia Woolf

Women still—although far less so—allow themselves to be defined by prevailing cultural priorities, such as home and hearth, as well as culturally crafted roles carved out by others. Immersed in a backwater of conflict in values and priorities, women find that the way out, the paths toward a more meaningful world, are often blocked by rusty gates. Many of these gates still require a passport stamped with traditional leadership skills: taking charge, being decisive, directing, dominating, delegating, commanding and controlling (being tough enough). It is time to open the gates more fully.

Studies of Women and Leadership

By the early 1990s, our cumulative experiences, drawn from the cultural milieu of childhood and barriers as young women teachers and administrators, led to a passion to study women leaders. By then, we were mentoring and observing graduate students, both men and women, serving in leadership roles. The different experiences and opportunities confronting our students moved us. Finally, we formalized insights from a lifetime of witnessing women who strived for leadership into a study of women's ways of leading.

The women with whom we talked were members of organizations of women leaders and women serving in leadership roles in education. Initially (1992), we spoke with 40 such women who were nominated by established women leaders and ourselves to participate in focus groups. From 1994-2003, we repeated the study with 300 women in the United States and Canada. We sought to understand how and why these women came into leadership, who influenced and supported them, what they valued, the unique struggles they encountered, what turning points made leadership compellingly necessary and allowed them to gather their own insights and beliefs and move them to action. In 2007, we duplicated the study with a group of 44 Moslem women at a regional leadership conference in Malaysia.

Over these past four decades, a growing body of research about human developmental and educational philosophy[2] supports our findings. Significant perspectives and themes emerged from our initial study...themes that would formulate the replication of the study throughout the United States and Canada. In Chapter One, these concepts will merge into a *Framework for the Development of Women Leaders.*

In the decade that followed our initial study, we began to investigate other career fields as well...business, the arts, science, government, sports and health. We were particularly intrigued by women who supported other women as mentors, models and pioneers in these fields. We investigated their struggles and conflicts. The stories of women in all stages of development, all situations of conflict and challenge, weave themselves throughout this text. We also investigated the lived experiences of hundreds of extraordinary women of international renown and selected those stories most nearly exemplifying the themes in our original study.

The study of women leaders in education was an experience in shifting consciousness for both the participants and us, requiring the redirection of re-examined lives more consciously toward leadership pursuits. To our delight, the study of women of international distinction affirmed the common collective experience of women.

From the passionate lives of these women leaders, echoed in focus groups, conferences and seminars, biographies and stories, we extracted the leadership perspectives, themes and skills that form the basis for this book. These perspectives and themes are recursive, not linear; interdependent, not separate. They can best be understood as an ecology, a networked, interrelated concept of leadership.

This book reframes women's leadership as an ecology of six interwoven themes. We propose that women who lead *commit to values, are conscious of their evolving selves, invoke passion and courage, arouse the imagination, create community and mentor the next generation.* These theme areas *can apply to men as well,* although we will argue that women tend to negotiate these themes differently, informed by unique values, dispositions, neurobiological structures and histories.

An Ecology of Leadership

Is it any wonder that we chose to redefine leadership? There are hundreds of books on leadership, six of them our own—so why write more? By leaving the definition of leadership to others, we reasoned, it would remain an ancient construct, keeping women separated from the actions of improving the lives of others. We were persuaded that the redefinition must be inclusive and available to all. Women have historically nurtured and served others; however, the organizations and policies essential for the systemic improvement of lives once lay beyond women's possible sphere of influence and participation. Some organizations still do.

In *The Constructivist Leader* we advanced a perspective on leadership that separates the broader notion from the individual and invokes a richer set of skills and dispositions. When leadership is viewed as *the capacity to engage in reciprocal, purposeful learning in community,[3]* the notion of leadership is moved into the network of learning relationships in an organization. This notion of leadership relies on equitable relationships, the exercise of collaboration, moral purpose and engaged learning communities. Women have a natural inclination for this way of being in the world.

The approaches involved in *leading as a form of learning* consist of: visioning, communicating, learning, relating, and sustaining. These are the approaches that permeate our findings about women in leadership, and these approaches are discussed throughout this book. Both men and women are discovering these capabilities within themselves. As we shall argue, research during the past decade gives us permission to pursue paths that may have been previously avoided. "The capacity to engage in reciprocal, purposeful learning in community" embraces a "new century" perspective on leadership.

...in a systems-seeking, co-evolving world, there is no such thing as a hero, not even a visionary leader. Everything is the result of interdependencies—systems of organization where we support, challenge, and create new combinations with others.

-Margaret Wheatley

Reciprocity enables the pursuit of learning and leading within patterns of relationships in which individuals are mutually committed to each other, rather than being dominant and submissive. For instance, when two leaders enter into a peer coaching relationship, they commit to the mutuality of learning. When a leadership team engages its members in deep dialogue toward shared understandings, reciprocal learning will enable the team to be smarter than any one of its members. The brain's capacity to find patterns and make sense of the world is liberated within relationships that tend toward mutual care and equitable engagement: *I am responsible for your learning and you are responsible for mine.* This emancipatory "social contract" reshapes the patterns of relationships within which learning and leading take place, freeing minds to explore openly together.

While learning and leading are *purposeful* by their very nature, morally engaged purpose is more than survival-driven purpose. To be morally engaged in the world requires that individuals bring to the surface values, perspectives and understandings that inform moment-to-moment actions, how others are treated, visions for a better world: equity, democracy, human rights, caring, social justice. When behaviors are value-based, discrepancies can provoke outrage; individuals cannot rest without addressing the differences observed. For instance, when school leaders value learning and the evidence suggests this is not occurring—that there is a huge lack of achievement among their students—a staff can rightly experience moral outrage. People are then driven to either find or work toward solutions or experience remorse. A sense of justice and care leads to investment in and tenacity about actions that are intended to right a wrong or create a better future. This is *purposeful learning.*

At the heart of effective societal leadership is a deep sense of purposefulness; that here is extraordinary power in a group committed to a common vision; that successful leadership depends upon a fundamental shift of being, including a deep commitment to the dream and passion for serving versus being driven by the pursuit of status and power.

-Joseph Jaworski, et al., Synchronicity

Further, learning and leadership occur in *community*. This community can be as intimate as an organization, a neighborhood, or a school. A community can be a gathering of kindred souls or friends. Ultimately, a community is related to the children of the world, including those brought into relationship by tragedy and those who are joined by oppression. At the heart of community are the concepts of care, inclusion, purpose, and lived experience. By *lived experience,* we mean the dailiness of lives, the moment-to-moment interactions, the meaningful dialogue and growing awareness about who is included in our lives, as well as the routines or behaviors that lead toward a larger purpose.

However, communities, by their very nature, are not necessarily morally purposeful. In the early 1980s, Lambert conducted a study of Synanon, a California cult working with victims of addiction. Synanon fancied itself as a community and in many ways, it was— similar lifestyle values, shared work, time spent in mutual interaction—yet, its purpose was intertwined with the messianic vision of its self-appointed "leader."

Organizations managed by paternalistic managers can suffer from some of the same problems as Synanon. "Community" should result in the growth and development of its participants rather than the smothering of initiative and imagination. Within our definition of leadership, purpose has a moral basis and fuses with reciprocal learning that has evolved collaboratively.

By assuming that leadership is a broader concept than leader, a new path is created. Everyone has the right, ability and responsibility to lead… leading means engaging in learning through the process of change. Leading enables all of us to realize meaning and purpose ourselves. When everyone takes responsibility for leading, the values manifest; participants awake to possibilities and are present in the world. Such "presence"[4] has long been seen as an individual spiritual journey; yet when this journey occurs within a reciprocal and purposeful learning community, presence can be a collective achievement as well.

When all of those involved take responsibility for leading, the *leadership capacity* of an organization ensures the creation and sustainability of improvement. When leadership and capacity are combined, they take on an organizational meaning. We have defined leadership capacity as *broad-based, skillful participation in the work of leadership.*[5] *Broad-based* means everyone in the community; *skillful participation in the work of leadership* means the understandings and actions that engage others in purposeful learning and leading.

Full participation means engaging those who have hesitated to see themselves as leaders in the past.

Leadership that is redefined as a reciprocal process of learning together in community, thereby growing the leadership capacity of the entire organization, is not only timely, but also prescient within the current climate of women's leadership. Women are moving boldly into leadership roles in which they can affect policy and practice: superintendent, principal, President, Minister, CEO, legislator, church leader. It is within this context that women in education and other fields are coming of age.

Women Activists Pave the Way: A New Context for Leadership

Through our study and experiences, we have learned that women demonstrated their strengths in these theme areas when they actively reached out to raise the *consciousness* of other women and translated consciousness into *action* and *policy*. Women in all walks of life, in all fields and in countries have laid the foundation so that other women can lead.

> *Today's women*
> *Born Yesterday*
> *Dealing with tomorrow*
> *Not yet where we are going*
> *But not still where we were.*
>
> *-Adrienne Rich*

A few remarkable women have framed the power of action for human rights. When the Fourth World Conference on Women adopted the Nairobi Forward-Looking Strategies for the Advancement of Women in 1996, it had been nearly 50 years since Eleanor Roosevelt led the world, through her work at the United Nations, to adopt the Declaration of Human Rights.

Between 1946 and 1948, Mrs. Roosevelt unrelentingly guided men of disparate beliefs toward the drafting and adoption of the

Declaration. Serene, competent and humble, her fierce adherence to democratic values and human rights accomplished a seminal victory in a divided world. Jean Monnet, father of the common market, summed it up:

> Fundamentally, I think her great contribution was her persistence in carrying into practice her deep belief in liberty and equality. She would not accept that anyone should suffer—because they were women, or children, or foreign, or poor, or stateless refugees. To her, the world was truly one world, and all its inhabitants members of one family.[6]

In the last half of the 20th century and the beginning of the 21st century, the groundswell of the women's movement brought remarkable progress. In many cases, women have been welcomed into formal leadership roles when they behaved or sought to behave as they perceived men to behave in a male-designed world; conversely, other women sought roles that could be transformed by the insights and behaviors of fully integrated women (see Chapter One). However, it is predominantly culture that grants or withholds permission to women to enter the leadership arena.

Internationally, by 2006, six presidents, seven prime ministers, and the President of the General Assembly of the United Nations were women. In spite of these developments, only four women in the United States—Shirley Chisholm, Patricia Schroeder, Carol Mosley Braun, and Hillary Clinton—have formally pursued the Presidency. Women occupy 16 percent of the seats in both Houses of Congress. Five women hold cabinet positions. And 16 percent of state governors' offices are occupied by women.[7] Nancy Pelosi became the first woman Speaker of the House of Representatives in 2007.

Surprisingly, only 16 percent of school superintendents are women, while 75 percent of teachers and 43 percent of principals are women. However, in 2006, 31 percent of the Great Cities school districts superintendents—large urban districts—-were women.[8] Nearly 50 percent of Ivy League university presidents are women, although only 13.8 percent of all university presidents are women.[9]

While women make up nearly half the work force, only 7.9 percent are top executives; only 1.4 percent of Fortune 500 companies have women as top executives (67 of those 500 companies have no women in the corporate office). A mere 14.5 of board seats in the top 500 corporations are held by women.[10] On the other hand, nearly half of all small businesses in America are women-owned: 10.4 million, versus 11.7 million owned by men.[11]

However, nearly 70 percent of program officers are women in volunteer and charitable organizations,[12] efforts that achieve great improvement in education, health, the performing arts, social and economic causes. Charitable participation is a double-edged sword for women. This is the arena that serves as an effective proving ground for women leaders, yet this is also where women can be side-lined away from formal power. The United States ranks only 69th in measures of women's political leadership. While women are gaining in the race for equality—one stunning example of this gain is Senator Hillary Clinton, now Secretary of State—overall equality for women remains a distant goal. Not all women leaders are manifesting the strengths of women's ways of leadership.

More than 60 years ago, Simone de Beauvoir vividly expressed this press for equality. With the publication of *The Second Sex* in England in 1953, de Beauvoir helped us to understand that fraternity (used in the French sense, to mean brotherhood and sisterhood) would not be possible without equality, and that equality required access to complex and challenging opportunities. Within the next few years, Betty Friedan wrote *The Feminine Mystique* in the United States and a new conversation began among women. Friedan's call to consciousness invoked women's passions:

> It was a strange stirring, a sense of dissatisfaction, a yearning that women suffered in the middle of the twentieth century in the United States. Each suburban wife struggled with it alone. As she made the beds, shopped for groceries, matched slipcover material, ate peanut butter sandwiches with her children, chauffeured Cub Scouts and Brownies, lay beside her husband at night, she was afraid to ask even of herself the silent question—"Is this all?"[13]

Is this all? Before de Beauvoir and Friedan, few had dared to ask that question of those who appeared safe and comfortable. While the question resonated with many women, the actions of Rosa Parks in 1955 made it clear that the experience of various women was very different. Asked to give up her seat on a Montgomery, Alabama bus to a white man, Parks refused. While she was being arrested, arraigned and convicted, the Montgomery boycott, already organized and awaiting the right moment, was set into motion.

There is always a moment in the struggle when one feels in full bloom. Vivid. Alive. One might be blown to bits in such a moment and still be at peace.... Sojourner Truth baring her breasts at a women's rights convention in 1851. Harriet Tubman exposing her revolver to some of the slaves she had freed, who, fearing an unknown freedom, looked longingly backward to their captivity, thereby endangering the freedom of all. To be such a person or to witness anyone at this moment of transcendent presence is to know that what is human is linked, by a daring compassion, to what is divine.

-Alice Walker

Moving forward from Montgomery required those who had historically been prevented from participating more fully in our democracy to develop many essential skills of leadership. Septima Clark, mentor to Rosa Parks and Marian Wright Edelman, developed an educational infrastructure for the Southern Christian Leadership Conference so that illiterate black citizens could learn how to read. She sought equal salaries for black teachers and was instrumental in developing the community capacity to translate legal rights into political realities.

When Malek Zaalouk, Chief of Education for UNICEF in Cairo, Egypt, proposed the establishment of Community Schools for Girls, she did so in response to credible evidence that such schools had the capacity to make a profound difference in Egyptian society.[14]

United Nations research found that the education of young girls is the most vital variable in a country's economic development, population control and environmental sustainability. These Community Schools bring education to girls in small villages who would not otherwise have access to schooling.

In the United States, the small schools movement took center stage through the work of Deborah Meier, when she initially served as principal of Central Park East in inner-city New York. Meier's passionate beliefs led her to establish a school characterized by engaged, active learning, foster a democratic community and promote a family-oriented system with student mentoring and advisement. Nurturing adults with high standards produced 90 graduates per year, 90% of whom went on to college. Next, Meier took on the challenge of creating 100 small schools throughout New York City, a vision that fell short of realization. Perhaps the most critical influence of this small schools model has been on educational structures throughout the country; they became shaped around the renewed consciousness that small is better, because improved relationships create better learning.[15] Yet, Meier's approach to charismatic leadership was not sustainable since it tended to limit the participation of others.

> *Until we fix our schools so that they are places where the elders are able to connect with the young in ways that can engage their hearts and minds they are almost irrelevant.*
>
> *-Deborah Meier, Principal, Boston*

Linda Darling Hammond has been a major force in translating consciousness and action into educational policy. These policies at the federal, state and local levels address the ongoing systematic inequalities that stand in the way of educational quality and outcomes. By insisting that all students must have equal access to quality education, she has formulated programs that enhance the capacity for schools and teachers to be responsible for student learning and responsive to student and community needs, interests and concerns.

Such policies speak to teacher quality and preparation, school structures and accountability.[16]

When Lawrence H. Summers stirred international controversy by suggesting that women may not have the intrinsic aptitude for math, science and engineering, the spotlight sought evidence of discrimination at Harvard. The evidence was quickly available. In the past 32 years, only four women had been granted faculty tenure in those disciplines.[17] It is no wonder that Drew Gilpin Faust was sought out as the new president at Harvard. As the successful President of Radcliffe College, she had demonstrated imaginative, collaborative and scholarly leadership skills. By designing and fulfilling a forward-looking agenda of institutional change at Radcliffe and at the University of Pennsylvania, she created a sense of common enterprise, set ambitious goals and fostered interdisciplinary collaboration. She is expected to accomplish similar "miracles" at Harvard.

> *Collaboration means more energy, more ideas, more wisdom; it also means investing beyond one's own particular interests or bailiwick. It means learning to live and to think within the context of the whole university.*
> *-Drew Gilpin Faust, President, Harvard University*

[handwritten margin note: PLC Collaboration / yr-2 focus]

Leaders such as de Beauvoir, Friedan, Clark, Zaalouk, Meier, Darling-Hammond and Faust consciously sought to influence others through their writing, speaking and actions. In so doing, they marshaled passions, stoked imaginations, galvanized resolve and strengthened courage in pursuit of human values. As activists, they stepped out ahead, taking inordinate risks to reputation, sense of self, career, and personal safety. They were successful in some domains, yet not in others. However, when women feel compelled to act out of a sense of self in response to rampant injustice, everyone benefits.

Charisma and sustainability do not go hand in hand. These contradictions in leadership among women and men in all walks of life created the fertile context in which women now choose to lead. *Women's Ways of Leading* suggests ways to confront and overcome the complications of activism while benefiting from the courageous stances that it takes to lead in a complex world.

Conclusion

As the reader observes the work of many remarkable women–leaders who brought intellect, opportunity and talent to bear on the great issues of our time—we would remind you that the women in our studies also exhibited these attributes. Readers may ask, "What about me? Can I set such high expectations for myself and others?" While we have chosen noteworthy exemplars in each dimension, many of them from our experiences in education, we are speaking to each reader, for we found no evidence that these qualities are the sole possession of the select few. Indeed, our studies of women tell us that each woman possesses the capacity to learn and to lead; the inner gems of values, capacity for self-understanding, passion, courage and imagination, a deep yearning for community and the desire to mentor others. We will suggest a pathway of arousing awareness for leadership possibilities, in which we suggest that women become aware of the need, opportunity and moral imperative to lead. And, as readers will learn, when women awaken, so does the world around them. Women are, by nature, constructivists, for they often seek to make sense of things through engagement of people and ideas.

Women's Ways of Leading may be used by the following groups and individuals: professional women and organizations; universities preparing women leaders in education, business, science, management, government and women's studies; institutions and agencies working with the concerns and issues of women; museums and academies for women; men working with women, for women or in therapeutic relationships with women; and book clubs.

The first four chapters of this book—Women's Leadership: Tomorrow's Legacy, Women Who Lead Commit to Values, Women Who Lead are Conscious of the Evolving Self, and Women Who Lead Evoke Passion and Courage—speak to who women are as individuals and who they are in the world. Chapter Five, Women Who Lead Arouse the Imagination, manifests consciousness into a sustainable, imagined world of quality. Chapter Six, Women Who Lead Create Community, describes how women engage others in the construction of meaning and action. Chapter Seven, Mentoring the Next Generation, suggests how women develop leadership in other women. Chapter Eight, On Becoming Transformational Women Leaders: Fulfilling the Promise, brings together ideas and practices for the preparation of women leaders in all fields. The Epilogue, *Desired Destiny*, summarizes the major concepts in the text and tells how women's leadership is a historical destiny that can no longer be denied. From values to practice to preparation, *Women's Ways of Leading* sets forth a pathway for women leaders and those who have yet to view themselves as leaders.

A Sufi tale…Once upon a time the disciples said to the Holy One, "Tell us what you got from Enlightenment. Did you become Divine?" "No, not Divine," the Holy One said. "Did you become a Saint?" "Oh, dear, no," the Holy One said. "Then what did you become?" the disciples asked. "I became awake," the Holy One said…to enable people to become awake and involved, involved and awake may well be the greatest thing that leadership can do for anyone.

- Joan D. Chittister, Spiritual Leader

Women's Leadership: Tomorrow's Legacy

Chapter One

*In order for women to emerge as powerful leaders who
can acknowledge the value of their femininity, many deli-
cate doors in the hearts of men and women will have to
be opened. Recognition that stereotypically "female"
qualities can add positive dimensions to leadership is
vital in helping women find a place in leadership.*

> *-Diane Ketelle, Educator*

The future of women in leadership is remarkably fresh and
hopeful. For thousands of years, women held second-class citizenship—if any citizenship at all. In many countries, it is still true.
However, the emergence of women leaders in Asia, Europe, Africa,
and South and North America provide an inspiring context for fledg-
ling leaders who may no longer be allowed to say, "I'm not a
leader...I don't see myself as a leader."

Why has women's leadership been such a difficult road to
travel? As we noted in the *Introduction*, many women, as well as
many men, have a deeply held bias against women leaders. Together,
women and men entered into a co-conspiracy that kept women cau-
tiously below the glass ceiling, or what Nancy Pelosi calls the marble
ceiling.

For years, many teachers told us they were not leaders. Their
experiences in hierarchical organizations with autocratic leaders
made this seem like a sensible response. *"We are not these kinds of
leaders,"* they might more accurately have said. In order for a significant number of women to liberate themselves from such haunting
experiences, the definition of leadership must be changed. We have
argued for a constructivist definition of leadership; in other words,
leadership as a form of reciprocal learning in community leading
toward a shared set of goals, a shared purpose.

when developing PLCs

At the end of our 2007 workshop in Malaysia, three women said: "But we don't want to be called leaders." "Why?" Linda asked. They were quick to respond: "Leadership is about power and authority, who makes the decisions, who's in charge." When leadership was explained as a form of learning, the response was: "If leadership were defined like that, we would be proud to be leaders." Others in the room agreed. In a follow-up e-mail from one of the participants, Sharifah Hadjarah Aziz told us:

> The workshop in Genting was an eye-opening affair for me. I discovered that I do have leadership qualities. It is alarming as well as exhilarating. Alarming because I fear the responsibility that comes with it. I would hate to think an error on my part can actually tarnish the image of the organization I work for. Exhilarating because I now realize that I can make a difference … I wish we had met earlier. But better late than never, right?[1]

In our studies, we had set about to talk to other women who had moved ahead in spite of obstacles—what their experiences had been, who encouraged them, how they handled the struggles and came through with new identities. In our graduate programs, we worked with women who changed their minds about becoming leaders. Some stopped short of that goal, others retreated, and still others felt that the journey might be too difficult. In our initial studies, we discovered five major leadership themes pertinent to all women: *Women who lead commit to values, are conscious of their evolving selves, invoke passion and courage, arouse the imagination, create community and mentor the next generation of woman leaders*. Of course, these themes relate to men as well; however, women tend to confront and negotiate these themes in different ways, with different styles and skills and alternative perspectives.

Women's leadership is a richly woven tapestry, the threads of which emerge from answers to challenging questions, complicated by the multiple factors that influence their development. When women negotiate this maze of inhibiting and facilitating factors, we propose that they move through a journey characterized by four

Leadership Theme

major *Perspectives* entitled: 1) The Denied Self; 2) The Nascent Self; 3) The Emerging Self; and 4) The Integrated Self.

In the *Introduction,* we described the historical background and context accounting for the current rise in formal[2] women's leadership roles. Although suffragettes assertively began the movement for the vote in the 1800s, intense preparation of the soil in which women would blossom began most dramatically in the 1950s. This rise, while still not representative of the potential number of women available for leadership positions, provided hope that a greater number of women would influence the next generations of women and their beliefs about possibilities.

As we studied the data collected in our study from women in the United States, Canada and Southeast Asia, as well as in our graduate programs, we identified the critical themes that women emphasized as well as common influences. It was no surprise that age, family and cultural norms played important roles as to when and how women began their paths into leadership. Most of the women leaders reported receiving strong messages at early ages about their capabilities. Parents and teachers often told them they could "do anything." At the same time, strong and often subtle messages encouraged them to "be a good girl" and follow the rules, be meticulous and compliant. Mothers, fathers, grandmothers, aunts, sisters, teachers, coaches or community mentors were often identified as those who encouraged them to develop their talents and believe in themselves. Conversely, these models can have a deeply detrimental effect if their message undercuts a young person's self-esteem and confidence. The role of family and mentors also held true for the women involved in our broader research, many of whom are included as portraits in the chapters ahead. Universally, having a mentor or someone who believed in them overrode prevailing cultural and religious messages about whether women should be leaders.

Louann Brizendine now suggests that many of the factors we often described as environmentally formed may be influenced more by biological "hardwiring" and hormonal surges. She claims that the female brain is genetically structured and shaped by evolution, biology and culture. By understanding these dynamics, Brizendine insists, we can use "our intelligence and determination both to cele-brate and when necessary, to change the effects of sex hormones on brain structure, behavior, reality, creativity and destiny." [3]

Brain research (handwritten in margin)

We are living in the midst of a revolution in conscious-ness about women's biological reality that will transform human society...The scientific facts behind how the female brain functions, perceives reality, responds to emotions, reads emotions in others, and nurtures and cares for others are women's reality...Women have a bio-logical imperative for insisting that a new social contract take them and their needs into account. Our future, and our children's future, depends on it.

- Louann Brizendine

Human dynamics (handwritten in margin)

One of the many compelling aspects of brain research regards cognitive style. Even in cases in which a vision may be shared, the decision about how to migrate toward that vision differs dramatically. We find two extremes of cognitive style most informative: concrete-sequential and abstract-random.[4] For instance, Lambert found that Madeline Hunter, Ralph Tyler, John Goodlad and Elliott Eisner shared an emancipatory vision for learning, yet were highly dissimi-lar in their approaches to planning learning for themselves and oth-ers. Hunter pursued a step-by-step, modularized and sequential approach, while the others insisted on more self-directed, contextu-ally-related and unpredictable paths.[5] What does this mean for women? We are not suggesting that women are more concrete-sequential. Madeline Hunter does not represent all women. Indeed, women are historically found to be more right-brained: holistic, cre-ative, inclusive.[6] However, the tasks to which women have often been relegated have required and valued concrete styles, with an emphasis on meticulous tasks and organizational duties, and thereby women have been given the message that the accompanying skills are required of women leaders. Certainly, cognitive style helps determine how women undertake the tasks of leadership, supervise others and relate to rules.

Further, the women in our studies, as with all women, lived in diverse family, societal and socio-economic situations and shouldered varied responsibilities, including the care of small children, aging parents or handicapped family members. These conditions influenced the age at which they began their leadership journey. In 2008, post-menopausal women comprised the largest demographic group in the U.S. Since age is no longer such a limiting factor to creative lifelong work and learning, lives need not be squeezed into a small number of vibrant years.

We're trapped in the assumption that work is unpleasant and should be stopped at 65.

-Mary Catherine Bateson

Some of the women reported short-term leadership roles in their school years, but few of the women reported that they set out with goals or drives to be leaders. Consequently, when they did enter into leadership roles, they were either invited in by someone who noticed their talents or aptitude for leadership, or were provoked into taking the lead, after an epiphany provoked by moral outrage. In the following chapter on values, the role of moral outrage will be explored in more detail.

Perspectives on Leadership

We deliberately choose not to use practiced terms in adult development, such as stage or phase, each of which suggests linear, predictable development. We make no such claims. Instead, we borrowed the notion of "Perspective" from Mary Field Belenky and colleagues[8] as a more apt term, meaning both a person's point of view about herself, based on her valuation of a situation, as well as an "artist's vista." The "artist's vista" captures the composed or constructed aspect of lives. Mary Catherine Bateson's *Composing a Life* suggests that the brush in the portraiture process belongs to the artist herself.[9]

Perspectives can be linear, but not necessarily so, for they may blend to form their own unique entity or period. Robert Kegan describes the "dignity of yearning" at each stage of development:

> Of the multitude of hopes and yearnings we experience, these two seem to subsume the others. One of these might be called the yearning to be included, to be a part of, close to, joined with, to be held, admitted, accompanied. The other might be called the yearning to be independent and autonomous, to experience one's distinctness, the self-chosenness of one's directions, one's individual integrity.[10]

Perspectives can become quicksand, keeping a woman stuck in one place—or they can serve as a launching pad for moving forward or backward.

Perspective One: The Denied Self

In our study, women frequently told of a period of silence in their development. Fear of creating conflict, or of not being able to defend a statement well enough, or of making a mistake, often caused them to remain silent in social situations and at school. They lacked the confidence to defend themselves. They remembered believing that other people were smarter, more sophisticated, more experienced—and so would defer to others' arguments and reasoning. Relying on authority is a safe place to hide if you're timid.

During this silent period, their beliefs regarding right and wrong (values) were dictated by parents, the church or strong cultural, societal "musts." Culturally expressed sex roles determined much of what they believed about themselves and other girls or women. "Little girls are seen and not heard." "Compliance is a woman's virtue." "Good girls don't get angry…it's not becoming." "Desirable women are submissive and passive." Snow White and Sleeping Beauty once awakened sought to marry the prince rather than conquer the world. Obedience to authority, at the expense of the self, is both protective and helpful.

In describing Loevinger's milestones of ego development, Sarah Levine argued that individuals in the conformist stage of development (similar to the Denied Self perspective of leadership development) believed that the right and wrong ways to understand and do things were the same for everyone at all times.[11] If these women thought differently from the group, they must be wrong. Many women in the study disclosed that conformity had been an important behavior for them. Acceptance and approval came from conformity and were critical to perceived survival and to being "chosen." In our graduate programs in educational leadership, women in this Perspective tended to be silent in larger groups but managed to find their voices in small groups and in journals.

Kristen Levine, a first-year teacher committed to the development of her students and herself, did not want her students to be frozen in Perspective One. She put into practice her learnings from the New Teachers' Institute at the Athenian School in Danville, California. On the very first day of instruction, Kristen engaged her students in dialogue by inviting them to listen, seek to understand and make connections with each other. She wrote on the board, "Silence shields wisdom."[12] Kristen is well on her way to becoming a Perspective Four teacher and leader.

Many organizations, such as schools, are established with male dominant norms. Bureaucratic hierarchies and rules, schedules and working agreements establish structures and policies that often colonize female employees. If a woman lives by the established norms of a male-dominated organization, she can become stuck (at least in this part of her life) in the Self-Denied Perspective.

While women may feel protected in such an environment, they can and do feel victimized, infantilized and blame others. Frozen in this perspective, women continue in silence, conformity and obedience. Or, these feelings can initiate behaviors that mediate the emerging self with institutional demands, Perspective Two: The Nascent Self.

Perspective Two: The Nascent Self

When the women in our study broke out of the Self-Denied Perspective and began to blossom as leaders in their schools, they often took on roles they believed would benefit both the school and themselves. Still not either conscious of their own values or "owning" their leadership skills, they were frequently "tapped" or invited in by someone in an organization, usually a male, who noticed a style or a skill that was believed to contribute to the organization.

Our observations are that women in business fall victim to Perspective Two thinking even more dramatically—and tragically—than educators. In 2002, Carleton (Carly) Fiorina, former Chair and CEO of Hewlett-Packard, said: "Women have to play by male rules and allow themselves to be judged by male standards; if they don't, they risk being marginalized."[13] In 2003, she modified her statement, saying that she had faced barriers herself and knows they exist for others, but prefers not to focus on them.[14]

Once initiated into leadership, many of the women were able to hone the desired skills pleasing to those in the organization. Respect from these other leaders (perhaps we should say "managers") gave them recognized success as a leader by the organization and led to strong loyalty and self-definition, based on the job. This perspective was much like Belenky's "procedural knowledge,"[15] an accommodation to the organization. In a retrospective conversation, the women described themselves as "conventional,"[16] tending to lead in the ways they *perceived* men to lead—rational, decisive, minimally collaborative. While these women entertained "input" from those below them in the hierarchy, their decisions were theirs alone. Often directed and reinforced by a conventional supervisor or mentor, the values they promoted were cherrypicked from their nascent array of values, many still unexpressed. Caught within traditional definitions of leadership, these Perspective Two leaders existed within a context made secure by the structure in which they found themselves.

However, these women often reported that they did not feel authentic. At times they felt they were "playing at being a leader." Since their leadership strengths were based on values and outcomes defined by the organization and their mentor or supervisor, they were surprised when teachers expressed a lack of confidence or trust in them. Seeking to avoid conflict at all costs, such opposition haunted them. Because loyalty, trust, gratitude and respect are driving needs in this Perspective, women selected values admired by the organization or role. Gradually, as they experienced more organizational success, they were able to identify and take credit for their contributions. It was at this point that their memories of leadership activities in Girl Scouts, sports, drama or debate in high school or college added to their recognition that they could be "good" leaders, often synonymous with "good girl." Many of them began to set leadership goals for the first time—goals that would eventually lead them up the career ladder.

So what was it that jolted some women into The Quest for Self that characterizes Perspective Three? Many things may occur: an enlightened mentor who challenges convention, a graduate program in leadership, a provocative workshop, dissonance caused by feedback from peers and staff that is contrary to her own self-perception, a violation of her own latent values that insinuates itself into her consciousness—any or all of these factors can provoke a shift to a different quest, a reflective quest.

Perspective Three: The Quest for Self

The genuine quest for self comes at a price. Having traveled the convoluted road through silence and rules and sometimes back again, a time may arrive when a woman looks into her mirror and asks: *Who am I? What has this all been about? At first I couldn't find my voice, and then I sacrificed it on the institutional altar. When policies were enacted that denied equity to children...where was I? When "No Child Left Behind" turned us into a nation of test takers, where was I? I was right there: the good girl, implementing policy without question. So now what? Am I angrier with myself, the institution, my mother, or all of the above? And, how do I get out of this quagmire?*

This internal dialogue can cause a woman to leave the profession, make a lateral career move, fight back, get stuck or adapt by "selling out" to the status quo. Dissatisfaction with the self can also lead to an assertive search for personal meaning and power. Belenky

— The 5-year break!

and colleagues describe this perspective as "subjective knowledge,"[17] noting attention to the inner voice and the diminution of other voices.

Social activism may be accompanied by fearless daring. No longer afraid of what others think, this is a time of experimentation and outspokenness. In the wake of her son's death in Iraq, Cindy Sheehan set up camp on the road to President Bush's home in Texas, and began an anti-war struggle that would sweep across the nation. Margaret Thatcher found recognized success as the Prime Minister of England by blending the more rule-bound nascent self of Perspective Two with the boldness of Perspective Three. Yet, as far as we know, she did not take the next step into Perspective Four. Such entrepreneurial behaviors are especially challenging within the public school system, but examples abound...the educator who strikes out and starts a charter school; implements a balanced reading approach in defiance of prescriptive requirements; insists on her singular, albeit legitimate, vision; or becomes president of the teachers' union.

Such righteous indignation energizes women toward boldness. They may relinquish connectedness for inward watching and listening, making a sharp differentiation between themselves and the voices of others. Individuality comes into prominence in pursuit of the essential self, although such a focus on self may mean an avoidance of mentoring responsibilities to others. For the women in our studies, such moral outrage often led them into a role such as union leader.

The boldness described here in Perspective Three may suggest an assertiveness that some women find difficult or unacceptable in certain cultures, even though they are encountering the same yearnings for individuation. We recognize that context may require a more gentle boldness (avoiding the celebrated feminine label, "bitch"). It is our experience that boldness can be packaged modestly through coaching, modeling and raising questions of practice. The audacity of individuation that characterizes Perspective Three—whether through assertive action or quiet guidance—can form the necessary dialectic that delivers women to the door of Perspective Four: The Integrated Self.

> *Georgia O'Keefe was unwavering in her points of view about herself and her art. This lucidity enabled her to look forward, not backward, thus remaining remarkably unconflicted about her chosen path. While the opinions of others were interesting, they seldom influenced her unduly.*
>
> *-Linda Lambert*

Perspective Four: The Integrated Self

Perspective Four is a portrait of a woman who has wisely constructed a self through the integration of inside and outside voices. Such balance is a function of maturity, although not necessarily age. As we noted above, the factors that influence a woman's experience can facilitate, inhibit or even derail such progression. Epiphanies that enable women to alter their perspectives and actions are usually longitudinal, garnered over time and often the result of struggling against the odds. For women in education, we rarely saw these qualities emerge before age 40, although anecdotal evidence in regard to age is always suspect.

The integrated woman is autonomous and inter-independent, capable of independent thought and action as well as reciprocal collaboration. Both autonomy and inter-independence are comfort zones as they now reside hand-in-hand. Collaboration evolves through relationships and work facilitated with informal authority; that is, authority derived from influence, associations, expertise, respect and experience. Instances of directive formal authority are rare.

No longer prey to dichotomized thinking or the wholesale relinquishment of the self in exchange for approval, and ascribing to universal ethical principles such as equity, justice and caring, women are no longer slaves to bureaucratic rules.

The Perspective Four woman is authentic, generative, evidences an unmistakable integrity, and projects a sense of personal power that is quickly recognizable even by those who have not yet attained that realm. A school principal who works collaboratively with teachers to honor their values while expressing her own is listened to—not because of blind agreement, but because her authentic voice assures teachers that she can be trusted under any circumstances.

Meg Whitman, former CEO of eBay, characterizes the reasons for the company's astounding success: strong teamwork, an informal working environment and non-hierarchical relationships epitomizing a community at work. The late Ann Richards drew people into her orbit when she was Governor of Texas, inspired them with confidence and walked with them into new territory, new possibilities. This networking orbit engaged others who yearned to be listened to, lightened with laughter, and warmed with passion. In a state known for Old Boys' Networks, a competing force came alive in Texas: the Old Girls' Networks.

The Perspective Four woman is liberated from old battles for the self, thereby unleashing a yearning to discover, create, contribute and lead. Reaching out to the world from an integrated foundation, such women generate learning, leading and hope.

As a Constructivist Leader, the Perspective Four woman engages those around her in the reciprocal pursuit of meaning, thereby forging remarkable results based on universal ethical principles or values. These strategies are explored in depth in the next chapter.

Themes from Our Studies of Women Leaders

The leadership understandings and actions emerging as themes in our study led us to realize that women who lead commit to values, are conscious of the evolving self; invoke passion and courage; arouse the imagination; create community and mentor the new generation. Women pursue these aspects of leadership as they negotiate different perspectives on the self. In order to lead well, individuals must **know and commit to their most deeply held value**s. Through a valuing lens, women become **conscious of who they are** and thereby hold a clear sense of identity in relation to others. This knowledge is an essential aspect of reciprocity and integrating the learning and expectations of others. Such consciousness or wakefulness is the necessary condition for pursuing purposeful learning.

Purposefulness stems from **values passionately and courageously sought, implemented and sustained.** We connect to learning when we **arouse the imagination, create community and mentor the next generation.** Taken together, these six themes engage leaders and those who are led through **reciprocal, purposeful learning in community.**

The realization of these themes is made possible by beliefs and assumptions; for instance:

- **Valuing:** means making a difference in the world. Further, women stalwartly believe they can make that difference. Moral imperatives frame the conversations. Values define who women are and what they will become.

- **Consciousness:** Women yearn to be more fully who they are, to understand that people continue to grow and develop. "I have the capacity to know who I am—both connected to and separate from other people." Consciousness encompasses identity...to know who women are as leaders and to be able to communicate that identity through words and actions.

- **Passion and Courage:** Women are willing to withstand suffering, struggle, pain and difficulties for what they believe in. These trials embolden, clarify purpose and strengthen identity. They can risk safety for the unknown, realizing that certainty binds them to old patterns and behaviors. Uncertainty is emancipating...freeing women from old habits and old beliefs.

- **Imagination:** Women possess a creative inner landscape that is the theater for imagining a better world. Imagination can invoke and deepen capacities for sympathy, empathy, compassion and spirituality. Imagining can make it so.

- **Community:** Women engage those around them in their work and in their lives in the reciprocal co-construction of meaning and action, thereby creating community, the essential task of leadership.

- **Mentoring:** Women make a difference in others' lives as well. Through support, modeling and coaching they enable others to grow beyond their own expectations. Women can deepen and enhance the learning process in others. Mentoring relationships are reciprocal… both learn in the process.

These six themes of leadership also play out in the development of organizations and societies. Each aspect leads us toward the transformation of institutions, including the essential strategies and skills for accomplishing such transformation. Chapters Two- Eight describe the manifestation of Themes and Perspectives into organization practice and policy.

These themes, together with the Perspectives on the self, merge to create a *Framework for Women's Leadership Development*. This Framework provides a loosely patterned overlay for each of the chapters that follow.

A Framework for the Development of Women Leaders

The Framework in Figure 1 builds upon the intersection or interrelationship between the self and life themes. As they intersect, the compelling tasks or preoccupations of evolving women leaders during different dimensions of their lives surface. The central dramas are the tensions between one's own voice and the often-competing sounds of other voices and the complexities of conflict avoidance. The more effective women leaders negotiate through these Perspectives by way of the tasks made evident by these themes.

Summary

More than two thousand years ago, Isis was the unchallenged primary goddess of the Egyptian, Greek and Roman worlds. She and her followers did not require leadership literature to embolden themselves or to build a rationale to step out into the world, take responsibility and model leadership for other women. However, since that time, a collusion of cultural and economic factors has erected canonized barriers and rules to suppress equity among men and women.

FIGURE 1.1: Framework of Women's Leadership Development

	Perspective 1	Perspective 2	Perspective 3	Perspective 4
Commit to Values	Unconsciously expresses values embedded in family, institutions, culture, and authority.	Expresses conventional values (loyalty, respect, trust, appreciation) in pursuit of organizational approval.	Articulates personal values that provoke assertive action.	Lives universal values (Equity, Care, Social Justice) from integration of inner and outer voices.
Evolving Self	Withholds personal voice: own identity is undefined; experiences shame and guilt; avoidance of conflict.	Defines identity by job, role, organization. Good leader=good girl. Appearance and social acceptability are of prime importance.	Differentiates personal identity from group identity; accepts self; accepts conflict as an essential part of change.	Bases authentic identity on self-reflection and the needs of others; aware that all humans are continuously evolving.
Passion, Courage	Fears of both conflict and revelation of incompetence prevents courageous action and keeps passion from surfacing.	Sees no reason to challenge convention; acting the "good girl." As a workaholic, denying self time for interests or passions.	Transforms passion and courage into "righteous indignation" and activism.	Uses courage to promote and defend universal values; passion ignites and sustains creativity and action.
Imagination	Uses imagination to figure out what others want from them. Sees the world from own perspective.	Innovates within narrow boundaries as prescribed by the organization; personal life may include creative endeavors.	Imagines a liberated self in order to pursue interest, talents, adventures and social change. Entrepreneurial.	Opens imagination to deepen compassion and empathy. Boldly creates new ideas, approaches, and solutions.
Community	Follows the lead of peers, group or those in authority. Attends and listens, but participates as a follower.	Manages non-democratic community; may solicit input but makes decisions on her own or in compliance with higher organizational demands.	Utilizes community as a strategy to accomplish goals, even when singular action is preferred.	Engages others in co-constructing meaning and action, thereby establishing community, the essential task of leadership.
Mentoring	Lacks awareness of others' needs, feels she has little to offer. Not seen as strong by others. Needs mentor.	Mentors both men and women into the expectations and rules of the organization and conventional values.	Models, rather than explicitly mentoring. The "accidental mentor."	Mentors the next generation of women leaders through personal relationships, writings, programs. Highly conscious of legacy.
	Perspective 1	Perspective 2	Perspective 3	Perspective 4

The history of women is one of starting over, often climbing the same mountain more than once.

The study on women in leadership that energizes and propels this book describes how women leaders have negotiated the paths before them. It is our conviction that all women can lead once they convince themselves that it is possible. However, an awakening does not happen in a vacuum, but in relationship, in community, in practice. In the chapters ahead, the perspectives and themes of women leaders will guide us toward a greater understanding of how women lead and how they overcome the stumbling blocks both within and without and illustrate their contributions to leading.

Suggested Exercise

Using Figure 1 as a guide to themes and perspective:
1. Circle the box most nearly like you are at this stage in your journey.
2. Give two examples that would cause you to choose this indicator.
3. Share with a colleague.

Note: at the end of Chapter Eight, we will ask you to complete this exercise for a second time and compare your results.

Women Who Lead…
Commit to Values

Chapter Two

The education system should be founded on "unveiling the mind." Unveiling means to remove the mask of igno- rance and unquestioning compliance to reveal the inner power and knowledge. …Women throughout the world wisely awakening to this call for unveiling find strength in their values and in themselves.
—Nawal El Saadawi, Egyptian feminist and author

The Meaning of Values

Why begin with values? Values can be as nebulous and as mys- tical as leadership itself. Yet it is values that describe who women are and what women stand for in the world. By defining Leadership as "reciprocal, purposeful learning in community," purpose or values form the heart of leading, as they are the heart of learning. The notion of universal values—principles or strongly held beliefs—turns atten- tion toward human rights ideals such as peace, caring, equality, uni- versal literacy, women's and children's rights, democratic citizenship and environmental care. These values are moral, yet not moralistic, suggesting to women what may be individually, and in community, just or "right."

Values *give meaning to lives, influence to relationships and power to actions.* Meaning is attributed to values as they become entangled within women's lived experiences. Nel Noddings sug- gested that the value of caring is a significant lens through which women, particularly, attribute meaning to experiences, build rela- tionships and frame action. Noddings encouraged teachers to give themselves permission to care about their students and other teach- ers, and to develop strategies for building reciprocal caring among students. Teaching and leading thereby derive meaning from the value of caring, characterized by receptivity, relatedness and engagement. Receptivity means allowing another into our lives; relatedness refers to whatever it takes to build a relationship; engagement means being reciprocally involved in what others care about. When schools are organized so that adults provide sustained advisement and mentoring to students, a significant medium for caring is established.[1]

Nel Noddings
Educator, Writer

"We should want more from our educational efforts than adequate academic achievement, and we will not achieve even that meager success unless our children believe that they themselves are cared for and learn to care for others."

Nel Noddings derived her deep value for caring from the influence of the compassionate teachers who taught her. These fortunate experiences led to a life-long interest in teacher-student relationships. "Care is basic in human life and all people want to be cared for," noted Noddings, who found meaning in the study, writing about and practice of care.

Some feminists might take issue with Noddings' commitment to domestic life: 10 children, a marriage spanning a half-century and a yearning for fresh flowers and clean linens. While being an "incurable domestic," Noddings managed to teach, direct the University of Chicago's laboratory school and serve as President of the John Dewey Society. The current chair she holds is Lee J. Jacks Professor Emeriti of Child Education at Stanford University. As a philosopher of education, she has written extensively on the value of caring, teacher preparation and peace education.

For Noddings, life is a moral quest and the most moral of those pursuits is the Ethics of Care. This quest seeks to transcend the Western traditional emphasis on individualism. Schools that are fragmented by rugged individualism and lack a collaborative culture are low leadership capacity schools, in which student achievement is polarized. As in many societies where the rich get richer and the poor get poorer, in low leadership capacity schools, students who face special challenges are tracked into patterns of failure.

Noddings has developed a noteworthy body of work by translating the natural caring of domestic life into a theoretical framework that works well for children and adults alike. She suggests four tenets to the Ethics of Care:

1. Model and demonstrate caring in relation to students
2. Engage students in dialogue about caring
3. Practice caring and reflection on that practice
4. Confirmation...affirm and encourage the best in others by building trust and ensuring continuity.[2]

We consider Noddings a leader. Her attention to reciprocal learning and care, and her persistent demonstration of these values rank her among the outstanding examples of constructivist leaders.

Gilligan pointed out that caring is the key value that provides added values to the moral development of women.[3] Kohlberg found that at the higher stages of development, humans converge around certain values.[4] For women, those values are consistently revealed as social justice, caring and equality; however, caring was not always on the men's list.

If societies accept the premise that each person has the potential for manifesting moral values, then the challenge is to discover how the fires get lit, what moves men and women toward these gold nuggets of shared values. Dialogue within schools can tap into the yearning for a shared moral purpose, giving *meaning to shared work*. Poplin and Weeres suggested that when teachers get back in touch with why they went into teaching in the first place, they find connections to shared values.[5] Individuals are certainly not drawn to education by salary, position, recognition or the potential for autonomy. It is most often values that lead women to devote their lives to others, particularly children.

Perspectives on Values and Activism

The women in our study told stories of values violated, values challenged, values fulfilled. For women in Perspectives One and Two, The Self-Denied and Nascent Self, respectively, values may be unexpressed or made to fit the expectations of the organization.

Figure 2.1 briefly describes the Four Perspectives of Values.

Figure 2.1   Perspectives on a Commitment to Values

	Perspective 1	**Perspective 2**	**Perspective 3**	**Perspective 4**
Commit to Values	Unconsciously expresses values embedded in family, institutions, culture, authority.	Expresses conventional values (loyalty, respect, trust, appreciation) in pursuit of organizational approval.	Articulates personal values that provoke assertive action.	Lives universal values (equity, care, social justice) from integration of inner and outer voices.

However, when we asked these extraordinary women why they had chosen leadership, we learned to expect a story of values violated: a child had been denied access to a highly successful program, turned away from a class about which she was passionate, or denied tutoring assistance for a serious reading problem—or a new teacher had failed to receive the administrative support she needed. These incidents and scores of other stories evoked a moral outrage that awakened women to the need to respond, and to recognize that responses can be more effective coming from a leadership perspective rather than from indignation alone.

Moral outrage derives energy from values that have been violated. When women ascribe to certain values that were violated or denied, a discrepancy is formed between what the women believed to be the right thing to do and reality, as set forth by "those in charge." For instance, a substantial number of the women in our study became involved with teachers' unions when they encountered an injustice, or a pattern of injustices. Before they chose to enter formal leadership roles, though, they had decided that unions were a legitimate medium for challenging school districts' decisions and conditions.

Martie Connor wanted to make a difference in how "gifted" students and those not so identified learned in the Saratoga (California) Union School District. She sought to become a teacher leader, initially through participation in the teachers' union. Such a move enabled her to influence the composition of district committees through union negotiation, which eventually led to the redesign of a flawed state program.[6]

Reaching Every Child:
My Adventures as a Teacher Leader
By Martie Connor, retired teacher

A few years after I began teaching, I realized that I wanted to be involved as much as possible in designing programs, choosing textbooks and making decisions that affected teachers' lives and classrooms. I became a "teacher leader," although teachers were not called leaders then. Beginning with the Saratoga (California) Teachers Association, I served on many committees and even chaired a few. Eventually, the association negotiated that teachers were to sit on all district curriculum and program committees.

During these early years, I taught various elementary grades and always sought to use new methods that would improve the quality of education for all children. Among my strongly held beliefs was the determined view that all children deserved exciting, engaging and strong instruction, with a correspondingly challenging curriculum. This belief was the main force that compelled me to volunteer for the committee established to evaluate, plan, and oversee the GATE (Gifted and Talented Education) Program. Since the Saratoga Union School District is a small entity in a middle-to-high socio-economic community, up to 40 percent of our students met the IQ (130+) criteria for the gifted program.

The funding level was meager——covering only 2 percent of our identified students. Historically, our district had a pullout program in which one-fourth to two-fifths of second through sixth graders would depart weekly for their GATE class. I firmly believed that this was not in the best interest of the students in our district. How could I explain to my second graders the purpose for this class, whether or not they were included? It distorted the concept and purpose of learning for all students.

After a great deal of research and parent interviews, our committee decided on a different, unprecedented direction. We chose to identify all of our students as gifted and talented, thereby integrating the GATE program into every classroom, for every child. The conversion did not happen overnight or without opposition. Initially, we presented our case in Sacramento and received a year-by-year waiver. A few parents were opposed to the lack of an individual, exclusive program. Parents on the GATE committee met with other parents, explaining the intent of the revised program. Ultimately, most parents supported the new program wholeheartedly.

We studied current successes, added new lessons based on our research, and designed professional development for all teachers. Each year the lessons were reviewed and evaluated by the teachers. For the first few years these lessons were modeled for new teachers, and in their second year, they were observed by the district GATE coordinator. We collected comprehensive data on student achievement for five years. It was a lot of work—-but so exciting, that we didn't stop.

At the end of the five years, we presented the statistical results to the state in order to show that we had improved learning district-wide and that our integrated program met the needs of our GATE students. With this evidence, we received a long-term waiver to continue the program, now considered a "best practice" for the state. Many districts visited our programs and used our lessons to begin similar professional development programs.

I believe this was a wonderful outcome. I was glad to have contributed to changing to a system that recognized the giftedness of all students and included all students in learning experiences that challenged and extended their thinking. Over the years, students have benefited greatly while learning from each other in interactive experiences and sharing their insights in all areas of the curriculum. Nearly twenty years later this program continues. I am proud to have played a significant role. Our common vision for students throughout the school community enabled us to learn ourselves into the leadership needed by teachers, administrators and parents alike.[6]

These gaps between values and action—perceived as injustice— inflamed professional sensibilities, which provoked these women to action. If they did not act to correct, or at least respond significantly to, the situation at hand, they experienced deep remorse that could not be easily shaken. These are turning points in women's lives that sometimes influence them to leave careers in education, but more often lead them toward formal leadership roles, such as school principal.

Remorse makes us lonely; we feel empty inside. When we walk hand in hand with our values we are no longer a stranger, we are no longer lonely. In the next chapter, we will see that our values form the basis of who we are, our consciousness, our essential self.

Values Integrated-Perspective Four

When the board of the National Accelerated School Network decided to respond to the national press for exclusive curriculum reform programs by adopting a classroom-only focus, Julie Biddle, Director of the Dayton Satellite Center for Accelerated Schools, had a tough choice to make. Heretofore, the Accelerated Schools model was a comprehensive reform initiative designed to build positive school cultures by taking stock of where they were, reaching consensus around a common five-year vision, and setting priorities based on the discrepancy between where the school was and where the school community wanted it to be. The new classroom focus veered the network away from whole school change and, therefore, the possibility of sustainability. Julie captured the dilemma:

In the comprehensive Accelerated Schools model, school personnel begin to see the students as "our" students, their school as "our school." They truly

> come to own both their challenges and their strengths as a school community. This "our-ness" maintains momentum when new challenges arise, new people join the staff, and when other schools in the district become jealous of their improved performance.[7]

Consequently, Julie decided to maintain the integrity of the program. She was also committed to honoring the network pledge to shared decision making. After polling the members of the network regarding the decision of the board, every school in the Dayton satellite, along with Centers in New York and Texas, chose to *continue the power of their actions* by maintaining the originally envisioned comprehensive model of school improvement.

Kenyan Nobel Peace Prize winner Wangari Maathai perceives the *influence that she exerts* as "touching hearts, convincing minds, and raising consciousness."[8] Maathai integrates values that inspire individuals and nations toward goals of environmental sustainability, human rights, gender equality and peace. These values enabled the Nobel committee to see the relationship between peace and the environment. Maathai makes the case that these values are interconnected. She explains it this way:

> Many wars are fought over resources, which are becoming increasingly scarce across the world. If we did a better job of managing resources and sustainability, conflicts over them would be reduced.[9]

Maathai selects and trains women to plant trees and gardens and to gain skills in democratic citizenship. When schools design professional development to address participatory, or shared, leadership skills, the leadership capacity of the school can ensure sustainable improvement. For instance, Leadership High School in San Francisco, a high leadership capacity school, uses rubrics to teach the skills of leading to students and adults alike. By creating a leadership curriculum, leadership comes vividly alive in the actions of everyone connected with the school.

Wangari Maathai
Recipient, Nobel Peace Prize, 2004

"When we plant trees, we plant the seeds of peace and hope[9]"

Wangari Maathai is a woman of firsts: the first woman in East Africa to earn a Ph.D. and win the Nobel Prize, and the first environmentalist to win the coveted Nobel Peace Prize. She is a woman of profound purpose and explicit values. Maathai integrates values that inspire individuals and nations toward goals of environmental sustainability, human rights, gender equality and peace.

Her commitment to the environment began as a daughter of a peasant farmer and a student of biology. Inspired by her parents to boldness and clarity, and given a compelling name such as Wangari ("Elder of the Burning Spear)," she was well equipped to become a determined woman of substance.

This path led inevitably to a Ph.D. in biology from the University of Nairobi. Maathai possessed the passion and the expertise needed to originate the Green Belt Movement in Africa.

Maathai and her followers in the Green Belt Movement embraced these major values: 1) love for environment and conservation; 2) self and community empowerment; 3) volunteerism; 4) a strong sense of belonging to the community of Greens; 5) accountability, transparency and honesty.

She has experienced Kenya both as an insider and an outsider. As an outsider, she was often jailed and abused for speaking out about governmental injustice and corruption. Now an insider, she is working for democracy, equality, peace and the environment.

Wangari Maathai is a remarkable leader who reciprocally engages others in her local and global communities, marshaling these energies toward multiple and integrated values. Maathai exemplifies a woman whose passion, courage and imagination are built upon a foundation of strong values.[10]

Linda Henke became Superintendent of Sycamore Heights School District at the edge of St. Louis, Missouri, realizing that this diverse urban district was alarmingly low-performing. This oldest district in the county had been dropping in performance since the 1960s. It was known for its disrepair (and despair), poor-quality programs, violence and gangs. The high school had dropped from over 1,100 to less than 300 students. The district had had four superintendents in five years; no one wanted to stay there. Then the climb into quality and pride began, the Sycamore Heights community was mobilized—80 people met weekly for three months. An intensive summer retreat ("Dwelling in Possibilities") was focused on learning communities, professional dialogue, reflection, inquiry and leadership capacity. "Understanding by Design" framed the new work in instruction and curriculum. K-8 looping (when a teacher stays with the same class more than one year) and block scheduling (large blocks of time such as two or more hours are scheduled for a class) at the high school served as the structure for sustainable relationships. Everyone was trained in leadership, and leadership teams guided the learning process.

New principals were found for five percent of the schools; 20 percent of the teachers were replaced. A new teacher evaluation system was designed, and extensive time for professional learning was built into the calendar. New behaviors and practices came as a result of Henke's uncompromising beliefs: everything is connected (systems thinking); dialogue and relationships in leadership are powerful avenues toward change; high- leverage priorities and actions move the system forward.

Sycamore Heights remade itself. On Missouri's Annual Performance Report, the school's total score grew from 57 to 91. High school attendance rose to 94 percent; the dropout rate fell to 2.4 percent. The school met state standards for the first time.

The Sycamore Heights District is an example of the power of a shared vision combined with the value-driven practice of all those involved. There are no excuses accepted for poor performance.[11]

"I've never spent a sleepless night wondering if I'm doing the right thing,"[12] notes Antonia Hernandez, President, Mexican-American Legal Defense and Educational Fund. "Doing the right thing" is unequivocal for this self-made Mexican immigrant. The *power of her actions* is derived from her deeply held value of access to educational quality for Latinos. This includes the promotion of free public education, a multi-cultural curriculum, engaging instruction, technology, and K-12 –through university support. When these principles are violated, she takes her values to court. Hernandez's passions energize her own values and the values of her organization, creating an agenda for action.

Antonia Hernandez
President, Mexican American Legal Defense and Educational Fund

"A solid education levels the playing field
for everybody.
It's the surest provider of equal opportunity."

Antonia Hernandez is passionate about civil rights. As president and general counsel of the Mexican American Legal Defense and Educational Fund (MALDEF) and president of the California Community Foundation, she has committed her life to promoting the civil rights of the Latino community.

At the age of eight, Hernandez and her family moved from El Cambio, Mexico, to Los Angeles. In 1956, immigrant children—including young Hernandez—were often the target of teasing and harassment. She not only survived these difficult times, but emerged with determination, intelligence and an unwavering belief that everyone "deserves to be treated with dignity and respect."

Hernandez' most persistent priority is educational quality and access for Latinos. This priority is framed by her resolute beliefs about the nature of education as the framework for unqualified mutual responsibility, including free public education for undocumented immigrant children. Schools must honor and celebrate diversity through a solidly relevant, multi-cultural curriculum. Students need to see each other as resources, engaging in reciprocal learning and support. Such an educational system needs

to prepare students for college and the workforce
while meeting the demands of a highly technological
society. Appropriate funding would make possible a
quality K-12 education, college, and support along
the way for underrepresented students.

Whether her advocacy is for educational quality and for bilingual voting assistance as an extension
of the Voting Rights Act, against racial profiling, or
in defense of individual violations of civil rights,
Hernandez' resolve is unswerving. Her demeanor
and determination are described as "sweetness and
fire." These apt descriptors reflect caring carried
forth in the passionate demonstration of deeply held
values.

Perhaps Hernandez describes her own influence best: "People can live, learn and work together
in a demonstration of common values—to protect the
individual freedoms we cherish, while giving great
value to characteristics that enable individuals to
show compassion and empathy, and to feel responsible for the conditions of others."[13]

Noddings, Biddle, Maathai, Henke and Hernandez possess what
we think of as "moral fiber" or "heart"…that compelling sense of
purpose guided by core values. Those values oblige us to ask: What
is my purpose in the world? How can I make it a better place? How
do I engage others in the pursuit of human rights and a sustainable
future? Moral purpose is the ultimate expression of an extraordinary
commitment to values.

In the best of worlds, we bring our personal values into group or
organizational settings and find a way to integrate them into collective action. Individuals, groups, organizations and communities
attribute meaning to values; wisdom transforms that meaning into
purpose. Where do those values come from?

The Genesis of Values

When we witnessed the work and heard the conversations of
remarkable women in schools, in government, in business and charitable endeavors, it was tempting to conclude that values are often

embedded in family genes. Values seem to be evident early in life for some women, while others struggle to find their moorings, those bonds that give a sense of emotional and physical security.

I'm doing what I think I was put on this earth to do. And I'm really grateful to have something that I'm passionate about and that I think is profoundly important.
                                                        -Marian Wright Edelman

---

For the women we studied, values were derived from their early family life, lived experiences, history, and a preponderance of compassion and passion. Frequently, their stories told of early responsibilities, such as taking care of younger siblings that gave young women a feeling of being both trusted and responsible. Mothers, fathers, grandparents, teachers and pioneers were mentioned frequently as mentors and sources of light who articulated and demonstrated commitment to moral values while simultaneously asking critical questions about their meaning. In many culturally diverse families, parents showed the way; in other families, questions about values provoked dissonance.

Although Linda's mother, Lucretia, had only completed the 8th grade, her imagination and fascination with learning helped shape her daughter's values. She was astute at pointing out discrepancies and inequities. She would casually observe: "That child has lost her father and seems sad. Have you talked with her?" "Have you noticed that those folks faithfully attend church but seem indifferent to others?" "I'm not sure why we are fighting a war in Korea." Lucretia seemed to innately recognize that discrepancies provoked caring, and commitment to a high set of values.

Mary's mother, Eloise, regularly demonstrated compassion and sympathy. In Mary's childhood years, the family lived on the campus of the University of Wyoming near the Laramie Cemetery. After sharing lunch under a nearby tree, Eloise would walk among the tombstones with her children, telling made-up stories of those buried there. Those who had enjoyed a short life had performed a valiant act that made them a special person—a brother who saved his sister, a young man who served in the war to protect our freedom. The legacy of those with a longer life included a profound fragment of wisdom. From these stories, her children entered the noble lives of others, selecting values that guided them all their lives.

Eloise died from cancer at the young age of 42. She left behind not only stories but memories of caring actions: being the first to care for an elderly or sick person in the church or neighborhood, organizing teams to take food to needy families, planting extra vegetables to share with others.

Margaret Atwood, the renowned Canadian author and teacher found herself the beneficiary of having grown up with a family of scientists in Nova Scotia, "the boys in the lab"… her father, an entomologist, and his graduate students…in a forest insect research lab in northern Quebec, and her non-traditional mother, who shunned tea parties for backwoods life. This family preferred to feast on topics such as intestinal parasites and sex hormones even at Christmas dinners. Atwood's non-traditional childhood left her with a burning desire to keep learning.[14]

More than one teacher in our study described their own conversations during their growing-up years as characterized by "curiosity and defiance," which served as a propelling force in insisting upon and acting out of their values.

A young Canadian teacher told us "As I developed a voice for 'at risk' adolescents,' my peers began to respect my passion for not giving up on kids whose disability was hidden."[15] Her colleagues began to perceive these special students differently, asking themselves questions about what more they could do to connect with them. Aware that voice gave strength to her values and those of her students, this teacher continued on a path into formal leadership.

The family environment provides a rich wetland for growth. Family is the original context through which women find the encouragement and inspiration to lead, by holding tight to their values. In these examples, family influences played a major role in the genesis of values. Conversely, women may eventually realize that the values with which they were raised were wholly or partly unsatisfactory. In the following chapter, this growth in consciousness may lead to a break from family values as a necessary part of the maturing process. Unable to evolve within the constricted or harmful values of some families, some women deliberately separate themselves from family beliefs in order to move toward a Perspective Four life.

As we noted in the Introduction, the values embedded in the report of the International Human Rights Commission found expression in the lived experiences of women leaders across diverse fields. More than 60 years after this report, the notion of the rights of children, of individuals with special needs, of parents, and of teachers are assumed to be a critical consideration in schools.

Barriers to Implementing Our Values: Perspectives One and Two

Whatever the genesis of values, sometimes our commitment falls short. Fears, needs and priorities intrude. If values are so important, so compelling, what gets in the way of listening to ourselves and trusting that our responses will be consistent with our moral character? Barriers abound; otherwise we wouldn't lament the conditions in many schools and districts today and the lack of success in meeting the learning and relationship needs of all children. We would even venture to say that the fundamental problem in schools and districts, as well as in business and societies in general, is the failure to act upon our values with integrity.

The suffragettes were jailed, attacked, and divorced in their quest for the American dream of full citizenship... Now, eighty years later, what will you make of their ideals?
                -Sandra Day O'Connor, Supreme Court Justice

The women in our study were remarkably forthcoming about what prevented them from exercising a full commitment to their values. They vividly described the fears, needs, reservations, lack of clarity, dependencies and competing priorities that kept them from acting on their values, finding it difficult to fully shed the fears of Perspective One and Two, which continue to affect the struggle for development. One participant summed up the fears that haunted her: "My fear of surrender and trusting each time I stepped out of the known, my fear of inadequacy, my fear of falling short of my purpose."[16]

In the years that followed, our research with hundreds of other women, as well as our personal lived experiences, served to confirm and explicate these issues. Several of these barriers are unique to, or are felt more heavily by, women. Here are several cases in point.

Sally became principal at Bellevue Middle School in the fall. She was fresh from a stunning career as a teacher leader and loaded for bear with the "right" values, including the value of equal access to the curriculum, and ready to take on the world. Within the first two weeks, Sally learned that the math department was strictly tracked so that at least one- third of the students would not take Algebra I by the time they entered high school. These students would fall short of the necessary math course of study for college.

Sally met with the members of the math department. Two forceful men teachers insisted that this was how math classes were organized in the school, and that certain (identified) students needed to stay in remedial math. One teacher in particular held her gaze, daring her to counter the decision. Her head was aching, her stomach tightened, and she fell silent. Her fear of instigating conflict with the math teachers ruled the day.

Maria, who had been asked by the principal to go to a regional workshop on whole language, was enchanted by what she learned. The workshop leaders laid out the value and theoretical framework for a constructivist, reciprocal approach to instruction that was highly compatible with Maria's beliefs. She was eager to fulfill the school expectation of presenting her new findings to her grade level teachers.

In preparation for the meeting, Maria met with a senior teacher, Grace, who had served as her mentor and friend. Grace told her that whole language would not only be a threat to herself and her way of teaching, and she even questioned whether whole language would actually strengthen test performance. Maria drew back, afraid to displease her mentor. Her presentation was perfunctory, formal and lacked advocacy.

Barbara, a midwestern superintendent of a K-8 school district, prided herself on the value she placed on student learning and on her ability to create a district in which student performance was steadily improving. In an area with a growing Latino population, she had worked with principals and teachers to honor the experiences, culture and language of all students. Together, they had developed a transitional bilingual program. Classroom visits had persuaded Barbara that children were blossoming under this approach. When two newly elected members joined the board, a new majority was formed. The board proposed an English-only approach to instruction. Barbara was taken aback by what she considered an affront to the value of diversity that was now established in the district. Yet, anticipating the loss of her position, she began to quietly dismantle the bilingual program.

Sally, Maria and Barbara struggle with fears that create barriers to the implementation of their values. These conditions are not irreversible. Indeed, they tell us where the learning needs to occur. For these women, a range of strategies enabled them to move forward. The first step is the realization that a fear is blocking action. These realizations or growth in consciousness often emerge from reflection and dialogue. Finding time for regular reflection and a trusted friend or colleague for dialogue can strengthen our resolve.

Once women realize the fear at hand (and stop rationalizing that fear, if possible), it is critical to consider what is at stake. Was it more important for Sally and Maria to please their colleagues or to promote programs that might eventually help hundreds of students? When such a question confronts our sensibilities, the answer is not difficult, although the prospect of altering entrenched behavior can still be very challenging. Rehearsing our actions, writing out an agenda or a plan, or taking a colleague into the conversation can often give the needed strength to overcome the barrier.

For Barbara, her risk was even more dramatic, since her prized possession, her position, depended on it. The board still held Barbara in high regard. Building on her own good will in the district, she would need to collect data on the success of the current programs in an effort to educate and persuade the board of the bilingual program's validity. If this approach did not work, Barbara might need to look for another position.   We will return to her case under the theme of examining the concepts of "passion and courage."

Value-Driven Practices and the World of Schooling

Equitable outcomes mean more than the same outcomes, having the same resources, the same curriculum and instruction, and the same access. The antithesis of the "bell curve," equitable outcomes represent a value-driven concept that means that everyone arrives in the general learning vicinity of everyone else, ready for a quality life of education, employment and citizenship. This value is one of three that underlie the practices listed in Figure Two. Value-Driven and Value-Violating School Practices are based upon the values identified by Gilligan[17] as at the higher levels of development for women: social justice, caring and equity. These examples represent Perspective Four, The Integrated Self, in action.

Practices and policies that are value-driven suggest to us that students are to be treated as individuals who possess interests, choices and passions of their own. They reciprocally care and learn from each other across grade levels and across ability and language groupings. For both peers and adults, this caring leads to sustainable relationships. Further, adults learn from each other and work together collaboratively, each having a voice in the governance of the school or district. The examples provided in Figure 2.2 are representative of these principles; the examples below explicate these values and embed them in stories of practice.

Figure 2.2 Value-Driven Curriculum Practices

Value-Driven Practices	Value-Violating Practices
1. Heterogeneous grouping	1. "Tracking" (remediation to advanced placement)
2. Full inclusion	2. Segregation-special education/language learners
3. Performance-based assessment	3. Standardized testing only
4. Block scheduling	4. Uniform 5-8 period days
5. Active Learning	5. Direct instruction only
6. Educators and counselors as advisers and mentors	6. Teachers deliver instruction/ Counselors as technicians
7. Collaborative governance	7. Autocratic governance
8. Inquiry-based decision-making	8. External originating reform
9. Teacher leadership	9. Administrator leadership only
10. Coherent, vision-driven programs	10. Fragmented, urgent-not important programmatic responses
11. Reflective practice	11. Compliant, traditional practice
12. Equitable outcome policies	12. Managerial policies

When Gerry returned to Poland Regional High School as a school coach she worked with the leadership team to design a school that met many of the "value-driven" features in Figure 2.2. Unlike any other public high school in the state, the school was organized into grade-level teams. Classes were heterogeneously grouped, with an advanced challenge available to each student. Students were placed in advisory groups and had the same advisor for their entire four years, thus ensuring sustainable relationships. Traditional letter grades were replaced by three designations: "Distinguished," "Advanced," and "Competent." Students had multiple opportunities to succeed…failure was not an option. In order to graduate, students conducted in-depth investigations in areas of their interest and presented them in the "senior celebration." The school was collaboratively governed through the leadership team.[18]

Each of the stories that follow portrays a dimension of value-driven programs and policies.

"It doesn't really matter much if you meet all the grade level standards or exceed them, if you don't contribute in a positive way to your community and to your school" says Rebecca Lindquist, California's Elementary Principal of the Year. She was chosen for this award as a woman who lives out her values, creating programs to promote character, community service and leadership. Early on, Rebecca recognized that giving attention to these values would bring increased academic success for all students. And she was right.[19]

Barbara Ryan, Vice President of Government Affairs for Children's Hospital and Health Center in San Diego has been a school board member in Santee, California, for 27 years. A mother of six children, she knew personally what it meant to hold high expectations and not settle for what could be "realistically expected." As a board member, high standards were a non-negotiable. "All children can learn," insists Ryan, "but we often lower our expectations because of socio-economic conditions or ethnicity. We must give all children a chance, provide the necessary resources and resist blaming failures on someone else." Resisting the temptation to have her own children tested for the gifted and talented program, Ryan deeply believes that all classrooms can and should meet the needs of all students.[20]

Denise Jay, principal of Bolsa Grande High School, turned around this large urban high school outside of Los Angeles. Denise believed emphatically that immigrant students could achieve at the same level as affluent suburban high school students if they were held to high expectations and provided with support. After seven years of steady support and improvement, Bolsa Grande is now one of the top ten high schools in the state.[21]

Kawsar Kouchok, an Egyptian leader and founder of the Centre for Curriculum and Instructional Materials Development (CCIMD) in Cairo has invested a lifetime of international education work to achieving active learning for children, often in societies where memorization, rather than engaged learning, has been the norm. Based upon her research and writing in active learning, Kawsar worked with Malak Zaalouk and UNICEF to establish Community Schools for Girls. Early in her career, Kawsar was chosen by the United

Nations to establish teacher-training camps in Palestine and to set up universities in Oman and Kenya. She later became the first woman dean of Helwan University in Egypt. Over a career that has spanned more than half a century, Kawsar has never lost sight of her values.[22]

At Glenlawn High School in Winnipeg, Canada, the student advocacy committee and principal Donna Burlow developed a comprehensive staff development plan to help teachers become more proficient at building caring relationships with students. In a long-range study of the school's effectiveness, all indicators pointed to the need for a more student-centered environment. The school subsequently implemented peer coaching, advisement, differentiated instruction, cooperative learning and portfolio assessment, and shared decision-making. Today, Glenlawn is recognized for its capacity to respond to changing times in an urban setting.[23]

The women above undertook value-driven practices with understandings, skills and competencies that enabled them to provide for choice, voice, inquiry and equitable outcomes. Such specific strategies were derived from core values of caring, social justice and equity. We found that valuing skills include at least the following:

- Identifying and articulating values;
- Facilitating community members in the development of a shared vision;
- Translating values and vision into goals and actions;
- Aligning own behaviors with values; being authentic;
- Providing feedback to others in relation to congruent implementation of vision;
- Designing and assessing curriculum and instruction or products consistent with shared vision;
- Integrating community talents and other resources into the pursuit of shared vision.

Conclusion

Even when women pursue values on a daily basis, nothing can be taken for granted. Yet the persistent pursuit of values, thoughtful attention to overcoming barriers, and the translation of those values into both personal and organizational visions, stoke passion and beget purpose.

In Chapter Three, the understandings about values will spiral into a deeper insight about who women are and who they are becoming. Women who lead attend to the evolving self and growing identity. That process of evolving integrates values into identity while building momentum for passionate action.

Remember?
I am the woman/with the blessed/dark skin/I am the
woman with teeth repaired/I am the woman/with the heal-
ing eye/the ear that hears.
I am the woman: Dark/repaired, healed/listening to you.
I would give/to the human race/only hope.
I am the woman/offering two flowers/whose roots/are
twin
Justice and Hope/Hope and Justice
Let us begin.

-Alice Walker

Reflections and Questions

This section has set forth our description of a value-inspired life and stories of women who are leading such lives, as well as the struggles of those who strive to lead such lives. We refer to values as "the genesis of leadership." Please consider and respond to the following questions in your journal or in conversation with other women. Select the questions that thoughtfully engage you in an exploration of your own life.

1. Do I see my own life reflected in these stories? In what ways?
2. What values form who I am?
3. Which Perspective (One through Four) best reflects my current development as a value-driven person? Why is that so?

4. How have my values given me strength, direction, focus?
5. What would I consider the major sources of my values?
6. Explore organizations dedicated to the values that I hold. How might I get involved?
7. To what extent does the district or organization in which I work reflect sound core values? How do I, or might I, influence that organization to evolve toward a more value-driven entity?
8. Think about my daily personal and work life. How can an awareness and strong commitment to a set of values resolve the struggles I encounter?

Values form your identity. In Chapter 3, *Women Who Lead are Conscious of the Evolving Self,* you will be asked to integrate your values into an awareness of how you are evolving as a woman leader.

Women Who Lead Are….
Conscious of the Evolving Self

Chapter Three

A crone is a woman who has a sense of truly being herself, can express what she knows and feels and takes action when need be. She does not avert her eyes or numb her mind from reality. She can see the flaws and imperfections in herself and others, but the light in which she sees is not harsh and judgmental. She has learned to trust herself to know what she knows.
-Jean Shinoda Bolen, Psychiatrist

Bolen captures the essence of this consciousness: self-expression, trust in self, a firm hold on multiple realities. Women who lead have a clear sense of who they are and who they are becoming. To become conscious of our evolving selves involves awareness, the capability to stand back and watch ourselves become different, more active and more integrated. This is a process of self-reflection.

Chapter Two described valuing as the embodiment of who we are; valuing as an expression of care. Women care about others, about issues of equity and participation, about the genuine quality and integrity of their work, about society and the future. Consciousness springs from the meanings derived from lives led and values attended to, while a lack of consciousness demands an adherence to values based either on the authority of others or on the unchallenged conventional values found in many organizations.

The struggles faced by Sally, Maria and Barbara in Chapter Two were primarily dramas involving growing consciousness as the pathway toward the genuine expression of values. The three women struggled with what others thought of their ideas and as individuals they were challenged with the need to mediate those ideas in order to move toward their own values.

Constructing Lives

To be conscious means to continually construct a life that reaches out and participates in the world. The women we studied were vividly aware of the growth occurring within themselves as they composed and lived out their lives. This awareness produced knowledge of both their strengths and limitations, enabling them to add value to other women's lives through their compassion, work and roles in the world. Understanding their journey assisted other women in constructing their own paths, integrating the needs and insistencies of others without losing themselves.

Mary Catherine Bateson refers to this process as "composing."[1] Composing a life occurs differently for women than for men, since women begin from a point of connectedness and attachment. The reflective journey is a dual process of consolidating connections while migrating away from these connections enough to gain perspective. Prior experiences are edited, allowing for an analysis of what we want to keep, modify or abandon…a struggle between harmony and dissonance.

Mary Catherine Bateson
Anthropologist, Educator, Author

"We are not what we know,
but what we are willing to learn."

Perhaps more than anyone else, it is Mary Catherine Bateson who teaches us to be conscious of our evolving selves. It was Bateson who insisted that composing or constructing our lives is a long-term improvisation of combining personal meanings that are found in both the familiar and the unfamiliar within the nuggets discovered in ambiguities. As we grow, we observe, assemble and reassemble the parts of our lives into new wholes. "A collection of broken beads can be joined in a necklace of beauty and grace,"[2]Bateson claims.

While Bateson understands that growing up is a slowly evolving process…and some of us never quite make it…she is eternally optimistic. Although we know that women who lead have a clear sense of who they are and who they are becoming—these insights do not come easily or quickly. Learning, reflection and dynamic relationships (including expectations that bind) all play an important role.

Bateson's life's work is about discovering and teaching us how to stay open to new learning.

Four of her books offer remarkable guidance in this journey of self-discovery and composition: *Composing a Life, Peripheral Visions, Willing to Learn and Full Circle*.[3] Each of these works tells us how she developed an anthropologist's eye, her assumptions about human development and pathways for composing and writing about our own lives. Through her work, parents, teachers, and children are more able to respond to epiphanies, to develop "the quality of attention that makes recognition possible: pattern matched with pattern, vagrant awareness welcomed, empathy established."[4] By mooring our lives to the shore of identity, we can ride and enjoy the swells and winds.

Bateson's writings help us to understand the connections among consciousness, identity and the world around us. "Major social change often involves fundamental shifts in identity," she argues, "including the acceptance of the role of learner struggling to function in a changed world."[5] We are all learners, and to the extent that we are purposely struggling toward a changed world, we are all leaders.

We have reasoned that leadership is a form of learning, learning together in purposeful ways. Our conception of leadership is ripe for the inclusion of Mary Catherine Bateson, a consummate learner and mentor of the next generation of women leaders.

"Composing" is a lifelong improvisation of combining personal meanings found in both the familiar and the unfamiliar with the nuggets discovered in ambiguities. Composing lives is the process of integration: integrating a sense of self and values with the expectations of others. While these expectations play a vital, sometimes demanding, role in the evolving self, if they are the dominant role, women can become permanently affixed in Perspective Two.

Power and Authority

During the process of composing lives, women evolve into and must come to terms with issues of power and authority. In our study of women this was named as one of the most challenging aspects of women's development. Why is that? Most of our interviewees have been uncomfortable with the expressions of power and authority they have experienced in families, churches, the workplace and society. Power and authority, though different, are often used to force, to control, to dominate.

We define *power* as first and foremost a personal, internal process, ranging from powerless to powerful, involving finding one's voice, growing in confidence and acknowledging personal authority. Externally, personal power is manifest in the influence of others' judgments, emotions and behaviors.

A closely related concept, *authority,* has two distinct branches: formal and informal. Formal authority is derived from laws or established rules that grant the right or give permission to direct others, make decisions and set policy. Derived or formal authority means that individuals in a particular position may retain rights over the behavior of others. A CEO, superintendent, director, priest or parent may derive authority from policy, ownership, canon, constitution, edict, or statute. How such authority is used will determine the relationships and participation patterns of its recipients. Formal authority can also be used as a crutch to achieve that which the holder thinks is not possible otherwise—"Do what I say because I am your superior."

On the other hand, informal authority is derived from credibility, knowledge, skillfulness, and the capacity to evidence a desired trait or moral example. Informal authority is a reciprocal social contract, since it is granted by the recipients based on their perception of the legitimacy of the other to lead. Such legitimacy is earned rather than legally granted.

The evolving consciousness of women suggests that *personal* power and *informal* authority are more effective ways to lead, retaining desirable reciprocal learning relationships.

> *A need for power has proven to be equally strong in men and women. However, men and women tend to think about power differently. Men construe it as more competitive and hierarchical and women as more cooperative and interdependent.*
>
> *Alice H. Eagly and Linda L. Carli*

The Four Perspectives of Women's Leadership

In Chapter One, Figure 1.1, four perspectives were introduced on being conscious of the evolving self.

Figure 3.1 briefly describes the Four Perspectives of the Evolving Self.

Figure 3.1 Perspectives on Evolving Self

	Perspective 1	**Perspective 2**	**Perspective 3**	**Perspective 4**
Conscious of the Evolving Self	Withholds personal voice: own identity is undefined; experiences shame and guilt; avoidance of conflict.	Defines identity by job, role, organization. Good leader=good girl. Appearance and social acceptability are of prime importance.	Differentiates personal identity from group identity; accepts self; accepts conflict as an essential part of change.	Bases authentic identity on self-reflection and the needs of others; uses informal authority to bring about change.

To understand how these four perspectives can play out in practice, consider the approaches governing the persistent national issue of adopting prescriptive reading programs. A *Perspective One* woman, not yet a leader, will seek to implement whatever program is handed to the school. A *Perspective Two* educator may aim to ensure that the prescribed program is implemented with integrity, as intended. A *Perspective Three* educator, on the other hand, will only implement the program if it is consistent with her own findings of effective practice; otherwise, she will refuse to take part in the new program or even leave the profession. A *Perspective Four* educator may work with others in the district and school to inquire into the effectiveness of the new program and help conceptualize a blended approach that draws on the strengths of approaches, as appropriate. Further, this leader will seek to disseminate information and educate others as an integral part of educational improvement.

Viewing consciousness through the lens of the Four Perspectives brings a realization of critical transition periods when women break through the inertia, re-interpreting earlier experience and rendering experience conscious, particularly between *Perspective Two*, The Nascent Self, and *Perspective Three*, The Emerging Self.

We don't accomplish anything in this world alone...and whatever happens is the result of the whole tapestry of one's life and all the weavings of individual threads from one to another that creates something.

-Sandra Day O'Connor

Perspectives One and Two

The central dramas of *Perspectives One and Two* often involve issues of conflict and responding to the expectations of others. Conflict can be terrifying; since attachment is so critical to women, conflict signals the possibility that attachments will be lost. Childhood experiences with parental conflict or violence often render the adult individual powerless. Yet, leaders cannot lead without being able to anticipate, surface, mediate and grow from anger and conflict. What a dilemma!

The second overriding drama of those characterized as in denial or nascent perspectives is the issue of responding to expectations. Again, it must be noted that since women were raised *in relationship to others*, rather than with the aim of *differentiating themselves from others* (as is true for men), the urge to please is often pervasive. Almost all women encounter this struggle...the tension between the authentic self and the self that others would have them be. This is often played out in schools and organizations when women receive messages from male superiors in the organizational hierarchy regarding the kind or intensity of work in which they should be engaged.

Combine this contradiction with the voices of parents that still resonate in women's heads, and the toxic mix slows progress toward the authentic self. There is a whirling nature, a spiraling process, to development—-not a march forward toward the Promised Land. Women tend to adapt and appease, accommodate, and, eventually, integrate.

Eugenia, an example of a *Perspective One* woman, was a graduate student in Linda's educational leadership program. Smart, sensitive and a successful manager, silence was her only refuge in groups. Repeatedly, Linda challenged her, in person and in journal responses, regarding the process of finding her own voice. While Eugenia could theoretically understand the notion of public voice and leadership, she froze in group settings. Toward the end of the academic year, she reported in her journal a life-altering experience. Eugenia had been sitting in a district administrative meeting when the name of a friend and colleague surfaced in the conversation. The friend was verbally crucified and scheduled for dismissal. Eugenia could not bring herself to speak up and defend her friend; the remorse she felt afterwards changed her life as an educational leader. She truly found her voice the hard way.

What does it mean to find your voice? Finding voice is more than talking. It involves the hope that one will touch others' emotions, that your thoughts will be heard. This requires confidence in the importance of what you have to say and in the trust that others will hear your message. Such insight requires a realignment of both the self and the other. For *Perspective One* women such as Eugenia, when she realized that her own silence was harmful to her friend, she was ready to move forward.

The professions are brimming with *Perspective Two* women. In fact, we would estimate that the majority of mid-level managers are in this phase of development, for they are the ones who make organizations work. Emboldened by the force of formal authority, women wield power over others. In education, such as the federally imposed program No Child Left Behind, these women are sometimes referred to "accountability queens." They do not question the goals of the organization or national direction, and in fact work hard to implement and preserve those goals against all odds.

When Geraldine was hired as assistant superintendent in a Texas school district, her major responsibility was to oversee testing and ensure that students were prepared to perform well. In the process, she oversaw the demise of the arts, science and much of the history curriculum, since the initiative exclusively focuses on reading and math. By taking the task at face value, Geraldine narrowed the curriculum.

In a nearby district, assistant superintendent Joanne led educators toward the development of an integrated curriculum that taught reading within the context of the sciences and the arts. The actions of Geraldine may be viewed as *Perspective Two*, while the actions of Joanne may be viewed as a *Perspective Three or Four*. Why is that? Because Joanne was able to step back and ask how educational goals could be combined so that students grew as critical and creative thinkers…as well as readers and mathematicians.

Once conform, once do what other people do because they do it, and a lethargy steals over all the fine nerves and faculties of the soul.

-Virginia Woolf

Condoleezza Rice, Secretary of Defense in the Bush administration, is a woman of deeply held values and sharply honed skills. Yet, she is an example of a *Perspective Two* woman. Confident, smart and successful, Rice personally admits that she is not self-reflective; in fact, she finds such indulgences a waste of time. When she joined the Stanford faculty as an affirmative action hire at the age of 26, it might have been natural for her to reflect upon whether she was good enough, but she never entertained these thoughts. Disciplined, focused and a great synthesizer of ideas, Rice is also a woman who never gives an inch and sees her opponents as attackers.[6] While she was living a life in which she sought personal power and held tightly to loyalty, personal transformation was not in her immediate forecast. As she returns to Stanford in 2009, a more relaxed woman with plans for writing two books, she may at last find self-reflection liberating.

An emergent world invites us to use our most human of all capacities, our consciousness. It asks us to be alert in the moment for what is unfolding. What is happening at this moment? What can we do because of what we just learned?

-Margaret Wheatley

Transitioning from Perspectives One and Two

Events and dramas that provoke change can be stunning, even shocking, such as in the case of Eugenia, who found herself propelled out of *Perspective One* by a singular event. Being dismissed from a position or dismissed as an individual, or even an overdose of weariness, can be the wakeup call. However, Bateson suggests that this journey of composing most often occurs longitudinally...over time. These changes may not seem dazzling until one day a woman realizes that the pathway itself was dazzling. Two stories represent this journey.

Anne Conzemius, co-founder of Quantum Leading and former Deputy Superintendent for Education in Wisconsin, learned to free herself from a life of rigidity, right answers and conforming ideas. Colleen Wilcox, Superintendent of Schools of Santa Clara County, California, evolved into the realization that the limits and boundaries that she had earlier accepted as a young girl from Mississippi were not only unnecessary, but a form of cultural bondage. Both Anne and Colleen freed themselves from their pasts, over time, through intense inquisitiveness and by responding to support systems within the environment, evolving from *Perspectives One and Two* into more fully integrated women.

Anne Conzemius
Co-founder, Quantum Leading

Having grown up the middle child of seven in a rule-bound Catholic family, achievement as a student could mean only one thing – good grades. Under the superb tutelage of my older siblings, I quickly learned that good behavior and figuring out how to take tests translated into good grades. What could be easier than this? So it should come as no surprise that as an adult, when faced with real-life issues and challenges in the workplace, if the right answer couldn't be determined through the use of a formula or found in a rulebook, I was at a loss.

The moment of truth came to me when I was Director of Employee Development for our state's Department of Employee Relations. I headed up a small staff of committed young men and women who were baffled by my regimented view of training – didactic, time and place-bound, and very traditional in content. Fortunately I had a team of strong-willed people with courage to challenge the "boss." They suggested I sign up for a class in creative thinking and problem-solving. When I examined my hesitation to take this class, I realized that I was afraid that it would be discovered that I had never had a creative thought in my life!

It was downright scary to think that I would have to step outside this comfortable me in order to stretch into some unknown potential called "creative thinker." At the age of thirty-six, I came into a new self-image. I took the class only to find out that I was actually capable of original thought (as opposed to original sin). That simple but profound moment freed me for life. I shudder to think what the rest of my life would have been like locked inside my former self.

Colleen Wilcox
Superintendent, Santa Clara County
Office of Education, California

When I was a child, growing up along the Mississippi, a girl in my class had a mother who was a doctor. That was quite an oddity at the time - and I can remember thinking, "Who would go to her? Why would anyone want to see a woman doctor?" I assumed she hadn't many patients.

My attitude was not unusual. Some professions were thought to be best-suited for men, not women. Typically, these were jobs of power, prestige and responsibility: doctors, lawyers, politicians, school principals and superintendents. There was an unquestioned attitude that pervaded my life-experience, holding that men could and should do these jobs - and that women couldn't and shouldn't.

This attitude stayed with me as I went through high school; got a bachelor's degree; did a stint in the Peace Corps; and even when I attained my master's degree. As I took jobs of increasing responsibility, some overstepped the boundaries of traditionally male occupations. But those old attitudes remained deep inside me. When I needed the services of a doctor, I chose a man. When I needed an accountant, I chose a man.

It wasn't until I was well into my 30s, with a Ph.D. in hand, that I finally began to question some of my long-held prejudices. It wasn't one single incident, but a series of observations over time. I kept bumping into situations where men in these prestigious positions were not working nearly as hard as their female counterparts. Some of these guys, frankly, were just skating. But their female peers seemed to be doing a lot more work, and in many cases, better work, too.

Eventually, when confronted with enough of these situations, the long-held beliefs and prejudices that had been so deeply ingrained in me as a child began to erode. It wasn't just a single epiphany. It was a series of small revelations, which, bit by bit, finally accumulated enough energy to cause a dramatic change of heart.

It was at that point that I realized: most of the women doing these jobs probably were as well or better qualified than the men—if for no other reason than they undoubtedly had had to work much harder to get to the same point. None of them could ever have skated. And that is why today, when I have the choice, I prefer to see a female doctor. I will seek out a female lawyer. I know they wouldn't be where they are unless they fully earned it.[7]

A powerful case in point is the longitudinal struggle for understanding by author Amy Tan. Much of Tan's writing was a quest for understanding— both of her parents and of her Chinese culture. Separating her own expectations from those of her mother was a long task. Her parents' expectations limited her scope of writing, until Tan came to realize that her parents were acting out of love rather than being disappointed in her. A trip to China with her mother redirected her thinking; by altering her perception of parental criticism, Tan was finally able to free herself. Writing fiction became her medium for finding out who she truly was.[8]

The journey from *Perspectives One and Two* is often a struggle of competing tensions. The co-author of this book, Linda Lambert, is on a lifelong journey—still far from complete—to resolve the battle between her natural tendencies for control and her value of democracy and inclusion. The maturing process requires the alignment and integration of values and behaviors that sometimes leads to the conquest of personality and cultural persistencies.

Perspective Three: The Emerging Self—Revolutionaries

As noted in Chapter Two, our study revealed that it is not uncommon for women who become aware of injustice to become union leaders. For instance, one woman joined a union to develop a new teacher evaluation system when a young teacher who had looked to her for guidance was unfairly denied tenure. Another teacher became an activist when she was provoked to confront her principal over what she felt was an inappropriate placement of a child in special education.

Georgia O'Keeffe, America's foremost woman artist, needed no provocation to become a strong individual with a clear identity. O'Keeffe's clarity was evident by the age of 12, when she declared that she wanted to be an artist. In 1909, that was a profession unheard-of for women. O'Keeffe mused of her early years: "Before I put brush to canvas, 'I question: Is this mine? Is it intrinsically of myself? Is it influenced by some idea or some photograph of an idea which I have acquired from some man?' "[9] As clear as O'Keeffe was about herself, she never desired the integration of self with others. Only after her long life ended did the Santa Fe Museum establish a leadership program for young women.

The *Perspective Three* woman differentiates herself from others and finds strength and a strong sense of personal power in her own resolve. Her values and passion sharpen her determination to separate from the crowd. One might ask, "Isn't being such a 'strong woman' what we want? Aren't these the women who will change the world? What is the advantage of moving into *Perspective Four*?"

Yes, *Perspective Three* women can and do change the world, but sometimes at the cost of leaving others behind. They may take their outrage and themselves too seriously, which may interrupt the process of reflection. Integration requires the capacity "to stand back and watch oneself becoming different" –challenging assumptions and laughing at oneself. A lightness of spirit can be a sign of maturity, and of an integrated self that does not personalize disappointments, indulge in regrets or avoid the unknown. Seriousness is often attended by conserving the images we hold in our minds, while lightness allows us to imagine ourselves in new stages, participating in new ventures.

Although the *Perspective Three* woman may be overly serious, she is growing in her capacity for reflection. When she realizes that she is blocked from achieving her goals by her failure to authentically involve others in her journey, she may open up to the broader world and realize that change is not a journey she has to take alone.

Perspective Four: Becoming a Transforming Woman

Sustainable change requires that the journey of development merge self and other—a woman must bring the inside world and the outside world together. Such women transform themselves as well as others through compassion, forgiveness and empathy and engage in what Coughlin, Wingard and Hollihan refer to as "Enlightened Power,"[10] the use of personal power with, not over, others to achieve results. Leading through enlightened personal power and informal authority is the appropriate realm of transforming women. Chapter Two described how Julie Biddle, Antonia Hernandez and Wangari Maathai achieved personal maturity and accomplishment by reframing their work as collective courageous action.

Christie Todd Whitman, a woman of deeply felt conservative beliefs and personal clarity, was appointed Director of the Environmental Protection Agency in 2001. She resigned her post in 2004 when the Bush administration directed her to implement relaxed industrial pollution guidelines that would have reversed the progress she had made when she was Governor of New Jersey. Whitman weighed the expectations held for her by the administration with her own sense of self, and found theirs wanting. Yet instead of leaving the Republican Party, she mediated her relationship by writing *It's My Party Too*, seeking to reform from within while maintaining her own integrity.[11]

The story of Elizabeth Reilly, Associate Professor of Educational Leadership at Pepperdine University, is an example of the role and nature of reciprocity for a *Perspective Four* woman. Opening up the conversation and believing in the gifts that everyone has to bring to the table brought forth a rapprochement of traditions and political tensions.

> *The joy of meeting someone you love, the sadness of losing a close friend, the richness of a vivid dream, the serenity of a walk through the garden on a spring day, the total absorption of deep meditative state—-these things and others like them constitute the reality of our experience of consciousness.*
>
> *- The Dalai Lama*

Elizabeth Reilly
Associate Professor, Educational Leadership, Administration, and Policy, Pepperdine University

An acquaintance of mine has said that he lacks a sense of terminal uniqueness, but I believe that each of us is indeed unique and gifted. From the women mentors in my life—principally graduate school professors—I learned years ago that it was my small gift to see the gifts in others, and this manifests itself through my teaching and my work in the world by being a muse and spreading the fairy dust as far and as widely as possible. Taking risks, seizing opportunities, however, is not always an easy matter, for the every day somethings and nothings of life can present both real and imagined obstacles. More often than not, however, it is fear that immobilizes me: the fear of failure or the fear of rejection that keeps me from taking the risk and of speaking up. At a recent international conference on school leadership held in Germany, I dined with two of the other conference attendees—one, a German Christian and the other, a Pakistani Muslim. With me, the American Jew in the mix, we made quite a trio. As we talked, I reflected inwardly at the unique-yet-fragile alliance budding among us three. We discussed social responsibility and the various minorities that suffer in our nations in diaspora. The subject moved to the essence of why we each do our work in the world, why it is that we

are educators. I offered, "Is it not so that your
children and mine—whether Christian, Muslim,
or Jew—might have a future?" Although their
eyes spoke volumes, both men nodded. I suggested we consider not sitting around waiting for
the politicians to take up this issue and that we
educators form an international symposium that
addresses diaspora within our own countries and
worldwide, and frame it through the lens of
social responsibility. We agreed to work toward
this vision together. I often tell my students that
both large and small things begin with a conversation. To be that muse in the world, we must
take risks, speak up, and be willing to imagine,
wonder, and accept liberal amounts of fairy dust
from like-minded travelers.[12]

Shirley Chisholm, the first woman to run for President in
the United States, had incredible boldness and confidence. A compelling story that demonstrates her consciousness involved a visit
Chisholm made to the deathbed of George Wallace, a man of deep
prejudice and racist actions. She had every right to shun him as he
did others. When she visited him in the hospital, he asked, "What are
your people going to think?" "I know what they're going to say," she
responded, "but I wouldn't want what happened to you to happen to
anyone." Her compassion moved him to tears.[13]

Shirley Chisholm
Legislator, Orator, Civil Rights Activist

"Unbought and Unbossed"

Shirley Chisholm was a woman of firsts:
the first African American woman in Congress,
the first president of the National Political Congress of Black Women, the first woman to run
for the United States presidential nomination in
the 20th century. Chisholm was a woman wholly
conscious of who she was….lived her life as she

saw fit…and saw her life writ large. As a life-long activist, she unrelentingly advocated for civil rights for people of color, women and children, people who were underrepresented by elected officials and society. Chisholm considered the ideas of others, resisted succumbing to outside pressures, adopted her own unique style and used her own voice.

The centerpiece of her unique style was her extraordinary and charismatic oratory skill. Later in life she claimed, "My greatest political asset, which professional politicians fear, is my mouth, out of which come all kinds of things one shouldn't always discuss for reasons of political expediency." This talent, and her intense interest in politics and history, was evident early. In junior high school, she identified her heroes: Harriet Tubman, Susan B. Anthony and Mary McLeod Bethune. The stories of these remarkable women helped her to realize that girls were as brave and bright as boys…and that perhaps a woman could be President.

Chisholm was a woman of surprises and also of great predictability. Deeply committed to a set of core values and courageous in the face of opposition, she could be counted on to take on the confounding problems of society and to create new solutions. Whether it was scholarships for needy Puerto Rican children, unemployment for domestic workers or a proposal to further the rights of women, she was tenacious and tireless in her support. "Women in this country must become revolutionaries," she declared, "We must refuse to accept the old, the traditional roles and stereotypes." Chisholm never minced words.

Chisholm prided herself on being "unbought and unbossed." This clarity, confidence and integrity served her well. It serves all of us well. Generations of women learned from Chisholm that they could lead with power and intensity, and that all issues are human issues and therefore "women's issues." Chisholm left

Congress in 1982 and summed up her desired
legacy in simple terms: "I'd like them to say that
Shirley Chisholm had guts." She sure did.[14]

Whitman, Reilly, and Chisholm were transformational women
because they asserted themselves in the world of others, thereby integrating their inner and outer lives.

Conditions that Provoke Transformation

Mary Warnock insisted that, "The primary purpose of education
is to deny people the opportunity for feeling bored or for succumbing to a feeling of futility, or to the belief that they have come to an
end of what is worth having."[15] One of the primary purposes of education, especially for women, is to build the hope and confidence that
leads to action. Organizations that invite women to evolve into
greater self- understanding are open, transparent and honest. Secret
codes or agendas, such as dominant male cultures, can derail the
reflective learning process by providing false or misleading information. Organizations that invite vulnerability, such as in problem- solving, enable women to honestly examine who they are.

Leaders have stories to tell, and by learning from these stories,
collective consciousness and values are created. Carol Witherell and
Nel Noddings argued that when communities encourage inclusive
dialogue, the result is an examination of the principles they hold, the
consequences of their actions, the history of our own beliefs and justifications for opposing points of view.[16]

Organizational leaders, and those in the process of becoming
leaders, grow and find satisfaction where learning, choice, discretion
and opportunities for multiple roles exist. We know from our work in
leadership capacity that roles can provide an enlarging context that
encourages self-perception and confidence. Many opportunities to
lead through multiple roles develop leaders who are constantly honing their skills and developing new insights.

We find "never being the same again" a code phrase for a
growth in consciousness. Experiences need to provide training
and practice in dialogue, self-disclosure, problem-solving, decision

making and new role performance. For instance, when teachers broaden their roles and become advisors, a new set of skills is needed; when governmental agencies value team leadership, a new set of skills is needed; and when a business asks employees to set personal development goals, a new set of skills is needed. We would suggest that the following skills and actions contribute to the growth of consciousness:

- Reflecting upon personal growth in relation to the work of leadership;
- Engaging others in reflection by modeling, providing time and structure, such as critical questions;
- Talking aloud about errors, personal growth goals, struggles, own journey;
- Coaching others through the process of growth in relation to values and behaviors;
- Challenging prevailing assumptions;
- Providing discretionary resources so that colleagues can pursue evolving goals.

Keep in mind that skill development or problem-solving without dialogue and conversation are empty pursuits.

Through reflection on actions, individuals can clarify what is known through talking and writing about their experiences and responses to those experiences, which is a compelling reason to include writing life histories and narratives as a way to understand the self. Understanding the self makes leadership possible.

Conclusion

Being conscious means experiencing and expressing empathy from different points of view. Such understandings result from a capacity for reflection, critically examining our experiences and actions. Self-reflection has the potential to change the way we make sense of our world. Reflection is a mirror into the soul, the act of facing ourselves squarely and honestly. It is raw truth, the kind of personal truth that allows us to say, "OK, here I am. I am in the processing of becoming the person I want to be. I will trust myself."

A healthy dose of self-doubt may remain, but the clarity derived from trust enables us to act upon our passions.

Women leaders becoming clear about their values and themselves are ready to unearth the passion and courage to proceed through life with vigor and intent. As you encounter the next section, entitled *Women Who Lead Invoke Passion and Courage,* you will be asked to integrate what you have learned so far about your values and yourself into a deeper awareness of how you are evolving as a woman leader.

Reflections and Questions

Women who lead are conscious of their evolving selves. By consciousness, we often think of the clarity that we hold about who we are and what our purposes are. As you reflect upon the stories and perspectives in this section, consider the following questions:

1. How important are the opinions or behaviors of others? How often do I find myself governed by the desire to please?
2. How do I approach problems when others are involved?
3. How comfortable am I with ambiguity?
4. In what situations am I able to express myself fully, authentically…thereby finding my voice?
5. In order to better understand myself, I'll make a list of my strengths and limitations…how can I use my strengths to lighten my load of limitations? Can I cast off "false limitations" …those that are archaic, or externally imposed?
6. Given my response to these questions, what is the storyline of my life so far?
7. What strategies will I use to continue to compose my life (journals, conversations, experiences, quiet reflection, mentors)?

A successful life for a man or for a woman seems to me to lie in the knowledge that one has developed to the limit the capacities with which one was endowed; that one has contributed something constructive to family and friends and to a home community; that one has brought happiness wherever it was possible; that one has earned one's way in the world, has kept some friends, and need not be ashamed to face oneself honestly.

-Eleanor Roosevelt, First Lady of the United States (1933-45), reform leader

Women Who Lead...
Invoke Passion and Courage

Chapter Four

From a timid, shy girl I had become a woman of resolute character, who could no longer be frightened by the struggle with troubles.
    -Anna Dostoevsky, wife of author Fyodor Dostoevsky

When Judy Vandegrift was hired as a team leader in a Wisconsin elementary school, she was unaccustomed to managing a whole class. It quickly became apparent that her skills as a math specialist did not serve her well enough as a classroom teacher. She soon shared her frustrations with the school psychologist, who offered to observe her class and give her critical feedback. This is where the real story started. Judy and the psychologist agreed that the feedback should be given in front of the whole team—a team that Judy had been hired to lead. After hearing the feedback, the team brainstormed suggestions for Judy on how she could better manage her class.

The results were profound. The atmosphere in Judy's class improved dramatically when she implemented the suggestions of her team. But in addition, there was a significant change in the way the team worked. Team members who had heretofore been defensive and secretive about their own practice opened up to team critique and significant changes in practice. This willingness to be open and vulnerable was a true act of courage on Judy's part, an act that resulted in shifts in perspective of each team member.[1]

Women who lead are courageous. By "courageous," we mean that these women confront conflict or difficulty, pain, danger or uncertainty without being overcome by fear. The passion that drives them transcends the momentary. Values provide a clear path, and an unambiguous sense of identity enables women leaders to act with resolve and tenacity. Courage, when most effective, is enduring and sustained. Remarkably, women find courage when they find themselves.

Courage doesn't always roar. Sometimes courage is the little voice at the end of the day that says I'll try again tomorrow.

-Mary Anne Radmacher

Standing up for the right thing often becomes self-evident to women who understand who they are. That is not to say that competing priorities of nearly equal merit do not create tensions. Yet women often surprise even themselves when they are moved to an action of unmistakable value. The "right thing" comes in many forms. Some women demonstrate their courage by working for children or peace in their own countries or in the world. Others mobilize communities to alter assumptions about who can learn and lead. Many provide sustained support to a noble cause. Still others have passionately organized others against an injustice that touches their deepest core and compels them to action. Such injustices might include inequitable outcomes in education, genocide, the rights of women and children, poverty, illness or the devastation of the environment.

It is often a lack of courage and passion that causes women to be risk-averse. We have found that women who lead undertake risks as a natural outgrowth of courage and passion. Risk-taking comes in many forms: creating a new school, composing literature from a unique perspective, undertaking a new career turn (such as when a teacher becomes an administrator), setting about to change the culture of an organization. Undertaking risk can lead to new adventures and innovation. Certainty is shed as women savor new possibilities, new learning.

Where there is no risk, the emotional terrain is flat and unyielding, and despite all its dimensions, valleys, pinnacles and detours, life will seem to have none of its magnificent geography, only a length. It began in mystery and it will end in mystery, but what a savage and beautiful country lies between.

-Diane Ackerman

From our four proposed perspectives, we draw differing points of view and capabilities regarding these fears, struggles and eventual achievements.

Figure 4.1 briefly describes the Four Perspectives of Passion and Courage.

Figure 4.1   Perspectives on Invoking Passion and Courage

	Perspective 1	**Perspective 2**	**Perspective 3**	**Perspective 4**
Passion and Courage	Fears both conflict and revelation of incompetence; prevents courageous action and keeps passion from surfacing	Sees no reason to challenge convention; acts the "good girl." As a workaholic, denies self time for interests or passions.	Transforms passion and courage into "righteous indignation" and activism.	Uses courage to promote and defend universal values; passion ignites and sustains creativity and action.

The Four Perspectives of Women's Leadership Development

We have argued that the four perspectives introduced in Chapter One are not linear, nor are they all a part of each woman's development. Never is that more true than with Courage and Passion. Like Athena, the Goddess of Wisdom, who was born fully formed from the head of her father, Zeus, some women seem courageous from the beginning. This is most often true when they have witnessed the trials of their parents in pursuit of a cause. For instance, Nobel Prize winner and Guatemalan activist Rigoberto Menchu Tum saw her mother, father and brother tortured and killed for their beliefs and actions against the oppression of indigenous people. Yet, she did not turn away. Injustice fueled her passion and resolve. Courage was her constant companion.

Rigoberta Menchu Tum
Guatemalan civil rights activist, diplomat, Nobel Peace Prize recipient, 1992

"There is no peace without justice;
There is no justice without fairness;
There is no fairness without development;
There is no development without democracy."

How much can any one individual endure? The life of Rigoberta Menchu Tum gives new meanings, new boundaries, to that question. Her mother, father and brother were tortured and killed for their beliefs and actions against the oppression of indigenous people. Yet, she did not turn away. Injustice fueled her passion and resolve to follow in the footsteps of her family. Courage was her constant companion.

A series of tragedies only strengthened Menchu's commitment to the rights of the indigenous peoples and social activism. She understood the women's rights movement as a cause integral to the broader agenda of equity and emancipation. By the age of 20, Menchu went to work for the Committee of United Campesinos (CUC). She fiercely sought to educate herself in Spanish and the court system so that she could be more effective in her work. She traveled throughout the region to organize Indians in remote villages and on plantations to secure fair wages for all workers; decent treatment for Indians; and respect for Indian culture, customs and religion. When the CUC was declared illegal, Menchu became an enemy of the state.

Menchu was awarded the Nobel Peace Prize in 1992 at the age of 33. The Nobel Committee recognized her work for social justice and ethno-cultural reconciliation based on respect for the rights of indigenous people. Soon after receiving the Nobel Prize, she established the Rigoberta Menchu Foundation and became a spokesperson for the United Nations International Decade of Indigenous People (1994-2003). The Foundation is dedicated to registering Indian voters in Guatemala, helping them to be part of the political process and establishing educational programs for refugee children.

By seeking to build a universal culture of peace, Menchu Tum has risked and invested her life in teaching others that the foundation of peace lies in the belief that "There is no democracy without respect for the identity and dignity of all cultures and people." As a leader, she frames the essence of change and transformation for all peoples who "search for specific and definite solutions to the deep ethical crisis that afflicts humanity." As a leader, she is a role model, a teacher and an icon for present and future generations of women.[2]

Also like Athena, we find young teachers like Kristin Levine (see Chapter One) who dared to use dialogue on her first day of teaching, thereby reaping the rewards of her courage. Judy Vandegrift dared to be vulnerable in front of new peers.

Perspectives One and Two, on the other hand, reveal courage that is muffled or viewed as unnecessary. *Perspective One* women often fail to see the imperative to act. Fear of conflict and the assumed revelation of incompetence prevent courageous action. It was not until Eugenia, whose story is described in Chapter Two, experienced a crisis that she was provoked to find her voice. Such an occurrence propelled her into *Perspective Three* of leadership development.

In *Perspective Two,* the defense and implementation of the status quo of accepted practice makes courageous action unnecessary, unless it is mildly executed in pursuit of organizational goals. If you are just doing what others in the organization wants you to do, little courage is required. Courage exercised as authority has the support of law, policy or firm practice, and therefore is less risky. However, a *Perspective Two* individual is capable of using anger to hold others hostage, to intimidate subordinates into compliance. When a principal is told that she must take a teacher assigned to her school, whether she thinks it is wise or not, a director of personnel can invoke policy, and if need be, the authority of the board to force compliance. If the principal still refuses, it is an act of high risk, an act of courage.

Margaret Thatcher, former prime minister of Great Britain, is a classic archetype of a *Perspective Two* leader. Her administration speaks to the point that merely electing a woman does not guarantee the primacy of women's issues or leadership approaches. The conventional wisdom that women are more collaborative and interpersonally sensitive does not prove true in all cases.

Women in our study said that decision-making is often labored because of their need to keep harmony; to make sure that everyone is happy with the outcome. This propensity to please, to not step on anyone's toes, gets in the way of two critical organizational needs: to make difficult decisions, and to make them effectively and efficiently.

What Else Gets in the Way?

It isn't just a lack of courage that gets in the way of expressing courage. Women deal with several unique issues that prevent courageous action. They experience isolation, loneliness and harassment in the workplace that do not plague men as often. Since few women have reached the upper echelons of formal leadership, there are fewer women models and mentors. Fewer women share their values and practices: for instance, the necessity to balance the needs of a special education child and the inherent costs of a business transaction that is economical but may violate essential values.

Sociologically, women are still in transitions that are difficult to negotiate. Societal and family expectations regarding the role of a woman as wife and mother can haunt women who also desire a demanding career. Formal leadership roles definitely demand more time and focus and there is an unsettling element of the unknown--factors that mitigate against family life. Women have unique health issues, both personally and within their families, such as breast cancer, ovarian cancer, and osteoporosis. They are more apt to be needed to care for a sick child or an aging parent, more apt to be the caretaker in any crisis. The results of courageous action can lead to unexpected consequences, risks that are seldom undertaken by women who are preoccupied with family or health issues.

A man in a workshop on women and leadership in Southeast Asia recently told us: "Men cognate (think), women feel." This perception of women by men is ubiquitous. Such prejudice pressures women to hide or deny their own emotions, even when those emotions spark passion for their values and goals. Women need to honor and legitimize their emotions as a natural, and desirable, part of who they are as leaders, because behaviors and impulses that are not expected tend to be submerged or denied.

My Gramma always said that fears are like nettles—if you grab them, wrestle with them, squeeze them—they won't bother you. But if you pick at them, they'll sting you.

-Granny G.

In Chapter Two, Women Who Lead Commit to Values, we introduced an array of fears described by women in our study. Below we specify the numerous fears that served as hurdles in their development as leaders:

- Feeling isolated, the only woman in an administrative role or department. "Breaking the mold" can be a lonely endeavor.
- Juggling multiple roles, such as career, marriage and motherhood. These conflicting demands lead to long hours and often-misunderstood tensions.
- Lacking women models or other women to talk to.
- Realizing "I was raised to please" and that you're still trying to please.

- Experiencing the "unknown," uncertainty, ambiguity as scary, particularly at certain stages of development.
- Being sexually harassed and the butt of jokes.
- Living and working with health issues unique to women.
- Being terminated without legitimate cause.
- Living with criticism and guilt related to conflicting expectations: wanting to be a leader, when parents and (some) men expect you to be a mother and wife.
- Staying true to ideals when those around you don't necessarily agree. Fear of being an outcast.
- Conflict arising from different perspectives in a male-dominated culture.
- Being uncomfortable with emotional responses in an environment in which emotion is considered weakness.
- Saying, "At my age, isn't it easier to just stay put, to do what I'm doing? Why take on something new?"
- Dysfunctional responses to anger.

In Chapter Two, we described how many of the women in our study were moved to "righteous indignation" when they encountered an injustice or unfairness. They could no longer be silent in the face of injustice and often joined unions as a means of righting a wrong. Such outrage is fueled by anger, a difficult emotion for women to express. Many women are raised to believe that anger is not ladylike, not appropriate. Anger brings on heart palpitations and tears. Clarissa Pinkola Estes in her book *Women Who Run with Wolves* encouraged women to accept rage as a teacher, "something not to be rid of so fast...something to learn from, to deal with internally, then shape into something useful in the world."[3] Estes believes that if a woman allows herself to be taught by her rage, thereby transforming and dispersing it, energy will return to be put to use in other areas, especially regarding creativity. Some stories we heard described how women transformed anger into new approaches to old problems, or began actions that changed the way things were done.

Recall Sally, principal of Bellevue Middle School, described in Chapter Two. Six months after she left the math department meeting feeling humiliated, she decided to try again. Her rebuff from the math teachers still weighed on her mind. In the meantime, however, she had worked with the faculty to establish a vision and norms for teacher dialogue. She had worked hard at building trust among staff and had established discussions with individual teachers in the math department, but had not yet approached the two most vocal teachers, or the department as a whole. She knew she had avoided them, just as they had avoided her.

Sally now had hard data that indicated that tracking students did not fit the school's vision. She and two new members of the department had done their homework on the progression of students, using test scores, and graduation and dropout rates. They interviewed high school students who had not taken Algebra 1. She was ready to approach the math department again, this time with "armor and sword." No matter how worried she was, she resolved to stay with the questions about equal access and the current strategy. This meeting was going to take all the courage she could muster.

You gain strength, courage, and confidence by every experience in which you really stop to look fear in the face. You are able to say to yourself "I lived through this horror, I can take the next thing that comes along."...You must do the thing you think you cannot do.

-Eleanor Roosevelt

Also in Chapter Two, we described the struggle of Barbara, a district superintendent in the Midwest who was directed to dismantle her school's bilingual program. As she proceeded to violate her own values, her energy decreased and she even had a hard time getting up in the morning. As her relationship with board members deteriorated over a six-month period, it became increasingly clear that she would have to engage in work that was meaningful for her. She started reading the ads in the state administrative newsletter for other superintendent positions. As she was beginning her research, the board called for her evaluation in closed session, and then informed Barbara that they were planning to terminate her contract. Her worst nightmare had come true; she was being fired!

Over the next few weeks, Barbara panicked. As a single parent, how was she going to meet her responsibilities to her family? Would her self-confidence be destroyed? Could she find another job? Would her family have to move? Fortunately, Barbara had made friends with Amie Tran, a superintendent in a neighboring district. She called Amie. With the help of coaching, Barbara reaffirmed her values and identified her strengths. Then, with renewed energy, she rewrote her resume. She still wanted to serve as a superintendent, but now she had the courage to deliberately seek a district aligned with her values.

Women experience fears that are often based on valid perceptions of organizational structures and cultural barriers. Historical role definitions prevail in most organizations, especially educational ones. Barbara was expected to take directions without question, even though they violated respected research, as well as her values and good judgment. Women in education are most apt to be assigned tasks concerning curriculum and instruction, counseling, and working with parents.

Women experienced in finance and personnel often prove inadequate to the demands of the future, including having a marketable resume, for roles such as the superintendency. Women invariably work longer hours, partly because they are assigned projects, evaluation and reporting that require extensive time beyond the normal school day. A "sports coaching culture" exists in many secondary schools, in which males regularly serve as coaches, creating relationships based on the language of competition and winning. It takes courage to challenge such a culture.

These challenges provide specific opportunities for women to change the culture and the dynamics of an organization. Donlan and Graves argue that, counter to the beliefs held in many organizations, "companies with the highest representation of women on their top management teams have better financial performance than companies with fewer women in these positions."[4] Even though education, especially at the elementary level, is dominated by women, there are fewer women at the superintendent level. A rigid hierarchy stands in the way of reciprocal engagement among both men and women in vertical roles. When women transcend these barriers, they are capable of transforming organizations.

Transforming Women: Perspectives Three and Four

In *Perspectives Three and Four*, women are propelled into activism through righteous indignation, often continuing their development to create an integrated, inclusive and sustained course of action. This may take the form of unrelenting resistance, pioneering, modeling, writing or practice. Women in our study were learning to live with courage and passion, as well as a high degree of consciousness and values.

Earlier, we discussed organizational and cultural barriers to leadership for women. It is our premise that women need to change cultures rather than the other way around. Transforming women employ a range of strategies to achieve this complex goal. Insisting on broader role definition is critical; for instance, tasks should include much more than curriculum and instruction (depending on career goals). Personnel, finance, public relations, and liaison with the district and boards can prepare women for desired positions.

Redefining leadership to a constructivist view—engaged learning toward a shared purpose—can move an organization away from "the one person in charge" model. Although self-promotion may sound egotistical, women need to be able to step forward and say, "I can do that, and I can do it well," rather than waiting to be asked. Women can lead an organization toward policies that allow for a more sane balance of work and family, such as rotating supervision and nighttime responsibilities. Ultimately, women must face the barriers within themselves as well, such as workaholism, reluctance to delegate, perfectionism, fear of conflict and the ability to say "no."

Recruiting and mentoring a larger number of women into top-level positions will, by its very nature, alter both culture and performance. The highly regarded 2004 Catalyst study, *The Bottom Line:*

Connecting Corporate Performance and Gender Diversity,[5] found several correlations linking performance and gender within 353 Fortune 500 companies:

- Corporations with large percentages of women on their executive teams gain returns 35 percent higher than those with fewer women in leadership positions.
- When 20 percent or more of the top positions in an organization are held by women, the agenda begins to change. For instance, in the U.S. Senate, women of both parties have worked together to enact critical legislation regarding women's and children's health, child support and health research.
- The number of women board directors in a company is a predictor of the number of women who serve as corporate officers and in line positions.

As more and more *Perspective Four* women gravitate to high-level positions in organizations and societies, those organizations—and societies—will become more equitable, collaborative and productive. For instance, Chile's President, Michelle Bachelet, kept her promise to fill half of her country's cabinet seats with women.[6]

Kawsar Kouchok, then Dean of the Faculty of Education at Helwan University in Cairo, Egypt, described what occurred when she and her staff members decided to make changes in the use of university rooms and labs:

> The President of the University cancelled my decisions. When I discussed the issue with him, he said 'I'm responsible.' I strongly replied: 'You are responsible to run the University, but I'm responsible to manage my Faculty.' And I gave him my resignation on the spot. He accepted it. The whole staff and student body refused to accept his action and took the issue to the Minister of Education. The Minister blamed him and took my side. I cancelled my resignation and continued in my post as the Dean. But, it really was a risk.[7]

Whether or not you agree with Kawsar's actions, she engendered the needed strength to take a stand even though she put her career on the line. She might have lost this battle. An experienced, battle-scarred woman in a culture where women do not often rise to prominence, she knew the risk she was taking. Shortly thereafter, she was appointed Director of the renowned National Centre for Curriculum and Materials Development by the Minister of Education.

When Linda Lambert, co-author of this book, accepted a position as the first woman secondary principal in a northern California school district, she soon found that male traditions in the district there—"how things are done around here"—were referred to as "Old Spanish Customs." Innovative practices in personnel, school organization, curriculum, student activities, and finances ran up against these "customs" and were usually discarded. Women elementary principals, teacher leaders and the Director of Personnel in the district joined with Linda to better strategize and innovate within the system.

Women Making History

Traditionally, courage has been linked with war and physical risk. These forms of courage include acts of extreme courage under fire while serving one's country and belief system, or heroic stories of rescue. Stories and books abound about men and a few women—such as Joan of Arc—who have shown courage in battle. While these acts are profoundly important and selfless, they may also be fleeting. Momentary acts of courage may not hold the enduring resolve needed to alter fundamental injustices. Our notion of courage, however, is sustainable.

Throughout history, women have demonstrated fervor for causes that led to bold, courageous action. As a result, whole movements were ignited because women responded with fury, acted with righteous indignation and intense passions. School integration was a result of a collective rage and the initial courageous legal action on the part of the Brown family of Topeka, Kansas. Rosa Parks' refusal to give up her seat on a Montgomery, Alabama, bus accelerated the civil rights movement. Parks was humble and unassuming in her attitude and behavior. Her form of selfless dedication sustained itself for a lifetime of service.[8]

I am really attracted to the earth. Caving gave me the confidence to be different. When I was young, the message was that only men can do the outdoor things. When I began caving I saw women going down into the Black Hole in Mexico, so I knew I could do it too.

-Louise Hose

Erin Gruwell, a first-year teacher in Long Beach, California, had the courage to break away from the traditional high school curriculum and to rebel against the department head's insistence that Erin teach the agreed-upon curriculum, even if it wasn't relevant to her students. Erin developed a curriculum about survivors of the Holocaust that engaged her "at risk" students and the community. Her story and the story of her 150 students is about changing the traditional curriculum into one that actually changed the students, Erin, and the world around them. The story is told in the book *The Freedom Writers Diary* and a major motion picture. As a result of her courage and determination to do what she felt was right for the students, she helped them understand the consequences of prejudice and racial hatred. A foundation has been established to share the Freedom Writers Methods with other schools.[9] What power one young teacher discovered when she invoked the courage to live her values!

It also takes courage to be the first woman, the pioneer, in any endeavor: head of state, elected official, a black student in an all-white school, superintendent, astronaut, sculptor, photographer, musician, painter, scientist, athlete or activist. As a young Latina in Chicago, Maria Hinojosa felt invisible. Although she wanted to be a journalist, she saw no role models, no faces like her own in the journalism profession. Yet she persevered, and eventually found her own voice and style. Today Maria is an award-winning journalist who tackles the tough issues.[10] Such pioneering actions, often considered risky to one's self-confidence, remind us that sometimes "to remain tight in the bud is riskier than it is to blossom."[11]

In 1927, Freya Stark, English by birth and raised in Asolo, Italy, became the first woman explorer of the desolate landscapes of the Middle East. Freya was a unique woman of courage who ultimately became involved in the political dynamics of the region and wrote with deep understanding and appreciation of the peoples she encountered.

Freya Stark, 1893-1993
Arabist, adventurer, writer, cartographer

"...the last of the romantic travelers."

Freya Stark had a rare voice. She saw the world as a romantic anthropologist...a lyrist...a journalist. Admirably escaping sentimentality, she wedded scientific inquiry with the expressions of a poet. Stark held a profound reverence for the Arabs, finding them to be thoughtful, giving and fascinating storytellers. These respectful relationships opened doors into spaces heretofore unavailable and unexplored. Stark, the adventurer, stepped through these doors and found a magical world.

At the age of 13, Freya's flowing hair became caught in the textile machinery, pulling her very near to death. Count Mario pulled her from the jaws of the machine, a rescue act that would tear off a large portion of her scalp, her right ear, and right eyelid. This damage would affect her feelings of personal esteem for the rest of her life. Many say that her style and personality allowed her to transcend these deformities. Further, she became the center of her mother's life, a position sweetly cherished and sought. Flora became her lifelong friend and mentor. Encouraging her daughter to pursue writing and adventure, Flora solicited her travel letters and typed her journals.

Stark most often traveled alone, accompanied only by camels and guides, through deserts, ancient cities, and uncharted domains. She fearlessly mapped the remote reaches of the Oriental world. As is so often the case, we can trace such fearlessness back to parents who encouraged bravery and endurance. Robert and Flora Stark were methodical in teaching these lessons, pushing and bribing their daughters to venture into frightening and dangerous situations. Freya came to embrace and enjoy that which she had feared.

During the Second World War, Stark served with the British in the Middle East. In 1940, there was little reason to believe that the British would win the war. It became Stark's job, in association with her work with the Ministry of Information, to convince Egyptians otherwise. Starting with a group of 12 friends, Stark amplified the message and the eventual involvement and commitment of 100,000 citizens. It is fascinating to think that the first "pyramid scheme" took place in Egypt.

Stark lived and ate like the indigenous peoples. Understandably, she contracted almost every disease that living so casually can bring. In her late 70s and 80s, she braved the Euphrates on a raft, crossed Afghanistan in a jeep, and trekked through Nepal on horseback. Given the life she led, it is astonishing that she lived to be 100 years old. In May, 1993, Dame Stark died at her home in Asolo, Italy.

Freya Stark found joy in the humanness of all peoples and things. She said:

If I were to enumerate the pleasures of travel,
this would be
one of the greatest among them—
that so often and so unexpectedly
you meet the best in human nature,
and seeing it so by surprise and
often with a most improbable background,
you come, with a sense of
pleasant thankfulness, to realize how
widely scattered in the world are
goodness and courtesy and the love of
immaterial things, fair blossoms
found in every climate, on every soil.[12]

Her adventurous spirit served as a prism through which she discovered life's surprises. By not taking herself too seriously, she was not bound by traditional boxes full of pre-set expectations that

> would stand in the way of learning. Therefore, she
> could not be disappointed. When others found fear,
> she found adventure; where others found problems,
> she discovered the rewards of humanity and history.

When Margaret Mead, a newly trained anthropologist, set off for a pioneering trip to Samoa at the age of 24. She was well aware that different cultures create different behaviors in the people who inhabit them. Mead found that Samoan men and women played varying roles regarding cooperation-competition and nurturance-violence, depending upon cultural norms. She concluded that our essential human nature is a result of the influence of our environments. Her findings changed the way the world understood gender and human development. While her conclusions have been altered or mediated in recent times, they influenced the field of social science for many years.

Jan O'Neill left teaching to pursue an entrepreneurial endeavor that would allow her to live out her values and would positively affect the lives of many adults and children. In partnership with Anne Conzemius, former Wisconsin State Deputy Superintendent, she formed Quantum Leading, a company involved in professional development, authorship, research and curriculum development. Jan told us:

> This business venture has been risky, often frustrating, and sometimes even terrifying, but it has always been a rewarding experience as we've watched our clients—who are now our friends and colleagues—catch fire with the possibilities of what they can do. The sacrifices have been worth it; there has been such a positive impact on kids, adults and even whole systems. I feel we're truly bringing joy to learning, and I can't imagine anything else more important.[13]

To bring about lasting change, we have seen women of quiet tenacity like Rosa Parks—a quietness not to be mistaken for lack of a personal voice—keep their focus, even though it has taken years for their actions to achieve results. Maya Angelou points out that leaving the room when someone talks disparagingly about another person is indeed an act of courage. Being present, being witness to and in moral support of, quiet acts of courage takes courage as well. A mother who devotes her life to raising a handicapped child is a person of quiet courage as is the child's teacher.

Aung San Suu Kyi
Burmese activist for human rights, Recipient Nobel Prize for Peace, 1991

*"To live the full life...one must have the courage to bear
the responsibility of the needs of others...
one must want to bear this responsibility."*

Aung San Suu Kyi has been under house arrest in Burma (also known as Myanmar) for 16 years. It is a fate freely chosen. San Suu—often referred to with the reverential "Daw" title—chose to return to Burma in 1988 after studying and working in England to struggle for equality and human rights, the promised path of independence. And, she chose to stay under house arrest for many years rather than accept the invitation to leave Burma without hope of return. By remaining in Burma, she continues to represent the non-violent protest for the rights of all Burmese peoples to political, economic, social and cultural self-determination; the right to peace; the right to live in a healthy and balanced environment; the right to share in the earth's resources. She has been the voice of hope for democracy and Burma's quest for freedom.

During her house arrest, she was isolated from family, other leaders of the resistance and the international community. She was unable to accept the Nobel Peace Prize in 1991 or to attend her husband's funeral.

Believing that hate and fear go hand in hand, Daw Suu claims that she never hated or feared her captors. She deeply believes that people cannot be frightened by people who they do not hate. These revolutionary ideas appear in her book, *Freedom from Fear*. Even though she suffered at times from malnutrition and illness, her commitment to non-violent and compassionate approaches never wavered. Aung San Suu Kyi continues to use her energy and resources to organize and support groups who are working for peace in Burma and other countries. She has been instrumental in the formation of PeaceJam to address the problems facing teenagers today by inspiring them to find meaning and integrity in their lives and to stand for nonviolent approaches to conflict.

Daw Suu symbolizes the tenacious passion and courage that has represented the women showcased in this section on Passion and Courage. Responsibility for the learning and development of others is an essential aspect of leadership, one that Daw Suu symbolizes. "To live the full life," she says, "one must have the courage to bear the responsibility of the needs of others...one must *want* to bear this responsibility."[14] Her leadership is framed by a coherent understanding of how values, philosophy and strategies can merge to form a united approach to social justice.

Evoking Courage and Passion: Understandings, Skills and Strategies

Courageous women such as Judy Vandegrift, Kawsar Kouchok, Jan O'Neill and Aung San Suu Kyi are not deflected from a course of action. The strategies applicable to each chapter are cumulative, spiraling through a personal and organizational labyrinth that will be summarized in Chapter Eight. Transforming women, women with an integrated self, display the following understandings and skills.

To understand that:
- Facing fears allow women to move through and beyond them. Our friend, Elizabeth Harris, on reaching the young age of 70, vowed to do something each day that makes her feel uncomfortable.
- Conflict is useful, even desirable. Conflict raises and resolves issues that would otherwise fester and destroy the culture and productivity. Fierce conversations, dialogue and focused collaboration can make conflicting ideas and beliefs surface before they get out of hand.

- Data and evidence are good partners for passion. Be prepared.
- Following your passions—doing work that energizes and gives you a sense of accomplishment and purpose—can bring about "flow."

Skills that support understandings:
- Process skills: dialogue, group problem-solving and facilitation, inquiry;
- Conflict resolution;
- Reframing, shifting perspectives on a problem;
- Yoga, meditation, deep breathing;
- Interest-based bargaining; interfaith dialogue;
- Journaling, all forms of reflective behaviors.

Conclusion

For the women described in this chapter, passion and courage are the energy sources of leadership. We might think of it this way: values provide the content and resolve of leadership, and consciousness gives us the confidence to lead. Passion and courage propel us forward. These are all facets of the learning process...learning toward our personal and collective purpose. In the next theme area, we will come to understand how imagination enables us to develop compassion and creativity in addressing the confounding issues of our time.

Reflections and Explorations

Passion and courage are those energy sources that enable us to realize our values and sustain our sense of identity. Moving beyond your own self-imposed limitations and breaking down organization/cultural barriers can take great courage. In this chapter, we have included women who have sustained their courage over a long period. Stepping into the unknown, being the first to do something, can build courage by engaging all of our senses, causing us to experience more fully who we are. As you think about the meaning of passion and courage and the women described here, reflect upon and explore the following questions.

1. In our book, we have invited you to understand yourself as a person guided by a set of core values. Ask yourself: have any of these values required me to act with passion and courage? Give an example.

2. Think of a time when I felt invisible. What were the circumstances? If I found my voice, what helped me? If I did not find my voice, what will I do the next time I am invisible?

3. Has fear ever prevented me from marshaling the courage that I needed? Recall a time when I was able to overcome fear and act courageously.

4. Are there women whom I admire because they were pioneers in a field?

5. Many women in these studies found their courage in collective action (e.g., a demonstration for some common cause, reaching out for guidance, participating in/leading union or organizational activities). When have I joined in a collective courageous act? What sustained my courage?

6. What actions (adventures) could I take that would push me beyond my self-imposed limitations?

7. Think of a time when I stepped out into the unknown, challenged my assumptions or made mistakes. What did it feel like? What did I learn about myself?

8. What approaches will I now undertake to further develop and sustain my passion and courage?

9. Name a past injustice that I remained silent about. Construct a new way I could address that injustice.

Your progress through this book has supplied you with a deeper knowledge of your values, yourself, and your passion and courage. As you prepare to explore the next section, "Women Who Lead…Arouse Imagination," open your heart to the imagination that enables you to create, to feel empathy and express compassion.

Women Who Lead...
Arouse the Imagination

Chapter Five

*...To insure that imagination will always, always be free
to light the slow fuse of the possible.*
–Maxine Greene, Philosopher

Imagination is the fire that ignites that slow fuse of the possible.
Just imagine how the world is changing, how women are changing,
how the possible can become probable—perhaps even inevitable.
Women who lead arouse imagination in themselves, in others and in
the world.

First, imagination—when inspired by life experiences and art
and literature—enables humans to become more compassionate and
more empathic by releasing our emotions as well as our intentions.
Second, such arousal enables creativity and innovation, including the
capacity to appreciate and share acts of creation.

---

*To my mind creativity is an innovative process which
embraces all the arts and sciences. It includes the love,
friendship and cooperation that people develop between
one another in the common effort aimed at achieving a
better life, and molding better individuals.*
-Nawal El Saadawi,

When we form images in our mind that were not known or
thought possible before, we are imagining. Bonita Calder, a retired
elementary school teacher and teacher union president, describes the
process of releasing her imagination:

> Surely one of the most rewarding and exciting expe-
> riences a teacher can have is to encourage and enable

> a child to unlock the mysteries of print. I set about to create a program that would help solve the problem of not enough time to engage students in the wonders of literature. The idea was to involve parents in the beginning reading process so they would not only enjoy watching their child learn to read, but they would be an integral part of the teaching and learning process.[1]

Bonita experienced such satisfactions many times in her career, redefining the role of teacher and teacher leader. Experiences such as Bonita's can occur in the classroom or in the home, or on a broader scale.

Human development occurs in a spiraling process that has been represented by a double helix. Kegan used such a helix to describe the evolutionary truces between independence and inclusion.[2] In Chapter One, we refer to these truces as yearnings.

The double helix defines the self as well as the universe. Rosalind Franklin, a British scientist, discovered the legendary double helix image through her work in X-Ray crystallography. When she saw the image under the microscope, combined with her deep knowledge and imagination, she knew that this image could represent DNA (deoxyribonucleic acid). Others (Watson, Crick and Wilkins) took her drawing and synthesized all that was known at that time about the human genome into an understanding of DNA.[3] The double helix DNA has become a metaphor as well as the reality for thinking about the world within and the world without. Launched by imagination, we are on a spiraling path upward as well as inward.

If only we can look in fresh ways, we can change the world by just that act.

- Zaha Hadid, Iraqi architect

Arousing Empathy and Compassion

As imagination separates individuals from the known, it also shifts perspectives. Experience provides the opportunity for meaning, through expressions of compassion and empathy. When humans imagine, images of new characters, language, cultural portraits, art forms and solutions are created. By transferring feelings to the character in a novel, a work of art or a tragedy, innate capacities for compassion and empathy give form and voice to those feelings. "The purpose of literature," argued Nabokov, "is to allow the reader to be in the presence of artistic expressions of justice, compassion, and hope."[4]

When women witnessed the struggles of other women in India or Sri Lanka during the 2004 tsunami or the 2005 Katrina hurricane in the southern United States, they entered those lives and became one with their struggle. Such connection helps to define empathy, the ability to identify with and understanding others' feelings and difficulties.

In *Poisonwood Bible*[5], Barbara Kingsolver alternately writes with the voice of each missionary family member in the Congo. Her vivid prose forecasts the horrific events that took place in the Congo in 2008. Readers feel a sense of shared humanity with the citizens of that war-torn country that no newscast, nor even photo, could arouse. Similarly, the on-going genocide in Darfur has touched the sensibilities of peoples of all ages and origins.

The flamboyant life of Isadora Duncan, the mother of modern dance, formed a soaring image of life fully lived for the women of the 1920s, while the poetry of Edna St. Vincent Millay gave language to the newly successful suffragettes. In *Women Warrior*,[6] Maxine Hong Kingston captured the experience of Chinese women in ways that gave voice to those who felt invisible. Portraits formed in people's minds make the invisible visible.

I learned to make my mind large, as the universe is large,
so that there is room for paradoxes.
-Maxine Hong Kingston, The Woman Warrior

In the novella *Uncommon Reader*, Alan Bennett describes the journey toward self-awareness of Queen Elizabeth of England, who discovers a bookmobile behind her palace. Guided in her selections by a kitchen worker, she begins to read…and read…and read. As her imagination is released, her perspectives about herself and the world change. Consequently, her relationships with the Prime Minister, her family and other workers are forever altered, becoming more sensitive and empathic. Freed from the bondage of ignorance, she herself begins to write.[7]

Toni Morrison engaged the world's imagination for empathy and compassion in *The Bluest Eye* and *Beloved*. Slavery and the plight and choices of women became personal. In her 2008 novel, *A Mercy*, she visits indentured servitude in late 17th- century Virginia, a continuing meditation on the varieties and degrees of enslavement and liberation.[8]

Toni Morrison
Author, recipient of the Nobel Prize
for Literature, 1993

*"…my project rises from delight,
not disappointment."*

Toni Morrison is a gifted storyteller whose characters seek to find themselves and their cultural heritage in a society that impedes them. Through Morrison's works of fiction and essays, we have come to understand what it is to be Black in America. Her language possesses the "luster of poetry," the rhythm of fine jazz, the texture of satin and the emotional complexity of notable literature. Through her imagination, we have been led down a spiraling staircase into great depths of compassion. For these gifts, we are a grateful nation.

It was not until her late 30s, after her divorce, that she began to write. Her first book was The *Bluest Eye*. From then on, the flow of her sensual, lush, musical language escorted us through Song of Solomon, *Beloved, Playing in the Dark, Jazz, Paradise* and *Love*. Each literary journey seeks to understand the quest for self, for identity, of the author, the characters and the reader. Readers are challenged to follow the narrative voice that shifts perspectives and examines multiple dimensions of the conditions in which her characters are found. Further, readers are confronted by the tension of competing emotions residing side by side. For instance, in Love, love and hate walk together; only in understanding both can we understand each separately.

In 1993, Morrison became the first Black woman author to be awarded the Nobel Prize for Literature. The Academy recognized that her novels were characterized by visionary force and poetic import, giving life to an essential aspect of American reality. Her epic power possessed "an unerring ear for dialogue and richly expressive depictions of Black America." Professor Sture Allen, Permanent Secretary of the Swedish Academy, noted in his introductory speech:

> *Toni Morrison's novels invite the reader to partake at many levels, and at varying degrees of complexity. Still, the most enduring impression they leave is of empathy, compassion with one's fellow human beings.*[8]

Morrison's influence on American life has been enormous. She advocates for human rights and dignity. She supports and mentors young writers, creating artists' workshops for students. The impact of her work and her writing is politically powerful. Morrison insists: "I don't believe any real artists have ever been non-political. They may have been insensitive to this particular plight or insensitive to that, but they were political because that is what an artist is—a politician."

Women who lead arouse the imagination. The ferocious imagination of Toni Morrison demanded that she be included in this dimension of women and leadership. Her characters evoke the empathy and compassion that arouse imagination in all who have the good fortune to read her remarkable writing.

In Chapter Three, *Women Leaders are Conscious of the Evolving Self*, the work of Mary Catherine Bateson describes openness to improvisation and ingenuity as enabling women to construct desired lives. Imagination and improvisation go hand in hand, like jazz, fine cuisine and the stories we tell to children.

The imagination needs moodling—-long, inefficient, happy idling, dawdling and puttering.
                                        -Brenda Ueland, writer

---

The reader may ask at this point, "But what you describe about imagination and the human animal…isn't this as true for men as for women? How is it different for men and women, if at all?" Let us examine those questions.

Do Women Use Their Imaginations Differently than Men?

As we described in Chapter One, Carol Gilligan taught us that women are raised in relationship to others. By being in relationship, girls learn the subtle, as well as not-so-subtle, cues that reveal the emotional state and expectations of others. Brizendine argues that women are especially good at reading visual cues, possess a larger emotional center, are more sensitive to the experience of pain in others and have the ability to be emotionally congruent with others.[9] These are the attributes of empathy.

The biology of empathy tells us that *mirror neuron circuitry*[10] connects us emotionally with others, especially through non-verbal expressions, allowing us to feel—or mirror—the emotions of others. This circuitry fires more intensely when people are cooperating. Reading nonverbal cues and cooperation are particular strengths of women. Goleman tells us that:

> Our mirror neurons fire as we watch someone else, for example, scratch their head or wipe away a tear, so that a portion of the pattern of neuronal firing in our brain mimics theirs. This maps the identical information from what we are seeing into our own motor neurons, letting us participate in the other person's actions as if we were executing that action…Mirror neurons make emotions contagious.[11]

Baron-Cohen devised a test referred to as the "empathy quotient." Women outscore men, often reading other's feelings from their eyes alone.[12]

Researchers have discovered that women have 10-33% more neuronal fibers in the corpus callosum than men, enabling them to be more aware of and express more feelings and understand the moods of others.[13] This enhanced awareness provides great field perception and communication.

Susan Pinker, author of *Men, Women and Real Gender Gap* and *The Sexual Paradox*, reports that "using the latest neurological and biological findings of brain-imaging and sex-hormone assays, it has been found that women are more consensus-minded and team-oriented, and are better at reading human visual cues, interpreting feelings, and maintaining relationships and relationship networks than men."[14] Like Brizendine, Susan Pinker brings scientific ballast to the transfer of truisms into probabilities.

George Lakoff argues that empathy is the core expression of a democracy. Such consciousness would mean a different political landscape:

We would understand that our brains evolved for empathy, for cooperation, for connection to each other and to the earth. We cannot exist alone…We would embrace the fact that empathy is at the heart of American democracy…It is why we care about fundamental human rights.[15]

Democracy and empathy are at the core of what makes us human; therefore they are deeply embedded in both learning and leadership.

Imagination and Innovation

When imagination emerges as creation, ideas, products, programs, and processes heretofore unknown become real. Therefore, "innovation" is the act or process of inventing or introducing something new. The story of Bonita Calder described an innovative approach to teaching reading. Morrison and Bennett created novels, recognizing that the novel, as invention, can tell deep truths by engaging the reader in journeys of self-discovery.

Sustainability is entirely dependent on innovation.
                                          -Darcy Winslow, CEO, Nike

---

Nancy Anthony, Library Media Specialist at Birch Elementary School, invented a process for thoroughly integrating the library's resources into the life of her school, thereby creating an open access library. This process required that all concerned, including teachers, administrators, and Nancy herself, alter their roles and uses of time.

The Open Access Library
By Nancy Anthony, Library Media Specialist

"Why did you build this very expensive facility?" I boldly asked Principal Richard Davidson by the end of my first year as Library Media Specialist in the newly expanded and renovated library media center at the Birch Meadow School in Reading, Massachusetts. I knew that I needed a clear purpose for my work. Although he circumvented the question, I still liked his answer: "That is why we hired you."

As impressive as this new media center was, it had not significantly touched the hub of the school itself. Classes visited once a week. Teachers dropped off students so they could have thirty minutes of planning time. If it was Tuesday, it was library day, and students needed to remember to return the two books they were allowed to check out on their scheduled day. They might listen to a story, do a library scavenger hunt, or watch a short video. Then they had ten minutes to check out books. Pretty routine. No research literature supports this kind of library program.

It had become very clear to me during that first year at Birch Meadow that Mr. Davidson had a clear sense of purpose in his job: students come first. When I presented to him a picture of what a library program could be when weekly scheduled classes are eliminated in favor of a system of open access, he accepted the idea with alacrity. After all, increased opportunities for student learning are at the center of an open access program. But what would the teachers think if they had to give up much needed planning time? [Fortunately, this planning time exceeded contracted planning time.] I made a proposal to the faculty, one that would no longer include a separate library period during which they could plan.

At an end-of-year staff meeting, I explained once again how using the library at the point of need was far more effective than isolated weekly visits. Teachers were willing to try this for one year and then assess its effectiveness. We never looked back. With open access, students use the library for "just in time" learning. Library use dramatically increased. With open access, I was able to schedule daily visits for students working on a project. I could teach in classrooms when that seemed to work better–or say, another teacher wanted to use the library for a project at the same time. And, since we were breaking down the barriers of library access, we also took off the limits to the number of books that could be circulated: unlimited; as much as you want!! After all, print-rich environments are what all educators strive to create.

Deciding to put student learning first in the library requires: 1) A library media specialist who recognizes that being proactive is key to a program's success; and 2) An administrator and faculty who perceive the library media specialist as a partner in curriculum development. Fortunately, we had both. With the crucial support of Mr. Davidson, who was named Massachusetts School Library Media Association Administrator of the Year in 2004, and with a faculty who recognized that their most precious resource – time – could be greatly "expanded" when two instructors were working together, the open access program developed into a lively center of learning and a true "hub of the school."[16]

Bena Kallick is a private consultant who provides services to school districts, state departments of education, professional organizations and public sector agencies throughout the United States. Her areas of focus include group dynamics, creative and critical thinking—the processes that enable individuals to invent together. One of the products of these rich processes is a Children's Museum.

Maria Clay of New Zealand developed the process of Reading Recovery, which is designed to provide the social interaction that supports students' ability to work in their "zone of proximal development"[17] just beyond their level of actual development—with a supportive adult who helps them solve problems and perform. Clay's theory of learning to read is based on the idea that children construct cognitive systems to understand the world and language. These cognitive strategies develop self-directing systems that generate further learning through the use of multiple sources of information.

Katherine Wagner, a parent in British Columbia, described her pathway to innovation:

> As a concerned parent of two small children in a small, remote Canadian community, I felt isolated from the ideas that would improve schools, initially for my own children. Public schools have always been reticent to provide parents with more information than absolutely necessary and I soon discovered that there is a lot of truth in the old adage "knowledge is power." Knowledge is also an essential component of leadership, an aspect requiring access to information.
>
> In this respect, my initial leadership opportunities would have been limited were it not for the Internet and email, a relatively new phenomenon in the early '90s. I emailed education researchers and became involved in learning dialogues that would have been impossible otherwise. I accessed journals previously only available in university libraries, the nearest of which was an hour away. I used listservs and bulletin boards to make virtual contact with like-minded parents across North America, and even the world. They provided me with advice, support and the confidence to realize that my perspectives and contributions were valuable. This knowledge helped me articulate my way to three consecutive terms as

an elected school trustee. Along the way, I met my greatest mentor, Helen Raham, through modern communication technology. A teacher and visionary, Helen invited me to be a part of her dream of creating an organization that would promote and fund public education policy research in Canada, The Society for the Advancement of Excellence in Education (www.saee.ca.) These days, I speak directly to parents as an education columnist.[18]

Entrepreneurs and Intrapreneurs

Women are among the fastest growth group for entrepreneurship. As of 2006, women businesses accounted for 30.4 percent of all privately-held firms in America, employing more than seven million workers.[19]

Bena Kallick, Maria Clay and Katherine Wagner, as well as Jan O'Neill, whose story is described in Chapter Four, are entrepreneurs. An entrepreneur is generally defined as someone who sets up and finances new commercial enterprises to make a profit. For our purposes here, we would add that when entrepreneurial enterprises are guided by a moral purpose, they can be transformative of the organizations being influenced and need not be created for personal profit.

Kallick, for instance, is co-founder of TECHPATHS, a company designed to facilitate teacher's networks and communications about performance assessment. She is on the Boards of JOBS for the Future and the Apple Foundation.

The Reading Recovery processes of Maria Clay, author and entrepreneur, have been used by millions of children worldwide. We would refer to Kathryn Wagner as an entrepreneur, even though The Society for the Advancement of Excellence in Education is a non-profit organization.

"Intrapreneur" is defined as "an employee with a flair for innovation and risk-taking that is given unusual freedom to develop products or subsidiary businesses within a company." Lavaroni and Leisey refer to such individuals as "Edupreneurs,"[20] thereby sharpening the definition to mean, "A person within the public school organization who takes hands-on responsibility in creating, developing and marketing a program, product, service or technology for the enhancement of learning consistent with the goals of and supported by the organization." All too often, organizations, especially schools, discourage creativity within the organization. Lavaroni and Leisey stress that: "The only successful education entrepreneurs we could identify had left the schools." Nancy Anthony and Bonita Calder are prime examples of intrapreneurs—edupreneurs—who work within systems, resulting in changed roles for everyone involved.

Translating Imagination into Organizations and Societies

When imagination takes form as innovation through the auspices of entrepeneurs, intrapreneurs or edupreneurs, everyone involved is altered through reciprocal relationships. Earlier, we described "reciprocity" as a critical aspect of leadership. The following story is told by Sheila Jordan, Superintendent of Schools, Alameda County, California, and represents a premier example of transforming an organization through imagination, leading to reciprocal relationships and an expansion of the arts:

> Restoring arts to the classroom is a central pillar in my tenure as Superintendent of Schools. Although I never questioned the importance of the arts as part of a complete education, my analysis was undeveloped. My partnership and subsequent warm friendship with Suzanne Lacy—- then Dean of the California College of the Arts—transformed and broadened my relationship to the arts. When, as a city council member, I announced my intent to support the development of an Oakland Youth Policy Initiative (OYPI), Suzanne convinced me of the potential for the role of art in policy development. The idea of the arts providing youth who are not identified as "leadership" types with a vehicle to have their voices be heard was appealing. The arts created a new palette of options. Meetings lack appeal and quickly get boring for young people. Performance art, alternatively, can deal squarely with the

issues young people are grappling with, opening the door for communication between kids from diverse backgrounds and different schools. Controversial issues, such as the relationship between cops and kids, can stimulate animated discussion and lead to creative problem-solving.

Later, as the first elected woman County Super-intendent in Alameda, it was my experience with Suzanne and other local artists that provided the impetus for me to propose the arts as a county office priority. Not only has our *Arts in Education* program evolved into a national model, but my work with the arts has provided me with the support I depend on to keep me afloat in the sea of bureaucracy that con-stantly threatens administrative creativity. I regularly turn to the leaders of our coalition for inspiration and support to steer a course that does not avoid but deals head-on with the main challenges we face as educa-tional leaders.[21]

Girls on the Run, a national program for girls in grades three through eight, empowers young girl's minds, spirits and bodies to help prepare them for their difficult adolescent years and to become strong, content and confident women. These girls meet for a 10-to-12 week curriculum that involves training for a five- kilometer fun run as the culminating activity, in concert with experiential learning about values, communication skills, being a good friend, making positive change, decision-making strategies, problem-solving and community service. In the Napa Valley Council, a group of local women successfully launched multiple sites in cooperation with the local schools in order to serve the growing interest in the program among the diverse families of the valley. Local fund-raising, espe-cially among women's groups, provide scholarships, so that any interested young girl is free to participate.[22]

The Children's Musical Theater of San Jose, winner of five National Endowment for the Arts awards, "is both the journey of a lifetime and the premier destination for Silicon Valley's young per-formers and audiences of all ages."[23] Its overreaching goals seek to inspire and teach compassion, teamwork, empathy, humility and life skills like communication and problem-solving, all in the process of integrating the arts into the lives of children. Remarkably, the theater casts everyone who auditions—no child is turned away. The CMT produces ten shows a year for differing grade levels. Parents and extended family volunteer in all stages of production.

The national organization, *Teach for America,* was founded by Wendy Kopp in 1990. It corps members see firsthand that educa-tional inequity is a problem that can be solved and gain a grounded understanding of how to solve it. They seek to lead their students to significant academic achievement, overcoming the challenges of poverty despite the current capacity of the school system.

Who are these passionate saviors of urban education? Teach for America is the national corps of outstanding recent college graduates and professionals in all disciplines who commit to teaching for two years in urban and rural schools—-and become leaders in the efforts to expand educational opportunity.[24]

Four programs—Arts in Education, Girls on the Run, Children's Musical Theater, Teach for America—what do they have in common? Each program broke with tradition by imaginatively reframing and integrating goals; each program grew in reciprocal relationship with the institutions and community of which they became a part, thus growing their strengths and values; each program influenced how teachers and parents teach and how the communities participate.

What Gets in the Way of Imagination?

We refuse to believe that some women are imaginative and oth-ers are not. Time and time again, we've witnessed the emergence of imagination when women are empowered and awakened. Our assumption is that imagination is inherent in all humans, just waiting to be activated and encouraged.

Mae Jemison
Engineer, scientist, physician, astronaut

*"I learned early in life not to limit myself due to
other's limited imagination."*

When Mae Jemison was in kindergarten, she
raised her hand to firmly declare that she wanted to
be a scientist. When the teacher asked, "Don't you
mean a nurse?" she indignantly placed her hands on
her hips and insisted, "No, I mean a scientist!" From
this early age, Jemison could imagine herself doing
things that were quite unexpected for an African
American woman from Alabama. This clarity and
determination has characterized a remarkable life of
achievement, including being the first African American woman astronaut.

Imaginative as she was, Jemison was still afraid
of the dark and of heights. Her mother, a mentor and
strong role model, taught her to confront her fears.
"You carry your own personal protection, your
strength with you," insisted Dorothy Jemison.

In addition to her valiant family, many heroes
and mentors influenced Jemison's confidence and
imagination. As a child, Wonder Woman and Cat-
woman represented women who did not need to be
saved. Linus Pauling garnered her admiration when
he worked to stop the atmospheric testing of nuclear
weapons. Che Guevara, Isaac Asimov and Shirley
Chisholm represented the symbols of courage, intelligence and independence that entranced this young
woman.

"Bruised and bloodied" by negative encounters
with professors who questioned her competence in
pursuing engineering, Jemison emerged stronger and

more confident. From medical school at Cornell University, Jemison traveled to Kenya to work with the African Medical Education and Research Foundation. After her internship, she continued to pursue her dream of working in the developing world. When she assumed a position as Area Peace Corps Medical Officer for Sierra Leone and Liberia, she was just 26 years old.

Jemison perceives herself to be a part of the universe—as much as any star, planet, asteroid, comet or nebula. "Don't my body and my mind contain the same atoms and energy as do the stars?" she queries.

Jemison never let the limited imagination of others deter her—and she never limited anyone else due to her own limitations. Her profound belief in herself and in others opened doors that may have rusted shut. By letting her own light shine, she reminds us, she gave others permission to do the same. "My life," Jemison imagines and hopes, "continues to hold secrets, new challenges and good times."[25]

While there are many reasons that imagination is kept from being activated, for our purposes we will focus on:

- **Low expectations on the part of others.** Mae Jemison learned early on not to limit herself due to others' limited imagination. When we co-authors of this book, Linda and Mary, were young women, we were accorded limited choices (but not by our mothers, by society). We could become either secretaries, nurses, or teachers. Other dreams were too audacious.
- **Lack of self-trust, confidence, failure to hear one's own voice.** Fundamentally, these are Perspective One limitations;

however, self-trust issues can quickly reappear under stress or conflict.

- **Fear of reprisal, disapproval.** Historically, women have been raised to please others—and are so good at it because they pick up clues even before the perceived authority figure has made a request or demand.
- **Organizational cultures with a pressure for conformity to traditional definitions of leadership.** Perspective One and Two women are especially subject to cultures that dictate behaviors, sapping the imagination from its members' souls.
- **Failure to understand the possibilities.** We've known many young women who have gone from home to college and into teaching or other lines of work, often experiencing consistent gender stereotypes in each setting. Under those conditions, the means to an imaginative life may appear more limited than they actually are.

What Facilitates the Imagination?

Assumptions lead behavior. Armed with the assumption that all women, all peoples, have imaginations, just as all peoples can lead, the opportunities for mining the full benefit from these potentials are endless. The following understandings and skills provoke the imagination:

- **Engagement in literature, the arts, and cultural experiences to extend empathy and compassion.** When women are involved in these experiences as a part of daily living, in and out of the work setting, they become more insightful, consequently transforming their relationships and approaches.
- **Reframe emotions as strengths rather than weaknesses.** Men who were frightened that the emotions of women would lead to family shame, wrong-headed decisions, and humiliation have created policies, laws and restrictions around the world designed to restrain women. For instance,

in Egypt an accident must be observed by three women in order to challenge the testimony of one man. It must be noted that women raise girls to submit and boys to dominate. As we have seen, emotions enable women to be empathic and compassionate and to lead with sensitivity. Mature women guard against impulsivity by channeling emotions in ways that are congruent with their values and inspire imagination.

- **Use of coaching and mentoring**. As we have seen, Katherine Wagner, Sheila Jordan, Anne Conzemius and Mae Jemison gained significant support, guidance and inspiration from mentors. In Chapter Seven, we will explore this topic in depth.
- **Fluidity of roles and responsibilities.** Nancy Anthony created a library system that resulted in the wide-scale refinement of roles. Such fluidity can respond to shifts in knowledge and maturity by framing roles that either grow with the individual or encourage individuals to grow into the roles.
- **Use of generative strategies to facilitate imaginative group problem-solving.** Such strategies may include inquiry, force-field analysis, brainstorming, Dewey's learning cycle (observe, discover, invent, produce), discovery—processes that evoke imagination and reframe meanings.
- **Opportunities for innovation and intrapreneurship.** Opportunities arise in open systems where value-laden dissonance can be felt and fully explored, such as the achievement gap with children of color. When such discrepancies are explored without timidity, reflection leads to innovation. This is a hallmark of a high leadership capacity school.

The Four Perspectives

We begin this section by reminding the reader of the remarkable story of Anne Conzemius told in Chapter Three. As a product of a rigid upbringing, Anne had brought her approach to life's problems into the work place, consulting the "rule book at every turn." When her co-workers suggested a workshop on creativity, Anne opened to the world of imagination and her life changed forever. It is significant that she already had the trust and respect of her co-workers, or they would not have felt free to make the recommendation they did. We witness Anne's story as a journey into creativity making possible her transformation.

Figure 5.1 briefly describes the Four Perspectives of Imagination.

Figure 5.1   Arouse the Imagination

	Perspective 1	Perspective 2	Perspective 3	Perspective 4
Imagination	Uses imagination to figure out what others want of them. Sees things from own perspective.	Innovates within narrow boundaries, as prescribed by the organization; personal life may include creative endeavors.	Imagines a liberated self in order to pursue interests, talents, adventures and social change. Entrepreneurial.	Opens imagination to deeper compassion and empathy. Boldly creates new ideas, approaches, and solutions.

In *Perspectives One and Two*, imagination is often used to over-react to others or the organization. For instance, a woman dwelling in *Perspective One* may not allow herself the imagination to formulate questions regarding the demands of reforms such as No Child Left Behind, while a *Perspective Two* woman may funnel her imagination into bureaucratic guidelines and rules to assure the accurate implementation of an initiative.

A *Perspective Three* woman may be the entrepreneur who has imaginative ideas and finds it necessary to leave the organization in order to make progress. She may be a keen observer of the organizational confinements, realizing that internal support for her innovations may not be forthcoming.

On the other hand, an imaginative *Perspective Three* woman may be able to garner sufficient power and authority to impose her ideas from above. When Mayor Adrian Fenty hired young Michelle Rhee as Superintendent of Washington, DC, in June, 2007, she hardly seemed a likely candidate, as she promised to make the city's school system one of the highest-performing in the country. As director of the non-profit New Teacher Project and her time with Teach for America, her lack of high-level line experience seemed to mitigate against success. Her most daring and controversial move so far has been the provision for a choice between higher salary without the security of tenure, or tenure without the benefit of a higher salary.[26]

We would question, however, whether such change is sustainable. It may be sustainable if 1) intense professional development, discretionary resources, and school community-building create a confident cadre of teachers, and 2) a larger number of educators and parents in the system support and continue the approaches and policies if Rhee leaves.

Perspective Four, transforming women, aptly describes the imaginative women whom we highlighted in this chapter. Empathy and compassion make them especially sensitive leaders; innovation extends their imaginations into broader realms, thereby transforming organizations through new ideas, approaches and programs.

Conclusion

As we moved toward the completion of this book, the United States and then the world moved into severe economic decline. While it is difficult to predict or even anticipate how this historical shift will alter who we are, Richard Florida in the *Atlantic Monthly* provided valuable insight into the road ahead by suggesting that it will be the areas that are "talent-rich ecosystems" that will emerge stronger than ever. Such ecosystems boast a "metabolic rate" that speeds up as food is converted into energy[27] (read: as imagination is converted into innovation). The essential factors? Education and innovation.

Nicholas Kristof has concluded that education—and women—are the foundation of recovery and future success. Women are the impatient resource ready to lead with learning and imagination within a reciprocal ecosystem.[28]

Each of the women in this chapter led by arousing imaginations. A poem, a radical notion, a blistering critique can move us to consider different paths, or a new approach to an old problem. When we are wide-awake, our imaginations are open to provocation. Arousing the imagination helps us commence a journey of self-discovery and realization. We lead through our personal manifestation of creativity, compassion and empathy as well as our capacity to evoke those responses in others.

We do not mean to say that everyone has a renowned author, artist or scientist buried within. We do suggest that almost everyone has an inner artist struggling to get free. Further, everyone can appreciate creative acts deeply, can share those with children and can creatively solve life's problems. When we explain to another person why we were moved by a poem, we arouse her imagination. And, when we figure out a new way to raise funds for a worthy cause, we are leading by arousing the imagination.

Imagination is thus stirred by art and literature, provocative ideas, unimaginable heroism and ordinary acts of lives fully lived. When we practice and apply imagination to our own lives, we are able to improvise, to take what we are made of and create new combinations, new strengths. Women cluster their talents in community. Chapter Six, Leading through the Creation of Community, will synthesize this book's themes into a collaborative action framework.

...But when the world becomes this flat, with so many distributed tools of innovation and connectivity empowering individuals from anywhere to complete, connect and collaborate—the most important competition is between you and your own imagination, because energetic, innovative and connected individuals can now act on their imaginations farther, faster, deeper and cheaper than ever before
-Thomas Friedman

Reflections and Exploration

We contend that passion and courage, coupled with imagination, lead to compassion, to be able to envision others' worlds as our own. Further, we have come to understand that imagination enables us to create, to invent, and to develop new answers to complex problems. Read and consider the following questions:

1. As I reflect upon a book I have read recently, its power still affects me. What did I learn about myself by reading it?
2. Have I been drawn into a recent event or story so much that I was moved to tears? How can I describe the connection that I felt with the persons directly involved in the event or story?
3. "Thinking outside the box" is an expression used to encourage new, imaginative solutions to a problem. This is creative problem-solving. When has my imagination helped me solve a problem in a new way? What circumstances and activities opened me to fresh ideas?
4. Imagine something that I think I cannot do but that I believe would heighten my understanding of myself, others or the environment. Using my own imagination and ingenuity, what could I do to construct the life that I imagine?
5. I would like to enlarge my opportunities for an imaginative life. How might I do that? What experiences will I seek? What books will I read? What people will I meet? What plays will I see? What ideas will I entertain? What music will I listen to? What art will I embrace?

Women Who Lead...
Create Community

Chapter Six

*Vibrant communities are sustained by a web of relation-
ships...*
                    -Fritjof Capra, The Web of Life, 1996

Communitarian Etzioni suggests that there are more than ninety
definitions of community. There are certainly at least that many definitions of leadership as well. While such diverse understandings may
appear chaotic at first glance, multiple definitions of a concept are
actually liberating. Singular definitions bind and restrict; not so with
notions about community or leadership.

Women in our study yearned for community. They repeatedly
found ways to create small and large communities, even when they
did not recognize what they were doing. The popularity of communities has strengthened in the past two decades, and these women
were pioneers in seeking out new community practices.

In this chapter, we bring forth our definition of leadership as it
relates to learning and to community, discuss how women are well-
suited to create community, and explore stories and programs that are
based on principles of community.

Defining Community

We have defined leadership as reciprocal learning in community toward a shared purpose. In this context, community is the field
in which meaning and knowledge are constructed and ideas are negotiated. The patterns, webs of relationships, matter, since learning in
community is an interdependent process. Leaders are invested in, and
committed to, each other's learning as well as to a shared purpose.
The women in our study and subsequent research experienced community in a few organizations, including unions and other groups

formed around a shared purpose, such as Women Leaders in Education. In a Canadian conference on women in which we were involved, the designers came together—at first temporarily—to acknowledge their struggles and support each other in their work. The success of this initial conference resulted in annual conferences on women in leadership, drawing from all fields of endeavor.

Community, therefore, can be defined as "an interconnected and complex web of reciprocal relationships sustained and informed by their purposeful actions."[1] Complexity is manifest in the many forms of diversity in the system—cultural, ethnic, beliefs, age, gender. The more diverse, the richer and deeper the possibilities for understanding. West African writer and teacher Malidoma Some insists that we all have an "instinct for community." "However, this instinct to be together is devolving into growing fragmentation and separation. We experience increasing ethnic wars, community battle grounds and self-serving interest groups."[2] Creating true communities becomes difficult when people are confronted with contending priorities of competition, self-aggrandizement, differing values, lack of skill and lack of time.

Although the pursuit of community is a basic human need, we need to learn to create the kinds of communities that promote human development. And we need to start creating communities early. We would propose that the purpose of an education is to engage children and adults in patterns of relationships in communities that serve as centers of growth—rather than to improve test scores. In Chapter Five, we described the Children's Musical Theater in San Jose, California. This theater company is such a growth community, with an overarching goal to provide a healthy environment where children are empowered and instilled with universal life skills and inspired to grow within a creative community.

Amitai Etzioni suggests a complementary way of viewing community:

> "Community is defined by two characteristics: first, a web of affect-laden relationships among a group of individuals, relationships that often crisscross and reinforce one another (rather than merely one-on-one

> or chainlike individual relationships), and second, a measure of commitment to a set of shared values, norms, and meanings and a shared history and identity–in short, to a particular culture."[3]

"Community" as a center for human development through shared purpose represents our fifth major leadership theme. As we will argue below, women are particularly adept at creating experiences and organizations that connect people and ideas. In this chapter, we will describe how to form communities that last.

Women and Community

In Chapter Five, we discussed women's unique capacity for empathy, a capability that is central to community. Reciprocity is not possible without empathy. Unless we can mirror the feelings of another, we have little hope of creating community. There is a danger to this empathy edge, however. Susan Pinker points out that because women can sense the distress of others, they often take the distress on themselves.[4] Ross and Mirowsky estimate that women experience distress 30 percent more than men.[5] Communities can dispel distress as well, since a woman's "social thermostat" spikes the release of the neurohormone oxytocin when social support is present. Oxytocin triggers and is triggered by intimacy, making the web of relationships in healthy communities essential to reciprocal learning.

Through nature and nurture, women are motivated to build community. A woman's aptitude for listening, caring, empathy and preference for collaboration over competition prepares them well for the work of creating community. For the past two decades, the research in brain science has lent validity to claims that women possess different dispositions and capabilities from men when it comes to building connections among people. Biology, hormones, brain circuitry, and early nurturing conspire to form a readiness for community. Brizendine argues that we are in the midst of a revolution in consciousness about women's biological realities. The scientific evidence behind how the female brain functions and perceives reality tells us repeatedly that women are especially sensitive to emotion, read emotions in others and nurture and care for others.[6] These are central aptitudes in the creation of community.

As noted in the discussion of Carol Gilligan's work in Chapter Three, women are raised to be connected to others; differentiation is not as highly valued as in men. This has both advantages and disadvantages as women move into leadership, a field that has historically prized individualism, adherence to authority and competition, the antithesis of community.

Everyone in this room has the answer. The purpose of this intense experience is to stimulate one, several, or all of us to extract and remember what we already know.
—Gail Taylor, Founder, Tomorrow Makers

Perspectives on Community

Women and men bring differing perspectives into the work of community, as participants and as originators and facilitators.

In Chapter Three, Eugenia was a silent *Perspective One* participant in district administrative meetings until her silence resulted in the non-defense of a friend and colleague. She was a follower who had not yet found her voice.

A *Perspective Two* individual may use or exploit "faux communities" either as a place to deliver edicts or policies, a convenient gathering of subordinates, or as a place to hide. In Chapter Three, we described the unique *Perspectives One and Two* journey of Beth at Jefferson High School. Beth had been offered the position of assistant principal because of her belief in collaboration. Even as a teacher, she had struggled with issues of decisiveness and the need to please. At Jefferson, Beth soon found herself taking more and more decisions to the faculty. When a teacher told her she didn't need to bring every small decision to the faculty, Beth realized that rather than conquering her perceived weaknesses, she was actually hiding them within collaboration.

A *Perspective 3* woman uses community as a strategy toward a larger goal, a cause. Often worthy, the cause brings people together and focuses energy toward the larger goal. As long as the goal remains unaccomplished, as with the union members in our study, people work closely together to persuade others and to implement techniques designed to succeed. In this category, we might find anti-war movements, professional learning communities (see below), and even teams aimed at narrowing the educational achievement gap.

Figure 6.1 briefly describes the Four Perspectives of Community.

Figure 6.1 Create Community

	Perspective 1	Perspective 2	Perspective 3	Perspective 4
Community	Follows the lead of peers, group or those in authority. Attends and listens, but participates as a follower.	Manages non-democratic community; may solicit input, but makes decisions on her own or in compliance with higher organizational demands.	Utilizes community as a strategy to accomplish goals, even when singular action is preferred.	Engages others in co-constructing meaning and action, thereby establishing community, the essential task of leadership.

Perspective 4—The Transforming Woman

Gail Taylor has spent over 25 years helping professional, scientific, corporate, and community teams discover deep patterns of interconnection, develop shared understanding, and self-organize at new levels of coherence. In 2003, she founded Tomorrow Makers, an organization that has since worked with such clients as Kaiser Permanente, Hewlett-Packard, the City of Orlando, The U.S. Navy and the World Economic Forum in Davos. Her assumptions about what leadership means and who can lead is congruent with the concept of constructivist leadership, and aligns her extensive work with organizations as the path of a transforming woman: engaging others in co-constructing meaning and action, thereby establishing community, the essential task of leadership.

Taylor's notion of self-correcting, or what she refers to as Sapiential Leadership, means that the person who can most clearly see the next step is responsible for communicating this step and facilitating or leading the group through it. She reminds us that:

> "In an age as complex as ours, it's unreasonable to imagine that any one person has all of the questions and all of the answers. To invest individuals with such responsibility creates unnecessary burdens and pressure and debilitates the creative edge of other members of the team...It is a kind of leadership that allows space to play, iterate, design and learn the art of flow as team."[7]

In Chapter Five, Bonita Calder described her new approach to reading that involved parents in a new kind of community. Caught up in the enthusiasm of imaginative planning, her colleagues expressed interest in the program as well. By spring of that first year, the other teachers at her grade level joined her in applying for grant money and deciding how to extend and enrich the original plan. As new first-grade teachers joined the staff, they were helped with their own "At Home Reading" center, now so successful that the PTA, Site Council and Educational Foundation supported its maintenance and growth. The success of this program was "due to the cooperation and respect among teachers, parents, administrators and funding groups and to the willingness of the school district to encourage teachers to try new approaches."[8]

In 2007, Drew Gilpin Faust was appointed President of Harvard University, with the expectation that she would repair, strengthen and build a strong community. Her previous leadership successes exemplified collaboration and community-building. In the Introduction to this book, we set forth these expectations. We caught up with her collaborative work through excerpts from a letter she wrote to the Harvard faculty, dated February 18, 2009.

Drew Gilpin Faust
Letter to Faculty, February 18, 2009

For Harvard, as for many other colleges and universities, our challenge is to confront the new economic realities and intelligently adapt ourselves to them, while at the same time affirming and strengthening the enterprise of learning and discovery that lies at the heart of what we do. Doing so will mean taking some difficult steps. At a time of new constraint, it will involve discipline and sacrifice…This challenge can seem particularly daunting…but we live in the moment that history has presented to us, and I am confident we will rise to this occasion as Harvard has so many times before. It is our collective obligation to face the situation with the right balance of short-term focus and long-term ambition, for ourselves and for the generations whose opportunities will be shaped by our choices…Wherever we work or study within Harvard, whatever the demands of our present moment, we share enduring ideals... And we are committed to upholding the values of free inquiry and expression, of excellence and innovation across the domains of knowledge that shape our University…I am grateful to faculty, staff, and students across Harvard who are working hard to consider how we can reduce budgets and how we can explore new ways of doing things that not only save costs but enhance our operations…The economic crisis, of course, has stressed the resources of many of our students and their families. With that in mind, we are working to make sure we restrain growth in tuition and fees for next year, while affirming our robust commitment to financial aid…In a time of dramatic and often disquieting change, it is important that all of us remember the enduring purposes of universities. We are a community of distinguished scholars, talented students, and dedicated staff — teachers and learners defined by our ideas and discoveries, not by our financial resources. Let us keep those purposes foremost in our minds as we pursue our work together in changing ways for changing times.[9]

The women in our study, along with numerous women whose stories are told in this book, sought and built community. Julie Biddle, then Director of Accelerated Schools for Ohio, used the concept of "leadership capacity" to build community within and among schools. Judy Vandegrift, through her expression of vulnerability, initiated a math coaching community in Wisconsin. Sheila Jordan, Alameda County Superintendent of Schools, created an arts community throughout the East Bay of the San Francisco Bay Area, while the founders of the Children's Musical Theater created a performing arts community in the South Bay. Below, the work of Ann Richards, Ann Lieberman and Ellen Malcolm will join in the line-up of transforming, *Perspective Four* women.

Below, we discuss various types of communities, as well as prerequisites to community, such as networking.

Communities as Centers of Learning and Achievement

As noted above regarding *Perspective Three*, communities are often used as a means, tool or strategy to achieve another goal, rather than as a learning center for the participants. This perspective, encountered regularly in education and business, can minimalize the role of community in human development. We would argue that communities can serve both *Perspectives Three and Four* purposes. As a medium for meaning making and knowledge development, community is the center of the maturation process, the locale for growing values, identity, courage, and imagination. Community can also be a conduit for other results, such as working on a national campaign for literacy or peace. Whatever aim is set forth for the use of community, it is skillful work.

Communities take many forms: teams, communities of practice, professional learning communities, organizational communities, on-line political communities, alliances and partnerships, and interest-based and informal learning communities.

Communities of Practice bring together people of shared purpose and passion who learn from each other to engage the issues that concern them all. This idea is as ancient as social order itself, although it has gained momentum in the past forty years. At the New Teachers' Center at the University of California in Santa Cruz, schools are designed as small learning communities to support teacher development *and* have a transformational effect on student achievement.[10] The design significantly reflects that of other education-based learning communities with a classroom focus. The process includes classroom observation, coaching and feedback, but adds the dimension of principal involvement and mentoring.

The *Professional Learning Community* is a descriptor now attached to the most prevalent education-based community in the United States. Its popularity—along with that of Leadership Capacity (see below)—speaks eloquently to the readiness of social institutions like schools to form community. Developed by Richard DuFour and Robert Eaker, such communities now include: 1) a shared mission, vision and value of student learning; and 2) collective inquiry through reflection, finding common ground and coordinated action. These collaborative teams are results-oriented.[11]

Joanne Rooney, Co-Director of the Midwest Principals' Center, described her experience in professional learning communities, persuaded that such communities can be at the heart of effective schools. "Both students and teachers enhanced their learning when they intentionally shared knowledge and talent in pursuit of their own professional development."[12]

Universities often use *"cohorts" as communities,* in which a group of students learn with the same professor over multiple semesters, thereby serving as the structure for degree or certificate programs. California State University, East Bay, organizes its

Educational Leadership Program around such cohorts, one professor with twenty to twenty-four students. Szabo described the cohort as a model learning community experiencing generative dialogue, inquiry, shared experience and emotional support. Such relationships build trust and enable honest self-disclosure and critiques of each other's thinking and work. The doctoral program at Wichita State University, Kansas, is also organized with cohorts, in which the students engage in field-based inquiry and teamwork. Faculty and participants work as peers and co-leaders, experiencing collaborative learning at its best.[13]

Meg Whitman's willingness to step into the unknown has set the path for her numerous journeys, the most recent and most impressive as (recently retired) CEO of eBay, the multi-billion-dollar on-line trading company. Whitman's vision for eBay was to build an *organizational community* of buyers and sellers. Community-building meant involving and listening to both buyers and sellers, many of whom had the opportunity to personally relate their ideas to her each month. While she made crisp, fast-moving decisions (and was often criticized for her style), she also listened, synthesized needs and desires, and put them into action. Whitman said about her own intent: "My job was to uncover what was going well. I think sometimes when a new senior executive comes into a company, the instinctive thing to do is to find out what's going wrong and fix it...You are much more successful coming in and finding out what's going right and nurturing that." Whitman continually readjusted and adapted to the market and the eBay community—seeking almost quarterly reinventions of the organization. Strong teamwork, an informal working environment and non-hierarchical relationships epitomize community at work. She firmly believed that the company needed "to have a sense of what issues are hot in the community. A cardinal sin is not knowing what the community's concerns are." This inclusionary style evoked loyalty to eBay from a community of strangers.[14]

Alliance, coalitions and *Networks* are growing. They are the first step in people finding like-minded others. They often lead to communities of practice. In regional, national or international networks, individuals see themselves as part of a broader profession, a broader world. They are listened to anew, with respect. The National Writing Project Network, studied by Ann Lieberman, is an excellent example of a network. The Network practices include: approaching every colleague as a valued contributor; viewing teachers as experts; creating forums for sharing, dialogue and critique; turning ownership of learning over to the learners; situating learning in practice and relationships; providing multiple entry points into learning communities; sharing leadership; and rethinking identities while linking them to professional community. The National Writing Project evolved into a community of practice.[15]

Ann Richards, late Governor of Texas, is said to have created the most diverse and inclusive administration in Texas history. Her style was charismatic and magnetic, larger-than-life qualities that often get in the way of community. However, she drew people into her orbit, inspired them with confidence and walked with them into new territory, new possibilities. Then, she connected them through networks. She engaged women who yearned to be listened to, lightened situations with laughter and warmed people with passion. In a state known for Old Boys' Networks, a competing force was born: the "Old Girls' Network." For years, Ann Richards built upon this network of talented Texas women and managed their campaigns. The network became her political power base, eventually enabling her to run for the highest state office.[16]

Ginger Rogers did everything that Fred Astaire did, but she did it backwards and in high heels.
—Ann Richards, late Governor of Texas

Emily's List, founded and still led by Ellen Malcolm, is both a national network and an intense political mentoring organization (see Chapter Seven). "Emily" is everywoman and stands for "Early Money is Like Yeast" (causing the bread—or the campaign—to rise). The goal is to identify and support women leaders who desire to be in political office. As a network, Emily's List communicates electronically with millions of women across the United States, keeping them informed about women candidates for political office, events of interest and fund-raising. Scores of women Cabinet members, members of Congress and governors accredit Emily's List with a major part of their success.[17]

Informal and interest-based communities abound: community gardens, coop nursery schools; book, service, professional clubs; quilting guilds; writing groups; political action groups; dog clubs; senior centers; church groups, to name a few.

For a community garden as a community, see Figure 6.1 below.

An intentional community is a planned residential community designed to have a much higher degree of teamwork than other communities. The members of an intentional community typically hold a common social, political, religious, or spiritual vision and are often part of the alternative society. However, such communities often become homogenous lifestyle enclaves. They also share responsibilities and resources. Intentional communities include co-housing communities, residential land trusts, ecovillages, communes, survivalist retreats, kibbutzim, ashrams and housing cooperatives. Though intentional communities do not claim to be "utopias" in the sense of *perfect* places, many do attempt to have a different and *better* sort of society.[18]

Each of the above communities possesses several shared features: a common mission or interest, a gathering of like-minded individuals (either in person or on-line), opportunities to learn together and a focus on accomplishing similar goals or conditions. A frequent drawback is the lack of diversity, an element that limits learning opportunities and sharpens conflict among groups.

What Gets in the Way of Community?

In previous chapters, we suggested lists of issues, often fears, from women in our study, and observed in our own practice. These barriers are pertinent here as well. However, there are unique impediments to creating community.

In the spring of 2009, a father-daughter basketball game was organized in the San Jose, California, area. Shortly into the game, the men stopped passing to their own young daughters as they became eagerly involved in competing with each other. The daughters stopped the game and drew a poster, pleading: DADS NEED TO PASS TO THE GIRLS! The fathers wouldn't...or couldn't...change their behaviors. "We don't want to do this again," declared the girls. "Unless it's volleyball," said one of the daughters. "We're better at volleyball."

The seduction of competition, most readily observable in men, is a major obstacle to community. Take, for example, the current addiction to the notion of merit pay for teachers based on the academic test results of their students. While this approach has surface appeal, in areas where it has been tried, it sets up competition, thereby making community nearly impossible. The idea undermines collaborative school cultures.

Competition ranks people and institutions, the essence of a win-lose mentality. *It is not possible to both rank and accomplish success for all.* Individuals tend to demonize "the other," the competitor. An alternative? Set standards high, require accountability, and reward successful schools and organizational teams, rather than individuals.

In organizations where leadership is defined by formal position and role, the assumption may exist that "the leader," rather than the group as a whole, is responsible for either achieving goals or forcing others to do so. Under these conditions, there is not a belief in the power of community. Aversion to community is often found in hierarchical cultures, where groups or teams without authority are placated and infantilized with extrinsic rewards (a party, a trip, a bonus).

Suppose that the above barriers are not in place, or desired, and that groups who yearn for community seek to establish them. The final challenge may be the lack of an interconnecting design, one that understands human dynamics and skill. Let's discuss the formation of communities.

What Creates Community?

Communities that are sustainable require a shared purpose or vision. What are we about? What is our intention? What do we want to achieve? Even in cases where the intent is almost solely the learning of the participants, such as university cohorts, a larger goal looms ahead.

Events, chaos, crisis can form communities around the sense of loss, heroism, experience that is theirs alone. A natural disaster such as a tornado or hurricane, war and national security initiatives (such as the Manhattan Project), bind people to each other with a sense of urgency, that can last for decades (e.g., veterans' groups). However, these groups usually come about through serendipity rather than intention.

In social institutions such as schools, businesses and nonprofit agencies, communities can make the difference between success and failure. We suggest the formation of communities of practice as centers of learning and human development and as centers of change, leading into the future. The following five principles and actions can be helpful.

1) Describe the beliefs or assumptions that lead to community. A number of beliefs underlie community, yet the most essential are: a) Community brings together those who share a purpose; b) Community is the context for reciprocal learning and leadership; c) Diverse communities are richer and more productive; d) Community enables people to accomplish goals that couldn't be reached alone. An interconnecting design describes the "who, what, when, where, why" of community.

2) Devise norms, agreements for working together. Decide on how: decisions are to be made, communication is to be designed, feedback is to be given and received, leadership is to be shared; as well as structural agreements, such as when and where to meet. Fundamental in developing webs of relationships is the agreement to respect and be fully present with each other, and to let go of worn-out assumptions (this will be a major outcome of dialogue).

3) Learn understandings and skills together. We find the essential skills for building community to be: facilitation for meaning making, empathic listening, dialogue, finding common ground, inquiry (discovering new information and posing questions), reflection, designing action plans and self-assessment. People learn quickly when the result is improvement in the quality of their lives, and achievement of the goals about which they are passionate. There are numerous resources for such learning described in Chapter Eight.

4) Deciding on resources required and needed. Many groups raise monies for various causes, although communities within organizations may need resources as well, such as release time, space, food, as well as written materials and a skilled facilitator, in the early stages of development.

5) Self-directing and assessing. Periodic assessment is essential for healthy communities. Regular reflection should be scheduled for community members to ask themselves: "How are we doing?" "Are we following our norms and attending to each other?" "How can we continue to improve?" The answers to such questions can result in continuous improvements in the community.

Margaret Wheatley suggests four key phases in the creation of community: Name the Community, Connect the Community, Nourish the Community and Illuminate the Community.[19] Using this framework, in Figure 6.2, we describe the Posh Squash Garden[20] and we describe a school community designed around the premise of "leadership capacity," defined as broad-based, skillful participation in the work of constructivist leadership.[21]

Figure 6.2   Examples of Created Communities

	The Posh Squash Garden[20]	**An American Middle School**[21]
Description	On the rugged Northern California coast is a decades-old community garden in the intentional community known as The Sea Ranch. While many cities, villages, towns, and regions have community gardens, the Posh Squash is an open, collective garden, available to anyone who is interested in participating (working) in the garden with other gardeners, sharing work and produce. Since it began in 1975, it boasts of having had over 600 gardeners in its community.	School communities emerge from many different sources: the determination of a principal, key teacher or district leader fresh from a university cohort, workshop, or reading; emerging from within—invented from the existing community; merging with another school or with an on-going community. Such communities are non-competitive, but cherish collaboration and share leadership as an essential aspect of sustainability. Two cases in point: in the Sacramento, California, and Syracuse, New York, school districts, a joint decision was made by district personnel and the teachers' unions to implement high-leadership capacity communities.

Name the Community	The Posh Squash began when a small group of residents in The Sea Ranch came together out of a mutual interest in gardening and a desire to participate in a collective enterprise. After locating an acre of property full of rocks and poor soil, but with enough sunshine to grow vegetables, greens and berries, the pioneering group of gardeners agreed on a set of core beliefs, values, precepts and practices. It became the Posh Squash. "The Posh Squash is organic, embraces stewardship of its soil, strives to sustainability by composting, recycling and using salvage materials wherever."	At American Middle School, reform commitments were *named* and written into policy at the district level: each school would have a highly trained leadership team that would in turn engage the whole staff in the learning and leadership of the school. The goal: to build the capacity of the school for improvement and sustainability. The interlocking web of leadership relationships would mean that when the principal left, the school would sustain its momentum.
Connect the Community	Over more than three decades, the gardeners have reconciled what they might want to grow and what would grow in its microclimate. There is a yearly cost of $130. per person, monies used for seeds and supplies. The Posh Squash offers both individuality and community. "A gardener may self-select favorite chores, adopt a particular plant or crop, undertake projects, or take on responsibilities for planning, supervising or decision-making. Always, the ethos of the garden instructs, gardening should be fun and fulfilling, and produce results." The participants stay connected by working alongside each other, planting, nurturing, harvesting and coming together for workshops and seminars and decision making meetings.	The trained leadership team developed its own purpose statement, beliefs, norms, facilitation responsibilities and ongoing learning plans. This team worked closely with the principal, also a team member, and created an interlocking design for the whole school that might include grade-level teams, action research teams and a book group. During the second year, peer-coaching teams were formed. Faculty meetings were designed as community meetings, using an agenda of dialogue, inquiry, reflection and action. Leadership Team members were chosen by the faculty as a whole, rather than by the principal.
Nourish the Community	Posh Squash employs several strategies to insure sustainability. Its "benignly coercive rules and admonitions are validated by experience and legitimated by the realities of successful gardening…. They invented and reinvented organizational structures and processes to harmonize the time, energy and skill, temperaments and expectations of highly individualistic gardeners." Shared leadership is an essential aspect of governance, involving a steering committee, monthly meetings of the membership and rotating individual responsibility for different days of the week, functions and products. Participants report, however, that individual leadership styles vary greatly from authoritarian to collaborative; for instance, a Tuesday can be quite different from a Friday. Communication, largely conducted through technology (website, newsletter and e-mail) keeps the group connected.	Once underway, each team had access to ongoing information and learning (personal, on-line and district-wide) about school communities, met the norms for open, responsive communication; and inquired into their own practice. Each person was viewed as a leader and grew in her or his own sense of identity about their capacities to lead their peers. The shared purpose of writing improvement was dialogue and inquiry. An action research project was established to discover the relative success of two complementary, but different, approaches, and the role of self-editing in writing improvement. The information was shared with the whole faculty, and an action plan was developed to blend the approaches.

Illuminate the Community	Most aspects of the garden are highly congruent with its core values and beliefs. The garden is celebrated by a Harvest Dinner, with recognition awards for outstanding service. Even the dedication of their very successful cookbook, *The Posh Squash, a community garden cookbook* demonstrates their community's cohesion and intent to go public as a means of community illumination.	Periodically, the Leadership Team, as well as other teams, met with teams from other schools to share ideas and coaching. District retreats brought people together to share stories and solve problems. Parents were invited. District policies were developed for supporting the tenets of leadership capacity, including a new evaluation process based on evidence of both adult and student learning. Student exhibitions were held to demonstrate to the broader community what the students were learning. The local university now works closely with American Middle School to prepare new teachers and principals.

Conclusion

Community can be understood as the field or medium in which reciprocal, purposeful learning and leadership occur. Women are particularly well-suited for creating such communities.

However, we would not be honest if we argued that communities represent crowning achievements for women. Communities are difficult to achieve, in their fullest and healthiest form. Our challenge to women is to improve and enhance communities of which they are already a part, and to launch communities that will meet the human yearning for relationships and purpose.

Reconnecting with the web of life means building and nurturing sustainable communities in which we can satisfy our needs and aspirations without diminishing the chances for future generations.

—Fritjof Capra

Reflections and Questions

1. Think of communities with which I identify. How effective
    are they? (Assume that the following four dimensions are
    continua, and mark each line where I would envision my
    communities reside.)
    Unclear intentions _____Purposeful
    Few opportunities to learn _____Many opportunities to learn
    Autocratic _____Shared leadership
    Exclusive _____Inclusive
2. What role do I most often play in these communities?
3. Review the definition of a *Perspective Four* view of com-
    munity (see Figure 6.1). What skills and understandings
    do I personally bring to the work of community?
4. If I were to initiate a new community, or set about to
    improve one of my communities, what approaches might I
    use?
5. How large is my world? Am I a part of any national or
    international movements, networks or communities?
6. President Barack Obama has challenged us to become part
    of a national community through participation and contri-
    bution. What part might I play?

Women Who Lead...
Mentor the Next Generation
of Women Leaders

Chapter 7

My grandmother had total focus, an attribute that deeply
impressed me. She also had the ability to make me feel
like I could do anything, that I could be a leader. She
focused all her positive spirit on me.
-Sandra Day O'Connor, former Supreme Court Justice

Mentoring is the reciprocal and intentional bridge that links one individual with another. In Chapters One through Five, we discussed the factors that distinguish and empower leaders: values, consciousness, courage and passion, imagination. In Chapter Six and Seven, leaders engage with others to form relationships and communal structures. These dual concepts, independence and interdependence, formulate a wholeness of leadership as reciprocal, purposeful learning in community.

Our mothers, Lucretia Todd and Eloise Jones, were the first to teach us about the value of mentoring. We didn't call it mentoring then, but we came to realize that caring and modeling, provoking and inspiring made us who we were. As we conducted our studies of women's lives, we learned more about our mothers as well. Their actions and words took on renewed meaning. The repetition of the message that we "could do anything we wanted to do" reverberated again and again. Our mothers insisted on drawing our attention to beauty in all of its forms—certainly the genesis of imagination. Questions shed light on observed inequities between men and women, the rich and the poor. Our mothers were our personal mentors and role models whose efforts at planned mentoring made sure that we, Linda and Mary, were the first women in our families to go to college.

Our colleague and friend Cindy Ranii, now a retired superintendent, told us that *every* major advancement in her career was preceded by a significant conversation with a caring, thoughtful mentor who prodded her to move on faster and further than she had ever imagined. Cindy learned that disposition and skill set were more important than climbing each rung of the "career ladder."

Cynthia Hall Ranii
Retired School Superintendent and University Instructor

Looking back over my 30 years in public education, I have come to realize what a powerful influence mentors had on my career. When I was just 32 years old and looking to re-enter the workforce after having two children, I gave a speech to a women's club. Having served in the Peace Corps in Iran, I spoke about their educational system and my experiences as an English teacher there. In the audience was Jean, a woman who had been a teacher in the high school I had attended. I hadn't even been in one of her classes, but she remembered me as an effective Student Body officer. She suggested that I look into English as a Second Language teaching or program coordination, since I had supervised training programs in Iran.

Within three months I had an exciting job as the Coordinator of the Indochinese Project at a local community college. That brief conversation with Jean, and her urging, propelled me into school administration. Several years later, Jean motivated me to apply for a job as a district-wide ESL coordinator. I said that I didn't have high school experience, but she insisted that I had the "skill set" and that was more important.

Once in the K-12 system, another administrator, Jim, suggested that I apply for a Special Projects/Grant Specialist position. With his encouragement, I served as a program coordinator and then director for the next five years.

Then, Les took me to lunch and asked if I had ever considered being a high school principal. I said,

"No, I have never been a high school teacher or an Assistant Principal." Again I heard, "Yes, but you have the skill set. That is more important." I became a high school principal and loved the whirl and challenges of that wonderful role for five years.

I was becoming a bit disgruntled and burned out when my high school history teacher Joan, invited me for lunch. We caught up on each other's lives. "Well, Cindy," she said, "what are you going to do next?" I didn't know. "You should be a Superintendent," she said. Again, I had set limitations on my own thinking and assumed that since I had not been an assistant, the superintendency was out of reach. Joan encouraged me otherwise. "You can do it," I remember hearing...and again..."You have the skill set to do it." I served as a high school district superintendent for 11 years.

Joan is now in her 80's and I'm in my 60's. We have known each other for some 45 years. In fact, she'll call me now and again to suggest that I teach wheelchair tennis (I have been in a chair since 2005) or...her latest idea for me...that I go to law school. I haven't rushed to take the LSAT, but ...

From each mentor I gathered confidence and courage that I did not have on my own. Thanks to my mentors, throughout my career I have never hesitated to pull talented colleagues or students aside and ask them, "So what are you going to do next?"[1]

We have learned through personal experience and our studies that mentoring the next generation of women leaders is the consummate leadership role. To reach out, to take responsibility for the learning and development of others, to mentor, is the true test of leadership value. Until this last step is taken, leading will not achieve its full expression. When women personally mentor others, plan structures for development and blaze the trails ahead, the generational connection is made. Women can then be confident that the path ahead will be paved by the experiences and commitments of those who have gone before.

Defining Mentoring

The Greeks taught future generations that mentoring referred to an enduring, sustained relationship, usually between an adult and a youth. This relationship, through continued and long-term involvement, provided support and guidance as the youth developed into an adult. Mentors invest in the potential, the future of another person, and stay around to see the potential realized. Mentees, or protégées, were often vulnerable, needed intimacy and were open to guidance.

Mentoring the next generation of women leaders requires this form of sustained relationship—as well as others that provide support and encouragement among peers and from a distance. The concept of mentoring has matured since the days of the Greeks. Today individuals of all ages are mentored, at all stages of development. But the notion of growth in the presence of another radiates a historical truth: that humanity resides in relationship. We can also place the concept of critical friendship in the realm of personal mentoring. Costa and Kallick defined a critical friend as "a trusted person who asks provocative questions, provides data to be examined through another lens and offers critiques of a person's work as a friend."[2]

Friends
You are the luck of my life
Whether deep laughter our mouths wide
Familiar jaws and teeth exhibited
Or the slow choke of tears, red eyes welled
I lean toward your confidence
Welcome the sturdy warmth

Your voices settle my stomach
Clear the air
Your handwriting relaxes me
I focus inward

Without such connections
I would stagger under the weight
Falter with each sentence
Nothing would make sense
And the closest I would get
To the inside of myself
Would be a tour through
My walk-in closet.

There is safety in the company we keep.
It keeps me alive, thank you.

-Barbara Joan Tiger

In our definitions, the concept of mentoring refers to several kinds of relationships, each unique, each affecting the individuals being mentored in ways that spur growth and development.

1) Personal mentoring. This definition is more loyal to the original meaning of mentor, with one exception. While parents, teachers and counselors provide close, one-on-one, sustained mentoring relationships, mutual mentoring, such as in friendships, is equally influential. Good friends help each other become more fully who they are. Personal mentors believe in the other person, commit to her welfare, and often help clear the way so that growth can take place. While these relationships are intentional, the influence is often more lasting than the mentor could have originally imagined.

2) Planned mentoring. To "plan" mentoring means to establish programs or structures that encourage and support the development of others. While also deliberate and intentional, the relationships are often less personal. An organization, professional organization, foundation, network, agency or university may be established to promote the development of women and might offer education and support, inspiration, awards, scholarships and recognition for accomplishments.

The concept of planning for mentoring on a large-scale basis is a relatively new idea that has come to fruition in the last three decades.

3) Trailblazing and Role Modeling. These are women who have been "firsts" in a profession or endeavor, are perceived as heroes, or have written or performed with such brilliance that others look to them for inspiration. This group also includes men, such as Mohandas Gandhi and Martin Luther King, Jr., who inspired through values that were translated into courageous action. Trailblazers and role models are often unaware of the influence that they are having on others. Relationships with trailblazers are rarely personal, although role models are often personal mentors. In our studies, parents are most frequently mentioned as role models and personal mentors.

It is these undeniable qualities of human love and compassion and self-sacrifice that give me hope for the future. We are, indeed, often cruel and evil. Nobody can deny this. We gang up on one another, we torture each other, with words as well as deeds, we fight, we kill. But we are capable of the most noble, generous and heroic behavior.

-Jane Goodall

Personal mentors engage in many forms of relationships. As Cindy mentioned in her story above, mentors may be teachers or friends who re-enter one's life at critical junctures. Or mentors may even be a group of co-workers who, as in the story of Anne Conzemius in Chapter Five, suggest a workshop in creativity, thereby enabling her to break out of the rigid reactions left over from an inflexible upbringing.

As we noted in Chapter Six, friendships not only reduce stress but also contribute to longevity. Two examples from these studies tell us a great deal about critical friendship: the relationship between Sheila Jordan and Susan Lacy and the relationship between Katherine Wagner and Helen Raham, both in Chapter Five. This relationship entered Sheila and Katherine's lives at an opportune moment: both needed to learn something new in order to move forward with their passions. For Sheila and Susan, the subject was art; for Katherine and Helen, it was public education policy research. Sheila told us, "Although I never questioned the importance of the arts as part of a complete education, my analysis was undeveloped. My partnership and subsequent warm friendship with Suzanne Lacy—then Dean of the California College of the Arts—transformed and broadened my relationship to the arts."[3]

In our studies, teachers, associates and husbands were personal mentors as well. Georgia O'Keeffe found mentors in her teachers and in her sponsor-husband, Alfred Steiglitz. It was Ann Richards' husband who encouraged her to run for political office and Barbara Jordan who monitored political ethics in her campaign. Rosa Parks' husband encouraged her to join the NAACP before they married and supported her courageous actions throughout her life.

Graduate student Eugenia, described in Chapter Three, was mentored by her University professor, Linda Lambert, to find her own voice, enabling her to stand up for her values. Our friend and colleague, Barbara Storms, assistant dean at California State University, East Bay, described for us the pathway cleared for her by personal mentors.

> Although I'd always dreamed of being a teacher, two female mentors saw my career differently. The first, a remarkable mentor—the first woman principal in a particular school district, and later the first assistant superintendent in that same district—who had encouraged me to student teach at the school where she was principal, sat with me to make a plan for going back to school. "I can see myself completing a master's degree," I commented to her. "A master's? You need to plan now for completing your doctorate!" Lois insisted, explaining that if I did so, I'd have more choices in my career.
>
> Years later, when I was working on my doctorate, another fabulous teacher-leader mentor, Sharilyn, encouraged me to think about moving into an administrative role. "But I like being a teacher," I explained. "Then you'll be a great school leader: one

who values good teaching!" she insisted. My decisions to complete a doctoral degree and to seek a variety of leadership roles changed my career trajectory. Without the (generally) gentle questioning of my female mentors (these two as well as others throughout my adult life) about my career goals, I would not have become a school administrator, educational researcher, college professor or mentor to other women. The *power of questioning and seeing the possibilities in others* are the special gifts that mentors give.[4]

Artist Delilah Montoya is a professor of photography and digital imaging at the University of Houston. She is a committed cultural worker whose purpose is to help students develop an expanding world vision and sustain their artistic sensibilities. When she collaborates with young artist she gives them a safe place to work, and she is inspired by their creative growth. Raised by her mother, Delilah Montoya testifies that women have empowered her family for five generations.[5]

Parents were the most critically important personal mentors for the vast majority of women whose cases appear in these six theme areas. Many of the women in our studies were isolated from society, colleagues and media. As a result, their parents were of paramount importance. Rigoberta Menchu, Rosa Parks, Aung San Suu Kyi and Toni Morrison experienced early deprivation that was filtered through the eyes of courageous and positive parents. Georgia O'Keeffe was isolated on the Wisconsin plain, yet her mother saw to her education, including art lessons. Mary Catherine Bateson was immersed in the intellectual milieu of her famous parents, anthropologists Margaret Mead and Gregory Bateson.

Each of the parents described above sketched out moral and cognitive schema of values and beliefs. They believed in themselves, their children and their own purposes in the world, instilling in each child the belief that they could do anything they wanted…a message that echoed throughout their lives. They modeled, sacrificed and questioned. Words and revelations inspired purposeful existences.

Women who were mentored effectively during their own lives consciously held fast to the need for mentoring as they came into their own. Such awareness led them to mentor other women, to plan mentoring programs and to blaze trails as yet unexplored by women of their own generations, thereby becoming the role models that they did not have. Below, an examination of the *Perspective Four* Transforming Women will lead to a fuller understanding of how these women mentor others.

As noted above, *Planned Mentoring* is a relatively new concept that has grown exponentially in recent years. The women who were featured in these studies were mentored personally and were witnesses to the path of pioneers. They were fortunate to have personal mentors and role models, although fewer opportunities for planned mentorship were available in their generations than today.

Established in 1912 by Juliette Gordon Low, the Girl Scouts had the first planned mentoring program, chartered by Congress in 1950. In 1976, Frances Hesselbein agreed to become CEO of Girl Scouts, at that time a failing organization. Her passion was to build an organization that provided diverse communities and equal opportunity for all girls to increase their contributions to others. Many women leaders today testify that in Girl Scouts they learned that "the quality of their ideas and the authenticity of their actions can shape the future." The world's pre-eminent organization dedicated solely to girls now has more than ten million members worldwide.[6] In subsequent years, peer-mentoring, often described as peer counseling, began to appear in schools. And sports began to play a significant role in developing young leaders.

Ruth Colvin saw a problem: pervasive adult illiteracy. Through her vision and tenacity, she established Literacy Volunteers of America (LVA) in 1962 in Syracuse, New York. The organization's uniqueness lies in its non-traditional approaches. Through community networks and mutual tutoring, she empowered learners to believe in themselves and in each other. The LVA has helped more than 400,000 learners in 40 states and 26 countries. Colvin was inducted into the National Women's Hall of Fame in 1993.[7]

In the early 1980s, California legislation established a statewide teacher mentoring program administered at the district level. The primary purpose of the program was to provide mentors for new teachers and teachers with special need. Although some relationships felt contrived, others grew into rich, reciprocal relationships.

Also in the early 1980s, the Principals' Center at Harvard began a movement that spread to other universities, intermediate units, states and countries. A critical aspect of this effort was the mentoring of school principals, a concept that joined with the cohort community concept described in the previous chapter, at many universities such as California State University, East Bay; Northern Colorado University and Vanderbilt.

The New Teacher Institute at The Athenian School, directed by April Smock, provides learning and mentoring experiences for first-year teachers. We discussed one participant, Kristin Levine, in Chapter One. Emboldened by the support from the Institute, Kristin bravely used dialogue on her first day, declaring "silence shields wisdom." Other teachers from all over the U.S. travel to Danville, California, to sharpen their teaching and leading skills before the start of their first year of teaching.

Ann Richards found inspiration and guidance in Girls Nations—a gift that she later gave back. Nichelle Nichols, the mentor who was instrumental in enabling Mae Jemison to become the first African American woman astronaut, worked with Women in Motion. Emily's List mentors promising women leaders into political office. Women's networks, both formal and informal, serve as co-mentoring forums.

Trailblazers and role models include those "firsts" in any of a multitude of fields. More than a half-century ago, Margaret Chase Smith of Massachusetts became the first woman to serve in both houses of Congress. In 1927, Amelia Earhart became the first woman to attempt a flight around the world. Julia Morgan not only designed exquisite buildings, but also cleared the path for women to enter the male-dominated field of architecture.

In Chapter Five, Nancy Anthony, Library Media Specialist at Birch Elementary School, described how she invented a process for integrating the library's resources thoroughly into the life of her school, creating an open access library. This process required that all concerned—teachers, administrators, and Nancy herself—alter their roles and uses of time. She modeled for other teachers several stages of school change: conceptualizing the improvement, co-planning with the principal, partnering with faculty to enable them to understand the changes in library use and how their roles would be altered by this change.

Role models are emerging in fields heretofore inhabited almost exclusively by men. For instance, only seven percent of musical conductors are women, a fact that makes the career of Iona Brown all that more amazing. Brown, born Elizabeth Iona Brown in Salisbury, England, in 1941, was one of the few women in the 20th century to move from bow to baton. Brown is best known for her association with the Academy of St. Martin in the Fields, the world's most recorded chamber orchestra. She insisted that the authority of her talent and commitment would inspire great performances rather than engender apprehension among the musicians. This remarkable and versatile woman has also conducted such far-reaching musical groups as the Norwegian and Los Angeles Chamber Orchestras and the London, Danish and Tokyo Philharmonics, thereby inspiring other women to follow in her footsteps.[8]

Although parents remain the most powerful role models, women have also sought and found trailblazers and role models in literature, current events, fashion and movies. Like many young women growing up in the forties and fifties, Mary and Linda, co-authors of this book, looked forward to Saturday afternoons at the movies watching emancipated Katherine Hepburn and Ginger Rogers, and rainy-day moments reading about Elizabeth Bennett in *Pride and Prejudice* or Jo March in *Little Women*. Eleanor Roosevelt, Germaine Greer, Betty Friedan and Gloria Steinem fueled our fervor, while teachers Marjorie Grant and Zina Steinberg showed us what strong women looked like in our daily lives.

What Women Bring to Mentoring

Mentoring the next generation of women leaders is a responsibility that belongs to all. In recent years, women have become more keenly aware of that responsibility. As we revisit the women honored throughout this book—both how they were mentored and how they mentor—it will become evident that things have changed. Women have become more conscious of their own strengths and capacities to make a difference in the world; consequently, they have turned their attention to the next generation.

We were gratified to find that Carol Spain Woltring and Carole Barlas had conducted a study remarkably similar to our own in the public health field. They sought to draw insights from leaders in the public health field and in turn show how those women were mentored and how they mentored the next generation of women leaders. This interview study of 36 high-profile U.S. leaders concluded that mentors gave these women permission to aspire, act and accomplish their great potentials. Further, these leaders nurtured other women, of all ages, through purposeful, informal mentoring as well as more formal mentoring involving "shadowing," interviewing, coaching, recruiting and sponsorship.[9]

Not surprisingly, our own studies, as well as those of Woltring and Barlas, reveal that women are particularly well-equipped to mentor others. Younger women are fortified with estrogen and oxytocin that prepare the brain's neuropathways with the capacity for communication, listening, caring, and empathy in all its forms. Although these hormones decrease with age, by the time women mature, they have refined their skills and found such deep satisfaction in, and wisdom from, relationships that they are natural mentors. Menopausal and post-menopausal women, often having attained personal and economic power, have the freedom and options to visualize projects of their own choosing. Both men and women now have time to define and redefine their relationships and roles and take on new challenges. Many organizations have found that the way to engage more mature employees is to ask them to mentor someone younger.

In all cultures, the role of grandmother is of primary importance in the survival and growth of children. They may be the primary caretakers and have a significant role as models and mentors. In the extensive, decades-long Kauai resiliency studies, it was most often the grandmother who enabled children to develop resilience[10]. Brizendine reflects on herself as a maturing woman, "I find myself excited and more determined than ever to try to make a difference in the lives of the girls and women I touch."[11]

The Four Perspectives and Mentoring

A *Perspective One* woman is in dire need of mentoring. To that extent, this chapter is very much for this woman. *Perspective Two* women play important roles in organizations today in establishing mentoring programs. These programs are often limited in impact, because they feel mechanical or scripted and lack the essence of learning relationships. However, these structured programs are important steps forward in settings where men have traditionally been mentored in the locker room or on the golf course and women have been treated as invisible. Companies that value mentoring build it into job expectations and provide valuable time for mentoring within the workweek.

> *Some days I stand on the ledge of life,*
> *Uncertain about tomorrow,*
> *Unsure about my destiny.*
> *You reach out to me...*
> *I see security in your hand.*
> *I gladly give mine to you.*
>
> *-Maya Angelou*

Our inquiry found that *Perspective Three* women, those fiercely independent women who often go it alone, are either significant "accidental mentors" or lend their names to planned mentoring programs that may have even evolved after their deaths. Georgia O'Keeffe is a prime example. She intentionally avoided mentoring anyone, including women, even though she was known as a strong feminist. Yet, her legacy includes the O'Keeffe Leadership Program for Girls at the Santa Fe Museum. It is unlikely, though, that she would have supported the program herself.

Figure 7.1 briefly describes the Four Perspectives of Mentoring.

Figure 7.1 Mentoring the Next Generation

	Perspective 1	**Perspective 2**	**Perspective 3**	**Perspective 4**
Mentoring	Lacks awareness of others' needs, feels she has little to offer. Not seen as strong by others. Needs mentor.	Mentors both men and women about the expectations and rules of the organization and conventional values.	Models and trailblazers, rather than personal mentors, are often "accidental mentors."	Mentors the next generation of women leaders through personal relationships, writings, and programs. Highly conscious of legacy.

Perspective Four Transforming Women are so conscious and deliberate in their mentoring that they often combine several forms. Sumedha Khannas served as Linda's mentor during a recent year-long women's development program. As a personal mentor, Sumedha learned about Linda's life and aspirations, shared relevant stories, posed challenging questions and tapped into Linda's interests and talents. As a pioneer, Dr. Sumedha Mona Khannas, gynecologist and international health worker, was a "Woman of Firsts" in the health and leadership fields worldwide. Sumedha begins her own story in her forthcoming book, *Integrating Body, Mind and Spirit Practices in Daily Life:*[12]

"Condolences...A Daughter is Born."

I was born in the Victoria Zanana Hospital in Daryaganj in Old Delhi, India. My parents, who already had one son and two daughters, were hoping for a boy to balance the progeny. Confident that I would be a boy, they had even chosen a boy's name long before my birth.

To everyone's disappointment, however, I was a girl, the third daughter. My father and his family, who were waiting outside the labor room, left the hospital when they heard that a girl was born. My mother cried tears of sadness as she held me in her arms. The nurses offered to take me into their care.

'No,' my mother proclaimed through her tears. 'She is my daughter and she will be better than all the sons of India.' This was an exquisite affirmation to receive at my birth. My mother's strong belief in me was her gift of love. It has supported me all of my life.

Early on, I also had an intuition that I would be a strongly independent woman in this life...

Sumedha was correct. Her fate was cast and she embarked upon a lifelong dedication to the lives of women. As a specialist in women's health, she has worked in more than 60 countries, often serving as the first woman to lead major initiatives in those locales. She planned highly acclaimed international leadership programs while serving in a top-level position with the World Health Organization. Sumedha founded the "Healing Well" in Northern California and is establishing a foundation aimed at improving the status of women by breaking cycles of poverty, ignorance and economic dependence[13]

A transforming woman attends to the leadership capacity of her organization by the very nature of her mentoring. When Anne Mulcahy handed over the reins of Xerox to Ursula Burns on May 21, 2009, it was an act of transition at the end of ten years of side-by-side mentoring. Both women are long-time employees of Xerox. Anne joined the company in the late 1960's, assuming the presidency in 2001. In the eight years to follow, Anne led this struggling company into the limelight again. Ursula was with her every step of the way. This is the first time that a woman CEO chose another woman to succeed her and the first time that an African-American woman has led a company as large as Xerox.[14]

From the beginning, Marian Wright Edelman's vision for a better world for children motivated her passionate journey. As a personal mentor, trailblazer and pioneer, Marian has served as a role model for thousands of women. She founded the Children's Defense Fund, along with a multitude of other programs designed to support and mentor children and young adults. A few years ago, a French diplomat explained to Linda that she had sent her daughter to live with Edelman during her daughter's high school years. She explained her rationale: there was no better mentor for a young woman than Marian Wright Edelman.

Marian Wright Edelman
Director, Children's National Defense Fund

"If you don't like the way the world is, you change it. You really can change the world if you care enough. You have an obligation to change it. You just do it one step at a time. I think we need to ask very basic questions about the kind of people we want to be and the kind of people we want our children to be."

By defending children from a world that renders violence in all of its forms as a pre-condition for living, Marian Wright Edelman has established mentoring as a process of creating a world in which children can thrive and learn. In 1973, after four years as a civil rights lawyer, Marian Wright Edelman established the Children's Defense Fund (CDF) as an organization that would advocate for all children. From the beginning, Marian's vision for a better world for children motivated her passionate journey. The work of the Children's Defense Fund is varied but consistently focused on one goal: the defense of children.

In 1994, she purchased the Alex Haley farm as the center for Freedom Schools, whose mission is to: "re-engage the whole community in the lives of its children and to reweave the kind of community that my mentors provided for my generation of children who faced a hostile, segregated world."[16] These schools train leaders of all ages and races across the country and provide fellowship, networking, technical assistance and mentoring. College-age mentors guide the children, establishing the relationships that Edelman has found vital in her own life.

Edelman's sense of identity and well-being began in the house that is now the center for the Children's Defense Fund. She was born to Maggie and Jerome Wright in 1939 in Bennettsville, South Carolina. The last of five children, she, like her siblings, was nurtured and supported by loving parents and community elders. Her life was to become a curriculum for what it is to be mentored. My parents expressed no sense of limits on my potential or on who they thought I could become…They saw me inside and not just outside and affirmed the strengths I had because I was blessed to be born a Black girl child." [17]

During her college years, three important people became mentors. Benjamin Elijah Mays, president of Morehouse College; Howard Zinn, who encouraged students to think outside the box and to question rather than accept conventional wisdom; and Charles E. Merrill. Jr., who not only provided a scholarship for study and travel at Spelman College, but engaged the students in long conversations, letters and visits. During her years at Spelman, Edelman learned empathy, a liberation philosophy, leadership and the means for action.

By 1963, the justice landscape was rich with mentors who further helped shape Edelman's life: Martin Luther King, Jr., Robert Kennedy, Bob Moses, Fannie Lou Hamer, Rosa Parks and Unita Blackwell. She looked to memories of historical heroes such as Harriet Tubman, Sojourner Truth, Mary McLeod Bethune and Septima Clark. In 1968 she married Peter Edelman; this was the first interracial marriage in Virginia.

In *Lanterns,* Edelman pays tribute to the extraordinary mentors in her life. By "Lantern," she means those who have shone the way, provided illumination, assisted others to find the path and carve out new roadways toward a purposeful life. Through her actions and her writings, we have come to understand mentoring in all of its manifestations: personal, planned, role modeling and trailblazing.

Bonita Calder's story of a unique, family-based reading program can be found in Chapter Five. Her journey as a mentor is more far-reaching, encompassing her life as an educator of young children, mentor advisor to new teachers, and pioneer. She was a mentor with the Silicon Valley New Teacher Project, designed to support new teachers during the first two years of their career. They seek to balance teaching to standards with helping children develop a love of learning. As a veteran teacher, Bonita welcomed the opportunity to try something new. She found the seminars for advisors exciting and energizing.[17]

Hillary Clinton began a life of mentoring as a girl of 14, caring for and mentoring migrant children while their parents worked. In January, 2009, Clinton explained to an audience of Emily's List women in Washington, D.C., about one of her major concerns as the new Secretary of State in the Obama Administration: the plight of girls and women in developing countries.[18]

Hillary Clinton
U.S. Secretary of State

"There cannot be true democracy unless women's voices are heard. There cannot be true democracy unless women are given the opportunity to take responsibility for their own lives. There cannot be true democracy unless all citizens are able to participate fully in the lives of their country."

When Hillary Clinton delivered the commencement address on the day of her graduation from Wellesley, she received a seven-minute standing ovation. She had spoken with clarity and forthrightness about the issues plaguing her university with a candor that delighted and amazed the audience. Hillary has been an important voice on the American scene ever since.

Hillary was born October 26, 1947, into a middle-class Midwestern family. Her mother was a homemaker, her father a small businessman. Yet her mother had a keen sense of her daughter's need to

defend herself and to become an activist through
school, Girl Scouts and church. Interested in politics
from an early age, Hillary entered debate, successfully ran for school offices and became active as a
Young Republican and later, a Goldwater Girl. In her
senior year, she ran for student government President
against several boys and lost. The Methodist Church
helped mold her sense of social responsibility and
"faith in action." Her youth minister took the young
people to hear Dr. Martin Luther King, Jr., an experience that accelerated her passion for social justice.

After her graduation from Yale Law School,
Hillary had many lucrative offers, but chose to follow
a path that would characterize most of her choices in
the years ahead. She joined Marian Wright Edelman
at the Children's Defense Fund in 1969; Edelman
became her most significant mentor. In 1974,
Hillary's first scholarly article, "Children Under the
Law," appeared in the Harvard Educational Review.
Twenty-two years later, now the First Lady of the
United States, Hillary would publish *It Takes a Village* in 1996 and again challenge us to make children's welfare our top priority.

Village appeared toward the end of her failed
effort to establish national health care while her husband, Bill, was president. She reminded us:

*"For the sake of the children, both personal and
mutual responsibility are essential...Let us stop
stereotyping government and individuals as absolute
villains or absolute saviors and recognize that each
must be part of the solution."*[18]

Health care was not her only painful disappointment during those White House years. Her husband's highly publicized adultery and impeachment
were aggravated by other scandals such as Travelgate
and Whitewater. It was during this time that she
became a powerfully polarizing individual in the
country, the object of criticism and ridicule. Washington and parts of the electorate were unforgiving.

Hillary was a pioneering First Lady: assertive
and articulate in expressing her values. Many were
not ready for a strong woman's voice emanating from

the White House. Yet, we would suggest that Hillary's experience made Michelle Obama's path more possible. At the 1995 United Nations Fourth World Conference on Women, Hillary's voice found an international audience. And, in her latter years in the White House, she played a pivotal role in the passage of legislation regarding children's health, adoption and foster care.[19]

In 2001, Hillary came into her own when she assumed the role of U.S. Senator from New York; she worked diligently in a bi-partisan manner. During 2001-2008, she gained respect from both sides of the aisle. *It Takes a Village* and *Living History* helped to set forth her own persona.

In 2008, Hillary ran for President, building a strong coalition of support and stating on the eve of her victory in New Hampshire that she had found her voice. She nearly won the election, coming closer to that coveted prize than any other woman in history. In 2009, President Obama appointed her Secretary of State.

Oprah Winfrey has defied definition while pioneering multiple roles of influence in film, television and personal development. Like so many others, she was successfully mentored by family members, especially her grandmother. She has lived a remarkable life as a personal mentor to other women, as a performer whose programs challenge others to improve their lives, as founder of the Leadership Academy for Girls in South Africa and as a political activist. As a trailblazer and role model, Oprah personifies a transforming woman who alters the lives of others.

Oprah Winfrey
Talk Show host, actress, producer and philanthropist

"I believe people must grow and change; they must, or they will shrivel up. Their souls will shrink."

"Sometimes I go into my closet when I'm feeling down and I stand in your shoes," one woman told

Oprah Winfrey. The woman had purchased Oprah's size ten shoes at an auction. Many women want to "stand in Oprah's shoes." Perhaps it is inevitable that entertainers will be role models. Some, such as Katharine Hepburn, bring us closer to being ourselves, to being able to hear our own voices, to unfettered expression. Oprah Winfrey represents such a significant role model for women in this 21st Century. Yet there is much more to Winfrey than modeling and trail-blazing. She is no accidental mentor.

Oprah Winfrey is one of the wealthiest women in the world and a renowned talk show host, actress, producer, philanthropist and public personality. As with many of the women in this book, she began life with the cards stacked against her. A Black girl born into poverty in Mississippi, she was moved from home to home, haunted by the lack of motherly love, sexually abused and cursed with food addiction. Things might have turned out quite different for Oprah.

What made the difference? Winfrey was born in her grandmother Hattie Mae's house on a small farm in Kosciusko, Mississippi, in January 1954. She credits her grandmother with "shaping her life the most." For the first six years of her life, she lived within the care and love of Hattie Mae, who taught her to read from the Bible by the age of three. Life was isolated and hard on the farm. Winfrey remembers thinking at a very early age, "My life won't be like this."

Teachers recognized her talent and intellect and recommended that she attend an Upward Bound school. During her adolescent years, she found solace and inspiration in books about courageous women like Anne Frank, Helen Keller and Sojourner Truth. At the age of sixteen, she felt validated by Maya Angelou's *I Know Why the Caged Bird Sings*. Winfrey said of her relationship with Angelou, now a personal mentor: *"Nobody makes it alone...and that's what Maya has been, a mentor and inspiration in my life. Everybody who gets through the tough times gets through the tough times because there is somebody standing in the gap to close it for you."*[21]

By purchasing the rights to her own acclaimed show and using it as a platform, Winfrey began to carefully and consciously create the streams of influence that would make her a remarkable mentor. She choose film parts (e.g., The Color Purple) and secured film rights to books such as Beloved, David and Lisa, Their Eyes were Watching God and The Wedding that communicated the messages of self-reliance, resilience and equality. Winfrey's personal stories turned out to be the most powerful of all. Her decision for self-revelation…sharing her childhood struggles with abuse and her life-long addictions…gave courage to countless others who could now say, "Perhaps I can also break through my bondage."

In 1997, Winfrey began a charity campaign called Oprah's Angel Network, which awarded 150 scholarships to young people chosen by the Boys and Girls Clubs of America. Two hundred "Oprah Houses" have been built by Habitat for Humanity. In 1998, Winfrey invested in Oxygen Media, a women's cable network, intended to bring women's issues to women. The Oprah magazine, "O," started publication in 2000 to bring stories and life strategies to women worldwide.

Winfrey is aware of the breadth of her influence and has more recently leveraged it to impact legislation. She has testified before the U.S. Senate Judiciary Committee and worked for the passage of the National Child Protection Act, which established a nation-wide database of convicted child abusers.

Oprah Winfrey is leading a joyful and deliberate life. Each action is weighted with her values and intention to help others create their own successful lives. She focuses each aspect of her media, philanthropy and politics on the goals that have guided her since she was a child.[22]

Maxine Greene became the first woman philosopher to be hired at Columbia University. From this position, she has leveraged other women into pioneering roles for several decades. As a mentor of the next generation of women, Maxine Greene invites commitment to values of equity, democracy and community. Her wakefulness and her passionate mind sustain her courage. She arouses the imagination in herself and others. She mentors as a role model, a teacher, a writer and a member of aesthetic communities.

Maxine Greene
Philosopher, educator, author

"Remember not to bow, not to submit, to choose, to be and to become."

Greene's life has been that of a pilgrim on a quest of becoming. She has been "on her way" since she first sought to carve the self from the challenge of being a Jewish woman amidst the prejudices against both. As a mother of two children, she often found the professional world hostile to women who wanted both a family and a profession. When Greene was hired as the first woman philosopher at Teachers College in 1966, she was not permitted into the faculty club. Over the following decades, Greene's persistence and imagination have helped women understand the nature of their quests for selfhood.

Two complementary pathways played a part in the construction of the woman who is now recognized as the most important American philosopher since John Dewey. The first path is paved with an intentional and enlightened philosophy of being. The second path suggests how consciousness can be awakened in others. This awakening, or releasing of the imagination, defines mentoring in its most powerful forms.

Greene believes that ideas that are worth learning have the capacity to awaken. And to what do we awaken? We awaken to the compelling need to build a just, compassionate, and meaningful democracy. By means of engagement with a project (experience), the attitude of wide-awakeness develops and contributes to the choice of actions that lead to self-formation. A project means the intentionalized vision or purpose of making or constructing the self and the world.

One of the major goals of education, therefore, is to nurture intellectual talents for the formation of our society into a more democratic, just and caring place. These talents and sensitivities are essential in order to help students and their teachers create meaning in their lives. Those who teach ought to be "those who have learned the importance of becoming reflective enough to think about their own thinking and become conscious of their own consciousness."[23] Democracy, Greene insists, is a way of life, not just a form of government. This way of life recognizes the capacity of everyone to choose, to act, to construct her own life. "The wonderful part about being a teacher," Greene argues, "is that we can free people to move toward an achievement of their own freedom, of their own expression, of their own pain, of their own hopes."[24]

Greene mentors the next generation through her teaching, writing, curriculum and Foundation. Her groundbreaking books, *Teacher as Stranger, Landscapes of Learning, The Dialectic of Freedom and Releasing the Imagination* have framed the journey toward wakefulness for educators. As Philosopher in Residence at the Lincoln Center Institute for more than 30 years, she encourages teachers to think in new ways about aesthetic experiences. Works of art, Greene believes, "often lead to a startling defamiliarization of the ordinary."[25] This dissonance awakens participants to a world that they have not seen before. They are compelled to action in their classrooms and in their communities by this new awareness.

The Maxine Greene Foundation provides "Greene Grants" of up to $10,000 for educators who are capable of inventiveness and go beyond the standardized and the ordinary, artists whose works embody fresh social visions and individuals who radically challenge or alter the public's imagination around social policy issues. Participants in all of these experiences enter into a dialogue that frames their own narratives. Greene's influence on educators has been profound. As a mentor of the next generation of woman leaders—much like Marion Wright Edelman—Greene combines the values, consciousness, passion and imagination essential for the creation of a future unlike the past.

How the Women Who Lead Mentor the Next Generation of Women Leaders

Our studies revealed a strong intention to mentor. *Perspective Four*, transforming women leaders, and many women in both the *Perspectives Two and Three* arenas were conscious of the need and responsibility to mentor other women.

Wangari Maathai, another transforming woman, *personally mentors* the women who volunteer in her Greenbelt Movement. She teaches and encourages, demonstrates and inspires. Maathai's aim is two-fold: to teach the skills of reforestation and environmental care while awakening the inner power of these women to pursue their values. In Chapter Three, Elizabeth Reilly, an American Jew, served as a critical friend to two men—one Christian, one Moslem—by challenging them to deal with the Diaspora within their own countries and to frame resolutions through the lens of personal responsibility.

Mary Catherine Bateson learns with and from her daughter as well as being her personal mentor and teacher. This mother-daughter journey has been a central aspect of her writing, often serving as the basis of personal anecdotes or stories that describe the learning process. In *Reading Lolita in Tehran*, Azar Nafisi invited young women to her home at great risk to herself and subsequently used literature to evoke young Iranian women's sense of possibility. As these women found their voices, Nafisi facilitated dialogues through which they were mentored by Nafisi and the other women.

Women who lead have significantly altered the face of *planned mentoring* for other women. Highly conscious of their own opportunities and accomplishments, they sought to give back—to mentor the next generation of women leaders.

In Chapter Two, Linda Henke, Superintendent of Sycamore Heights, mentored school district personnel through professional development by assuming that personal empowerment can lead to community empowerment. Professional Development as a form of planned mentoring can be also found in such programs as Courage to Teach and Courage to Lead. Such professional development begins with the evocation of voice and personal strength and evolves into new understandings of the mission at hand.

In 1993, Mae Jemison left NASA to establish the Jemison Group, Inc. an organization designed to focus research on the beneficial integration of science and technology into daily life. This research focus advances technologies suited to the social, political, cultural and economic context of the developing world. During this same period, Jemison founded The Earth We Share (TEWS), an international science camp for students ages 12-16.

At Poland Regional High School, described in Chapter Two, school coach Gerry is an example of how new roles such as coach, mentor, and advisor can influence and shape a school faculty and school structure. In this case, Gerry worked directly with the leadership team to bring about significant improvements through personal and team coaching and mentoring.

U.S. National Soccer Team player and Olympic gold medalist Mia Hamm created the Mia Hamm Foundation. It is dedicated to raising funds and awareness for two very personal issues for Hamm: researching bone marrow diseases and encouraging and empowering young female athletes. Following her brother Garrett's death in 1996 from aplastic anemia, Hamm pledged to make a difference by helping people who suffer from that illness and other bone marrow diseases. Realizing that her opportunities were the result of the tireless work of pioneers, Hamm has dedicated much of her time to mentoring other young women in sports.[26]

Other examples of planned mentoring abound in the stories of women in this book. They include:

- Girl Scouts – Frances Hasselbein
- Greenbelt Movement- Wangari Maathai
- Arab Women's League – Nawal El Sadaawi
- Girls on the Run-Molly Barker
- Teach for America- Wendy Kopp
- Rosa and Raymond Parks Foundation-Rosa Parks
- Writer's Unions of Canada-supported by Margaret Atwood
- Earth We Share –Mae Jemison
- Arts in Education, Alameda County, California-Sheila Jordon

- Girls Nation and women's networks - Ann Richards
- The Dialogue Project – Azar Nafisi
- Roots and Shoots- Jane Goodall
- Whitman College at Princeton-Meg Whitman
- Maxine Greene Foundation at the Lincoln Center for the Arts
- Leadership School for Girls, Namibia-Oprah Winfrey
- Emily's List-Ellen Malcolm
- The White House Project- Marie C. Wilson

The power of mentoring and its effect on employee satisfaction and retention has encouraged many organizations to plan mentoring programs, either for women alone or for both men and women. We recommend the latter approach since mentoring for one gender only can be divisive. The dominant organizational hierarchy in each setting greatly influences the mission and result of such programs. Riane Eisler refers to "hierarchies of domination" and "hierarchies of actualization," labels that speak for themselves. The first designation refers to those that are imposed, rigid and ruled by fear; the latter designation is based on mutual values and benefits, respect, caring and accountability.[27] In a domination culture, the aim of mentoring leads to *Perspective Two* thinking, while in an actualization culture, mentoring can lead to transformation (*Perspective Four*).

Stacy Blake-Beard describes two successful mentoring programs aimed at the retention and satisfaction of women employees: Proctor and Gamble's Mentor Up program and Deloitte and Touche's Initiative for the Retention and Advancement of Women. As a result of the programs, which also changed the gender culture of the organizations, P&G reduced women employee losses by 25 percent while Deloitte and Touche increased women partnerships by nearly 400 percent over a seven-year period.[28] Although these programs began as business strategies, they resulted in improved productivity, socialization and commitment.

Professional associations often recognize the significance of mentoring. The National Association of Women Lawyers grants the Margaret Brent Award to outstanding lawyers nationwide. Brent was the first woman lawyer in America, arriving in the colonies in 1638. She was a master negotiator, an accomplished litigator, and a respected leader. Brent was involved in 124 court cases over eight years, and won them all. Over 250 years later, *Harper's* magazine noted: "By this action, Margaret Brent undoubtedly placed herself as the first woman in America to make a stand for the rights of her sex." This particular reference to Ms. Brent relates to the pertinence of the criteria for lawyers receiving the Margaret Brent Award for professional excellence in their field. They must have:

- Influenced other woman to pursue legal careers,
- Opened doors for women lawyers in a variety of job settings that historically were closed to them, and/or
- Advanced opportunities for women within a practice area or segment of the field.[29]

The women with whom we have taken our journey are most often *trailblazers and role models*. They are trailblazers, in that they engaged in activities and work that heretofore was denied to women—or that women themselves have avoided. They were role models through their writings, public performances and demonstrations, heroic actions, oratory, and by the very positions that they occupied. While they were often conscious and deliberate in accepting these roles— we often encountered women for whom such roles were secondary. When passion ignites action, how others experienced them became less important. Yet, trailblazing and role modeling converge with, and often create, legacy. "Legacy as mentor" means that what we leave behind, our space and voice in the world, serves to mentor future generations.

Women educators throughout our studies served as role models. Barbara Ryan, School Board Member in Santee, California, insisted that expectations for student performance not be lowered because of social economic conditions or ethnicity. Judy Vandegrift, newly hired math team leader, modeled openness and vulnerability by holding up her own teaching to criticism and analysis, thereby allowing others to open their classroom practice to observation and feedback. And Martie Connor modeled lessons for teachers to use based on the assumption that all students are gifted. Armed with this provocative belief, Martie became a trailblazer in her district's new approach to gifted education.

The worlds of literature, art, and science also abound with women trailblazers. Nawal El Saadawi often said or wrote the unsayable in her writings and teaching on women and sexuality, and women and power, in the Middle East. Frida Kahlo's frank, bold lifestyle was a stunning example of courage and passion to women, especially Mexican women, who had not allowed themselves such visibility and choice. Georgia O'Keeffe knew at an early age that she would be an artist and allowed nothing to interrupt that goal. Women artists were virtually unknown at that time, certainly not women artists who painted for public showing.

Toni Morrison was the first African American woman to be awarded a Nobel Prize. Mae Jemison was the first African American woman astronaut. Rigoberto Menchu, a Guatamalan Quiche Indian with no access to literacy or political power, has challenged 500 years of colonial rule to demonstrate that personal will and tenacity can supersede traditional means of power in bringing about change. After forming a new indigenous political party, Encuentro por Guatamala, she ran for president. As noted above, Sumedha Khannas was a trailblazer in the field of international health.

Skills and Understandings of Mentoring

Women who mentor other women find a rich landscape of possibilities embedded in *Perspectives One through Four*. Even though a woman may appear to function with a limited perspective, it is important to keep in mind that all women need and benefit from mentoring. Believing in each person's potential for growth is a strikingly optimistic path. Once, peoples held a static view of one another.

Today, we can be confident that individuals grow and change—that they are capable of evolving into their better selves. Such optimism encourages us to be aware of the many skills and understandings that contribute to high-quality mentoring, particularly of the next generation:

- Demonstrate strong collegial skills—including critique, support and reciprocity;
- Understand and communicate knowledge related to the field in which you both work; stay aware of the "cutting edge" of knowledge;
- Provide solid experience as a context for examining ideas and actions; use cases and stories;
- Demonstrate flexibility in thinking and learning;
- Serve as a model adult learner yourself;
- Understand persuasion, facilitation and change processes;
- Demonstrate curiosity, inquiry, discovery;
- Display role flexibility by understanding when to teach, facilitate, listen, inquire;
- Evidence capacity for mutual trust and regard;
- Orchestrate dissonance and consonance through questioning, feedback and coaching;
- Foster self-direction in others by encouraging independence and self-analysis;
- Understand the stages of a mentoring relationship, altering interactions in response to growing autonomy.[30]

When organizations establish mentoring programs, training is vital for success. The skills and understandings above can serve as a starting point to develop an effective, field-sensitive program.

On our climb to power, with each step up the ladder we make, let's be sure to become the kinds of leaders who reach down and give a helping hand to those behind us. That's real power—power that can dispel fear and promote freedom and equality.
-Pat Mitchell, former CEO of PBS

Conclusion

Mentoring captivates the imagination and evokes the *power to bring about change* that is embedded in all women...as well as in all men. As humans, we await the growth in awareness that change necessitates. We suggest that the waiting is over. Women need to initiate, reach out, and invite the mentoring that will facilitate their journeys toward transformation.

Mentoring is a win-win, reciprocal relationship. Mentors learn as those who are mentored learn. As we talked with women, we found this truism repeated over and over. The later stages of transformation are made possible when women reach out to assist other women into leadership.

Openness to mentoring is key. We are saddened when we hear someone say, "I've never had a mentor." Perhaps the receptivity factor is not as open as it might be. Stacy Blake-Beard expressed it beautifully: "I enter each mentoring relationship with the thrill, the sheer possibility that I am going to be transformed by my partner."[31]

As Grandmother-Mentors, we hold great expectations for our grandchildren. We wish for them a transforming journey of fulfillment characterized by unassailable values; a clear sense of who they are; the courage to pursue their passions and make the world a better place; an active and liberated imagination; and loving families and communities. We trust that, in turn, each grandchild will mentor the next generation of learners and leaders. It is our honor to listen and question, inspire and model, blaze new trails and love our grandchildren unconditionally.

Reflections and Questions

Mentoring the next generation of leaders asks women to foster the leadership qualities in others, to support and reaffirm while challenging and provoking. Reflect upon and explore the following questions about your past and present experiences with mentoring. If you are keeping a journal, write your responses.

1. Who were the mentors in my life?
2. In what ways were they of help to me?
3. Who are my role models? Why?

4. If I were advertising for a mentor now, what description or criteria would I use?
5. Am I mentoring anyone now? Describe that relationship.
6. Review the skills and understandings of mentoring above. Which of those come easily to me? Which require new attention and learning?
7. Do I currently have a mentor? If I were asked to honor her or him at an event, what might I say?
8. Do I work within an organization that has a formal mentoring program? How would I evaluate its success?
9. If I were to design the ideal mentoring program, what would it entail?

On Becoming Transformational Women Leaders: Fulfilling the Promise

Chapter Eight

We can be a part of changing the way women are viewed in this country, and build a government that doesn't just encourage women to dream big, but one that provides women and young girls with support and resources to pursue those dreams. I want that for my daughters. I want that for your daughters. I want that for this country.
*   -Michelle Obama, April 18, 2007*

This book has been driven by several assumptions; foremost among them are: 1) All humans have the right, responsibility, and capability to be a leader. 2) Leadership is reciprocal, purposeful learning in community is best fulfilled by transforming women, an integrated individual who has many *Perspective Four* qualities and characteristics. 3) All women are capable of becoming transforming women and, therefore, consummate leaders. We now return to these assumptions to more fully discuss the process of becoming transforming women. By way of refinement, we offer:

It can be said that a transforming woman leader—one who has evolved into a wholeness honoring both self and others— is one who: *Lives and leads from universal values, passionately and courageously pursued. Aware that she, as well as others, is continuously evolving. The woman leader invokes imagination in the search for compassion and creative action. Learning and leading for the betterment of the world occurs in community. She tirelessly mentors the next generation of women leaders.* We can fairly say that most women in our studies already were, or were on a conscious path to becoming, transforming women leaders. In fact, we drew the Per-

Figure 8.1 Perspectives of the Transforming Woman Leader

Values	Evolving Self	Passion and Courage	Imagination	Community	Mentoring
Lives universal values (equity, care, social justice) from integration of inner and outer voices.	Bases authentic identity on self-reflection and the needs of others; uses informal authority to bring about change.	Uses courage to promote and defend universal values; passion ignites and sustains creativity and action.	Opens imagination to deepen compassion and empathy. Boldly creates new ideas, approaches and solutions.	Engages others in co-constructing meaning and action, thereby establishing community, the essential task of leadership.	Mentors the next generation of women leaders through personal relationships, writings, and programs. Highly conscious of legacy.

spective paradigm from this evidence, combining what we knew about women leaders with the extant research on human development.

> *You don't have to put an age limit on your dreams, I just want people to feel inspired and motivated to go out and do things that maybe they had put off because they thought they were too old.*
>
> *—Dara Torres*

Our aim in this chapter is to propose pathways toward becoming transforming women leaders. First, by nominating "Women to Watch," then suggesting skills and understandings, organizational strategies, and approaches to bring full circle the journey advanced in this book. We also suggest ways to think about rejoining the lives of women and men as partners in the creation of a more integrated world.

It is our belief that women leaders are nearing a critical mass in many fields in "developed" countries. The concept of "critical mass," while originating in the areas of science concerning the amount of radioactive material needed to produce a nuclear reaction has been used repeatedly to suggest the amount of participation needed to reach a tipping point of change, a sustainable alteration in the direction of an idea or a society.[1] Everett Rogers suggests that it takes thirteen percent of the population to accept a new idea, while adoption rates between five and twenty percent can make an innovation self-sustaining.[2]

It would be naïve of us, however, to suggest that women's leadership within dominant Moslem and Catholic countries has reached, or is even nearing, a critical mass. While a woman sometimes serves in high positions in these countries, it is usually because she is the daughter or widow of a prominent or martyred male leader.

However, we do observe a dramatic increase in awareness and actual opportunities for the education of young girls, a condition that is the most promising move toward an international future for women leaders.

Women to Watch

Given our premises about women leaders and the qualities and perspectives that characterize them, we offer a few "Women to Watch," women whose behaviors thus far suggest that they already evidence two or more of the descriptors offered in Figure 8.1 above. This grouping is meant to encourage the reader to bring other nominees, including themselves, to light. In order to create shared understandings, we have nominated women who are somewhat well known. However, these criteria apply to the women in our daily lives as well—to our daughters and granddaughters, our sisters and cousins, our friends and colleagues. Our nominees are:

Katharine Jefferts Schori, the first woman to serve as presiding bishop of the Episcopal Church, as well as the first woman bishop of the global Anglican Communion. Katharine's capacity to respectfully hold competing and diverse ideas in balance and to negotiate for common ground makes her the right person at the right time in history for this vast Anglican religious community. Her blessing of same-sex couples and the ordination of gay clergy stems from her belief that "God is asking us to build a society where people can live together in peace with a sense of justice, where people can develop their gifts to the fullest."[3] Katharine supports a "pause" (a fasting period) on these actions in order to "...lower the emotional reactivity in the midst of this current controversy, so we just might be able to find a way to live together."[4]

Selection criteria: Values, Self-Understanding, Courage, Community, Mentoring

---

Religion is at its best, I think, an invitation into relationship. It's not necessarily a set of instructions for how you deal with every challenging person you run across in the world. It has that at its depth, but it does not give one permission to say, "This person is out, and this one's okay and acceptable." And it continually invites us into a larger understanding of that relationship.
                    -Bishop Katharine Jefferts Schori

Indra Nooyi, CEO of PepsiCo, is considered a caring visionary who "can relate to people from the boardroom to the front line." Indra has pledged that fully half of Pepsi's U.S. revenue will be derived from healthful foods by 2010. By reinventing the company to focus on healthy food, eschewing fossil fuel in favor of wind and solar power, and campaigning against obesity, Indra symbolizes organizational transformation. She has also created a "team of rivals" by inviting her top competitor to become her "right-hand man." What is next for this dynamic leader? "Washington," she claims. "I want to give back."[5]

Selection criteria: Values, Self-confidence, Courage, Imagination Community, Trailblazer

Ellen Johnson Sirleaf, the first woman President of Liberia, is an heiress to a long line of suffering, powerless and oppressed, yet spirited women. Although considered a member of the elite class, Ellen was always in the middle of fierce political storms and thrown into prison repeatedly for her courageous defiance. Three revolutions later, this sensible and pragmatic woman—formerly the country's finance minister— is now seeking the means for Liberia to bring itself into the 21st century and provide leadership to other trouble spots in Africa.[6]

Selection criteria: Values, Courage, Self-confidence, Nation as Community, Trailblazer

From nuclear proliferation to genocide in Darfur, U.N. Ambassador **Susan Rice** places her values front and center. A scholar, activist and athlete, she was always a woman to be reckoned with. A Rhodes Scholar who earned a doctorate in international relations at Oxford University, Susan joined the Clinton team at the age of 28 and has developed a powerful network of value-driven individuals, including her mentor, Madeleine Albright, former Secretary of State.[7]

Selection criteria: Values, Self-Confidence, Courage, Imagination, World as Community

Shirley M. Tilghman, President and Professor of Molecular Biology at Princeton University, is a world-renowned scholar, an exceptional teacher, and is respected worldwide for her pioneering research and advocacy of women in science. Her research into mammalian and human genomes makes her a champion of discovery and a contributor to the U.S. Human Genome Project. Her recognition that burdensome loans discourage students from choosing among the helping professions has led Princeton to eliminate the use of such loans. She does not hesitate to take provocative positions on a number of topics, including the governmental policy on science, stem cell research, and the Katrina hurricane.[8]

Selection criteria: Values, Courage, Innovation, Mentoring, Community

Michelle Obama has been vividly clear that her career choices reflect her values. Rejecting corporate law, the Princeton and Harvard graduate turned to community service at Public Allies (Aerators) and the University of Chicago, where she created the first community service program and served as vice president of community and external affairs for the U.C. Medical Center. Michelle was an energetic and articulate campaigner for her husband in 2007-08. Since becoming the first Black First Lady, she has continued to signal her values loud and clear by working with military families, the homeless, women and girls, and national service. Michelle's capacity to balance family life with the other issues she cares about makes her a remarkable model for women everywhere.[9]

Selection criteria: Values, Self-confidence, Passion and Courage, Imagination, Trailblazer, Community

Michelle Rhees, the controversial Chancellor of Washington, D.C., promised Mayor Adrian Fenty that she would make the city's urban school district into one of the highest-performing systems in the nation. Coming from the national teacher center movement, she understands the value of adult learning and mentoring; her current strategies are to find and reward strong teachers, purge incompetent ones and weaken the tenure system. While the jury is still out as to whether she can keep her promise, she has made bold changes in her two years of tenure. Michelle has closed 15 percent of the city's schools, fired more than 100 workers, dismissed 270 teachers and removed 36 principals. This bold action has created many enemies, and many admirers.[10]

Selection criteria: Courage, Self-confidence, Innovation, Mentoring

Christiana Amanpour, CNN's chief international correspondent, has reported on all the major crises from the world's many hotspots, including Iraq, Afghanistan, the Palestinian territories, Iran, Israel, Pakistan, Somalia, Rwanda, the Balkans and the United States during Hurricane Katrina. She doesn't hesitate to move deftly into areas involving famine, genocide, and war. Her daring work has earned her multiple awards, including four Peabody Awards and the Edward R. Murrow Award. In 2007, Her Majesty Queen Elizabeth II made Christiana a Commander of the Most Excellent Order of the British Empire (CBE) for her "highly distinguished, innovative contribution" to the field of journalism. She has managed to secure interviews, sometimes under the most harrowing conditions, with the world's most prominent leaders. An Iranian and a brilliant scholar, Christiana is conversant in Persian, French, and English. Her most deeply held values have been reflected in the CNN specials she has hosted, examining issues of religious radicalism and terrorism, the Israeli and Palestinian conflict and the historical roots of the world's most miasmic problems.[11]

Selection criteria: Passion and Courage, Values, Self-confident, Imagination, Trailblazer, World as Community

Skills and Understandings Identified Most Often in Women Leaders

The women described above, like the vast majority of the women in our studies, possess, or seek to possess, a flexible and evolving set of skills and understandings. Drawing from each of our chapters, we selected the most potent of these factors, grouping them into theme areas in Figure 8.2. These are the skills and understandings of the Constructivist Leader, those that invite and engage, support and guide, contribute to reciprocal learning and build community.

In Chapter Seven, Cindy Ranii described the echo of her mentors as they insisted that even though she may not have direct line experience, she possessed the skills and understandings essential to the next career position to be considered. These leadership skills and understandings make possible organizations that successfully promote human development.

Design Organizations that Promote Human Development

In order to realize the quality of women we nominated above, organizations, cultures and societies need to recognize, nurture and release women's gifts. These gifts include values, voice, passion and courage, imagination, desire for community and a willingness to

Figure 8.2   Leadership Skills and Understandings

Commit to Values	Evolving Self	Passion & Courage
• Identify and articulate values • Translate values and vision into goals and actions • Align own behaviors with values; authentic • Facilitate community members in the development of a shared vision • Provide feedback to others in relation to implementation of vision • Design and assess actions and programs • Integrate community talents and other resources into the pursuit of shared vision	• Reflect upon personal growth in relation to the work of leadership • Engage others in reflection • Talk aloud about errors, personal growth goals, struggles, own journey • Coach others through the process of growth in relation to values and behaviors • Provide discretionary resources so that colleagues can pursue evolving goals	• Use process skills: dialogue, group problem solving and facilitation, inquiry • Learn conflict resolution • Express constructive anger • Reframe, shift perspectives on a problem • Practice yoga, meditation, deep breathing to manage stress and maintain balance • Employ interest-based decision making; interfaith dialogue • Journal; use all forms of reflective behaviors

Imagination	Community	Mentoring
• Engage in literature, the arts, and cultural experiences to extend empathy and compassion • Reframe emotions as strengths rather than weaknesses • Use coaching and mentoring • Practice role fluidity • Use generative strategies to facilitate imaginative group problem-solving • Provide opportunities for innovation and intrapreneurship	• Describe the beliefs or assumptions that lead to community • Devise norms, agreements for working together • Organize team learning of community skills • Provide needed resources • Conduct self-assessments of community successes	• Demonstrate strong collegial skills—including critique, support and reciprocity • Communicate knowledge related to the field • Provide experience as a context for examining ideas and actions • Demonstrate flexibility in thinking and learning • Serve as a model learner • Understand persuasion, facilitation and change processes • Demonstrate curiosity, inquiry, discovery • Evidence mutual trust and regard • Orchestrate dissonance and consonance • Foster self-direction in others • Understand the stages of a mentoring relationship

mentor other women into leadership. Organizational cultures can encourage risk-taking, innovation, imagination and boldness—or they can manifest the reverse responses. We have selected a few strategies and approaches that provide supportive and evocative environments. They are meant to be viewed as exemplars that can lead the reader to identify successful approaches already at hand and new ones yet to be invented.

The section above on skills and understandings will now be integrated with environmental strategies. Women's sense of personal power, "enlightened power," is best accessed in environments where the following characteristics are present:

- **Listening**, that demonstrates care and respect for others' needs and our own.
- **Integration** of personal stories, that brings people together within a framework of logical meaning and emotional coherence.
- **Reflection** that creates a space in which to cultivate community, goodwill, shared contribution, and connection.
- **Dialogue** that fosters curiosity and wonder rather than judgment and blame.
- **Nurturing** the human spirit, through alternative forms of expression, such as drawing, storytelling, and movement
- **Creating space** for healing, by defining organizations as human social systems formed from a spectrum of bodies, minds, and spirits—not a mere collection of tasks.[13]

Organizations that invite women to evolve into greater self-understanding are open, transparent and honest. Secret codes or agenda, often found in male-dominated cultures, can derail the reflective learning process by providing false or misleading information. Organizations that invite vulnerability, such as in transparent problem solving, enable women to honestly examine who they are within the context of those organizations. Carol Witherell and Nel Noddings argued that when communities encourage inclusive dialogue, the result is an examination of the principles they hold, the consequences of actions, the history of our own beliefs and justifications for opposing points of view.[14]

Our experience is that management meetings have historically been one of two types: listening to others talk about administrative mandates or issues, or "show and tell." When Tony Alvarado was Superintendent of District Two in New York, he required administrators to bring unresolved problems to district meetings. These were uncensored problems, ones that were unsolved and required their presenters to honestly open the floor to alternative solutions, some of which required changes in the beloved and familiar approaches of the administrators involved.

An expectation and attitude of accountability to constituents can also require that leaders go public with both the good and the bad news. Such a public display of honesty can result in genuine reflection. Organizations like this create vertical as well as lateral domains through which critical thought and provocative questions can be posed. Often we have noted that hierarchical authority generates a nearly rigid caste system, blocking critical voices from accessing the sacred lines of power. Rarely can individuals raise questions about goals or budget priorities, so critique is transformed into blame, voiced in staff rooms or at the water cooler.

Developing policies that promote learning, equity, autonomy and choice as well as sustainable relationships and community support human development. When human needs are met through thoughtful and well-implemented support strategies, individuals are invigorated by the values that give meaning to their work. Such policies are revealed within the following areas: personnel practice, professional development, continuous improvement and resource allocation.

Susan Scott described principles for conversations as ways of expressing who we are and what we believe. In *Fierce Conversations*, she provided strategies for authentic conversations; confronting challenges with courage, compassion and skill; handling strong emotions; and building relationships. This is the nature of the context in which sensitive, democratic decision-making should be made.

Design Organizations Based on Values

Translating personal values into shared organizational visions through a planning process codifies the public expression of composite values for an organization. Once personal values are disclosed and understood, core values can be developed to help create a shared vision, a mission or set of core beliefs. Such action does not require that the vision is the sum total of the individual values; it does mean that the essence of individual values are reflected in organizational visions. "Buying into" the CEO's or management's vision, regardless of how good it is, does not qualify. If it is clear, inspiring and effective, the vision mirrors those who act upon it on a day-to-day basis and gives direction to the organization as a whole.

Select, Evaluate and Sustain Personnel Who Serve through the Expression of Personal and Organizational Values

The selection of personnel who will contribute to the values of the organization is more than the result of an interview process, although questions can be framed to elicit value narratives (see Chapter Two). Applicants can be asked to participate in conversations, to present dilemmas confronted and resolved, and can be given simulated problems to work through.

Evaluative approaches that involve self-analysis; peer, customer, student and parent feedback, accompanied by a portfolio of participatory activities, can bring a three-dimensional view to employee performance. Outstanding personnel are more likely to be retained when there are opportunities for continual participation, learning and imaginative expression. Leaders and managers, and those in the process of becoming leaders, grow and find satisfaction in institutions where learning, choice, discretion and opportunities for multiple roles exist. We know from our work in leadership capacity that roles can provide an expanded context that encourages self-perception and confidence. Many opportunities to lead through multiple roles, as opposed to merit pay, develop leaders who are constantly honing their skills and developing new insights.

California State University, East Bay, has long used a means of selecting graduate students for their programs in educational leadership that asks this question: "What is your track record in teacher leadership?" The program seeks students of initiative, courage and passion—-not candidates who are waiting to be certificated in order to exercise their natural leadership.

Organizations can establish similar expectations. Leadership "track records" are key to understanding the path of leadership that is likely to be followed in the future. Leadership scenarios drawn from casebooks, Girl Scouts, 4-H, sports, apprenticeship programs, church or the performing arts may reveal such a record.

Establish Governance or Management Models that are Broad-based, Democratic and Transparent

Governance approaches need to permit a fluid flow of ideas and critiques, encouraging voices from all participants to reach others in the organization. Democratic models or approaches integrate access and communication both vertically and horizontally. Groups of individuals, such as teams, focus groups, and committees—along with community organizations—generate and influence decisions and policies. Guided by organizational values, participating groups and individuals formulate ideas and actions that create organizational direction. For instance, programs that require employees or students to make contributions to the broader community illustrate that when talents and resources are shared, equity becomes a reality. Many organizations have few or no processes through which employees or customers/clients communicate with administration, management or boards, let alone participate in governance.

Cupertino Union School District, home to the top-rated schools in California, developed a circular rather than a hierarchical organizational chart. The goal was to level the playing field so that teachers and support staff, through their school leadership teams, could participate in the important discussions of the district.[16] Such access, accompanied by well-developed leadership skills, contributed to the remarkable leadership capacity in the district.

In many parts of the United States and Canada, collective bargaining or other union negotiation processes bring additional strain to the relationships among personnel and boards. These tensions prevent the meaningful types of dialogue described above. In 1992 when co-author Mary was hired as superintendent of the Saratoga Union School District, the district had recently ended a year of contentious and angry negotiations. Employees felt disenfranchised from decision-making and unappreciated, Board members felt they were giving as much as they could, and administrators described the teachers and staff as "spoiled." Mary asked the Board to set aside budget concerns and explore the viability of Interest-Based Negotiations (IBN)[17]. After extensive and inclusionary study and planning, IBN was initiated on a trial basis. Today, IBN continues to be used as the district's approach to negotiation.

While not all conflict was eliminated, the Saratoga Union School District now had ways to approach conflict. The process helped build strong relationships that served in times of crisis and moved the District through difficult periods of school funding. All groups were involved in major district decisions, budgeting, curriculum, professional development, and school construction, within committees established to hold conversations and arrive at interest-based decisions. The techniques of interest-based negotiations became interest-based decision-making. The district became a safe place for disagreement and alternative perspectives because it now had an embedded culture that encouraged dialogue and diverse approaches to solving difficult problems. This led to contract, policy and practice changes that eventually included parents and students in the process of building a community with mutual trust.

The world needs courageous, committed leaders with a "genuine desire to reach compromise" to tackle the world's most thorny issues, especially where religion and politics intersect.

-Christiana Amanpour

Provide Professional Learning Opportunities

Leadership capacity is understood as broad-based, skillful participation in the work of leadership. The vision, shared governance and professional learning dimensions of organizational behavior above address vital aspects of this concept. Leadership capacity assumes that everyone has the right, responsibility and ability to lead. Professional learning is most powerful when embedded in the work itself, rather than delivered as a separate training workshop. For instance, communication skills are developed most effectively through the use of team operating agreements and feedback.

The critical minds of courageous and passionate women can be nurtured by several sound approaches to professional learning. Five are particularly noteworthy: 1) inquiry; 2) team-building, including coaching; 3) Planned Mentoring Programs (described in Chapter Seven); 4) Courage to Teach and Courage to Lead; 5) Outward Bound.

Consciousness is provoked by inquiry as a constructivist approach to learning. Dialogue is framed by genuine questions of practice and leads to inquiry: "Why is it that girls respond differently to issues of war and peace? How has the changing economic climate altered views about our product?" The uses of data and evidence may be said to have begun with the work of Edward Deming's "Quality Circles," first in Japan, then in the United States, where they were adapted by multiple organizations and institutions. At its core, inquiry creates knowledge, while the emanating dialogue creates meaning.

Courage to Teach, now joined by *Courage to Lead*, represents the very essence of this theme regarding women and leadership. It focuses neither on "technique" nor on school reform, but rather on renewing the inner lives of professionals in education. Developed by Parker J. Palmer and the Fetzer Institute in 1994, *Courage to Teach* frees inner courage and imagination through:

- Renewing heart, mind, and spirit through the exploration of the inner landscape of a teacher's life
- Reconnecting to one's identity and integrity—identifying and honoring gifts and strengths, and acknowledging limits
- Creating a context for careful listening and deep connection that also honors diversity in people and professions

- Helping educators create safe spaces and trusting relationships in their schools, with their students and colleagues, and within their communities
- Exploring the connection between attending to the inner life of educators and the renewal of public education[18]

Programs based on *Outward Bound* can develop physical as well as psychological and emotional courage, trust and mutual regard. At the Athenian School in Danville, California, the Athenian Wilderness Experience (AWE) requires students in their junior year to spend about 25 days in either Death Valley or the High Sierras (three of those days are spent alone). These experiences are transformative. Arlene Ustin, founder and former director of the program, claimed after 23 years of observation and careful evaluation that students develop a deep and active compassion, maturation and self-confidence, a moral compass that guides their decisions, skills for taking care of each other in a multicultural context, a perspective that helps them understand the difference between necessity and privilege, reflective practices, clarity regarding their next steps in life and unique leadership qualities.[19]

Policies and practices that support professional learning may include internships, graduate programs, sabbaticals, travel, research, shared readings, and professional writing. Technology now occupies many learning arenas: as a work product in and of itself, as a means to connect and communicate (Web bar, Webcast, video conferencing, Skype, Facebook, Twitter), and as a means to access individuals at all hours. Information can be acquired anytime, anyplace. The implications for the future of learning are just being imagined.

Allocate Resources for Equitable Outcomes

Money, knowledge, talent, technology, and time are all resources. Discretionary funds can motivate teams to seek imaginative approaches. "Intrapreneurship"—energetic, grass-roots leadership from within the organization—requires budgetary flexibility.

If teacher quality is to be ensured for inner-city schools, it may be necessary to provide differential staffing, incentives and professional learning, as well as an adequate salary, in order to reach this goal. Businesses have long understood the need for differential compensation.

Time enables values when organizational policies provide women, and men, with family leave to care for children or a dying parent. Time enables values when teachers build relationships with and guide students, and when teachers have opportunities for essential dialogue. Ultimately, time invested underwrites sustainability.

The leadership capacity of an organization is the key to its sustainability. We know a great deal about how organizations improve; yet sustainability is just beginning to be understood.[20] Values become manifest over time; without a commitment to sustainability, however, values become hollow and tainted.

Women and Men, Together Again

Throughout this book, we have drawn distinctions between women and men in order to highlight differences in biology, temperament, nurturance patterns, and experience. Our chief aim has been to describe how women can be viewed as separate entities, strong and flexible in their own right, not as inadequate men. In order to clarify these distinctions, we have related recent brain research, historical paths, work patterns and oppressive policies. We believe that we can now say that women are especially well- equipped to play the role of leaders for an emerging world in need of compassion, collaboration and unity.

...crone wisdom has been so far represented by exceptional men who are crones, such as Nelson Mandela, Mahatma Gandhi, His Holiness the Dalai Lama, and Jimmy Carter.

-Jean Shinoda Bolen

That said, we now seek to bring women and men back together. We appreciate that humans are more alike than different, and that most of the differences are in degree not in kind. Women and men

share most of the same yearnings, desires for a peaceful world, experiences of the pain of separation and loss, aspirations for their children. The 72-year longitudinal Grant Project study concluded
recently that the most important factor in men's lives was *relationships.*[21] This insight alone brings men and women together once and
for all: *relationships* are the most important element in life.

It is not our intent to secure a "gender-free" world. Quite the
contrary. We do not want to erase critical distinctions, for the richness
of diversity lies in the subtleties and complexities of differences that
are blended to achieve fully integrated individuals and cultures.

Our shared responsibility is to learn from each other, to enter
into reciprocal relationships—what Simone de Beauvoir referred to
as "fraternity"—in order for each to learn what the other has to offer.
Such a process would require profound mutual regard, attributing
desirable strengths and qualities to the other gender. Men have much
to teach women about decisiveness, political will and remaining aloft
so as not to over-personalize issues and get emotionally bruised.
Women can teach men about securing and sustaining relationships,
translating empathy into action and productive collaboration.

If these approaches to mutuality were to occur more consistently, we might imagine a world such as the one that Marilyn Ferguson envisioned in 1980: the dawning of a new age, with people
exercising their talents to the fullest, social and professional hierarchies reduced, societies impelled forward by ever-more-thrilling scientific discoveries. Ferguson suggested that we will see a burst of
creativity that would make the Renaissance pale in comparison and
would require women and men to learn together in new ways.[22]

On Becoming: Traveling through this Book as a Transformative Journey

Each of the previous chapters includes "Reflections and Explo-
rations" intended to spiral personal reflection through a deepening
process of self-discovery. From your initial assessment of *perspectives*
into an examination of *values*, we ask that you reflect upon your *evolving self* in relationship to values expressed. *Passion and courage* suggest
a personal energy source that gives form and power to purposeful action,

while *imagination* stirs empathy and frames innovation. Now empowered to create communities, we ask that you do so. Finally, *Women's Ways of Leading* expects that you will *mentor* other women into leadership.

Reflections and Explorations

Return now to Figure 1.1 in Chapter One: *A Framework for Women's Leadership Development.* Questions to ask yourself within the context of your network of women leaders are:

1. How did I originally assess myself? Where am I now?
2. What are the areas of need that arose during my reading of this text?
3. What is my plan for creating more learning experiences consciously designed to strengthen the areas that I've identified?
4. What resources will I need? (See the Selective Bibliography and Appendix A)
5. How will I next challenge myself?

Women Who Lead Seek a...
Desired Destiny

Epilogue

A woman is the full circle. Within her is the power to create, nurture and transform. A woman knows that nothing can come to fruition without light. Let us call upon woman's voice and woman's heart to guide us in this age of planetary transformation.
-Diane Mariechild, Spiritual Leader

On March 11, 2009, President Barack Obama gathered Cabinet members, family members and women leaders from many fields of endeavor in his conference room at the White House to establish the White House Council on Women and Girls. He began:

> The purpose of this Council is to ensure that American women and girls are treated fairly in all matters of public policy...I am proud that the first bill I signed into law was the Lilly Ledbetter Fair Pay Restoration Act. But I want to be clear that issues like equal pay, family leave, childcare and others are not just women's issues. Our progress in these areas is an important measure of whether we are truly fulfilling the promise of our democracy for all people.[1]

This significant day in history was 161 years since the Declaration of Sentiments, a plea for an end to discrimination against women in all spheres of society, was written. March 2009 marked 233 years since the Declaration of Independence was written.

Turn back time to 1862 London. The West family becomes converted by a passionate young Mormon missionary. So enamored are they by the promise of a Mormon "Mecca" in Salt Lake City, Utah, the West family bundles up their two daughters, nearly six-year-old Ann Lydia and her ten-year old sister, Caroline, and sends them with another family to America, to join a covered wagon train to Utah, during the American Civil War. Ann Lydia West was Mary Gardner's great-grandmother.

After the rugged trip west, during which she lost her adopted mother, what else could the young and daring Ann Lydia expect of her life? She could expect to lose both her innocence and her self-confidence as she grew older, like many other women of her time. According to the Declaration of Sentiments written at the Women's Rights Convention held a Seneca Fall, NY July 1848, she:

- Could not vote or participate fully in civic life, submitting to laws, in the formation of which she had no voice;
- Was required to adhere to moral codes that did not apply to men;
- Had no voice in her church, which claimed Apostolic authority for her exclusion;
- Once married, in the eye of the law, she was civilly dead: she could not own property, be educated (women were not known as teachers of theology, medicine or law), keep her children if a separation occurred, or have a say over any money that she may have earned; she must obey her husband or be deprived of liberty and expect punishment.[2]

As a Mormon, she could have been expected to share her husband with one or more other women. Ann Lydia's dreams of writing plays would remain a fantasy, remaining a secret in her private thoughts, destiny denied.

Fortunately, the historical journey from 1848 to the present has been rife with both struggle and achievement for women. Appendix C situates the Lambert and Gardner women on a timeline of the achievements of women. The women in our families have been born and raised in the vibrant climate of growing equity and social change. Our children and grandchildren are the beneficiaries of those who have gone before. It is our hope that all of us will remain conscious of this struggle as we encounter the work yet to be done.

The passage (some would say an organized expedition) is far from complete, although women today enjoy continually improving conditions and self-governance. Jean Shinoda Bolen is a psychiatrist and spiritualist who elegantly imported the concept of "crone"—the aging wise woman— into the vernacular of maturing women. Jean reminds us that our journeys are richer and more liberated because of the awakening that we as women have sought for ourselves.[3]

Women in the third phase of life—now often characterized as women after age 60— entered childbearing years with the invention of the "pill," and the landmark decision of Roe v. Wade. Control over our reproductive organs was accompanied by new choices in career options, education across diverse fields, religious beliefs, and the possibility of raising children while pursuing other passions. We expected equal pay for equal work, although we waited for Lilly Ledbetter to lead the fight. We long for quality child and health care. Women artists, authors, performers, conductors exploded onto the scene in the last 50 years. Each achievement was, and will continue to be, guided mainly by women leaders, women who are clear in their values and self-confidence, passionate and courageous in their actions, imaginative in envisioning the paths ahead, creators of community of support and purpose and mentors of the next generation.

So what is the *Desired Destiny* now? How will we recognize the signs when they appear? Do women desire things that are more different and new than ever before? Have our expectations reframed what is desirable? To some extent, though, we women may still want what we've always wanted.

Maureen Murdock retells the 14th century English tale, "Sir Gawain and Lady Ragnell." One day, King Arthur returns from the northern lands and an encounter with the fearsome Sir Gromer, and relates a troublesome story to his nephew Sir Gawain. It seems that Sir Gromer had agreed to spare Arthur's life if he would return in a year with the answer to the question, "What is it that women most desire, above all else?" Sir Gawain assures Arthur that together they will find the answer. After almost a year, they fail to do so.

King Arthur turns to the grotesque Lady Ragnell, an animal-like sorceress. She agrees to give him the answer if Sir Gawain will willingly marry her. "Impossible!" rages Arthur. But Arthur relents and relates the demand to his generous nephew, who promptly agrees to marry Lady Ragnell. After all, his uncle's life is at stake. Arthur reluctantly agrees and receives the answer from the fiendish Lady.

When King Arthur relates the answer to Sir Gromer, he is enraged because the answer is correct: "What a woman desires above all else is the power of sovereignty—the right to exercise her own will." Ah. The reader will not be surprised that the ugly Lady Ragnell, upon her marriage to Sir Gawain, turns into a beautiful damsel.

But the story does not end there! The now-beautiful Lady informs her husband that he has a choice. "I can only be beautiful at night or during the day," she explains. "Which do you prefer?" The wise Sir Gawain ponders the question, drops to his knees, takes her hand and replies: "It is your choice to make, my Lady." "You have broken Sir Gromer's wicked spell," she tells him excitedly...and the now fully beautiful Lady and her young knight live happily ever after.[4]

Women still desire free and conscious choice above all else. And, we would add, women also want to see themselves as leaders who experience reciprocal relationships, learners who construct meaning and knowledge, and passionate and purposeful creators of community.

A few indicators we expect to find when a *Desired Destiny* is arising:

- Women leaders in significant enough numbers to make a difference in organizations and societies;
- Democracy and civic life will expand as participation in leadership grows;
- Cultural and educational practice will assume that everyone has the right, responsibility and capability to lead;
- Young girls will freely go to school in most parts of the world;
- Quality and accessible child care, family leaves and health care;
- Fluid and flexible work schedules and roles;
- Organizational cultures/environments that encourage leadership;

- Increasing numbers of enlightened males supporting and joining in the journey toward gender equality.

Women can be guardedly optimistic about the future, because much of the world is opening to new possibilities, even as some of the world is still tight in a bud. All women everywhere are sisters, and each country has women and men leaders who are ushering in a new enlightenment. We remind the reader of Spiritual Leader Joan Chittister's retelling of a Sufi tale...

> Once upon a time the disciples said to the Holy One, "Tell us what you got from Enlightenment. Did you become Divine?" "No, not Divine," the Holy One said. "Did you become a Saint?" "Oh, dear, no," the Holy One said. "Then what did you become?" the disciples asked. "I became awake," the Holy One said...to enable people to become awake and involved, involved and awake may well be the greatest thing that leadership can do for anyone.[5]

Women's Ways of Leading is an awakening.

Mary and Grandchildren

Linda's Grandchildren and Great-grandchildren

End Notes

Introduction

1. Simone de Beauvoir, *The Second Sex*, p. 686,1961.
2. These authors informed our thinking. Brizendine, 2006; Bateson,1989, 2004; Cochran-Smith and Sytle, 1993; Senge, 1992; Belenky et al., 1986; Levine, 1989; Cross,1982; Noddings, 1984; Gilligan, 1982; Kegan, 1982; Greene, 1978; Loevinger, 1976.
3. Lambert et al., The first and second editions fully develop the concept of constructivist leadership as a new definition of leadership. *The Constructivist Leader*, 1995 and 2002.
4. Senge, Scharmer, Jaworski, Flowers, *Presence*, 2004.
5. Linda Lambert, *Building Leadership Capacity in Schools*, 1998; *Leadership Capacity for Lasting School Improvement,* 2003.
6. As quoted in Joseph P. Lash. *Eleanor: The Years Alone.* p.337, 1972.
7. Center for American Women and Politics at Rutgers University, www.cawp.rutgers.edu. 2007.
8. Urban Indicator. June 2006.
9. Vicki Donlan, *Her Turn*, p.139. 2007.
10. Catalyst, www.catgalystwomen.org. 2007, 2009.
11. Donlan, p.77, 2007.
12. Ibid, p.145.
13. Betty Friedan, *The Feminine Mystique*,1963.
14. Malek Zaalouk, personal communication, 2005
15. Deborah Meier, *The Power of Their Ideas*, and personal communication. 1995, 2006.
16. As presented in Ann Lieberman, *Teacher Leadership*, 2004.
17. Onlinefocus.org, 2007.

Chapter One: Women's Leadership: Tomorrow's Legacy

1. Sharifah Hadjarah Aziz, personal communication, 2007.
2. "Formal" here means paid leadership roles that hold power and authority to make decisions in the arenas of education, business, health, governance, politics and policy.

3. Louann Brizendine, *The Female Brain*, p. 7, 2006.
4. As reported in Robert Sternberg and Eleana Grigorenko. "Are Cognitive Styles Still in Style?" American Psychologist. Vol. 52:No.7, July, 1997.
5. Lambert, Unpublished Dissertation, 1983.
6. Leonard Shlain, *Sex, Time and Power: How Women's Sexuality Shaped Human Evolution.* 2003.
7. Savage, 2007.
8. Mary Fields Belenky et al. *Women's Ways of Knowing.* 1986.
9. Mary Catherine Bateson, *Composing a Life.* 1989.
10. Robert Kegan, *The Evolving Self,* p.107, 1982.
11. Sarah Levine, Loevinger's milestones of *Ego Development* as discussed in *Promoting Adult Development,* 1989.
12. Kristen Levine, personal communication, 2008.
13. Marie Wilson, *Closing the Leadership Gap,* p. 2, 2007.
14. Ibid.
15. Belenky et al. term, 1986.
16. Loevinger's term, 1976
17. Belenky et al. term, 1986.

Chapter Two: Women Who Lead Commit to Values

1. Nel Noddings, *Caring: A Feminine Approach to Ethics and Moral Education.* 1984.
2. Nel Nodding's story is derived from reading, Noddings, 1984; Noddings, 2002; Flinders, 'Nel Noddings' in Joy a Palmer. Ed. Fifty Modern Thinkers on Education. From Piaget to the Present, 2001; and M.K. Smith, "Nel Noddings, the ethics of care and education," in the encyclopaedia of informal education, www.infed.org/thinker/noddings.htm. Updated: April 17, 2005.
3. Carol Gilligan, *In a Different Voice*, 1982.
4. Lawrence Kohlberg, *The Psychology of Moral Development.*1976.

5. Mary Poplin and J. Weeres, *Voices from the Inside. A Report on Schooling from Inside the Classroom.* The Institute for Education in Transformation, Claremont Graduate School, 1992.
6. Martie Connor, personal communication, 2007.
7. Julie Biddle, personal communication, 2006.
8. Wangari Maathai's story is derived from reading Wangari Maathai, p.33, 2004. "Rise up and Walk," Fall of 2007. Her Nobel Lecture, 2004 printed on the Official Website of the Nobel Foundation, http://nobelprize.org. 2004 and The Green Belt Movement International Publication, www.greenbeltmovement.org.
9. Ibid. 2004.
10. Ibid. 2004.
11. Linda Henke, personal communication, 2006.
12. As quoted in Sylvia Mendoza, *The Book of Latina Women: 150 Vidas of Passion, strength and Success.* p. 3, 2004.
13. Antonio Hernandez's story is derived from reading Sylvia Mendoza's book and Latina MS, at www.latina.ms. Accessed 2008 and an article found on findarticles.com, Antonia Hernandez: The Leading Legal Eagle for Civil Rights, Civil Rights Journal, Fall 1998.
14. Margaret Atwood, web.net/owtoad/bio.html; retrieved 2006.
15. Participant in Canadian Women's Conference, Personal communication, 2003.
16. Ibid, 2003.
17. Carol Gilligan, *In a Different Voice*, 1982, and Gilligan, *Mapping the Moral Domain*, "Remappng the Moral Domain: New Images of self in Relationship," pp. 3-19, 1988.
18. As told in Ann Lieberman and Lynn Miller's book on *Teacher Leadership*, p.71-80, 2004.
19. Rebecca Lindquist, EdCal, Association of California School Administrators newspaper, 2006.
20. Barbara Ryan, personal communication, 2008.

21. Nicole Ashby, U.S. Department of Education, about Denise Jay, "High Expectations Help California Students Reach Higher Levels of English Fluency, Academic Proficiency." The Achiever: Vol 5, No.2 February 2006.
22. Kawsar Kouchok, personal communication, July 15, 2006.
23. Donna Burlow, personal communication, June 10, 2006.

Chapter Three: Women Who Lead Are Conscious of the Evolving Self

1. Mary Catherine Bateson, *Composing a Life.* 1989.
2. Mary Catherine Bateson, *Willing to Learn, 2004.*
3. Mary Catherine Bateson's story is derived from her four books, *Composing a Life, 1989; Peripheral Vision,* 1994; *Willing to Learn*, 2004; *and Full Circles, Overlapping Lives,* 2007.
4. Bateson, *Peripheral Vision*, pp.111-126, 1994.
5. Bateson, 2004.
6. Marcus Mabry, *Twice as Good. Condoleezza Rice and Her Path to Power*, 2007.
7. Ann Conzemius, personal communication, 2005.
8. Colleen Wilcox, personal communication, 2008.
9. Academy of Achievement Biography of Amy Tan, www.achievement.org. 2005. Amy Tan's books *The Joy Luck Club*, *The Kitchen God's Wife*, 1991, *The Hundred Secret Senses*, 1998, and *The Bonesetter's Daughter*, 2001 helped her understand herself, her culture and family. *The Opposite of Fate*, 2004.
10. Quote is printed on the wall of O'Keeffe Museum, Santa Fe, New Mexico.
11. Linda Coughlin, Ellen Wingard and Keith Hollihand, *Enlightened Power.* 2005.
12. Christine Todd Whitman, *It's My Party Too*, 2005.
13. Susan Brown Miller, *Shirley Chisholm*, 1972.
14. Shirley Chisholm story is written from Susan Miller's book and eSSortm, www. essortment.com. Shirley Chisholm biography. Accessed 2008.

15. Mary Warnock as quoted in Maxine Greene *Releasing the Imagination: Essays on Education, The Arts and Social Change*, p.22, 1995.
16. Carol Witherell and Nel Noddings, *Stories Lives Tell: Narrative and Dialogue in Education,* 1991.

Chapter Four: Women Who Lead Invoke Passion and Courage

1. Judy Vandergrift, personal communication, 2006.
2. Rigoberto Menchu Tum's Story is derived from Julie Schulze, *Rigoberta Menchu Tum, Champion of Human Rights,* 1997, and Rigoberta's autobiography, *I Rigoberta Menchu An Indian Woman In Guatemala*, Edited by Elisabeth Burgos-Debray and Translated by Ann Wright, London: Verso, 1984.
3. Clarissa Estes, *Women Who Run With Wolves*, p. 352,1992.
4. Donlan and Graves, p. 56, 2007.
5. Linda Coughlin, Ellen Wingard, Keith Hollihan, Eds. *Enlightened Power, How Women are Transforming the Practice of Leadership,* p.xxv; Catalyst study, on-line ref. 2007.
6. Barbara Kellerman, p. 18, 2007.
7. Kawsar Kouchok, personal communication, 2006.
8. Rosa Parks' Story is derived from *Quiet Strength: The Faith, the Hope and the Heart of a Woman Who Changed a Nation,* 1994 and *Rosa Parks: My Story,* 1992.
9. Erin Grunwell, *The Freedom Writers Diary,* 1999.
10. Maria Hinojosa, *Raising Raul, Adventures Raising Myself and My Son.* 1999.
11. Anais Nin, "And the day came when the risk to remain tight in a bud was more painful than the risk it took to blossom." www.brayquote.com.
12. Freya Stark's story is written from Freya Stark, "Strolling on Alone, Hatless," in Women of Discovery, pp. 78-80, 2001; Freya Stark, "The Southern Gates of Arabia: A Journey in the Hadhramaut," 2001.
13. Jan O'Neill, personal communication, 2007

14. Aung San Suu Kyi Story is written from her autobiography *Freedom from Fear* and Bettina Ling, *Aung San Suu Kyi, Standing Up for Democracy in Burma,* 1999. The quote is from her Nobel Peace Prize acceptance speech delivered by her son in *Freedom from Fear,* p. 238, 1995.

Chapter Five: Women Who Lead Arouse the Imagination

1. Bonita Calder, personal communication. 2007.
2. Kegan, p. 109, 1982.
3. Sources used to reference DNA were: Wikipedia, en.wikipedia.org. Nobel Prize Foundation, nobelprize.org, and David Ardell, Rosalind Franklin, The National Health Museum, Resource Center website, www.accessexcellence.org.
4. Vladimir Nabokov, *Lolita,* Epilogue, 1955.
5. Barbara Kingsolver, *Poisonwood Bible*, 1998.
6. Maxine Hong Kingston, *The Woman Warrior*, 1977.
7. Alan Bennett, *The Uncommon Reader*, 2007
8. Toni Morrison, *The Bluest Eyes*, 2007, *Beloved*, 2006, *A Mercy*, 2008 to name a few.
9. Toni Morrison story is written from her books listed above, as well as Playing In the Dark, 1992; "Toni Morrison," Ohio Reading Road Trip, www.ohioreadingroadtrip.org; 2005; and Marilyn Miller Interview with "Toni Morrison," 2009.
10. Louann Brizendine, 2007.
11. Daniel Goleman, *Social Intelligence*, 2006.
12. Baron-Cohen, 2003 as quoted in Goleman p. 139, 2006.
13. Leonard Shlain, *The Alphabet Versus the Goddess*, p. 23, 1998.
14. Susan Pinker. *Atlantic Monthly*, "Should Women Rule?" Nov. 2008, pp. 125-126, Nov. 2008.
15. George Lakoff, *The Political Mind*, p.266. 2008.
16. Nancy Arnold, personal communication, 2008.
17. Lev Vygotsky, Zone of Proximal Development as defined in *Mind in Society*, 1978.
18. Katherine Wagner, personal Communication, 2007.

19. Marie Wilson, pp. 3-4, 2007.
20. Lavaroni and Leisey, personal communication, 2008.
21. Sheila Jordan, personal communication, 2006.
22. Girl's On the Run, www.girlsontherun.org.
23. Children's Musical Theater of San Jose, www.cmtsj.org/about.
24. Teach for America, www.teachforamerica.org.
25. Mae Jemison story is written from her book, *Find Where the Wind Goes; Moments from My Life,* 2001. and Female Frontiers, "Meet: Mae Jemison, first African-American women to fly in Space," quest.arc.nasa.gov/space/frontiers/jemison.html,
26. Amanda Ripley, "Can She Save Our Schools?" about Michelle Rhee, Time Magazine, December 8, 2008.
27. Richard Florida, "How the Crash Will Reshape America," The Atlantic Monthly, March, 2009.
28. Nicholas Kristof, "Economic Stimulus/Education and Schools," New York Times, Feb. 15, 2009.

Chapter Six: Women Who Lead Create Community

1. Linda Lambert, et al., p.51, 1995.
2. Margaret Wheatley, *Finding Our Way, Leadership for an Uncertain Time*, p. 45, 2005.
3. Amitai Etzioni, *The New Golden Rule: Community and Morality in a Democratic Society,* p. 127, 1996.
4. Susan Pinker, *The Sexual Paradox*, 2008.
5. Ross and Mirowsky supported this in Pinker, p. 120, 2008. Also discussed in on-line study UCLA, www.sciencedaily.com, 2000.
6. Louann Brizendine, 2006.
7. Gail Taylor. www.tomorrowmakers.org web site, and personal communcation, 2006
8. Bonita Calder, personal communication, 2008.
9. Drew Gilpin Faust, Letter to Harvard faculty, February 18, 2009. www.president.harvard.edu
10. Gary Bloom and Robert Stein, "Building communities of Practice," Leadership September/October 2004.

11. Richard DuFour and Robert Eaker, *On Common Ground; The Power of Professional Communities,* 2005.
12. Joanne Rooney, "The Principal Connection/Who Owns Teacher Growth?" Educational Leadership, ASCD Newsletter, p. 2, April, 2007.
13. Szabo Chapter in Lambert et al. pp. 225-227, 2002.
14. Meg Whitman's story is taken from "Meg Whitman," www.businessweek.com, 2000. "Meg Whitman," dir.salon.com, 2001, Robert Harbison, "Peerless Leader," 2004, and Notable biographies, www.notablebiographies.com 2008, and Harvard Business Review, *Meg Whitman and eBay Germany.* 2001.
15. Ann Lieberman. Diane Wood, *Inside the National Writing Project; Connecting Network Learning and Classroom Teaching*, 2003.
16. Ann Richards, *Straight From the Heart, My Life in Politics and other Places*, 1989, and Texas State Library and Archives Commission *www.tsl.state.tx.us* accessed 05, also Shropshire and Frank Schaefer, *The Thorny Rose of Texas,* 1994,
17. Emily's List, www.emilyslist.org.
18. Fellowship for Intentional Community, www.ic.org, and Wikipedia Utopias en.wikipedia.org/wiki/utopia, accessed 2009.
19. Margaret Wheatley, *Finding our Way*, 2005.
20. Posh Squash, *A Community Garden Cookbook*, pp. 4-5. 2004 and personal communication, 2009.
21. Linda Lambert, *Building Leadership Capacity in Schools*, 1998, *and Leadership Capacity for Lasting School Improvement*, 2003.

Chapter Seven: Women Who Lead Mentor the Next Generation of Women Leaders

1. Cindy Ranii story personal communication, 2009.
2. Art Costa and Benna Kallick, "Through the Lens of a Critical Friend,"p. 150, 1993.

3. Sheila Jordan, personal communication, 2006
4. Barbara Storms personal communication, 2006.
5. Delilah Montoya Biography, "Teaching Philoso-phy,"www.delilahmontoya.com/educator, Accessed 2009.
6. Girl Scouts of America Official Website, www.girlscouts.org. France Hesselbein, former CEO continues to mentor and support nonprofit organizations as chairman of the board of governors of the Peter F. Drucker Foundation for Nonprofit Management. She has been lead editor and has contributed to many books on leadership (see Bibliography). One that speaks to women's ways of leading is *On Creativity, Innovation, and Renewal*, San Francisco: Jossey Bass, 2002.
7. Ruth Colvin, personal communication, 2006.
8. Anne Inglisi, Obituary on Iona Brown, The Guardian Weekly, www.guardian-weekly.com. June 10, 2004.
9. Carol Spain Woltring and Carole Barlas, *Women Leaders in Public Health,* 2001.
10. Emmy Werner et al., Kauai Pregnancy Study, (this initiated the longitudinal work on Resiliency), Pediatrics, AAP Grand Rounds, pediatrics.aapublication.org, 1968.
11 Louann Brizendine, p. 152, 2006.
12. Sumedha Khannas, unpublished manuscript, 2009
13. Sumedha Khannas, personal communication, 2009.
14. Ashley Vance, "At Xerox, a Transition for the Record Books," New York Times, May 22, 2009.
15. French Diplomat, personal communication, 2008.
16. Marian Wright Edelman, *Lanterns,* p. 19, 1999.
17. Marian Wright Edelman, *Lanterns,* p. xvii, 1999.
18. Bonita Calder, personal communication. 2008.
19. Hillary Clinton, *It Takes A Village to Raise a Child.* p. 311, 1996.
20. Hillary Clinton, *Living History*, pp. 22 and 48, 2003.
21. Oprah Winfrey's story is derived from books, magazine article and newspaper reports collected over many years. To name a few — *The Uncommon Wisdom of Oprah Winfrey, a Portrait in Her Own Words,* Edited by Bill Adler.

Katherine Krohn Biography, *Oprah Winfrey*, Academy of Achievement, Biography and interview www.achievement.org. 2005

22. Maxine Greene, *Releasing the Imagination,* p.65, 1995.
23. Linda admiration for Maxine Greene is demonstrated in this story which synthesizes Greene's writings as well as videos, essays and interviews about her. To name a few, *Exclusions and Awakenings: The Life of Maxine Greene*, Hancock Productions, LLC. "The Educational Theory of Maxine Greene," Rosalie Shaw and E. G. Rozycki, 2000.
24. Maxine Greene, *Releasing the Imagination*, p. 4, 1995. The Maxine Greene Foundation, www.maxinegreene.org.
25. Mia Hamm, Women's Soccer World, www.womensoccer.com. And Mia Hamm Foundation, www.miafoundation.org. accessed 2008 and 2009.
26. Riane Eisler, *The Real Wealth of Nations*, p. 29, 2007.
27. Stacy Blake-Beard, "The Inextricable Link Between Mentoring and Leadership," p103-105, In Coughlin, et al. *Enlightened Power*, 2005.
28. Margaret Brent Award website, www.abanet.org.
29. Morgan Lambert and Linda Lambert, "Mentor Teachers as Change Facilitators", adapted from Thrust, p. 29, April-May, 1985.
30. Stacy Blake-Beard, p. 109, 2005.

Chapter 8: On Becoming Transformational Women Leaders: Fulfilling the Promise

1. Patricia Aburdene and John Naisbitt, *Megatrends for Women*, p. xvi-xvii, 1992.
2. Everett Rogers in *Megatrends*, p. xvi, 1992.
3. Katharine Jefferts Schori, Interview with Bill Moyers, www.pbs.org/moyers/journal, June 8, 2007.
4. Katharine Jefferts Schori, Divine Impulses, TheWashington Post, www.washingtonpost.com, 12-2008.
5. Michael Useem, "New Ideas from this Pepsi Generation," *US News and World Report*, December, 2008.
6. Ellen Johnson Sirleaf, Helene Cooper, "Madame President, a memoir by Liberia's Ellen Johnson Sirleaf, 2009.

7. Susan Rice, Charlie Savage, "The New Team Susan Rice," The New York Times, 2008. Christina Corbin, "U. N. Ambassador Susan Rice Faces Her First Test as Top U. S. Diplomat." FOXNews.com, 2009.
8. Shirley M. Tlighman, Charlie Rose, "A Conversation with Shirley M. Tlighman," March 16, 2009. And Shirley M. Tilghman, President, Professor of Molecular Biology," www.princeton.edu. May 2005
9. Michelle Obama, Transcript from Video of Michelle's Speech at Women for Obama Luncheon, Sacramento, my.barackobama.com. 2007.
10. Michelle Rhees, Amanda Riplet, "How to Fix America's Schools," Time magazine, December 8, 2008.
11. Christiana Amanpour, Forward in *Women of Discovery*, 2001. Christiana Amanpour, Wikipedia, en.wikipedia.org. 2009.
12. Anderson and Shafer. "Deeper Power" in *Enlightened Power*. 2005.
13. Ibid, p.62
14. Carol Witherell and Nel Noddings, *Stories Lives Tell*, 1991.
15. Susan Scott, *Fierce Conversations*, 2002.
16. Linda Lambert, p. x. 2002.
17. Interest-Based-Negotiation (IBN) is an approach to labor-management bargaining designed to bring problem solvers on both sides of an issue together in a relationship that encourages cooperation instead of competition. Glaser and Associates, 1995.
18. Parker J. Palmer and the Fetzer Institute, *Courage to Teach,* 1994.
19. Arlene Ustin, personal communication, 2008.
20. These authors have written about sustainability: Hargreaves, 2006, 2007; Collins, 2002, 2007; Lambert, 2003, 2007.
21. *Atlantic Monthly*, June 2009.
22. Marilyn Ferguson, *The Aquarian Conspiracy*, 1980.

Epilogue: Women Who Lead Seek a Desired Destiny

1. Barack Obama, " Obama creates women's council," posted by Foon Rhee, Political Intelligence, www.boston.com, March 11, 2009. Executive order, establishing A White House Council on Women and Girls, my.barackobama.com, March 11, 2009.
2. Declaration of Sentiments, Report of the Woman's Rights Convention Held at Seneca Falls, NY, July 19-20, 1848. www.thelizlibrary.org.
3. Jean Shinoda Bolen, 2003.
4. Maureen Murdock, *The Heroine's Journey*, pp.131-133, 1998

Appendix A

Leadership Study Interview Questions:

1. Recall a time when you began to display leadership behaviors. Tell us about it.
2. What do you think initiated your entry into leadership?
3. What are two major influences that supported your emergence into leadership?
4. If someone else invited or supported you in your entry into leadership, describe that relationship.
5. What and/or who supported and helped sustain your work in leadership? What were their behaviors?
6. Were there special challenges in this journey into leadership? Please describe.
7. Think of a time when your perception of yourself as a leader or your leadership style was challenged by others, thereby causing conflict. How did you work through the situation? Now project five years into the future, how might you handle this situation in the future?
8. What words would you use to describe yourself as a leader?
9. Is there a metaphor that captures your sense of yourself as a leader?
10. What gifts, talents, or skills do you bring to the work of leadership?
11. As you consider your own leadership journey, what support do you believe women need in order to fully express their leadership styles and abilities?

Appendix B

Partial Resource List for Organization Supporting Women's Leadership and Research

Institute for Women's Leadership: Dedicated to examining issues of leadership and advancing women's leadership and involvement in decision-making in all arenas. (iwl.rutgers.edu)

Old Girls Network: For mid to senior level business and professional women who nurture, understand and appreciate the concepts of giving and sharing their contacts, ideas and support. (www.oldgirlsnetwork.net) There is a Young Girls' Network too.

Emily's List: Members are dedicated to building a progressive America by electing pro-choice Democratic women to office. "We believe in the power of women as candidates, as contributors, as campaign professionals, and as voters to bring about great change in our country. Emily's List will win today and build for tomorrow. We are making a long-term investment in women to develop their political skills and cultivate resources so that we can bring more women into politics and elected office. Only then can we build a progressive majority and construct a society built around equal opportunity for all, civil rights, diversity, and compassion. By working together, we can make a difference — and change the face of American politics." (www.emyslist.org)

The White House Project: The White House Project is a nonpartisan, nonprofit, organization that aims to advance women's leadership in all communities and sectors—up to the U.S. presidency—by filling the leadership pipeline with a richly diverse, critical mass of women. (www.thewhitehouseproject.org)

Catalyst: The leading nonprofit membership organization working globally with businesses and the profession to build inclusive workplaces and expand opportunities for women and business. (www.catalyst.org)

Center for Women's Business Research: Provides data-driven knowledge to advance the economic, social and political impact of women business owners and their enterprises worldwide. (www.nfwbo.org)

MentorNet: One-on-One E-Mentoring program; To further the progress of women and others underrepresented in scientific and technical fields through the use of a dynamic, technology-supported mentoring network and to advance individuals and society, and enhance engineering and related sciences, by promoting a diversified, expanded and talented global workforce. (www.mentornet.net)

National Federation of Republican Women: We strengthen the Republican Party by recruiting, training and electing candidates; advocating the Party's philosophy and initiatives; and, empowering women of all ages, ethnicities and backgrounds in the political process. (www.nfrw.org)

La Herencia and Las Adelitas: Dedicated to mentoring the next generation of leaders and to the advancement of Democratic women in New Mexico (www.herencia.com).

The Institute for Inclusive Security: Includes the Women waging Peace Network: Advocated for the full participation of all stakeholders, especially women, in peace processes. (www.huntalternatives.org)

WAPPP (Women and Public Policy Program of Harvard Kennedy School): Creates gender equality and improves the lives of women and men throughout the world. (www.hks.harvard.edu)

Appendix C

*A Historical Timeline of Women's Rights in America**
and
Seven Generations of Lambert and Gardner Women

1848 At Seneca Falls, New York, 300 women and men sign the Declaration of Sentiments, a plea for the end of discrimination against women in all spheres of society.

> *1854 Mary's Great Grandmother Ann Lydia West was born. At age five she crossed the Atlantic Ocean from England to American and then joined a wagon train to Salt Lake City.*
> *1886 Linda's maternal grandmother Nell Cox Lashmet was born.*
> *1888 Mary's maternal grandmother Carrie Hatch Neville was born.*

1890 Women in Wyoming were granted the right to vote.

> *1908 Linda's mother Lucretia Lashmet Todd, was born. (Simone de Beauvoir was born.)*

1920 Nineteenth Amendment was passed, giving women the right to vote.

> *1921 Mary's mother Eloise Neville Jones was born. (Betty Friedan was born.)*

1937 The U.S. Supreme Court upholds Washington State's minimum wage laws for women.

> *1939 Linda Todd Lambert born*
> *1940 Mary Jones Gardner born*

1948 Universal Declaration of Human Rights passed by the United Nations.

> *1955 Linda's stepdaughter Laura Lambert Pintane was born.*
> *1958 Linda's stepdaughter Ellen Lambert Johnson was born.*
> *1960 Linda's daughter April Green Smock was born.*
> *1962 Mary's daughter Deirdra Gardner DiNapoli was born.*

1954 *Brown vs. the Board of Education* strikes down "separate and equal" concept, integrating schools for African Americans and white students.

1963 The Equal Pay Act is passed by Congress, promising equitable wages for the same work, regardless of the race, color, religion, national origin or sex of the worker. *The Feminine Mystique* written by Betty Friedan.

1964 Title VII of the Civil Rights Act passed, including a prohibition against employment discrimination on the basis of race, color, religion, national origin, or sex.

> *1965 Mary's daughter Kimberly Gardner Mulcahy was born.*

1971 Reed v. Reed, 404 U.S. 71 (1971): The U.S. Supreme Court holds unconstitutional an Idaho state law establishing automatic preference for males as administrators of wills. This was the first time the court strikes down a law treating men and women differently.

1972 Title IX (Public Law 92-318) of the Education Amendments prohibits sex discrimination in all aspects of education programs that receive federal support.

1973 Roe v. Wade, 410 U.S. 113 (1973) and Doe v. Bolton, 410 U.S. 179 (1973): The U.S. Supreme Court declared that the Constitution through the concept of the right to privacy protects women's right to terminate an early pregnancy, thus making abortion legal in the U.S.

1973 Women's Educational Equity Act funds the development of non-sexist teaching materials and model programs that encourage full educational opportunities for girls and women.

1973 The Equal Employment Opportunity Commission, the Justice and Labor Departments, and AT&T sign a consent decree banning AT&T's discriminatory practices against women and minorities.

1981 The U.S. Supreme Court ruled that excluding women from the draft is unconstitutional.

1984 Roberts v. U.S. Jaycees, 468 U.S. 609 (1984), sex discrimination in membership policies of organizations, such as the Jaycees, is forbidden by the Supreme Court, opening many previously all-male organizations (Jaycees, Kiwanis, Rotary, Lions) to women.

1984 Mississippi belatedly ratifies the 19th Amendment, granting women the vote.

1984 Hishon v. King and Spaulding, 467 U.S. 69. The U.S. Supreme Court rules that law firms may not discriminate on the basis of sex in promoting lawyers to partnership positions.

> *1984 Linda's 1st granddaughter Jessica Johnson Fuller was born.*
> *1990 Linda's 2nd granddaughter Chloe Smock was born.*
> *1991 Linda's 3rd granddaughter Keely Lambert was born.*
> *1992 Linda's 4th granddaughter Shannon Pintane was born.*
> *1992 Linda's 5th granddaughter Ashley Lambert was born.*

1993 The Family and Medical Leave Act went into effect.

> *1993 Linda's 6th granddaughter Catherine Lambert was born.*
> *1995 Mary's 1st granddaughter Olivia DiNapoli was born.*

1997 Elaborating on Title IX, the Supreme Court ruled that college athletics programs must involve approximately equal numbers of men and women in order to qualify for federal support.

> *1998 Linda's 7th granddaughter Madeline Lambert was born.*
> *1998 Mary's 2nd granddaughter Claire Mulcahy was born.*
> *2000 Mary's 3rd granddaughter Ella Mulcahy was born.*
> *2001 Mary's 4th granddaughter Grace DiNapoli was born.*

2003 *Jackson v. Birmingham Board of Education.* Supreme Court rules that Title IX, which prohibits discrimination based on sex, also inherently prohibits disciplining someone for complaining about sex-based discrimination.

> *2003 Mary's 5th granddaughter Camille Mulcahy was born.*
> *2006 Linda's 1st great granddaughter Emily Fuller was born.*

2009 President Obama signs the Lilly Ledbetter Fair Pay Restoration Act, which allows victims of pay discrimination to file a complaint against their employer within 180 days of their last paycheck.

2009 President Obama signs an Executive Order creating the White House Council on Women and Girls.

National Women's History Project www.legacy98.org/timeline.html
And Info Please www.infoplease.com/spot

Women's Ways of Leading Selected Bibliography

Aburdene, Patricia, Naisbitt, John. *Megatrends for Women*, New York: Villard Books, 1992.

Ackerman, Diane. *An Alchemy of Mind*. New York: Scribner, 2004.

Alspaugh, Nancy, Kentz, Marilyn, Photography by Halpin Mary Ann. *Fearless Women: Midlife Portraits*. New York: Stewart, Tabori and Chang, 2005.

Amanpour, Christiane: Foreword in *Women of Discovery, A Celebration of Intrepid Women Who Explored the World*. New York: Clarkson Potter/Publisher, 2001.

Angelou, Maya. *I Know Why the Caged Bird Sings*. New York: Random House, 1975.

_____. *Phenomenal Woman*. New York: Random House. 1994.

_____. *Even The Stars Look Lonesome*, New York: Random House, 1971.

Ashby, Ruth, and Ohrn, Deborah Gore. *HERSTORY, Women Who Changed the World*. New York: Viking, 1995.

Bateson, Mary Catherine. *Composing A Life*. New York: The Atlantic Monthly Press, 1989.

_____. *Peripheral Visions*. New York: HarperCollins Publishers, Inc., 1994.

_____. *Willing to Learn, Passages of Personal Discovery*. Hanover: Steerforth Press, 2004.

Beilenson, Evelyn and Tenenbaum, Ann, Editors. *Wit & Wisdom of Famous American Women*. New York Peter Pauper Press, Inc., 1986.

Belenky, Mary Field; Clinchy, Blythe McVicker; Goldgerger, Nancy Rule; Tarule, Jill Mattuck. *Women's Ways of Knowing, The development of Self, Voice and Mind*. New York: Basic Books, Inc., 1986.

Bellavance-Johnson, Marsha. *Georgia O'Keeffe in New Mexico*. Ketchum: The Computer Lab, 1998.

Bennett, Alan. *The Uncommon Reader*. London: Faber and Faber, 2007.

Bernstein, Carl. *A Woman in Charge, The Life of Hillary Rodham Clinton*. New York: Vintage Books, 2008.

Blake-Beard, Stacy. "The Inextricable Link Between Mentoring and Leadership," In Coughlin, et al. *Enlightened Power.* San Francisco: Jossey-Bass, *2005.*

Bolen, Jean Shinoda. M.D. *Crones Don't Whine, Concentrated Wisdom for Juicy Women*. York Beach: Conari Press, 2003.

Bloom, Gary and Stein, Robert, "Leadership," *Thrust for Educational Leadership*. ACSA, 2004.

Brizendine, Louann, M.D. *The Female Brain*. New York: Morgan Road Books. 2006.

Capra, Fritjof. *The Web of Life*. New York: Anchor Books, 1996.

Case, Chester, "About the Posh Squash." in *The Post Squash Cookbook*, Morris Press Cookbooks, 2004.

Clinton, Hillary Rodham. *It Takes a Village and Other Lessons Children Teach Us*. New York: Simon and Schuster, 1996.

_____. *Living History*. New York: Simon and Schuster, 2003.

Cochran-Smith and Lytle, Susan L. *Inside/Outside. Teacher Research and Knowledge*. New York: Teacher College Press, 1992.

Collins, Jim, *Good to Great: Why Some Companies Make the Leap and Some Don't*. New York: Harper Business, 2001.

Conzemius, Anne and O'Neill, Jan. *Building Shared Responsibility for Student Learning.* Alexandria: ASCD, 2001.

Cosman, Carol; Keefe, Joan; Weaver, Kathleen, Editors. *Women Poets.* London: Penguin Group, 1978.

Costa, Art and Kallick, Bena. "Through the Lens of a Critical Friend." Educational Leadership, pp. 49-51, Oct. 1993.

Coughlin, Linda, Wingard, Ellen, Hollihan, Keith, Editors. *Enlightened Power, How Women are Transforming the Practice of Leadership.* San Francisco: Jossey-Bass, 2005.

Cross, Patricia K. *Adults as Learners.* San Francisco: Jossey Bass, 1981.

Daloz, Laurent A. *Effective Teaching and Mentoring, Realizing the Transformational Power of Adult Learning Experiences.* San Francisco: Jossey-Bass Publisher, 1987.

Davies, Brent Editor. *The Essentials of School Leadership.* Thousand Oaks: Corwin Press, 2005.

Deak, JoAnn, with Barker, Teresa. *Girls will be Girls, Raising Confident and Courageous Daughters.* New Work: Hyperion, 2002.

De Beauvoir, Simone. Translated and edited by H.M. Parshley. *The Second Sex.* New York: Bantam Books, 1961.

Dietz, Mary E. *Professional Development Portfolio, Continuous Learning.* San Ramon: Frameworks, 1993

_____. *Journal as Frameworks for Change.* Arlington Heights: SkyLight, 1998.

Donlan, Vicki, Graves, Helen French. *Her Turn, Why it's Time for Women to Lead in America.* Westport: Praeger Publisher, 2007.

DuFour, Richard, Eaker, Robert. *Professional Learning Communities at Work, Best Practices for enhancing Student Achievement.* Virginia: ASCD, 1998.

DuFour, Richard, Eaker, Robert, DuFour, Rebecca, Editors. *On Common Ground; The Power of Professional Communities.* Indiana: Solution Tree, 2005.

Eagly, Alice H., Carli, Linda L. *Through the Labyrinth, The Truth About How Women Become Leaders.* Cambridge; Harvard Business School Press. 2007.

Edelman, Marian Wright. *Lanterns, A Memoir of Mentors.* New York: Harper Collins Press, 1999.

Eisler, Benita. *O'Keeffe and Stieglitz: An American Romance.* New York, Penguin, 1991.

Eisler, Riane. *The Real Wealth of Nations, Creating a Caring Economics.* San Francisco: Berrett-Koehler Publisher. Inc., 2007.

Ellison, Sheila, *If Women Ruled the World: How to Create the World We Want To Live In.* Maui: Inner Ocean Publishing Inc. 2004.

El Sa'adawi, Nawal, Translated by Marilyn Booth. *Memoirs from the Women's Prison.* London: The Women's Press Ltd, 1991.

El Sa'adawi, Nawal, Translated and Edited by Hetata, Sherif. *The Hidden Face of Eve.* London: Zed Books Ltd., 1980.

Estes, Clarissa Pinkila. *Women Who Run With the Wolves, Myths and Stories of the Wild* Wolman Archetype. New York: Ballantine, 1992.

Etzioni, Amitai. *The New Golden Rule; Community and Morality in a Democratic Society.* New York: Basic Books, 1996.

Felder, Deborah G. *A Century of Women: The Most Influential Events in Twentieth-Century Women's History.* New York: Citadel Press, 1999.

Ferguson, Margaret, *The Aquarian Conspiracy.* Los Angeles: J. P. Tarcher, 1980.

The Fourth World Conference on Women. *Covenant For the New Millennium.* Santa Rose: Free Hand Books. 1996.

Flinders, David. "Nel Noddings" in Palmer, Joy, Ed. *Fifty Modern Thinkers on Education from Piaget to the Present.* New York: Routledge, 2001.

Fisher, Roger, Ury, William, and Patton, Bruce. *Getting to Yes: Negotiating Agreement Without Giving In, 2nd edition.* New York: Penguin Books. 1991.

Fitzgerald, Tanya. "Interrogating Orthodox Voices: gender, ethnicity and educational leadership. In Fidler, Brian, Ed. *School Leadership and Management.* Oxfordshire: Carfax Publishing Vol. 23, Number 4, November 2003.

Friedan, Betty. *The Feminine Mystique.* 3rd edition. New York: W.W. Norton, 1997.

Geniesse, Jane Fletcher. *Passionate Nomad, the Life of Freya Stark.* New York: The Modern Library, 2001.

Gilligan, Carol. *In A Different Voice. Psychological Theory and Women's Development.* Cambridge: Harvard University Press, 1982.

Gilligan, Carol, Ware, Victoria, Taylor, Jull McLean, Editors. *Mapping the Moral Domain. A Contribution of Women's Thinking to Psychological Theory and Education.* Cambridge: Harvard University Press. 1988.

Glaser, John and Associates. "Planning to Bargain: An Introduction to Effective Negotiating and Problem Solving." Unpublished document prepared for Saratoga Union School District. Yountville, CA. 1998.

Goleman, Daniel. *Social Intelligence, The Revolutionary New Science of Human Relationships.* New York: Bantam Books, 2006.

_____. *Emotional Intelligence, Why it can Matter More than IQ.* New York: Bantam Books, 1995.

Goodall, Jane, with Berman, Phillip. *Reason for Hope a Spiritual Journey.* New York; Warner Books 1999.

Goodrich, Nora Lorre. *Heroines.* New York: HarperCollins, 1993.

Greene, Maxine. *The Dialectic of Freedom.* New York; Teacher College Press, 1988.

_____. *Landscapes of Learning.* New York: Teachers College Press, 1978.

_____. *Releasing the Imagination.* San Francisco, Jossey-Bass, 1995.

Harvard Business School. *Meg Whitman and eBay Germany.* Boston: President and Fellows of Harvard College, 2001.

Hesselbein, Frances. *Hesselbein on Leadership.* San Francisco: Jossey-Bass, 2002.

Hesselbein, Frances and Cohen, Paul M., Editors. *Leader to Leader.* San Francisco: Jossey-Bass Publisher, 1999.

Herrera, Hayden. *Frida: A Biography of Frida Kahlo.* New York: Perennial, 2002.

Hinojosa, Maria. *Raising Raul, Adventures Raising Myself and My Son.* New York: Penguin Books, 1999.

Jackson, Stevi, Ed. *Women's Studies, Essential Readings.* New York: New York University Press, 1993.

Jaworski, Joseph. *Synchronicity, The Inner Path of Leadership.* San Francisco; Berrett-Koehler Publisher, Inc. 1996.

Jemison, Mae Dr. *Find Where the Wind Goes. Moments from my Life.* New York; Scholastic Press, 2001.

Johnson, Robert A. *SHE, Understanding Feminine Psychology.* New York: Harper Row, Publishers, 1989.

Kegan, Robert. *The Evolving Self. Problem and Process in Human Development.* Cambridge: Harvard University Press, 1982.

_____. *In Over Our Heads: The Mental Demands of Modern Life.* Cambridge: Harvard University Press, 1994.

Kegan, Robert, Lahey, Lisa Laskow. *How The Way We Talk Can Change The Way We Work; Seven Languages for Transformation.* San Francisco: Jossey-Bass. 2001.

Kellerman, Barbara, Rhode, Deborah Ed. *Women and Leadership: The State of Play and Strategies for Change.* San Francisco: Jossey-Bass, 2007.

Kincheloe, Joe L. Steinberg, Shirley. *Thirteen Questions: Reframing Education's Conversations.* New York: Peter Lang 1992.

Kingsolver, Barbara, *The Poisonwood Bible.* New York: Harper-Collins, 1998.

Kingston, Maxine Hong. *The Woman Warrior, Memoirs of a Girlhood among Ghosts.* New York: Random House, 1977.

Kohlberg, Lawrence. *The Psychology of Moral Development.* San Francisco: Harper and Row, 1984.

Kyi, Aung San Suu. *Freedom from Fear.* London: Penguin, 1995.

Lakoff, George. *The Political Mind.* New York: Viking, 2008.

Lambert, Linda; Walker, Deborah, Zimmerman, Diane P. Cooper, Joanne E., Lambert, Morgan Dale, Gardner, Mary E. Slack, P.J. Ford. *The Constructivist Leader,* New York: Teachers College Press, 1995.

Lambert, Linda; Walker, Deborah; Zimmerman, Diane P.; Cooper, Joanne E.; Lambert, Morgan Dale; Gardner, Mary E.; Szabo, Margaret. *The Constructivist Leader,* second edition. New York: Teachers College Press, 2002.

Lambert, Linda. *Building Leadership Capacity in Schools.* Alexandria: ASCD. 1998.

_____. *Leadership Capacity for Lasting School Improvement.* Alexandria: ASCD. 2003.

_____. *"A Critical Analysis of the Assumptions held by Policy-makers, Researchers and Staff Developers about Adult Learning."* Unpublished dissertation, San Francisco: University Press, 1983.

Langley, Andrew. *Barbara Hepworth.* Oxford: Heinemann, 2003.

Lash, Joseph P. *Eleanor: The Years Alone.* New York: W.W. Norton and Company, Inc. 1972.

Levin, Sarah L. *Promoting Adult Growth in Schools, The Promises of Professional Development.* Boston: Allyn and Bacon. 1989.

Lieberman Ann, Miller, Lynn. *Teacher Leadership.* San Francisco: Jossey-Bass, 2004.

Lieberman, Ann, Wood, Diane. *Inside the National Writing Project; Connecting Network Learning and Classroom Teaching.* New York: Teacher College Press, 2003.

Lindbergh, Anne Morrow. *Gift from the Sea.* New York: Vintage Books, 1978.

Ling, Bettina. *Aung San Suu Kyi, Standing up for Democracy in Burma.* New York: The Feminist Press, 1999.

Lisle, Laurie. *Portrait of an Artist: A Biography of Georgia O'Keeffe.* New York: Pocket Books, 1986.

Loeb, Paul R. *The Impossible Will Take a Little While.* New York: Basic Books, 2004.

Loevinger, Jane. *Ego Development: Conception and Theories.* San Francisco: Jossey Bass, 1976.

Lyons, Nona Plessner. In Gilligan, et al, *Mapping the Moral Domain.* "Two Perspectives: On Self, Relationships, and Morality." Cambridge: Harvard University Press. 1988.

Mabry, Marcus. *Twice as Good, Condoleezza Rice and Her Path to Power.* New York: Modern Times, 2007.

McLeish, Kenneth, Trans. *Aristophanes, Clouds, Women in Power, Knights.* Cambridge: Cambridge University Press, 1979.

Meier, Deborah. *The Power of their Ideas: Lessons for America from a Small School in Harlem.* Boston: Beacon Press, 1995.

Menchu, Rigoberta. Edited by Elisabeth Burgos-Debray, Translated by Ann Wright. *I...Rigoberta Menchu: An Indian Woman in Guatemala.* London: Verso, 1984.

Mendoza, Sylvia. *The Book of Latina Women: 150 Vidas of Passion, Strength, and Success.* Avon: Adams Media. 2004.

Miller, Susan Brown, *Shirley Chisholm*. New York: An Archway Paperback, 1972.

Moller, Gayle, Pankake, Anita. *Lead with Me: A Principal's Guide to Teacher Leadership*. Larchmont: Eye on Education, 2006.

Morrison, Toni. *Playing In The Dark: Whiteness and the Literary Imagination*. New York: Vintage Books, 1992.

——————. *Bluest Eye*. New York: Plume, 1994.

——————. *Love*. New York: Vintage, 2003.

——————. *A Mercy*. New York: Alfred A. Knopf, 2008.

——————. *Beloved*. New York: Plume, 1987.

Murdock, Maureen. *The Heroine's Journey: Workbook*. Boston and London: Shambhala, 1998.

Nabokov, Vladimir. *Lolita*. New York: Vintage Books, 1955.

Noddings, Nel. *Caring, A Feminine Approach to Ethics and Moral Education*. Berkeley: University of California Press, 1984.

——————. *Starting at Home: Caring and Social Policy*. Berkeley: University of California Press, 2002.

Olsen, Tillie. *Silences*. New York: Delacorte Press/Seymour Lawrence, 1965.

Palmer, Parker J. *The Courage to Teach: Exploring the Inner Landscape of a Teacher's Life*. San Francisco: Jossey-Bass, 1998.

Parks, Rosa with Jim Haskins. *Rosa Parks: My Story*. New York:Puffin Books. 1992

Parks, Rosa with Gregory J. Reed. *Quiet Strength: The Faith, the Hope and the Heart of a Woman Who Changed a Nation*. Grand Rapids: Zondervan Publishing House, 1994.

Pinker, Susan. *The Sexual Paradox; Men, Women, and the Real Gender Gap*. New York: Scribner, 2008.

Pipher, Mary. *Reviving Ophelia, Saving the Selves of Adolescent Girls*. New York: Ballantine Books, 1994.

Polk, Milbry, Tiegreen, Mary. *Women of Discovery: A Celebration of Intrepid Women Who Explored the World.* New York: Clarkson Potter/Publishers, 2001.

Rennolds, Margaret, Editor. *The National Museum of Women in the Arts.* New York: Harry N. Abrams, Inc., 1987.

Richards, Ann. *Straight from the Heart, My life in Politics and other Places.* New York: Simon and Schuster, 1989.

Schaef, Anne Wilson. *Meditations For Women Who Do Too Much.* New York: Harper San Francisco, 1990.

Schulze, Julie, *Rigoberta Menchu Tum, Champion of Human Rights.* USA: John Gordon Burke Publisher, Inc., 1997.

Scott, Susan. *Fierce Conversations; Achieving Success at Work and in Life, One Conversation at a Time.* New York: Viking. 2002.

Senge, Peter. *The Fifth Discipline: The Art and Practice of the Learning Organization.* New York: Doubleday, 1992.

Senge, Peter, Scharmer, C. Otto, Jaworski, Joseph, Flowers, Betty Sue. *Presence, An Exploration of Profound Change in People, Organizations, and Society.* New York: Currancy Doubleday. 2005.

Shenk, Joshua Wolf. "What Makes Us Happy." *The Atlantic*, pp. 36-53 June, 2009.

Shlain, Leonard. *The Alphabet Versus The Goddess.* New York: Viking,1998.

Shlain, Leonard. *Sex, Time and Power: How Women's Sexuality Shaped Human Evolution.* New York: Viking, 2003.

Shropshire, Mike and Schaefer, Frank. *The Thorny Rose of Texas.* New York: Carol Publishing Group, 1994.

Tan, Amy. *The Opposite of Fate. Memories of a Writing Life.* New York: Penguin Books, 2003.

Tannen, Deborah. *The Argument Culture: Moving from Debate to Dialogue.* New York: Bantam Press, 2003.

Teacher, Janet B (Ed.). *Women of Words* (2nd Ed.). Philadelphia: Running Press. 2002.

Tenneson, Joyce. *Wise Women: A Celebration of Their Insights, Courage, and Beauty*. Boston: Bulfinch Press, 2002.

The Freedom Writers with Erin Gruwell. *The Freedom Writers Diary*. New York: Broadway Books. 1999.

The Posh Squash Community Garden; *The Posh Squash Community Garden Cookbook*, Sea Ranch: 2004

Turner, Elizabeth H. *Georgia O'Keeffe: The Poetry of Things*. Washington, D.C. and New Haven: The Phillips Collection and Yale University Press. 2000.

Von Waberer, Keto. *Frida Kahlo, Masterpieces*. Munich: Schirmer Art Books 1994/2003.

Vrato, Elizabeth. *The Counselors: Conversations with 18 Courageous Women Who Have Changed the World*. Philadelphia: Running Press. 2002.

Vygotsky, L. S. *Mind in Society. The Development of Higher Psychological Processes*. Edited by Cole, Michael et al. Cambridge: Harvard University Press 1978.

Walker, Alice, *Her Blue Body Everything We Know*. San Diego; Harcourt Brace, Jovanovich, Publishers, 1991.

Warner, Carolyn. *Treasury of Women's Quotations*. Englewood Cliffs: Prentice Hall, 1992.

Wheatley, Margaret J. *Leadership and the New Science*. San Francisco: Berrett-Koehler Publishers, 1992.

_____. *Turning to One Another: Simple Conversations to Restore Hope to the Future*. San Francisco: Berrett Koehler Publishers, 2002.

_____. *Finding our way, Leadership for an Uncertain Time*. San Francisco: Berrett-Koehler Publishers, 2005.

Whitman, Christine Todd, *It's My Party Too: Battle for the Heart of the GOP and The Future of America.* New York: Penguin Group, 2005.

Wilson, Marie C. *Closing The Leadership Gap, Why Women Can and Must Help Run the World.* New York: Viking, 2004.

Witherell, Carol and Noddings, Nel (Editors). *Stories Lives Tell, Narrative and Dialogue in Education.* New York: Teachers College Press. 1991.

Wollstonecraft, Mary. *A Vindication of the Rights of Women.* New York: Alfred A Knopf, 1929.

Woltring, Carol Spain, Barlas, Carole. *Women Leaders in Public Health.* Seattle: Artists-Writers Publishing, Inc. 2001.

Woolf, Virginia. *A Room of Ones Own.* San Diego; Harcourt Brace Jovanovich, Inc., 1929.

Zichy, Shoya. *Women and The Leadership IQ, The Breakthrough System for Achieving Power and Influence.* New York: McGraw-Hill. 2001.

Breinigsville, PA USA
08 February 2010
232191BV00004B/34/P

WILLIMANTIC

INDUSTRY AND COMMUNITY

The Rise and Decline of a Connecticut Textile City

THOMAS R. BEARDSLEY

WINDHAM TEXTILE & HISTORY MUSEUM

WILLIMANTIC, CONNECTICUT

First published in 1993 by the Windham Textile and History Museum,
157 Union-Main Street, Willimantic, CT 06226

Second Printing, 1994
Third Printing, 1999
Fourth Printing, 2003

Library of Congress Catalog Card Number: 92-83719

ISBN 0-9634524-0-1

Fourth printing funded in part by a grant from the

CONNECTICUT LIGHT & POWER COMPANY

For Mam and Dad

CONTENTS

PART II: COMMUNITY

ACKNOWLEDGMENTS

No work of this kind is produced in isolation. Consequently, I would like to thank the following: Sheila Biddle at the Ford Foundation in New York City for her support of the Museum's Oral History Institute; Bruce Fraser and the Connecticut Humanities Council for continuing support of the Museum's scholar-in-residence program; Laura Knott Twine and the staff and Board of Directors of the Windham Textile and History Museum for supporting this project in difficult economic times; Congressman Sam Gejdenson for his hard work on the Museum's behalf; David Shuldiner for his advice in oral history technique; members of faculty at the University of Sheffield, England, particularly Harry Barnes, Karl Hedderwick, Colin Holmes, David Martin and Tony Sutcliffe for invigorating lectures and course work; the faculty of the University of Connecticut's History Department, particularly Bruce Stave and Bill Hoglund for guiding me, a culture-shocked Englishman, in the late 1980s; Susan Tepas for making sense and order of the diverse materials collected in my primary source data base, which provides the core for Industry; Lucy and Kevin Crosbie, the publishers of the Willimantic *Chronicle,* for their continued assistance and access to their old newspaper files; Bob Beaudreault, the property manager of the vacant American Thread Company site in Willimantic, for his advice and guidance; the staffs at the Connecticut State Library, the Connecticut Historical Society, Eastern Connecticut State University, University of Connecticut, Willimantic Public Library, Windham Town Hall and the Windham Historical Society; Bill Scheidley and Feenie Ziner in the University of Connecticut's English Department for supplying a long line of committed, talented student interns to the Museum's programs; the students themselves, Michelle De Rigo, Jill Tuozolla, Tracie Molinaro, Susan Morgan, Britt Gustafson, Lara Allen and Cristina Marques; Linda Riquier and Jennifer at L & R Marketing; the Museum's librarian, Linda Kate Edgerton, and projects manager, Kate Waitte, for proof-reading; Richard Twine for the map of old mill sites; Billie Salter and Nancy Spiegel for their insightful advice during the final stages of manuscript preparation; Fran Funk and Roland Laramie for their assistance with the photographs: François Gamache for access to his excellent collection of historic Windham postcards: David Geary for editing the early drafts: fellow Englishman Peter Tuffrey for editing the final draft; my parents, Ron and Vera Beardsley for their lifelong support; my wife"s parents, Martin and Betty Henry; and last, but not least, my wife Margaret, for her support during her months of isolation when I was researching and compiling this work. I hope I have not forgotten anyone.

Tom Beardsley, Willimatic, Spring, 1993

INTRODUCTION

Part I

Industry

This book consists of two parts, *Industry and Community*. Part I, *Industry*, is a review of Willimantic's industrial developments since 1822, compiled from primary and secondary sources. It is far from comprehensive, but fills a chronological gap as virtually nothing has been published in recent years concerning Willimantic's rich textile and industrial history. Numerous urban-booster pamphlets and books appeared between 1868 and 1920, when Willimantic was expanding, but no single work has addressed the overall picture since Allen B. Lincoln's *History of Windham County* (1920).

I have specifically avoided collating a 'dry' list of the numerous industries which sprang to life and disappeared in Willimantic during the last 170 years. This list does need compiling, but *Industry* focuses upon the cotton and silk industries which dominated Willimantic's economy for so long. The old cotton and silk industries began to decline during the early twentieth-century, and were replaced by the manufacture of velvet cloth, synthetic textiles and mica-capacitors. The Rossie and Leiss velvet companies, and the Electro Motive Company, which produced television and radio parts, filled the gap in the local economy created by the collapse of the city's textile industries. Willimantic's remaining textile giant, American Thread, went over to the production of synthetic textiles during the 1950s and 1960s.

Willimantic prospered and grew as America industrialized after the Civil War. Its local government was dominated by a powerful Democratic political machine, thanks to the community's large Irish-American population. Willimantic's colorful mayor, Daniel Patrick Dunn (1859 - 1922) was a legend in his own lifetime. He and his fellow Democrats resided in City Hall continually between 1905 and 1917. In the 1880s, a local politician predicted that Willimantic would one day become the capital of Narragansett, a large New England state consisting of a combination of Eastern Connecticut and Rhode Island. Such optimism was well founded as the city's booming cotton and silk industries were firmly placing Willimantic on the national and international map.

The Willimantic Linen Company and its successor, the American Thread Company (ATCO), dominated the city's social and economic life for more than 130 years. Because of this, Willimantic was long regarded as a one-industry city. This dependence held obvious risks, and appeals for industrial and economic diversification were first heard just after the Civil War.

This reliance upon one industry was worrying. For example, in 1910, the American Thread Company was suffering from an acute shortage of labor, despite the large influx of Austrian-Polish immigrants into town. The Company advertised nationwide for "125 girls." An investigation conducted by a local Roman Catholic priest revealed that despite the favorable "breeding habits" of the French Canadian and Polish population, there was a shortage of 'girls' to fill the vacancies at American Thread. The Priest, St. Joseph's Arthur De Bruycker, pleaded for people to stay in town, and the Thread Company renovated its boarding-house, the 'Elms,' to attract single out-of-town female workers, aiming "to make the place as homelike as possible for girls and women."

Willimantic's male heads of households were leaving Willimantic in droves - and taking their wives and daughters with them. The local textile industries, particularly American Thread, paid poor wages to men not lucky enough to be employed in the lucrative trade of machine-fixer. The Thread Company's low pay was only acceptable to 'girls.' Local men could not find jobs in Willimantic outside of the textile industry, and potential low-income female labor left town with them, leaving a large hole in the local economy. Willimantic's politicians convinced a local silk-loom manufacturer, the Willimantic Machine Company, to stay in town, and pleaded for a well-known local inventor, W. J. Asher, to bring his Windsor Locks-based washing-machine factory to his hometown - if not, at least let Willimantic manufacture his mangles.

In the early years of this century, a group of local businessmen formed the Willimantic Development Company, which ultimately built factories on South Street, Moulton Court and Wilson Street, to attract new industries to town. Two of the most successful organizations attracted by the favorable leasing terms offered by the Development Company's new industrial buildings were the Rossie Velvet Company, which occupied the South Street factory, and the S. C. S. Box Company, which made wooden boxes for chain stores, packers and butter and egg dealers in its Moulton Court factory. At their height, the two companies provided 400 jobs for local people, away from the traditional silk and cotton industries - but both companies were early victims of the Depression. The cry for diversification was particularly loud as Willimantic's silk mills also began to close during the traumatic 1930s.[1]

As the twenty-first century approaches, Willimantic is a community in decline and flux, an old industrial city in a post-industrial epoch. Its low-paying textile industry finally left in 1985. Nevertheless, post-industrial Willimantic possesses much potential, particularly if Route 6 to Hartford is developed into a continuous highway, and if *Amtrak* further develops its ridership through the community.

Willimantic's greatest strength lies in its geographical position. It is located conveniently between New York City and Boston, and within easy reach of Hartford and Providence. Diversified small industries, called for in the years when the textile industry was well established, might be attracted to a town with such excellent transport links. Furthermore, tourism could be nurtured in Willimantic's vacant mills, workshops and factories.

Part I looks back at Willimantic's prosperous industrial epoch. It utilizes information gleaned from local nineteenth and early twentieth-century newspapers, providing an anecdotal, human dimension not revealed by official figures and statistics, and often ignored in purely scholastic studies. Willimantic's cotton and silk industries are discussed within the city's nineteenth-century social and cultural milieu. This particular New England industrial community has too often been ignored by the documenters of Eastern Connecticut's rich history. It is remembered in detail in Part II by the people who lived and worked there.

Part II

Community

The picture of Willimantic missed by the compilers of statistics and newspaper reporters is completed here by memories of the community's working people. This section's subject matter is based on a series of oral history interviews conducted in 1979/80 and the early 1990s. The study and practice of oral history has generated much controversy, but this work avoids any esoteric debates about function, bias or myth, and does not discuss the subject's close relationship with anthropology and folk lore. Those fields have been expertly discussed elsewhere.[2]

In 1979, Dr. Bruce Stave organized an oral history project, "The Millworkers of Willimantic" for students studying in the Department of History at the University of Connecticut. Dr. Stave's students interviewed people who had worked for the American Thread Company in Willimantic. The inspiration for his course lay in a recently published anthology of oral histories, which has become a classic. Tamara K. Haraven's and Randolph Langenbach's *Amoskeag: Life and Work in an American Factory-City* (1978), explored the lives of workers in the Amoskeag mills in Manchester, New Hampshire. Dr. Stave, who is now the director of the University of Connecticut's Center for Oral History, bequeathed the transcriptions of the 1979 interviews to the Windham Textile & History Museum in 1989. I have edited those interviews into one essay, which is included as Chapter 1. The interviews in Chapters 2 through 14 were conducted as part of the Museum's Oral History Institute, which began operating in March, 1990. I have edited out the questions posed to each interviewee to provide individual biographies in the first person.

Both sets of interviews cast light upon the decline and fall of an industrial city in the large, relatively unexplored, Connecticut hinterland east of Hartford. The story is mainly related by people who worked in Willimantic's textile mills, but a useful background to life in the community is provided by several individuals not directly involved with the textile industry.

I have translated slang to facilitate an understanding of the narrative. Colloquialisms remain where they do not detract from the subject matter. Correct grammar is important, but I have attempted to retain each individual's manner of speaking. I take full responsibility for the editing. Each transcription fully reflects the oral content on the tapes.

At this point, a brief word about the practicalities of the oral history process is necessary. I was conversant with the recorder, tapes, and batteries - or so I thought. Batteries quickly lost their power, tapes became entangled. I often placed the recorder too far from the interviewee, and several re-interviews were necessary. The secret of proficiency in oral history interviewing in one word? Practice.

Oral history is restrictive because of its obvious time limitation. Elderly people interviewed today can recall the early years of this century, but how revealing it would have been talking to an elderly Willimantic resident in the 1920s. For example, the June, 1924 issue of the American Thread Company's official magazine, the *Atco Star,* includes a short article about John Curry, who had just retired as the assistant overseer in Mill Number Two's ring and mule spinning department. Save for a two-year stint in a Providence mill, 79 year-old Curry had worked for ATCO in Willimantic for 57 years. He began work at age 10, in 1865: "He has never been late to work and the only medical attendance he has ever received was one office visit to a local physician." An interview with this fellow might have been informative, to say the least.

My personal interest in oral history began during the early 1980s at the University of Sheffield, England, through an educational program financed by several northern universities and the National Union of Mineworkers. Students were encouraged to interview local coalminers, and several years later, the advantages of those interviews became obvious. They revealed an unrecorded history, unavailable from any other source. Paul Thompson, a leading British oral historian, has challenged the orthodoxy that *single* sources, such as unsupported interviews, need careful corroboration.[3] Thompson asserts that discrepancies between oral and written sources does not mean that one is more reliable than the other: "The interview may reveal the truth behind the official record. Or the divergence may represent two perfectly valid accounts from different standpoints, which together provide vital clues towards the true interpretations."[4] It is impossible to qualify every remark from alternative sources, so I have consequently chosen interviews which hopefully provide some balance between individual bias and perception, and actuality.

The Museum's oral history collection is far from comprehensive. The experiences of the community's large Latino population needs to be fully cataloged. This is high on the Museum's list of priorities, and the study will go ahead as soon as funding can be secured. The Museum's collection will also benefit from more interviews with the community's displaced persons (DPs) population. The Latinos and DPs can be considered as relative newcomers to the area, and I have attempted to discover how the community's older, established groups, such as the Irish and the French Canadians, felt when the new groups began to settle in town in the 1950s and 1960s. Racial prejudice is a thread weaving through some of the interviews and several interviewees requested that certain derogatory remarks regarding race be deleted; but some remain, so those who crave political correctness beware. Conversely, some of the interviews reveal varying degrees of racial integration.

I thank all the interviewees for inviting me into their homes and giving up their valuable time. I hope the reader will enjoy the contributions. If you have any comments, suggestions or criticisms, do not hesitate to contact the Windham Textile & History Museum.

Funding for this publication was provided by the Windham Textile and History Museum, the Connecticut Humanities Council and the Ford Foundation. The completed transcriptions and tapes can be studied on request at the Museum. A Finders Guide to the Museum's entire collection of interviews is also included.

PROLOGUE

Rapid Growth and Slow Decline

A few words about this embryo city may not be amiss. Twenty years ago it was called a smart little village but, it was always added, business is overdone there. The Willimantic Linen Company had just completed their No. 2 Mill and laid out a village of their own near the junction of the Natchaug and Willimantic rivers.

They immediately entered on an era of prosperity which has benefited the borough exceedingly, and which has continued until the "Thread City" is known all over the civilized world. They now operate four mills, one of which bears the distinction of being the largest building on the ground floor in the world. Here are also the Windham and Smithville cotton mills, the Holland and Chaffee silk mills, the Morrison Machine Co., and several smaller manufactories, all of which, with its superior railway facilities, help on the perpetual boom which seems to have struck the town.

They now claim nearly 10,000 population, and are growing at the rate of a thousand a year. A system of water works has recently been completed, and contracts are out for electric lighting; surveys have been made for sewerage, and two new buildings for fire purposes have been erected.

The *North East Grocer*, August 10, 1888.

Today, Eastern Connecticut is a blur to those passing through the State on its interstate highways. Willimantic is off the beaten track, a backwater, the only major urban area in Connecticut not served directly by an interstate. Its *raison d'être,* the textile industry, has virtually disappeared. This once proud and famous manufacturing city and railroad hub has one remaining active railroad connection.

The railroad arrived in Willimantic in 1849, and launched the area into the industrial era. A fascinated crowd assembled to watch the first passenger locomotive depart Willimantic for New London. The small town had seen nothing like it before. Hundreds of people jostled for a free ride on the first train to New London. "The village was all astir," crowds of people were, "joyously anticipating their first ride...fun, frolic, noise and laughter abounded."[1]

The railroad gave the outside world access to Willimantic, and introduced an ethnic diversity unknown before. Many of the Irish laborers, who constructed the line to New London, settled in Willimantic and found work in the growing cotton industry. The native Yankees and new Irish settlers lived uneasily together.

Within a few years, several railroads passed through the town. The power of the Willimantic River had initially attracted investment capital from Rhode Island and Massachusetts during the 1820s, to manufacture cotton cloth, and the industrial revolution gained a footing in the area. Several local cotton mills amalgamated to form the Willimantic Linen Company in 1854. Windham's population tripled between 1840 and 1890, rising from 3,392 to 10,032.[2]

The Willimantic Linen Company boomed after the Civil War. Its magnificent Mill Number Two was built in 1864, and Willimantic quickly became known worldwide for the finest spool cotton thread manufactured west of Manchester, England. "Thread City" also became known for its high quality silk thread and cloth. Silkworms were nurtured in nearby Mansfield. Orchards of mulberry trees also became a common sight in Windham and Lebanon. The area's silk industry declined by the 1840s, but a revival, fired by the rapid expansion of Willimantic, began in the 1860s.

In 1881, a conference of local farmers and industrialists hoped to re-invigorate Mansfield's silk industry. At the meeting William Atwater recalled that, in his youth, his family made great profits from silk culture, producing around 130 pounds of raw material every year. He was sad that the culture of Mansfield silk had finished. The Chaffee Company's Joseph Conant told those present that whilst American-grown silk was the best in the world, it was too expensive, and his company was forced to import their requirements from abroad.[3]

Mansfield's initial agricultural interests in the mulberry bush ensured that the first mechanized production of silk thread took place in America at Hanks Hill and Gurleyville. Despite numerous antebellum attempts to manufacture silk in Mansfield, the industry grew in the urban environment of the expanding "Thread City." Willimantic's silk firms and silk loom manufacturers became known nationally, and internationally - a reputation based upon the enterprise nurtured in nearby Mansfield, Connecticut, in the area occupied today by the University of Connecticut's pastoral campus.

PART I

INDUSTRY

FORMER MILL SITES OF WILLIMANTIC, CONNECTICUT

1 Windham Manufacturing Company ———— 1823

2 Smithville Manufacturing Company ———— 1845
   (Previously the Lee Mill, 1822)

3 Turner Silk Mill ————————————— 1889

4a Holland Silk Mill 1 ——————— East Mill 1864

4b Holland Silk Mill 2 ——————— West Mill 1873

5 Natchaug Silk Company ——————— 1888

6 Chaffee Silk Company ——————— c 1870

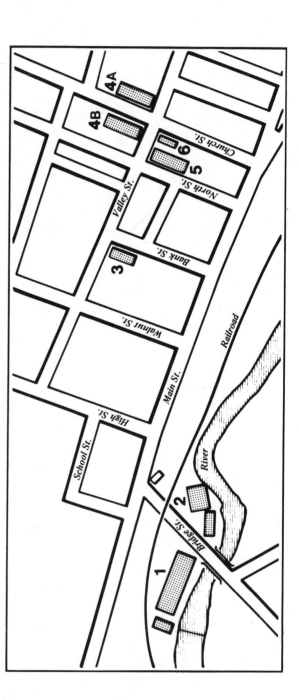

Part I

INDUSTRY

Among her manufactories, Willimantic sits supreme.
Between her lofty hills, on her own native stream
With Prospect Hill upon the north - near old Mansfield's line.
While on the south stands Hosmer's Hill, that old landmark so fine.

Down through the valley that they form, the river winds its way,
Turning the wheels of the different mills from morn till close of day.
The steady hum of the spindles is heard throughout the day.
With the regular beat of the weaver's loom where the busy shuttles play.

Way on the western border where the river runs deep and slow,
Stand the Windham Company's granite mills, built many years ago.
About half a century now, they have run day after day.
And many a yard of cotton cloth these mills have sent away.

We wondered down deep in our minds as we were passing through,
If there were any in these mills that commenced when they were new.
Not one! we think the echo came, that wrought here in days of yore;
While there are many we could name, who are on the other shore.

We pass along to Bridge Street now, - a few rods down the stream;
Here we find a noble work in the stone arched bridge is seen:
It spans the stream to bank to bank; - 'tis proper here to state,
It was built by Lyman Jordan in the year eighteen sixty eight.

On a point below Bridge Street, where the River bends I say,
Are the Smithville Company's granite mills where the busy shuttles play:
You can hear the hum of the spindles from morn to eventide,
With the merry hum of the bobbin boy as he pieces up back side.

'Tis nearly fifty years, now, since first these mills did start;
They have furnished work in all that time to many a youthful heart
Who in later years looks back I say, to those early days gone by,
When he tormented the overseer, and his patience sorely tried.

We wander down the river now, a half a mile or more,
To the Linen Company's mammoth mill, built in eighteen sixty four.
Mill Number One stands just above, built at an earlier date;
Still above stands the old spool shop, built in eighteen twenty eight.

They manufacture cotton thread of every hue and grade,
From three cord up to six cord, as good as ever was made.
The Company now stands ahead. The highest award was fixed
Upon their six cord cotton thread at the Centennial in seventy - six.
One and all, they are agreed 'tis the best thing ever seen
For use upon that household pet - the family sewing machine.

As we pass on, now, down the stream a little further still,
At the eastern end of our village, stands the Austin Dunham mill.
For years they've manufactured warps for other mills to make
Up into cloth of every grade - of every hue and shape.

Here we will pause - we stop and gaze at the river's onward flow,
Ready to turn more factory wheels in villages down below.
As we go down the valley of time, let us do the best we can -
Strive to win an honored name and assist our brother man.

If I made mistakes in dates as downstream I did go
Have charity - for the best will err, and so might L.P.0.

Willimantic *Enterprise*, February 12, 1878.

CHAPTER 1

Cotton City 1822 - 1926

In 1876, the Willimantic Linen Company received worldwide acclaim when it demonstrated its high-quality, six-cord cotton thread and manufacturing processes at the Philadelphia Centennial Exposition. By 1882, it was Connecticut's largest manufacturing company.[1] The American Thread Company, a British Trust, took control in 1898 and operated on the site until 1985. While its imposing granite mill buildings continue to dominate the physical appearance of the downtown area, the significant role played by preceding and rival companies in the local textile industry's development has been largely overlooked.

In 1706, colonial settlers built a saw and grist mill at the junction of the Willimantic and Natchaug Rivers to take advantage of water-power provided by a 90-foot drop in little more than a mile of the Willimantic River's length. Local Native Americans referred to the area as 'Wilimentuck', the "Land of the Swift Running Waters." However, nearby Windham's more favorable position on the old turnpike led to its steady growth during the colonial and early American period. By the early nineteenth-century, Windham Center was populated by farmers, artisans and traders. It was the area's political and economic base, a well-established prosperous community.

With little warning, a vibrant colorful industrial community exploded at nearby Willimantic Falls during the 1820s. A Rhode Islander, Perez O. Richmond, had recognized the potential of the fast-flowing Willimantic River. He erected a cotton mill, replete with a state-of-the-art water-wheel, on the site of the old saw and grist mills. Within a matter of months, several mills were built west of Richmond's. The industrial revolution had arrived. A nineteenth-century historian noted that, "the few previous residents of the hitherto quiet valley were almost dazed by the onset...Chaos and confusion seemed to reign supreme for a time." Willimantic's first public building was a "grog-shop," which "diffused a most lurid light." The village built to house the workers at

Richmond's new mill became known for its decadence, and was named "Sodom."[2]

In 1826, Willimantic's prosperity and America's fiftieth birthday were celebrated by local businessmen and manufacturers. A toast was proposed to the Willimantic River. Its "swift flowing waterway" was compared to the autumnal harvest, providing "...rich treasures to repay the labors of industry and art...embracing the farms, manufactures and mechanics through the country it flows." The combination of two geographical advantages - a fast flowing river, and proximity to Providence, Rhode Island, a source of investment capital, launched the area into the industrial revolution. The railroad's arrival in 1849 rapidly accelerated the process.

EARLY MILLS

In 1877, the Willimantic *Journal* recorded the abandonment of the borough's Congregational meeting hall on Main Street, built by Charles Lee in 1828. The old hall's demolition unearthed a time capsule buried in the foundations. Its contents revealed that between 1822 and 1828, Willimantic Falls had gained almost a thousand new inhabitants, plus "six cotton factories, six stores, three groceries, two shoe shops, one druggist, five blacksmiths, one millinery, two schools, two taverns and forty houses." [3]

In 1866, a "gentleman from Providence," an investor in the area's early industrial development, described Willimantic as, "too much warp with too little filling." Willimantic then stretched two miles from "Wellsville" in the east to the cemetery in the west.[4] The Rhode Islander's observation elicited a response from a long-time local resident who explained that Willimantic was a combination of four small industrial communities, built around the town's first mills in the early nineteenth-century. He recalled a jingle from his schooldays which listed Willimantic Falls' manufacturing villages: "Richmond Town, Jillson Hill, Leesburg, Tingleyville."

Richmond Town, later known as Sodom and Wellesville, was built in 1822 around the area's original cotton mill erected by Perez O. Richmond at the junction of the Natchaug and Willimantic Rivers. Richmond constructed, "a small structure of wood some 35 x 65 feet, one and a half stories in height," and filled it with cotton machinery. This small mill laid the foundation for the "immense business in manufacturing cotton" which would soon dominate the local economy.[5]

Jillson Hill was named after Asa, William and Seth Jillson who came to Willimantic from Dorchester, Massachusetts in 1824, and completed two small mills on the site occupied today by the American Thread Company's 1916 concrete warehouse. A generation later, the Jillsons employed 100 hands, 75 women and 25 men, and annually produced some $40,000 worth of print cloth from 40,000 spindles and 100 looms. The $1,400 expenditure on wages was split somewhat unevenly between the men and women, as 25 men earned $700, the same as 75 women.[6]

Leesburg was named for Charles 'Deacon' Lee who built a stone cotton mill on the east side of Bridge Street, Willimantic in 1822. Lee purchased four acres of land and water privileges extending from the river to Main Street, from Elizabeth Fitch on May 14, 1822, and "With commendable energy and perseverance he built (a) dam flume and wheel pit and erected a three-story and attic stone mill, with 36 looms."[7] Perry Richmond beat 'Deacon' Lee by a few months to become the area's first textile industrialist.[8] In 1827, Lee constructed the large granite structure, still extant, on the southeastern corner of Main and Bridge Streets, and went into partnership with Royal Jennings to sell dry goods and groceries to his millworkers. Leesburg became known as 'Smithville' after 1845, when two brothers from Providence, Rhode Island, Amos and James Smith, purchased the site.

In 1823, Mathew Watson and brothers Nathan and Arunah Tingley went into partnership and established the Windham Manufacturing Company on a site west of Bridge Street, "for the manufacture of cotton cloth,"[9] bringing 'Tingleyville' into existence. Watson and the Tingleys purchased the land to build their mill on November 4, 1822, paying $189 to local landowner Anna Fitch for eight acres of ground and water privileges south of the Willimantic River, and a further $34 for 59 rods of land and water privileges further to the east. They sealed their rights by purchasing 59 rods on the south bank of the Willimantic River for $50 from Thomas Gray, Samuel Byrnes and David Smith. The Windham Manufacturing Company also completed 62 tenement houses, which became known as the "Yellow Row."[10]

Richmond Town and Jillson Hill were absorbed by the Willimantic Linen Company in 1854. But those communities, along with Leesburg and Tingleyville had led Willimantic's charge into the industrial revolution a quarter of a century before the formation of the Willimantic Linen Company.

THE SMITHVILLE MANUFACTURING COMPANY

These cotton mills stood on the east side of Bridge Street, and were originally erected by Charles 'Deacon' Lee in 1822. Extensions were added in 1846 and 1852. The buildings were subsequently occupied by the Smithville Company, 1845-1895, the Willimantic Cotton Mills Corporation, 1895-1907, the Windham Manufacturing Company,1907-1911, and the Quidnick-Windham Manufacturing Company, 1911 - 1926. *WTHM*

The Charles Lee mill was purchased in 1845 by Amos and James Smith of Providence, who put it under the control of a wealthy local landowner, Whiting Hayden. The old community of Leesburg subsequently became known as Smithville. James Smith later became the Governor of Rhode Island.

In 1848, the Smithville mills became the site of Willimantic's first attempt to produce cotton thread, some six years before the establishment of the Willimantic Linen Company. The Smithville Company was sued for breach of patent by the Coats Cotton Company of Manchester, England, and forced to cease production.[11] Despite that setback, the Smithville Company rapidly expanded. Stone-built mill additions were erected in 1846 and 1852. In 1850, its 136 strong workforce, consisting of 81 women and 55 men, worked 176 looms, and produced $85,000 of print cloth.[12]

Three years later, the Smithville Company built stone cottages for their operatives, and provided Willimantic with its first public water pipe system, laying "a three inch diameter iron pipe, with hydrants at suitable points, from their mills down Main Street...and up High Street to Valley Street."[13] Production capacity was further increased in 1857 after another granite extension was added. At that period, the Smithville cotton mills were the most extensive in Connecticut.[14]

The Company suffered at the outset of the Civil War, when its workers joined the Union Army, and the working hours of those remaining were cut because of a shortage of raw cotton. Skilled help was rare, and to persuade weavers to stay in Willimantic, the Smithville Company allocated plots of land to cultivate vegetables, free of rent. The Windham Company followed suit to keep the "help" in town, "ready to resume labor when the state of affairs render it prudent to get into full operation again."[15]

By the time of the Civil War, the Smithville Company's operatives were mainly composed of Irish-born men and women. In early 1862, the Company suspended operations for several weeks due to an outbreak of smallpox among its "Irish" workforce. Later that year, this latter group entered into a "pitched battle" with French Canadian operatives employed at the Windham Company. There was much animosity between the Irish and the 'Canucks,' but relationships became more civilized over the years. A generation later, instead of fist fights and clubbings, differences between the companies' employees were resolved by a baseball, a bat, and a diamond.[16]

The Smithville Company prospered after the Civil War. In 1866 it was agreed that the highway approaches to the Smithville and Windham mills should be improved. The companies fully supported the borough of Willimantic in its plans to replace the old wooden bridge, which had provided southern access to the mills and Willimantic since 1828. The old bridge was constantly being rebuilt or repaired because of floods. Lyman Jordan, a local mason, built a fine stone-arch bridge from the granite located in the adjacent river banks. The bridge was opened for traffic in 1868 and, at that time, the 80-foot arch made it the second largest of its kind in Connecticut. The State's longest stone-arch bridge, of 103 feet, was built on Main Street, Hartford, in 1833. Jordan's fine structure is still in use today, and remains the third largest stone-arch bridge in Connecticut.[17]

The Smithville Company's existence was checkered by boom and bust. In 1877, it raised its dam by two feet, and installed new water wheels and flumes to increase its motive power. Production increased, and during that year it manufactured three million yards of print cloth from 428,500 lbs. of cotton.[18] By 1879, it had ceased production announcing $600,000 of debt. Over 225 hands were thrown out of work, and the local economy slumped. A local farmer complained that his milk sales had fallen by 25 quarts a day.[19] Cotton cloth manufacture was resumed in May, 1880, thanks to a financial package organized by the Chelsea Savings Bank of Norwich, Connecticut.

In 1887 the late Whiting Hayden's controlling interest was sold to Oliver A. Washbourne of Providence, Rhode Island. Despite this new owner, and others which followed, the mill was always referred to by locals as 'Hayden's mill.' Washbourne's Smithville Company peaked around 1890. Its buildings were fitted with state-of-the-art machinery, including three water wheels and a large double Corliss engine driving 20,856 spindles and 508 looms. Some 300 employees produced top quality cotton goods, including twills and prints which were distributed across America and around the world.[20] The Smithville

Company was refinanced by the Chelsea Savings Bank in May, 1891, but it was further hit by the financial panic of 1893, and went on to short-time work. It was subsequently liquidated in February, 1895, and more than 300 hands were thrown out of work.

The abandoned Smithville Company was revived by the Willimantic Cotton Mills Corporation, a company organized in November, 1895, by Englishman Joseph Mercer, a well-known proprietor of cotton mills in Greenville, Rhode Island. The following year, Mercer's new Willimantic company was providing employment for 400 local hands. Joseph Mercer operated the old Smithville mills until March, 1907, when the site was purchased by the Windham Company. Mercer had entered 1907 with debts of $80,000, and he was forced to sell the Willimantic Cotton Mills Corporation's entire stock for $75,000. It was purchased by the Windham Company's chief shareholder, Frank Sayles of Providence. Mercer's massive inventory included two Hercules water wheels of 125 and 100 horse power, and a Collins 125 hp water wheel. The Windham Company also obtained a 500 hp Corliss steam engine, and 281 weaving looms. A further influx of capital from Rhode Island enabled Willimantic's ancient mills, east and west of Bridge Street, to consolidate into one Company on November 5, 1907. The new enlarged Windham Company, now owned by a Mr. J. H. Hambly of Providence, Rhode Island, appointed Walter B. Knight, as its agent and manager.[21]

THE WINDHAM COTTON MANUFACTURING COMPANY

The Windham Cotton Manufacturing Company, more commonly known as the Windham Company, was organized in 1823, and gave birth to the Willimantic manufacturing village of 'Tingleyville'. The Company's 1825 ledger provides an intriguing glimpse of its earliest history, along with contemporary life in Willimantic Falls.

The ledger reveals that the Company employed 376 full-time and part-time hands during 1825. The men were mainly full-time workers. A male weaver made $2.50 a week, but could expect some form of gratuity payment in lieu of wages. For example, Phillip Hopkins was given rye-whisky, gin and brandy at six cents a shot. He also accepted a goose valued at 40 cents, and some nails, sugar and cheese. His annual income, including cash and 'in-kind' payments, amounted to $184.33. Alfred Robinson also received a few shots of rum, but his annual payment of $198.21, was mainly paid in "wood, lard, flour and potatoes."

The women provided a part-time workforce, and also received payment in-kind. Charlotte White made $101.34 during that year, paid in "mutton, sugar, apples, cabbage, cinnamon and salt." Her board was deducted from what little cash she received. However, Maria and Matilda Holt collected all their pay in cash. Maria was hired from August until October, and paid $15.75. Matilda

Top: The Windham Company's "east mill," erected in 1828. It was later occupied by the Quidnick-Windham Company (1911-1926) and the Willimantic Silk Company (1928-1937). The building with the mansard roof, situated behind the horse-and-cart, was built in 1873 and housed the Company's offices. It is extant and located at the western end of the Bridge Street shopping plaza. *François Gamache*

Bottom: Looking west over Bridge Street, beyond Lyman Jordan's 1868 stone-arch bridge, to the Windham Company's mills. *WTHM/Laramie*

was hired between September and November, and paid $29. 70.

The Company's largest expenditures were $1,441. 92 for "lambs, cucumbers, rice, corn, butter, wood, lamps and apples," for their boarding house; $340 for new looms; $165 for a schoolhouse, and $45 for a "yoke and oxen." The ledger details every item used to pay the workers. The itemized goods, purchased from local merchants, included, "rum, brandy, tea, nails, combs, sugar, paper, mutton and ginger."[22]

Three years later, in 1828, the Windham Company erected a granite mill, which subsequently became known as the 'east mill'. It measured 46 x 118 feet, and was equipped with "improved machinery." The Company's water power was augmented by the building of "a substantial stone dam across the river." A wooden bridge was also financed and built during that summer - and Bridge Street came into being. In 1845, a further mill extension was added, 50 x 100 feet, along with a number of brick tenements. This small community of worker-housing was known as 'Tingleyville' or the 'Yellow Row,' covering an area of 37 acres adjacent to the Willimantic River.

The growing Windham Company made a permanent impact on antebellum and postbellum Willimantic. It laid out new streets, built a company store, houses, instituted a bank, and was the first local Company to employee 'Papists,' (Roman Catholics). The Founder, Arunah Tingley, retired to Providence in 1840, and John Tracy took charge. He organized the Willimantic Savings Institute in the Company's offices in 1842, "encouraging operatives to lay up their earnings and make solid investments."[23] Tracy served unpaid as secretary and treasurer until being succeeded in 1874 by the Smithville's old agent, Whiting Hayden, who held the post until his death in 1886.

In 1847, suffering from a labor shortage, Tracy recruited five Irish laborers working on the new local railroad. This "opening wedge" of Irish immigration was described by Ellen Larned: "Hibernians settled...like an army of grasshoppers. Shanties were set up wherever they could find a footing."[24] The large influx of Irish into Willimantic led to the building of a magnificent new church, St. Joseph's, in 1874. Writing in 1920, Allen Lincoln recalled Willimantic during the late 1860s. He remembered how the Irish families, residing in his father's newly-built tenements on Center Street, fascinated and horrified everyone in town. The Yankee boys' baseball games were often interrupted by the shrill screams of Irish women announcing "hog killing time." Pigs' blood gushed from severed throats, and provided the main ingredient for an Irish delicacy called "blood puddin."

Lincoln also writes of the large steam shovels building a railway embankment in Willimantic for the Boston, Hartford and Erie Railroad. His attention was attracted to the colorful men working there, "...who were almost entirely the new-coming Irish. (They) lived in shanties near the then dense pine woods on the North Windham Road, and some lively times they used to have o' nights."[25]

The Windham Company's postbellum economic growth funded the building of an impressive structure, replete with a stylish mansard roof, to house new offices. Erected in 1873, this historic building still stands at the western end of the Bridge Street Plaza, one of the few reminders that vast granite mills formerly stood nearby. [26]

By 1877, the Windham Company had expanded its production, and was manufacturing "lawns, twills, forty-inch cotton sheets, pocketings, crinkle goods and 70,000 yards of print cloth per week." Spur railroad tracks were built to connect its premises with the New England and New London Northern railroads.[27] This expansion created a demand for new residences, and a row of brick tenements was built. Railroad travelers coming from the west into Willimantic commented favorably on the, "neat and tasty appearance of the row of new brick houses built by the Windham Company for their help. They are neat, solid and comfortable."[28] These houses, built in 1880, are still extant, and are located on Willimantic's Vermont Drive.

In 1881, the Windham Company built two large brick tenements north of Main Street. It laid curbing and a new road northwards to connect Main Street with Valley Street. The new thoroughfare was completed in November 1882, and named Windham Street. Two more streets were opened up soon afterwards as Valley Street was extended to meet Mansfield Avenue. They were named Tingley Street and Watson Street in honor of the Windham Company's founders.[29]

In 1887, the Windham Company was prosecuted for not complying with Connecticut's child labor laws. The charges were withdrawn when the agent, Thomas Chandler, explained how difficult it was detecting whether or not a child was under thirteen years of age. And what could be done if parents forced their children to work? Chandler paid a nominal fine of $54.73.[30] Willimantic's authorities did not wish to rock the boat, as the Windham Company owned some of the most desirable land inside the towns limits. This diplomacy was repaid in 1889 when the Company donated a large tract of land to accommodate Willimantic's bid to become the site of Connecticut's newest State Normal School. Norwich put in a strong claim, but the school was granted to Willimantic. Normal School classes commenced in offices in the Willimantic Savings Institute's offices, and in the 'Oaks' school, while the new school building was being constructed on the Windham Company's Valley Street lot. This forerunner of Eastern Connecticut State University opened for business in its new premises in 1896.[31]

The Windham Company hit hard times in the late nineteenth century, and was re-financed by an influx of capital from Providence, Rhode Island. The Company's owners, the Rhode Island Hospital Trust, demanded the payment of an outstanding $75,000 debt, held by a number of Rhode Island banks. This obligation was met by Charles Merriman, Robert Knight and H. I. Wells from

Providence, who put the Company on a sound financial basis. In 1907, these gentlemen purchased 'Hayden's mill,' operated by the Willimantic Cotton Mills Corporation since 1896, and built a boiler house, "fitted with the latest power-producing apparatus."

In February, 1910, Walter B. Knight, the agent of the new expanded Windham Company, announced plans to connect its east mills - the Smithville Company's two old mills - with a four-story high, 35 x 70 foot building. But, by August, 1910, Willimantic's oldest surviving cotton manufacturer closed its doors for the last time, throwing over 500 hands out of work. The closure was blamed on a shortage of raw cotton, caused by speculators hoarding it and forcing prices to rise.[32]

The Windham Company experienced difficulties recovering from this set-back, and in June, 1911, it was taken over by the Quidnick Manufacturing Company of Providence, Rhode Island, a consortium of several Willimantic businessmen, and the Windham National Bank which issued 2,500 shares priced at $100 each, guaranteeing a 7 per cent return. The new organization was named the 'Quidnick-Windham Manufacturing Company'. It operated successfully in Willimantic's historic Bridge Street cotton mills for the ensuing 15 years, giving regular employment to more than 500 locals.

On May 21, 1926, the Quidnick-Windham Manufacturing Company went into receivership, "unable to meet its obligations as they become due," and the mills east and west of Bridge Street were gradually wound down. On July 26, 1926, the Company's 79-year-old master mechanic, George B. McCracken retired after 58 years of service. He had worked with the Windham Manufacturing Company since 1868. During those 58 years, the Company often suspended operations, depending upon the economic climate, and McCracken was forced to find temporary employment in several various locations, including a cotton mill in Georgia; Stonington's Atwood-Morrison Machine Company; South Windham's Smith-Winchester Company; East Hampton's Brown Machine Company; Willimantic's Smithville Company and Holland Silk Company. But McCracken always returned to the oldest cotton company in Willimantic, where he had worked for seven different superintendents. During his faithful service, McCracken patented a steam-trap, spindle, shuttle-guard and valve - all being used by the Quidnick-Windham Manufacturing Company at the time of its demise.

The Quidnick-Windham Manufacturing Company's east mills, the old Smithville mills (1856-1895), were closed during the summer of 1926, and the west mills, occupied by the original Windham Company (1823-1911), ceased production on November 1, 1926, ending 104 years of cotton cloth manufacture in Willimantic. The final employees were overseers, Charles Clark, Daniel Cremin and James Catlow. The closure of the Quidnick-Windham Manufacturing Company, along with 52 other New England mills in 1926, was blamed upon "southern competition."[33] Cotton City was no more.

Willimantic reigned as a 'Cotton City' for more than a century, manufacturing cotton cloth and sheets from 1822 until 1926. A young man, employed as a spinner at the Windham Company during Cotton City's early days, laid the foundations for the Willimantic Linen Company to become the nation's premier producer of six-cord cotton thread. That young man, Origen Hall, was born in Mansfield, Connecticut in 1806, and worked for Tingley and Watson's Windham Company between 1824 and 1839. Hall found opportunities to be limited in Willimantic, and in 1840 he organized the Willington Thread Company with Elisha Johnson and Marshal Dimock. Origen Hall later formed a partnership with Timothy and Austin Merrick, and manufactured thread at Mansfield Hollow. He died at his Church Street, Willimantic, home in his 82nd year.[34]

The Willington Thread Company is credited as being the first American cotton thread manufacturer to finish its product with glaze. In 1855, Origen Hall sent his partner Elisha Johnson to Plymouth, Massachusetts to investigate the rumor that a recent German immigrant, John M. Heck, had built a machine which performed this task. Johnson subsequently hired Heck, and his process was employed in the Willington Company's mills. A series of revolving brushes removed the superfluous size from the cotton thread, which was then dried by hot air. Hall's glazed thread drew a great deal of envious attention from Willimantic, where two Hartford gentlemen, Austin Dunham and Lawson Ives, were unsuccessfully manufacturing linen from flax. This was in a mill not too far away from where Hall had learned all about the cotton industry.[35] The foundations for Thread City had been laid.

CHAPTER 2

Thread City 1857 - 1985

Derricks and materials begin to arrive, and soon some 200 men will be at work here, making this quiet portion of the village the theater of bustle and activity such as it never witnessed before.

Willimantic Journal, May 29, 1863

It is tempting to suggest that the history of the Willimantic Linen Company is that of Willimantic. This is untrue, as many of the Linen Company's well-publicized schemes regarding education, company stores and worker housing were initially instigated in Willimantic, albeit on a smaller scale, by the Smithville and Windham Companies. Few people today can recall the Bridge Street cotton mills, wherein the latter two companies operated for more than a century. The Willimantic Linen Company, and its successor, the American Thread Company, have become the focus of interest because the eye-catching granite mills in which they operated dominate the local skyline.

The name "American Thread" is synonymous with twentieth-century Willimantic and its current residents, but that British-owned organization can trace its roots back to several small cotton manufactories which operated in Willimantic well before the Civil War. This chapter demonstrates the Willimantic Linen & American Thread companies' links with the early industrial history of Willimantic, and the community's resultant rapid growth and increasing social problems. Two wealthy capitalists from Hartford, Connecticut initiated events in the years leading up to the South's secession. If those Dixie States had stayed in the Union, the name Willimantic would probably have not been synonymous with high grade, six-cord cotton thread - and the "Thread City" might have become better known as "Silk City."

This woodcut originally appeared in the *New York Daily Graphic* in 1877. The three-year old St. Joseph's Church can be seen on the horizon. The Willimantic Linen Company mill buildings depicted are, from left to right; Store House (c1860), Mill Number One (1826), Spool Shop (1826), Mill Number Two (1864), Mill Number Three (1877) (originally the Welles Company, 1845), the Dunham Manufacturing Company (1858). The Linen Company's newly-built store and library can be seen just to the left of Mill Number Two's chimney. *Courtesy of the New York Historical Society, New York City.*

Top: The Willimantic Linen Company's Mill Number Three stood on Recreation Park in Willimantic. The structure was built in 1845 by the Welles Company. It was taken over by the Dunham Manufacturing Company in 1858, and became the Linen Company's Mill Number Three in 1877. It was demolished after World War One. *François Gamache*

Bottom: This photograph was published as a stereo-optic view. It features Willimantic's lower Main Street, circa 1870. The photographer positioned himself on the roof of the Linen Company's Mill Number One and took this picture looking west. The building with the bell tower is the Linen Company's spool shop, originally the Jillsons' 1828 cotton mill. It was demolished in 1916. The turn-off to Jackson Street can be seen opposite the spool shop. The granite building below Mill Number One's dormer windows was utilized as a store house, and as tenement housing for workers. The steeple of the Methodist Church on Church Street can be seen in the upper-right hand corner. *WTHM/Laramie*

IVES AND DUNHAM

Lawson Ives was born in 1804 in Bristol, Connecticut, where he eventually manufactured brass clocks and mined copper, accumulating a "handsome property." Ives moved to Hartford in 1848 and engaged in the businesses of wool, sewing machines and steel manufacturing. According to his obituary, Ives "had an almost infallible intuition in the selection of the best talent to aid him in the development of the many schemes which he began, and to this faculty he himself attributed a great degree of his success." He died in Hartford on July 2, 1867.[1]

Austin Dunham was born in Mansfield, Connecticut in 1805. As a young man, he worked in a country store, and in cotton manufacturing in Coventry. He moved to Hartford in 1834, and organized A. Dunham and Sons, "dealers in cotton goods and manufacturers in cotton fabrics." Dunham invested his capital in several successful ventures across Connecticut. He died in Hartford on March 15, 1877.[2]

Ives and Dunham became involved in Willimantic industry in 1845, when they went into partnership with William L. Jillson and John H. Capen to form the Welles Manufacturing Company. These gentlemen financed the building of a three-story mill on the site of Perry Richmond's original premises, along with a number of row houses. Richmond's 'Sodom', named after the wicked biblical city in ancient Palestine, briefly became known as 'Wellesville.' The more colorful name has stuck, however, and locals still refer to this area, on Willimantic's Lower Main Street near its junction with Routes 14 and 6, as 'Sodom'.

In 1858, Austin Dunham bought out Capen and Jillson, and formed the Dunham Manufacturing Company. He built on a couple of stories and expanded the mill's productivity. By 1861, Dunham, apart from his growing interest in the Willimantic Linen Company, was employing 44 hands and producing 352,000 yards of cotton warp. In 1870, Dunham employed 60 men, 30 women, and 20 children under 16 years of age. They produced almost $200,000 worth of yarns and warp each year in a mill powered by two water wheels and one 250 hp steam engine.[4]

Dunham's health began to fail and in March, 1877, he relinquished his interest in the Hop River Warp Company in Columbia, and sold the Dunham Manufacturing Company to the Willimantic Linen Company, for $288,380.[5] Dunham's mill became the Linen Company's Mill Number Three, and was destined to be the scene of some exciting experiments in electrical lighting, carried out by his son. In 1889, Mill Number Three, the old Dunham mill, was described as being 175 feet long, 40 feet wide, with five floors and a mansard roof.[6]

Lawson Ives and Austin Dunham invested their capital wisely, until they mistakenly financed a linen manufactory in Willimantic. Yet that misjudgment

These postcard views reveal the Willimantic Linen Company's 1857 Mill Number One, and early twentieth-century developments at the American Thread Company. The top view dates from 1913. The 1828 Jillson mill, on the extreme left, was utilized by ATCO as a spool shop. In the the bottom view, circa 1920, a concrete warehouse has replaced the 1828 mill and 1860 storehouse. Mills Five and Six are connected by a new building. An enclosed concrete bridge, completed in 1918, spans Route 32 to connect Mill Number One with Mill Number Five. *WTHM*

laid the foundations for an organization which grew to quickly become Connecticut's largest industry. Ives and Dunham invested in the production of coarse linen goods and formed the Willimantic Linen Company on February 18, 1854, with capital of $75,000.[7] Historian Allen Bennet Lincoln contended that Ives and Dunham did not solely produce linen at this time. They organized the Company "to manufacture flax or cotton into yarn or cloth."[8] No trace of this early cotton venture has been located, but it is well documented that Ives and Dunham manufactured linen in a section of Asa & Seth Jillson's 1828 granite mill between 1854 and 1856.

Numerous sources attest that Ives and Dunham's short-lived venture failed because the Crimean War in Europe deprived their operation of flax. However, a nineteenth-century textile historian, Reverend William R. Bagnall, contended that Ives and Dunham, who were ordinarily acquainted with huge returns, moved into cotton thread manufactory because of the linen venture's poor profits, not because of any scarcity of raw materials. Bagnall explained that the nascent Willimantic Linen Company was unable to compete with linen manufactories in Ireland, Scotland, and "other foreign countries," which produced linen at much lower cost.

Elisha Johnson, Origen Hall's partner in the Willington Thread Company, convinced Ives and Dunham of the profitability of cotton thread manufacture. Consequently the Hartford businessmen abandoned flax, but continued to rent a portion of Jillson's mill to spin cotton thread, finishing it by the Johnson/ Heck technique[9] in a small wooden structure nearby.[10] In 1857, Johnson, who subsequently became a chief stockholder in the Willimantic Linen Company, moved his machinery from Willington, and installed it in a massive new granite mill, financed and built by Lawson Ives in Willimantic for the expanded manufacture of the Company's highly profitable and popular glazed, three-cord cotton thread.

The building of the new mill in 1857, later to be known as Mill Number One, attracted a great deal of attention. It was noted by a visitor from Hartford that Willimantic's residents merely had to scrape off the earth to find the finest granite. He welcomed the building of the large new mill, but he criticized the local authorities for allowing an alder swamp to stand between the railroad depot and Main Street. "It makes their village look more like Kansas City, rather than an old and thriving borough of New England." The swamp was drained and the mill was quickly built. It was designed to be three stories high, with a 70 foot tower. "The structure will be 300 foot long with excellent arrangements for securing good air and complete ventilation. A new stone bridge is to be built on the site of the old Iron Works Bridge."[12] The new mill was ready for operation in July, 1858.

Johnson later returned to Willington and sued Ives and Dunham for substantial damages, claiming that they had illegally patented the 'thread-finishing' technique which he had introduced to them in 1857. He demanded royalties for all the work done by the machine, originally invented by his German employee, John Heck. It was calculated that if Johnson had been successful, the Willimantic Linen Company would have owed him approximately $50,000.

In 1878, an Englishman killed his wife in Norwich, Connecticut. The subsequent lurid press reports of his trial provide an alternative account of the origins of the Willimantic Linen Company. William B. Riddle poisoned his wife so he could marry his mistress. The trial report revealed that Riddle had been hired by Dunham and Ives in 1857 to install the latest English cotton machinery in their newly-built granite cotton mill. Riddle had apparently convinced Ives and Dunham that cotton thread would be a more profitable item than linen cloth. It may have been because of Riddle's observation that Ives and Dunham approached Origen Hall and Johnson in Willington for advice and permission to produce cotton thread in Willimantic. Austin Dunham promoted Riddle to paymaster, but the Linen Company dismissed him soon afterwards when he falsified the payrolls, and pocketed the difference. Riddle moved on to Norwich and opened a twine and yarn manufactory employing 30 women. In May, 1878, shortly after the discovery of his wife's body, he was apprehended in New London while arranging to ship his machinery to New York City.[12]

Ives and Dunham recruited the services of Gardiner Hall, Origen's younger brother, to oversee their new mill. Gardiner was born in 1809 in Mansfield, Connecticut. In 1814 he started work in Mansfield's Eagleville mills, and the five-year old's weekly wage of 50 cents was paid to his parents. Gardiner became an accomplished mule spinner and found employment in Asa and Seth Jillson's Willimantic cotton mill, where he rose to become Assistant Superintendent. He left the Jillsons in 1842 and entered into several profitable ventures before being lured back to Willimantic in 1857 by Ives and Dunham, to superintend Mill Number One's erection. He remained in charge at the Willimantic Linen Company until 1864.[13] The Jillson family had laid the solid foundations upon which Ives and Dunham built the Willimantic Linen Company - a name it kept, despite its abandonment of flax manufactory, until it was taken over by the American Thread Company in 1898.

By 1828 the profits from the Jillsons' small wooden mill, at the confluence of the Natchaug and Willimantic Rivers, enabled them to construct an impressive granite mill with an ornate bell tower, which was later used as the Linen Company's wooden spool manufacturing shop. The name Jillson was synonymous with Willimantic in the years before the Civil War. The town was greatly saddened by the death of Asa Jillson's son, William Lawrence Jillson, in 1861. W. L. Jillson arrived in Willimantic in 1826, from Scituate, Rhode Island, to learn his father's trade. He subsequently became a partner in the

Jillson & Capen Cotton Machine Manufacturing Company, which prospered in antebellum Willimantic. W. L. Jillson was also the agent for the A. & S. Jillson Company, the Willimantic Duck Company and the Dunham Manufacturing Company - all Jillson family affairs.[14] In 1870, William Lawrence Jillson's son, William Curtis Jillson (1833-1898), and Ames Burr Palmer (1820-1887), patented the highly efficient 'Jillson and Palmer Cotton Opener'. This state-of-the-art carding machine cleaned 60 bales of raw cotton per week. It was manufactured in Willimantic, and large orders were shipped to cotton mills across America,

The Jillson family dominated Willimantic's economy for almost three generations. But Ives and Dunham slowly took over from them after 1865. The Willimantic Linen Company wisely stockpiled raw materials during the late 1850s, in anticipation of the Civil War. The subsequent shortage of raw cotton greatly increased its value, and Ives and Dunham made massive profits, augmented by strict protectionist measures which limited competition from abroad. The Linen Company's cotton thread was sold, at a massive profit, to fulfill a large U. S. Government order for Union Army uniforms. Thanks to its stockpile, the Linen Company was immune from the cotton famine being experienced in other New England mills. "...the (Willimantic) Linen Company have been driving every spindle in their thread mills all the past season and cannot begin to fill their orders." That was 1862, and things improved.[15]

MILL NUMBER TWO

Large war-time profits enabled the Willimantic Linen Company to expend over one million dollars to build a new mill, a boarding house and a large number of rowhouses for its growing workforce. In April, 1863, Ives and Dunham purchased the paper mill privilege in Willimantic from John Campbell of New York City. Nasin Olin, a Plainfield stonemason, was instructed to build a substantial 18-foot high granite dam to increase the already considerable water power at this point. It was east of their 1857 mill, at a location locally known as the 'Oven Hole.' Olin quarried gneiss granite from the Willimantic River bed, a type of granite ideally suited for mill construction, and began work on a "mammoth mill."[16]   Construction commenced in June, 1863. It was revealed that the new mill would be 640 feet in length, second in size in Connecticut to the Sprague mill at nearby Baltic. A grist mill, paper mill, and a saw mill, dating from the colonial period, were torn down to facilitate the construction of the vast new granite mill which subsequently became known as the Linen Company's Mill Number Two. A new road was laid connecting 'Sodom' to Lyman Jordan's "new bridge." This stone-arch bridge is still used to provide access to eastern Willimantic from Connecticut Route 32.

Olin's large granite dam was completed by September, 1863. According to the Willimantic *Journal*, it was able "to withstand the rushing floods of the rapid

The summer of 1992. Bob Beaudreault, the manager of the vacant American Thread mill site, stands on the bridge built over the Willimantic River in 1880 to connect the existing complex to the new mill, Number Four. The Linen Company's Number Two Mill (1864) can be seen in the background. *Fran Funk*

Willimantic River. It is 18 feet high, 10 feet thick at the base and six feet at the top, of solid masonry. It consists of Willimantic granite laid in water cement. It is well worth a visit before the water covers it. Now is a good time to examine it."[17]

The construction of Mill Number Two went ahead, but not without incident. Work on the walls was suspended in December, 1863, because of the severe winter weather, but more than 300 hands were retained to grade the area's new roads, and to fill in water-clogged sections with stone and gravel. A strike by carpenters slowed progress the following Spring, but the militants were "weeded out" and work resumed in late April, 1864. That incident was followed by a walk-out of laborers grading the new roads and preparing the grounds of the new mill. They were out for a week, demanding a raise in wages. The Willimantic Linen Company capitulated and paid the strikers an increase. Several weeks later, a young mason called Harvey Skinner, who had recently arrived from Monson, Massachusetts, was killed during blasting operations. His colleagues collected a sum of more than $200, a virtual fortune in 1864, for his widow and children.

By September 1864, the mill's fourth story was under construction. It drew much attention and interest, as this floor had no supporting posts. It was suspended from the roof above, providing a vast, clear space, 400 feet x 70 feet. When the looms on Bridge Street fell silent because of war-time shortages, the Willimantic Linen Company was roofing its new mill. Much work was completed during 1864, and a reporter from the local paper visited the site at the end of the year:

The largest building erected, from the foundations which were laid last year, is the new thread mill built by the Willimantic Linen Company of stone, which is 404 feet in length, 69 feet in width and four stories high, each story 12 feet high. It has two towers, one in front and the other in the rear, about midway of the main building. The front one when entirely completed, will be 125 feet high from the foundation. 100 foot of stone which is completed and 25 feet of wood which will be put on in the spring. A large water tank will be built in the tower, about 80 feet from the ground which will furnish water for washing purposes and safety against fire. The Linen Company have laid the foundation to the wheel house, which is 45 x 80 feet. They have finished their boarding house which is 96 x 45 feet, and three stories high. They have moved and fitted for tenements, two houses and have built 18 one story and a half tenement houses, each designed for two families, besides doing an immense amount of grading and other work. We do not know how much money the Company have expended during the past year, but it has been quite a pile. Considering the war, the times and especially the high cost of building materials and labor, we think we have done pretty well, but this is only the beginning. Willimantic is bound to go ahead and we only need manufacturing prosperity to make still more rapid progress.[18]

Indeed, Willimantic did "go ahead" thanks to the Linen Company's vast expenditure which transformed the eastern section of the town. Four more large mills were added during the next half-century, and Willimantic cemented its reputation as America's Thread City. Mill Number Two's impressive gothic architectural lines still dominate eastern Willimantic, and the village built to house the mill's workers is still a vibrant part of the community.

IVERTON

Mill Number Two's gothic-style tower drew national acclaim. Equally notable, however, was the "new village" being erected across the road to attract experienced cotton mill workers to Willimantic. The Linen Company initially erected a large boarding house, resembling a "fine hotel," during the Fall of 1863, for single women workers. It was completed with the frontage facing east, but was later lifted and wheeled around so that this elevation faced Mill Number Two, and was used to lodge the new mill's construction workers. At Christmas, 1866, the boarding house's managers, Mr. & Mrs. Bartlett, provided "music, mimickry and games" for the first female residents.[19]

By the spring of 1864, the Linen Company had built more than 40 two-family houses. Locals named the area "Threadville," but the Company, persuaded by a campaign conducted by the Willimantic *Journal*, named its "new village" in honor of Lawson Ives. "Iverton" became a much sought after address:

> The cottages are each calculated for two families and are neat, pleasant and convenient. They are located on parallel streets running east and west. Those on the front extend almost to Wellsville. They are set at a sufficient distance apart and each has an ample yard in the rear. The surface, to the depth of several feet, has been graded by sandy gravel and it will always be dry and clean about the premises. The dwellings completed are occupied, and already the locality is assuming the appearance of a habitable village.[20]

Iverton was a unique name in the United States. The Linen Company conducted a nation-wide search and discovered that the closest-sounding name of a village, town, city or post office, was Louisiana's Iverson. The Company's publicity department produced an interesting pamphlet in 1868. Purported to be a history of the 14 year-old company, it includes an interesting description of Iverton:

> The houses, methodically arranged, present a fine and cheerful appearance, so different from that to which the eye of the dweller in the great city is accustomed, that the mind turns back to those pretty white cottages with a sense of restness and quietness almost unknown to the residents of a city like New York. The rent of these houses is a mere nominal sum. For similar accommodations in New York or vicinity, five times the amount of rent would be demanded.[21]

The Linen Company's postbellum motto was "spend, spend, spend." The new mill's capacity demanded increased water power, and Dunham and Ives had no hesitation in investing capital to build a large dam at nearby Columbia to back up the water, creating a vast lake which could be drawn upon when summer droughts reduced the Willimantic River's water power. The dam was constructed during the summer of 1865 by Palmer Sessions and Charles Baldwin. They employed 25 men and five teams of horses to build the 20-foot tall, 130 foot wide dam, which created Columbia Lake over 278 acres of local meadow land. Once operational, the Willimantic Linen Company had access to water power unsurpassed in New England.[22]

THE NEW OFFICE

The addition of fine new office premises was an ideal finishing touch to the new mill. Gneiss granite was also used in its construction, work beginning in October 1865. The building was completed, and fully furnished and decorated, by the end of the following year. In 1867, Eugene Stowell Boss, a future mill agent, gave a local reporter an extensive tour:

> By the politeness of Mr. E. S. Boss, the book-keeper of the (Willimantic) Linen Company, we were shown around the new office which the Company have just completed. It stands within the grounds of the company's new mill and is built of "gneiss" or "Willimantic" granite. The outside is well finished and looks quite substantial. The inside is equally as substantial and is finished in a superb manner. There are three principal rooms, viz, Director's, Agents and Book-Keepers. Besides a capacious passage way, wardrobe, cellar, attic, etc; The Director's room which is in the South Western corner of the building is magnificently furnished with sofas, easy chairs, center table, Brussels carpet, marble mantel and open fire grate. It is connected by heavy folding doors with the Agents's room which is furnished in a somewhat plainer style. The book-keeper's room is in the opposite side of the building and is well furnished with desks, tables and safe and carpets in the same manner as the other rooms. The woodwork of the doors and that around the windows is of chestnut, profusely paneled with heavy black walnut moldings and all finished with a rich furniture gloss. The ceiling is finished with molded work, and in each room a heavy chandelier hangs from it. The windows are large, the sash of cherry with black walnut casings held to them, placed by silver headed screws, and the light of the sun is let in or kept out at will by a combined blind and curtain. The woodwork was superintended by Mr. Dwight Potter, the boss carpenter of the company, and reflects considerable credit upon his taste and skill in that department. The office is considered to be the finest in the state. The Linen Company, which is now the largest thread manufacturing establishment in the United States, employs between 500 and 600 hands, but with only half of their space for machinery occupied, and they are constantly increasing their working force and adding new machinery. [23]

In 1894, many of the office's original functions were transferred over the road to the building which now houses the Windham Textile & History Museum. The Linen Company's directors met in the granite office for many years. It also housed the Company's design engineers and draftsmen, and was later utilized by the human resources staff. Today, this fine structure serves as offices for the vacant mill site's property manager, Bob Beaudreault.

SOCIAL IMPLICATIONS OF RAPID ECONOMIC GROWTH

Willimantic, the "quiet, industrious village" visited by the Connecticut historian John Warner Barber in 1835, was totally transformed by the formation of the Willimantic Linen Company after 1854. However, the area's rapid physical and economic growth created problems. During the 1860s, the local newspaper recounted much drunkenness and debauchery. Intemperance was seen to be "alarmingly on the increase in Willimantic, and has been for some time." The town's "saloons and groggeries" never closed, not even on the Sabbath. A "notorious Irish groggery" on Jackson Street sold "liquid fire" on the "Sabbath." Jackson Street was full of "noisy" and "beastly drunken" men, causing a constant nuisance to the "quiet people" in the neighborhood. Crime and disorder was on the increase: "Of the last 30 criminal cases brought before the (Willimantic) court, nine were for intoxication and twelve were for assault and breaches of the peace where liquor was a direct, inciting cause."[24]

The Irish mill builders worked and played hard. They labored for $1.25 a day. Seventy-five of them went on strike in the spring of 1864. Ives and Dunham refused their demands for a 25 cents a day raise, and sacked them. The workers, many of them from County Kerry, resided in an unsightly shanty-town located on the aptly named "Kerry Hill." The dwellings stood in stark comparison to the handsome new village of Iverton. Lawson Ives purchased the hill and tore down the Irish workers' crude abodes, located in the area known today as "Carey Hill." Needless to say, the Irish families were somewhat displeased at the destruction of their homes.

Tensions between the Irish workforce and the Willimantic Linen Company came to a head when a dozen Irishmen, armed with clubs, planned to murder their foreman, a "Mr. Roberts," while he was alone tending the horses in the Company barn. They were distressed by Roberts' continual mistreatment of the Irish building laborers, and launched a murderous attack on him in the darkened barn. The foreman grabbed a club, and fought his way out of their midst, finding safety in a small room in the barn. When Roberts' assailants tore the door down, it alerted other workers sleeping in the recently-built boarding house, and they charged to the foreman's rescue. Roberts refused to identify his assailants, but from then on he worked armed with a pistol.[25]

Despite the attendant social problems, the Willimantic Linen Company experienced unprecedented growth after 1866. British cotton thread dominated the antebellum domestic market, but restrictions on imports, and the dollar's wartime devaluation increased the price of British cotton fourfold, enabling Willimantic spool cotton to dominate the home market during the war and reconstruction years. The thread was considered to be:

> ...equal to the finest English cotton imported. It runs in sewing machines as well as silk twist and has the additional merit of cheapness.

When the (Linen) Company get their large and splendid new mill in operation with their improved machinery, large experience and unrivaled facilities we believe that they will turn out six corded cable cotton superior to any produced in Europe or this country.[26]

A young man named William Eliot Barrows arrived in Willimantic in 1874. He was interested in the social problems caused by America's rapid industrialization during the years after the Civil War. Barrows believed he could resolve the confusion emanating from a society being torn apart by the painful transition from agrarian to industrial production. The wealthy Willimantic Linen Company provided Barrows with an experimental stage to exercise his fertile mind. Another chapter in Willimantic's colorful history was about to begin.

CHAPTER 3

William Eliot Barrows

*This mill and these people are my life, my career, the next greatest
responsibility I have in the world after that of my own family*

W. E. Barrows, 1883

William Eliot Barrows, circa 1895

A man born in Ohio in 1842 left an indelible mark on Connecticut's postbellum history. Between 1874 and 1883, William Eliot Barrows, the son of a Connecticut-born theologian, attempted to 'civilize' a rapidly growing textile community. The potential agent of change at the time was socialism. Barrows despised socialism, but he knew that modifications had to be made to the nation's social fabric during the difficult years of rapid industrialization and political and economic reconstruction. He looked upon America's problematic industrial classes as misguided children, who required some fatherly discipline and guidance. Barrows strongly believed in the reforming powers of education and culture. If the mainly immigrant workers were exposed to these things, they might be somewhat less inclined to riot, strike and drink.

When 32-year-old Barrows arrived in Willimantic in the mid 1870s, to organize the Linen Company's finances, it resembled a frontier town. Violence and drunkenness was a way-of-life. Willimantic's central position, in the northeast corridor between New York City and Boston, meant that the numerous railroad routes passing through the community often deposited the flotsam and jetsam of American society on its doorstep, much to the chagrin of its predominantly hard-working Irish Catholic community, who were attempting to shake free from Yankee prejudice.

Barrows and the Willimantic Linen Company were made for each other. Barrows arrived in Willimantic full of ideas. The Linen Company's six-cord cotton thread was so successful that shareholders received astronomical returns. The wealthy Company constantly looked for ways to further invest in its future growth. It paid excellent wages and provided first class accommodation for its workers. The Company's progressive reputation increased after founder Austin Dunham passed control to his liberal-minded son, Austin Cornelius Dunham - who was responsible for hiring Barrows in 1874.

A. C. Dunham was in control. Barrows had the ideas. The Company had the resources. All the ingredients were present, and Willimantic was to become the scene of some dramatic activity. Before examining Barrows' social programs, it is worthwhile to briefly examine the influences in his early life which may have shaped his paternalistic attitude to those less fortunate than himself.

GETTYSBURG, LOWELL AND WILLIMANTIC

William Eliot Barrows was born on July 14, 1842 in Hudson, a small town between Cleveland and Akron, Ohio, the eighth of Elijah and Sara Barrows' 10 children. William's early life was shaped and tempered by a strict Christian upbringing. His father, Elijah Porter Barrows, was born in Mansfield, Connecticut in 1805. He graduated from Yale in 1826 with a degree in divinity, and taught in schools and colleges until 1835, when he was appointed pastor of the First Free Presbyterian Church in New York City. From 1837 until 1852, Elijah Barrows was professor of sacred literature at the Western Reserve College in

Ohio. In 1853, he was appointed professor of Hebrew language at the Andover Theological Seminary in Massachusetts. By 1866, the distinguished and widely admired professor had retired to Middletown, Connecticut, where he produced several religious tracts. In 1872, he returned to Ohio, and taught at the Oberlin Theological Seminary. E. P. Barrows died in Oberlin in 1888, aged 83.[1]

William was born while his father was teaching at the Western Reserve College in Ohio. When the Civil War broke out, the Barrows family were living in Andover, Massachusetts. Nineteen year-old William signed on as a hospital steward, holding the rank of private, in the 19th Massachusetts Volunteers. The letters he wrote home to his family between 1861 and 1865 reveal much about his character. Those to his mother are chatty and relaxed; to his father somewhat stiff and formal.[2]

Barrows detested army life. He was horrified by the stench of piled, decomposing bodies; bemoaned the quality, and lack, of food, the awful weather, the ruthless execution of deserters, and the endless marching through knee-deep mud. He became despondent and asked his father to arrange a transfer to the navy. Elijah assured his son that he was better off in the army because there were no chaplains or religious privileges in the navy. William explained to his father that his regiment had no chaplains, and that the very hard army life was much worse than the navy, and wrote that he could not think of more than four men in the whole regiment with whom he chose to associate.

William Barrows hated life in the ranks with a passion. But in March, 1863 he was promoted to second-lieutenant, and his quality of life improved dramatically. His desires for a maritime life declined. The letters home became more cheerful and positive. He confessed to his mother that he never smoked, drank liquor, chewed tobacco or swore and, as far as he knew, only one other man in the regiment could say the same. He wrote his father and apologized for not having any formal education.

Between March, 1862 and March, 1864, Barrows was assigned to the Army of the Potomac and became known personally by Generals Alexander S. Webb and George M. Meade. In 1863 Lieutenant Barrows was appointed Webb's aide-de-camp and a close friendship developed between the two men.

Alexander Stewart Webb (1835-1911) graduated from West Point in 1855, and is renowned for holding the "bloody angle" or the "stone wall corner" during Pickett's famous charge at the Battle of Gettysburg. In 1865, Webb was appointed Chief-of-Staff to General George Meade and took his young aide-de-camp with him. After the war, Webb became professor of ethics and history at West Point. In 1869, he was appointed President of the College of the City of New York, a post he held with distinction until 1902. Webb's progressive philosophy impressed his young aide-de-camp, and probably provided some of the basis for Barrows' subsequent social experimentation at Willimantic.

Barrows became well-known in industrial circles, but his war-time actions also drew some attention. At the height of the Battle of Gettysburg, Lieutenant Barrows took command of three Vermont companies and performed a successful flanking operation. This was his first taste of action, and William proudly sent his father a Confederate officer's sword, and made a walking cane from the captured flag staff of a Virginia regiment, which he used for the rest of his life.

Barrows' formative years were spent in an élite Yankee culture. Upper-class life in nineteenth-century America mirrored that in Great Britain, where paternalism was defined as *noblesse oblige* - those more fortunate being obliged to look after the lower orders. Barrows' perception of his own social standing is revealed in a December, 1864 letter to his sister Sara, in which he thanked her for making him a new cap with fancy braid. The cap greatly impressed his commanding officer, Captain Pelton, who asked Barrows if Sara would make him a similar one. Barrows wrote to Sara that he thought Pelton, of Middletown, Connecticut, was a "first-rate, good looking fellow," but he also suggested that Sara should not make Pelton a similar cap, because, "...he has no birth."

Shortly after Gettysburg, Barrows was promoted to First Lieutenant, and quickly attained the position of Brevet Major when working with General Meade's Staff. Barrows was mustered out of service in July, 1865, and he used two of the nation's most popular and well known war heroes as references as he sought employment. George Meade wrote: "...Captain Barrows served at my HQ, Army of the Potomac...I knew him to be a young gentleman of high character and a most gallant and meritorious officer, and if you can find him the appointment he seeks, I shall consider it a personal favor for which I will be duly grateful."[3] Alexander Webb recommended Barrows for a job as an instructor at the West Point Military Academy:

> William E. Barrows...desires some temporary employment. He has been for some time in the Lowell Machine Shop, and is now ready to take charge of some works, but would in the meantime like the position of assistant to you...General Meade is very fond of Barrows since he found him to be a valuable as an officer of the General Staff. For my own point of view I can hardly say enough in his favor. He is well educated, intelligent, industrious and most trustworthy.[4]

Back in October, 1864, Barrows had informed his father that one of his commanding officers was "an extensive wagon manufacturer" and had offered him a job after the war. His interest in manufacturing processes led to his decision to fully learn the engineering trade at the Lowell Machine Shop in Massachusetts.

Barrows' wartime letters reveal his warm personality, his high moral standards, his genial relationships with his family - and an intense respect for the family's strict, religious patriarch, Elijah. His outlook was further honed by

Alexander Webb, and by postwar work at the Lowell Machine Shop, where his interests in the welfare of America's industrial classes began. Barrows later admitted that he had been highly interested in the workers' living conditions at Lowell, just as he had been by the welfare of the soldiers under his command during the Civil War.

When the war was over, Barrows worked as an engineering apprentice at the Lowell Machine Shop. In 1872, he was appointed manager of the Ivanhoe Paper Mills in Paterson, New Jersey, and became involved in the importation of industrial machinery from Great Britain. Barrows' skills and business acumen attracted the attention of the Willimantic Linen Company, which hired him in 1874, and put him to work in Hartford as an assistant-treasurer. When Austin Dunham died in 1877, Barrows became vice-president, general manager and treasurer. Barrows was appointed president in May, 1882, on the death of the post's previous incumbent, Thomas Smith. He now wielded considerable power - too much for his opponents in the Company who considered him to be an overspending eccentric. By 1883, Barrows had redirected much of the Willimantic Linen Company's extensive wealth away from its stockholders, and invested it in several controversial schemes.

In 1877, America's industrial communities were aflame with radical political ideas imported from Europe. The foreign creed of socialism took root in the country's industrial communities and alarmed America's establishment. But Barrows had no wish to shoot or bayonet the nation's revolting and striking workers. He believed he could groom them to sophistication, and subsequently displayed a great deal of paternalistic benevolence towards Willimantic's "uneducated and primitive" French Canadian and Irish workforce. But Barrows was no egalitarian. He didn't believe in worker empowerment - he just created more subtle ways to control them.

Barrows provided free food and drinks, which he distributed to his workers during extended coffee breaks, and built a company store-and-library, a dance pavilion, advanced housing, and the largest mill in the world, containing a special ambience thanks to the colored glass in its windows and its numerous tropical flowers and plants. This mill was also the first designed specifically to be illuminated by electricity. Barrows also provided social and educational programs. The cost was astronomical, but this persuasive and charismatic hero of Gettysburg argued that the Company's investment would be repaid tenfold.

William Barrows also greatly impressed Richard T. Ely, an up-and-coming young economist. But he also managed to alienate many of America's leading industrialists and economists, including George M. Pullman, and William Graham Sumner - to say nothing of profit-starved directors at the Willimantic Linen Company during the early 1880s.

DANIEL PIDGEON

Numerous sources recall William Barrows' achievements in Willimantic between 1876 and 1883. One of the most informative was published in England in 1884. Daniel Pidgeon, an English engineer and travel writer, had toured America's rapidly industrializing Northeastern states during 1883. He believed that the future of the American people was the greatest question of the "modern world" and perceived that answers would be provided by America's "men of English blood." He was impressed by conditions in the industrial towns he encountered, compared to those in Britain. Pidgeon was surprised by the relatively high standard of living enjoyed by the American working class. He published his thoughts and observations in a volume entitled *Old World Questions and New World Answers*, wherein Americans were defined as "social alchemists" employing "democracy" to transform workers from "base metal" into "precious metal." According to Pidgeon, America modified inferior national traits by separating "obstinacy from English courage, superstition from French thrift, indolence from Irish shrewdness, want of enterprise from Scandinavian industry, shiftlessness from negro docility and indifference from Chinese skill and patience."[5]

Pidgeon had traveled widely around New England and Connecticut before arriving in Willimantic in the spring of 1883, but he had met no one quite like Anglophile William Barrows, or seen such impressive textile mills or innovative social programs. Barrows was the personification of Pidgeon's 'social alchemy' - experimenting in his own personal laboratory called Willimantic. Pidgeon entitled Chapter 13 of his book: "The Willimantic Thread Company - Benevolent Mill Owning," wherein he introduced Barrows' innovations:

> Let us now go and look at (Barrows) work. The mill will invite us first, then the library, reading rooms, schools, and art schools, next the splendid co-operative stores, where his people - I had almost said his family - supply all their wants. Afterwards we will visit the industrial village of Oakgrove (the "Oaks"), enter some of its pretty houses, and last, not least, spend a few moments at the president's own simple but charming home, which, accessible to all Oakgrove, crowns a little eminence in the very centre of the operative settlement.[6]

Profitability and worker control lay behind the benevolent facade. Barrows' company store was no cooperative. The workers did not share in its profits or benefit from lower prices. After a promising start it failed badly and soon folded, earning Barrows numerous enemies. The bitter pill of the store was sweetened somewhat by the introduction of a library and reading rooms, which survived until 1941. The store, which now houses the Windham Textile & History Museum, was forced upon the workers.

THE LINEN COMPANY STORE

William Barrows' imposing 1877 building served as a company store from 1877 until 1884. It was leased to private parties in 1885. The stores, on the first two floors, were converted into company offices in 1892. The company library, located on the third floor, operated between 1878 and 1941. The Windham Textile & History Museum took over the building in 1988. *WTHM*

In February, 1877, the Willimantic Linen Company was hit by a massive $345,000 increase in city taxes.[7] Company Treasurer Barrows planned to recoup some of that money by cornering the Willimantic market in food, clothes and dry goods. The Company demolished a saloon at the junction of Union and Main Streets, and commenced to build a large store. Its dramatic architectural lines attracted much attention, as it approached completion. The new building was designed in a style which Barrows believed to be typical of Elizabethan England. A library and reading room would be installed in its loft, replete with vaulted ceiling. But revenge was in Barrows' mind during the summer of 1877, and the reading rooms could wait a while.

Barrows' store opened for business in October, 1877. He hired George Purinton as supervisor, and put him in charge of 17 clerks. The first floor featured a meat-and-oyster market and an extensive grocery store. The second floor housed a dry goods and boot-and-shoe department and a millinery shop. In 1878, the new store's turnover exceeded $125,000.[8] The Hartford *Courant* was duly impressed:

> On the first and second floors is a store, unsurpassed in all New
> England for convenience and neatness, where meats, groceries and dry-
> goods of the best quality are bought at lowest market rates, are sold low
> for cash, customers getting the benefit of the company's high financial
> standing in the purchase of their goods. [9]

The *Courant* failed to notice that the Linen Company's workers were not
allowed to pay in cash. The goods sold in the store were of the highest quality,
and every customer received correct weights and measures - but the Company's
hands were virtually forced to shop in Barrows' new all-purpose supermarket.
Barrows had devised a system of "pass-books...ingenious order-cards...as good
as cash." Each individual card was punched to represent the price of the goods
purchased by the employees. The cash value was then deducted from their
wages.[10] Barrows also reduced the store's cash prices for those people not
employed by the Linen Company - which took more business away from the
local merchants who, as selectmen, had hiked his company's taxes.

Willimantic's traders and businessmen responded by instigating a price-war
with the new store. The price-cutting was welcomed by consumers, but in April,
1882, Barrows was forced to cut the store's inventory in half. His critics argued
that the dry goods, boot-and-shoe and millinery departments were deterring
outside businesses from locating in town. A month later, the dry goods
department was closed, and Barrows converted the millinery shop into a large,
spacious office, which he occupied during his remaining months in Willimantic.
Only the grocery and meat departments were fully maintained, as they
produced the largest profits.[11] The Willimantic *Chronicle* was delighted, and
hoped that the Company would quickly:

> ...abolish the whole establishment...and...remove a widespread local
> enmity which has sprung up against the company on this account...That
> the interests of the Linen Company and Willimantic are identical is
> mythical, for little of the earnings go into the pocket books of our
> citizens - the stock is owned abroad...Abolish the store and become one
> of the real factors in the town's prosperity![12]

After Barrows resigned in October, 1883, the store was closed down, and on
January 1, 1884, it was officially wound up as a Willimantic Linen Company
Corporation. Its vacant departments were leased to private concerns. Initial
negotiations with Norwich businessmen, Messrs. Stead and Setchel, to lease the
vacant store, fell through, and it lay unused for more than a year, save for the
third-floor library and Barrows' old office.

On April 15, 1885, the vacant store was purchased by Julius Pinney of
Hartford, who converted it into a meat and grocery market. Pinney had
managed the Cheneys' company store in Manchester, Connecticut, but even his

vast experience failed to make Barrows' old store into a profitable concern. In May, 1889 Pinney sold it to W. E. Amidon and Charles Dimmick, the proprietors of the Windham Company's store, located at the junction of Bridge Street and Main Street. They too met with little success, and abandoned the business in 1892.

Several weeks after the departure of Amidon and Dimmick, the Willimantic Linen Company brought in an army of workmen. The store's interior was completely overhauled and remodeled. Offices were built on the first two floors to accommodate the agent, the superintendent and his assistant, clerks and draftsmen.[13] A fireproof vault was installed. Hot-air heating was supplied through a 24-inch conduit which ran underground from Mill Number Two's boiler room. The second floor was converted for general office work. The mill agent, Eugene Boss, moved from the stone office building in front of Mill Number Two into a new "light and roomy private office" on the same floor. The old meat-and-oyster market on the south side of the first floor was converted into an office for the Company's purchasing agent, chief clerk and paymaster.[14] The renovations were completed by March, 1893. The store's tempestuous, eventful 15-year history was over. The Dunham Hall Library continued to be highly popular, and it helped the Linen Company recoup some of the good will lost in the community by the introduction of a store designed to coerce its workers to shop there, and undercut Willimantic's merchants.

DUNHAM HALL LIBRARY

On Saturday, March 2, 1878, Barrows opened his pet project in the top story of his new store - a company library and reading rooms. He explained in an interview at the time that he had been impressed with similar schemes developed in England by Sir Titus Salt.[15] Barrows stocked his library with 600 volumes, all gifts from wealthy benefactors enriched from being Willimantic Linen Company shareholders. Four hundred books were checked out on the opening day. The library was dedicated to the memory of the Company's founder, and named Dunham Hall. It was open daily from five in the afternoon until nine-thirty in the evening, and was considered to be, "one of the most charming rooms of its size in the State...lighted with gas...beautifully finished in wood (with) two open fireplaces with wood mantles." The reporter further enthused that, "the sight of it is a temptation to sit down and enjoy it... The lack of places like this is what has so seriously affected the morals of our manufacturing towns."[16]

The library grew quickly. Its opening hours were extended in 1879, and the number of texts had more than doubled to 1,300. By 1889 it had grown to 2,500 volumes; in 1920, the collection numbered 7,000 works, consisting of essays, biographies, poetry and fiction, "all carefully selected." The "convenient and warm" reading room was furnished with comfortable seats so patrons could,

Barrows' Dunham Hall Library, photographed October 1, 1896. Charles Noel Flagg's portrait of Austin Dunham, the Willimantic Linen Company's founder, can be seen at the right of the picture. The library was used by three generations of Willimantic people. *WTHM*

"...read to their heart's content." Adjoining the main hall was a small room used for lectures and games where visitors played chess and checkers, but gambling was strictly prohibited.[17]

The library's visitors worked and chose their books under the austere stare of Austin Dunham. It was said that Dunham's eyes followed borrowers and readers around the library. In 1880, the Company spared no expense and commissioned Charles Noel Flagg to paint the late Austin Dunham's portrait. Flagg was considered to be Connecticut's leading contemporary portrait painter. He was studying at L'Ecole des Beaux Arts in Paris when he received the lucrative commission. Barrows mailed photographs of Dunham to Paris, and several months later the completed portrait was briefly exhibited at the Company's Hartford offices before being hung in the Dunham Hall Library, where it intimidated several generations of library patrons.[18]

The library was dominated by a fearsome custodian named Jenny Ford. Born in Norwichtown in 1840, she had been employed by the Linen Company as a clerical worker since 1859, and was librarian from 1878 until her death in 1904. Her successor, Hattie Gates, was equally as strict.[19] Despite Dunham's 'all-seeing eyes' and the formidable Misses Ford and Gates, everyone was welcome, whether or not employed by the Linen Company.

Barrows arranged a number of cultural programs in his library, including a free drawing school and a series of educational lectures. His most popular institution was a school, where the Company's most talented vocalists received free singing lessons. The classes, held on Monday and Thursday evenings, were often attended by more than 200 operatives. Several choirs were formed and Barrows hired the Loomer Opera House [20] to stage a grand concert. It was attended by a packed house of 1,500 consisting of invited guests and Company employees.[21]

In October, 1882 Barrows gave Dunham Hall over to Sadie Bailey, a labor organizer from Philadelphia. She lectured about labor reform, and asserted that institutions like Dunham Hall existed because of newspapers such as *Labor World*, and work done by labor organizers. She added that: "the spirit of advancement and humanitarianism exhibited by the (Willimantic Linen Company) has been made possible and practicable by the progressive influence of labor reformers who are spreading the light of truth and justice all o'er the earth ringing out the glad tidings of joy that 'Labor is Honorable.' "[22]

Barrows' progressive ideas regarding labor reform were underpinned by a strict, Protestant moral code, inherited from his father. In April, 1878, he hired a pastor, the Reverend Lemuel Wells, to organize weekly Episcopalian church services and a children's Sunday school in the library, at ten in the morning, two in the afternoon and seven in the evening. By 1882, the school and services were highly popular, and Barrows rewarded the Sunday school's 125 members with outings, entertainments and picnics.[23] He believed that Willimantic's next generation of millworkers, those now under his influence as children, would be easier to control than those currently enriching Willimantic's saloon keepers each evening. He "civilized" his wayward French Canadian and Irish operatives by teaching them to read, speak and write in English. If he was successful, the Company would be able to deploy its workforce much more efficiently. In the 1880s, workers were often placed in ethnic groupings, to assist communications. This practice continued for many years, but it was considered to be somewhat inefficient.

In the summer of 1882, Barrows announced that all Linen Company employees who could not read or write in English by July 4, 1883, would be dismissed. He hoped that this threat would accelerate the Americanization of his mainly foreign-born workforce. Daniel Pidgeon thought this was an excellent idea: "If Barrows knows that if he is to make Americans of his alien operatives, he must begin by educating them. There is not, however, a man, a woman, or child in the mill who will be qualified for discharge under this notice."[24] Pidgeon was wrong.

Barrows provided free night classes in the Dunham Hall Library, conducted by Charles and Mary Emma Peck, on Tuesday and Thursday evenings to teach "the rudiments of reading and writing." On the first night Dunham Hall was over run with applicants, so two more classes were organized on Monday and Wednesday evenings for female instruction. Males attended on the original two evenings. Twenty-four double schoolroom desks were installed in the games room to accommodate 172 illiterate millworkers. Nevertheless, a large number of operatives lost their jobs after the literacy deadline.

Barrows' critics believed that his literacy drive was a plan to weed out undesirables. Unfortunately, 'the baby was thrown out with the bathwater' as some valued and highly skilled employees were forced to leave, fueling further opposition to his schemes. Barrows could not win. He was also criticized for showing favoritism to some workers. A local newspaper noted that "discrimination is being made in favor of those who have been long in the company's service and are too far advanced in years to learn and they are being retained."[25]

Although the Willimantic Linen Company dispensed with Barrows' store after his departure in 1883, it continued to invest in his library. In 1886, the library staged an operetta with piano accompaniment, performed by America's most accomplished singers, including Katie Carroll, of Providence, Rhode Island, who brought the house down with her rendition of "Way Down Upon The Suwannee River."[26]

The library continued to be a community focal point for three more generations. In 1925, American Thread employees were strongly encouraged to visit the Dunham Hall Library and read some of the 25 newspaper and magazine titles to which the Company subscribed. They were reminded that, "A college education is not necessary...if you have not got a good education, you can get it at no cost. It is all in the books, and inspiration and happiness as well." Each employee was urged to possess at least three books, the Holy Bible, a Savings Bank Book, and the works of Shakespeare.[27] Barrows' influence was still apparent, some 42 years after he had left the Company. The Dunham Hall Library was closed to the public in 1941. The American Thread Company donated 600 of the library's volumes to the American armed forces preparing for Second World War action.[28]

FOLLIES?

Many of William Barrows' projects, such as free uniforms and meals for workers, were abandoned by the Linen Company after he departed in 1883. Several of his projects, however, could not be disposed of so easily. Barrows' opponents pointed to his so-called follies, such as the "Oaks," a worker housing project centered on Quercus Avenue in the southern suburbs of the town, the Willimantic Fairgrounds, Mill Number Four, and the Barrows House. However, these 'follies' greatly interested the Company's new British owners when they arrived in town.

A British conglomerate, the American Thread Company (ATCO) absorbed the Willimantic Linen Company, and other New England cotton mills in 1898.

The house which Barrows built. His Willimantic residence overlooked his "Oaks" development. This photograph was taken in 1909, when the house was occupied by Dr. Louis I. Mason and utilized as a private hospital. Extensive renovations were undertaken in 1911, when Mason built a large three-story extension which contained operating rooms, kitchens and convalescent rooms. The 1881 building, along with its 1911 extensions, was demolished in the 1960s. *François Gamache*

ATCO invested heavily in Willimantic's material and human stock to improve the workers' social and cultural welfare, while resisting the attempts of the American Federation of Labor to organize its employees.

ATCO discovered that William Barrows had laid some firm foundations. Leading engineers and managers from England were installed in Barrows' "Oaks" cottages. In 1915, Barrows' Willimantic Fairgrounds were improved, and re-named "Recreation Park." The area was subsequently sold to the City of Willimantic in 1939 for one dollar, and "other considerations." ATCO also financed and supported Barrows' Dunham Hall Library until 1941.

ATCO added machinery to unused space in the mammoth Mill Number Four, and began new construction. Mill Number Five was built in 1899, Mill Number Six in 1907, a bleach house in 1910, a connecting mill between Five and Six, and a concrete warehouse in 1916. ATCO also continued to finance and maintain Barrows' "Oaks" development until 1938, when all company housing was disposed of by auction.

THE OAKS

The Linen Company's "Oaks" cottages on Quercus Avenue near completion in early 1881.
Canadian Center For Architecture, Montreal (CCAM)

Worker housing built locally by the Willimantic Linen Company, Iverton (1864) and the "Oaks" (1880), compares well in design and originality to any erected during the nineteenth century in America or Europe. William Barrows designed and constructed some 40 unique single-family homes to attract skilled workers to the Willimantic Linen Company's expanding business. Their innovative appearance attracted much favorable attention, and muted early criticism. Ground was broken in June 1880 at an area south of the town historically known as the "grove of oaks." The main thoroughfare of this "city of cottages" was named Quercus Avenue ("Quercus" can be translated from Latin to mean "appertaining to oaks"). The inspiration behind the "Oaks" came from four sources: Lowell, Massachusetts; worker housing built in Bradford, Yorkshire by Titus Salt; the designs of "gingerbread cottages" in the nearby Methodist Campground; and contemporary developments in city and urban planning.

After the Civil War, architects and urban planners such as Alexander Jackson Davis, Frederick Law Olmsted and Calvert Vaux, were commissioned to design the new suburbs radiating from American cities. The ideal of the countryside appealed to America's growing middle class. They yearned to escape over-crowded, unsanitary, and violent urban areas, and live in a more pastoral environment. And the rapidly growing national economy meant they now had the means to do this.

Urban planners broke with tradition by providing many of the new suburban communities with curvilinear roads, snaking through bucolic scenery, depositing rustic houses in their wake. This was a significant break away from what Kenneth T. Jackson has described as the "psychological significance of the clean, efficient, utilitarian grid."[29] The grid system had dominated American city planning since George Washington's days. But planners such as Olmsted and Vaux, who designed New York City's Central Park, organized their suburbs to convey a feeling of spontaneity. They insisted that houses be set back thirty feet from the street, to give a sense of openness, and required homeowners to maintain immaculate gardens, thus suggesting prosperity and elegance.[30]

Barrows planned his "Oaks" estate in 1879. The single-family houses were ready for occupation in April, 1881. They were provided with a large garden, and built in four different styles situated in such a way as to break repetition. Barrows trained the occupants in the arts of floriculture and vegetable growing. The grid design of streets, seen to its best advantage in Iverton, was abandoned. Barrows' cottages were placed on curving roads. The influence of Davis, Olmsted and Vaux upon Barrows' Willimantic suburb is obvious. The winding streets, gardens and architectural styles of the "Oaks" impressed Federal investigators compiling the U.S. Government's tenth manufacturing census. Published in 1883, it featured the "Oaks" in a glowing report. In 1882, Barrows erected a large dance pavilion adjacent to the "Oaks." It became Willimantic's social center for a decade, housing dances, concerts, Shakespeare performances and demonstrations of Barrows' latest gadgetry. It was torn down in 1892 because of vandalism and rowdyism.

The Willimantic Linen Company provided the finance for Barrows to build a new house in Willimantic. He surprised many when he announced that the house would be built in the midst of his "Oaks" development. Ground was broke for his "new house over the river" in October 1880, at a location considered to be "the most pleasant in the village." The plans revealed that the property would cover considerable ground and be constructed from "colored stone." It was only one story high, "in the fashion of the new mill," with a large cellar. Barrows moved his family from their Hartford residence into the "fine and unique residence in the Oaks" in August 1881.[31]

The house was constructed from Mill Number Four's waste materials. It was called a "whimsical man's extravagance," and a "grotesque eyesore." When the Company decided to dispose of it in 1887, a realtor's skilled use of adjectives transformed it into an "ingeniously planned, thoroughly built, and in all respects a first class and desirable property." Barrows gave Daniel Pidgeon a tour:

> We reached the door of one of the most tasteful but oddest houses I have ever seen...the walls are made of old materials, or, rather overburned and distorted bricks...pretty climbers make the straggling Elizabethan cottage still more picturesque. The woodwork of the doors, windows and staircases have no mouldings...the unpolished surfaces of native walnut and chestnut...replace all paint.[32]

The house was not exactly in the midst of the workers' cottages; it stood on a hill overlooking them. Daniel Pidgeon was surprised that Barrows did not mind the "white flutter of washing days...or the shouts of children at play." Barrows replied that his place was to be among his hands - as their natural and appointed leader.

Before being torn down in the 1960s, the house was subsequently used as a hospital and a base for Willimantic's Elks Club. However, a large part of its fine stone boundary wall and ornate gateway can still be seen.[33]

MILL NUMBER FOUR

The Willimantic Linen Company's vast Mill Number Four was considered by many to be Barrows' greatest folly. It was the largest factory building, in terms of ground area, in the world. When construction got underway in 1880, the Linen Company's public relations machine claimed that the building was so vast, its designers had to take the earth's natural curvature into consideration. However, an engineer writing in the *Boston Journal of Commerce* exposed that as a myth.[34] Nevertheless, the new building's vast dimensions and unique design grasped nineteenth century imaginations. It was the first textile mill to be built entirely on a single story, with special underground chambers to accomodate driving shafts and belts, which were normally positioned above the looms and machinery. The unsightly pulleys and belts were out of sight, so the mill could be illuminated by the new electric arc lights hung from an unencumbered ceiling. The directors of the local gas company were devastated when they discovered that the company was to employ this new technology to light its mill. They had expected a massive contract for lighting the new mill by the traditional method.

The surrounding forest was quickly cleared and ground was broken in early March, 1880. Construction went ahead with amazing speed:

> The new structure will be located on the opposite side of the river from the other mills, and will be 840 feet long and 168 feet wide, one story with a basement, which will be occupied by the shafting. It will be lighted with fifty-one windows, each thirteen feet wide, or 663 running feet of windows out of 840. There will be two ells attached to the building each 75 feet long, which will contain the engine, picker and

Top: Mill Number Four, pictured upon completion in 1880. This view was originally captioned, "The largest cotton mill on the ground in the world."

Bottom: Inward ambience. Several of this series of photographs, commissioned by the Linen Company in 1880, stressed the pleasant working atmosphere within the new Mill Number Four. This is a view of the ladies' changing rooms, replete with colored glass and exotic plants. *(CCAM)*

finishing rooms. The mill when completed will cover an area of about three and a half acres, which is said to be the largest of any cotton mill in the country. The electric light will be employed in lighting the mill. The erection of this important addition to the company's property will necessitate a corresponding increase in the number of dwelling houses— and that number is reported to be eighty. Their payroll numbers between eleven and twelve hundred hands; and the number of hands required to operate the new mill cannot fail to have a healthful impression on the business interests of the village.[35]

A local building contractor, George Jordan, was put in charge of construction. Over 150 men excavated the mill's foundation in the north-west corner. A special railroad track was laid to accomodate the delivery of building materials. Five steam-driven derricks were put into position to hoist the granite, stone and bricks from the railroad cars. The granite and stone came from two sources. The Company purchased land adjacent to its mill site from a local landowner, Chipman Young, and dug a quarry. It also purchased a quarry in Monson, Massachusetts, and shipped some special stone to the site. Sheds were built on site to house workers and horses. A portable 10 hp Baxter steam engine supplied the power for the wood lathes which turned and shaped the new mill's ornate woodwork.

The Willimantic Linen Company had experienced numerous industrial relations problems during the construction of Mill Number Two in 1864, and 1880 proved to be no exception. A large number of laborers employed to build the new mill were Swedish. They received $1.25 per 12 hour workday. Barrows was impressed with their progress and gave them a 25 cent a day raise. However, those employed in digging the mill's foundations went on strike in protest. Why were the Swedish workers treated so well? Barrows refused to increase the strikers' wages, and 40 of the 75 shovelers, "a turbulent element," drew the pay owed them and left the site. The strike was considered to be "indefensible on any reasonable grounds." The culprits were identified as a "few young fellows who had come in from other places and presumed the company were at their mercy and would pay any price demand, but unfortunately such was not the case and the places of the men dismissed were readily filled."[36] The atmosphere was tense, and the Company hired a force of special constables to guard the site, and requested that licensed dealers in intoxicants refuse to sell liquor to any stranger for the duration of the strike.

Despite this setback, the mill was almost completed by the late summer. Work went on during the night, thanks to the Company's arc lights. The bridge across the Willimantic River, connecting the new structure to Mill Number One and Mill Number Two, was mainly built during the night under electric arc floodlight. The first machinery was installed in August. The grand opening, which also served as a Republican Party rally, took place soon afterwards. Ex-President Grant came to see the new mill in October, 1880, and Barrows instructed the operatives to dress for work. The local press noted that: "The employees of the Willimantic Linen Company's new mill are required to wear uniforms. The females wear a white overskirt fitting closely and belted about the waist with a band of red ribbon. The males wear white coat and pantaloons with cap to match."[37]

Mill Number Four cost the Willimantic Linen Company a fortune, but it did not work to full capacity for many years. People came from across America and around the world to see this wonder of the modern world. However, Barrows' gigantic cotton mill added to the list of his enemies and critics. When Barrows departed for Pullman in 1883, it was hoped that his mill could be quickly disposed off:

> A rumor has been very extensively circulated about the village this week to the effect that the New York and New England Railroad are negotiating for the purchase of the [Willimantic] Linen Company's Number Four Mill and will use it for car shops. It would be one of the best things that could possibly happen for prosperity of this village because it would import a large number of mechanics. It seems to be the general opinion that Mr. Barrows made a gigantic blunder when he built the mill to manufacture thread in, but if this rumor should have any foundation its disposition will be fortunate for the company, it is thought, and surely will be for the village. [38]

It was a hoax. Mill Number Four was not to be transformed into railroad workshops. Nevertheless, the rumor created much excitement. Indeed, Mill Number Four was under-utilized for many years, and its size and design was considered to be an unnecessary extravagance. It reached full production after the American Thread Company took it over in 1898 - and Barrows' vast mill subsequently proved to be a great asset to the British-owned Company. It is of interest to note that Mill Number Four's unique design, on one level, facilitating single-line production, was widely used by the American textile industry when it gradually began to relocate in the South during the early twentieth-century. It was argued that nineteenth-century, multi-storied New England mills were unsuitable for the latest techniques in textile manufacturing.

PULLMAN, ELY AND SUMNER

Despite Barrows' unpopularity among certain directors of the Willimantic Linen Company, his numerous innovations and social experiments came to the notice of Yale University, which awarded him a prestigious honorary M. A. degree in June, 1882. Barrows surprisingly resigned from the Linen Company and left Willimantic in October, 1883, to supervise George Pullman's paternal-istic schemes in the suburbs of Chicago. His departure was not greatly mourned:

> The general opinion about here is that Mr. Barrows has spent more money for beauty than for practicability. Personally, Mr. Barrows is, however, a perfect gentleman, always on the side of good morals and an advocate of elevation of public sentiment, but we think the Linen company needs a manager less revolutionary in his ideas.[39]

Barrows was lured to Illinois by a $12,000 salary, 500 shares in the Pullman Land Association, a new house in the Pullman community, and the position of company vice-president. George Pullman, the president and founder of the Pullman Palace Car Company, had closely followed Barrows' social experi-ments in Willimantic, and was greatly impressed. Pullman had purchased 4,000 acres of land outside Chicago, and built a private city, 'Pullman', to house his employees. It was three-years-old, with a population of over 8,000 when Barrows arrived there.

George M. Pullman organized the Pullman Palace Car Company near Chicago, in 1867, to build sleeping and restaurant cars for the nation's expanding railroad system. When Barrows was building his company store-and-library in Willimantic, Chicago experienced a violent railroad strike. Pullman was greatly disturbed by this event, and he planned an ideal workers' community, hoping to eliminate worker unrest. Ironically, Pullman's Com-pany was the site of one of the most violent strikes in American history in 1894, when it cut wages and challenged Eugene Debs' American Railway Union.

Barrows arrived at Pullman in the fall of 1883, and was shocked by the undemocratic, dictatorial nature of the community. The following year, a young professor from John Hopkins, Richard T. Ely, was commissioned by *Harper's New Monthly Magazine* to write an article about the place.[40] Ely was initially impressed by Pullman's clean appearance, but he quickly discovered that it had no soul. Ely compared the power of the Pullman Palace Car Company with that enjoyed by Bismarck in Germany, and explained that Pullman's community represented "benevolent...feudalism (to) please the authorities," and that its occupants were surrounded by "constant restraint and restriction."[41]

Ely's initial investigations proved to be fruitless. No one living in Pullman was allowed to speak to him. However, a "disgruntled employee" opened up to Ely, and expertly dismantled Pullman's tactics and organization.[42] Ely's *Harper's* article referred to "a warm hearted official" who showed "momentous concern" for the welfare of Pullman's "laboring classes." This official congratulated workers who had planted flowers in their gardens, and he gave one lady two potted plants for her attractive, colorful displays.[43] Ely's "warm hearted official" was probably Barrows, who was well known for his interest in floriculture. He had often awarded prizes to the occupants who kept the best gardens at the Willimantic Linen Company's tenements and houses.

Barrows resigned his post at Pullman on December 5th, 1884, claiming that George Pullman had not fulfilled his part of the contract regarding shares in the Pullman Land Association. Barrows wrote to Ely in March, 1885. The tone of this letter strongly suggests that Barrows was Ely's confidante in Pullman. Barrows promised to give Ely some points he had missed in his *Harper's* critique, and explained that George Pullman was greatly displeased with his article, and had fired the people he suspected had talked to Ely. George Pullman's paternalism was far too dictatorial for Barrows. He was highly gratified by Richard T. Ely's exposure:

> Of all your thousands of readers of the Feb. Harpers...Mrs. Barrows and myself are your most interested readers, and if proof were needed, my only reason for leaving the service of the Pullman Palace Car Company was because I could not sink myself to be melted up and ran into his mould...when I am asked why I left Pullman, I refer to the Feb. Harpers.[44]

William Eliot Barrows had a habit of bumping into significant figures in American history. Richard Ely became known as America's most controversial political economist. He called for a 'New Deal' long before President Roosevelt entered the White House. Ely argued that laissez-faire economics were "unsafe in politics and unsound in morals."

Richard Theodore Ely was born in Chautauqua, New York, in 1854. He attended Columbia University and subsequently gained a Ph.D. in political economy at the University of Heidelberg, Germany, in 1879. He was appointed professor of political economy at John Hopkins in 1881, and met Barrows at Pullman in 1884. Ely wrote a treatise on the labor movement around this time, which was considered highly subversive. It led to calls for his removal from John Hopkins. In 1885, Ely organized the American Economic Association (AEA), along with several other economists including a promising graduate student called Woodrow Wilson. The AEA challenged the political and economic orthodoxy of the time. It argued that "least government was worst government," and that society should protect its women and children from the cruelties caused by supply and demand and free contract. More controversially, it proposed that workers were better off when organized in a union.

Between 1892 and 1925, Ely worked at the University of Wisconsin, where he formed the Institute for Research in Land Economics and Public Utilities. He became the chief political and economic adviser to Wisconsin Governor Robert "Fighting Bob" LaFollette, and Wisconsin became a proving ground for

Ely's radical economic theories. Richard T. Ely's controversial ideas were eventually taken on board by the political mainstream after the Wall Street Crash in 1929. By the time of his death during World War Two, Richard T. Ely was known as the "dean of American economists." He died in 1943, aged 89, after seeing many of his ideas come to fruition.

Ely campaigned all his life for careful regulation of the national economy. This flew in the face of the laissez-faire ideology espoused during the late nineteenth century by establishment figures such as Yale University's professor of political economy, William Graham Sumner (1840-1910), who believed that the national economy should be totally unfettered, the one iron law of economics.

Sumner crossed swords with Barrows in 1883, shortly after the President of the Willimantic Linen Company had been awarded his honorary M. A. by Yale. Sumner was furious at his college's decision to honor a man whose Company openly supported the tariff on imported cotton. In Sumner's view, such tinkering was ruining the American economy. In January 1883, Sumner bitterly attacked the Willimantic Linen Company in a famous speech to the Brooklyn Historical Society in New York, where he referred to Barrows' Company as a "tariff-built fraud." Sumner claimed that Willimantic's major employer was not an industry but a "poor house" and "insane asylum" supported by taxation.

Barrows was furious, and responded by inviting Sumner and all members of Yale's senior year for a conducted tour of the Willimantic mills. Sumner declined, but this invitation gave the Linen Company a great deal of free national publicity. Two hundred and thirty one Yale students arrived in Willimantic on February 21, 1883, and were treated like royalty by the Company. Two were almost drowned while inspecting a water wheel, and several others were involved in debauchery with "pretty mill girls." Sumner remained unimpressed by Barrows' theatrics, but two weeks later, the Yale students thanked Barrows by sending their Glee Club to Willimantic. The Linen Company's operatives enjoyed a fine musical performance, free-of-charge, at the Loomer Opera House.[45]

Barrows' nine year stint at the Willimantic Linen Company was highly eventful, not to speak of his experiences at Pullman in 1884. In 1885, Barrows was hired as a special commissioner to that year's Industrial Exposition in New Orleans. He was based in Lima, Peru, as he searched South America for suitable exhibits. Between 1886 and 1888, he managed the Hinckley locomotive works in Boston, Massachusetts, which repaired and built steam railroad engines. In 1889, Barrows became a leading shareholder and manager of the Welsbach Incandescent Gas Burner Company of Gloucester, New Jersey. He also became involved in early experiments to produce domestic electric refrigeration units. After a long and distinguished career in industrial and social experimentation and innovations, William Eliot Barrows died in his home at Haverford, Pennsylvania on July 30, 1901, shortly after his 59th birthday.

This chapter has merely recounted Barrows' influence on Willimantic. It is neither a promotion nor a critique of his methods. But it does act as a case study which demonstrates how the United States dealt with the economic and social dislocation created by rapid industrialization. It contrasts with the methods employed in Europe, where much more political and economic power was ceded to working-class organizations to lessen the revolutionary potential created by the impact of industrialization. Nevertheless, American paternalism had many faces, as revealed by Barrows' treatment of strikers in Willimantic, and by his subsequent experiences in Illinois, where he deplored the dictatorial methods of George Pullman.

William Eliot Barrows left his mark on Willimantic. Whilst not underestimating his revolutionary designs in worker housing and mill building, nor his progressive social experimentation, Barrows was greatly involved with America's first experimentation to light an industrial workplace with various types of electric lights. The following chapter recounts the period when the Willimantic Linen Company was known worldwide as a pioneer in electric lighting.

CHAPTER 4

Electric Lighting Pioneers

The superintendent stepped up to the desk and touched a button,
and two hundred little globes made the room as bright as day

Electrical Review, October 11, 1883

The activities of chemists in Cleveland, Ohio, and Newcastle, England, coupled with the experiments and machinations of a New Jersey tinkerer and a Connecticut entrepreneur, all came together on a cold February evening in Willimantic, Connecticut in 1879, and altered the course of world history.

In 1876, Charles Francis Brush developed an electric arc light in Cleveland, Ohio. Electric arc lamps were so named because an arc of intensive light was created by jumping an electric current between two sticks of carbon. For a time, electric arc lighting looked to be the ideal replacement for candle, oil and gas light in stores, homes and factories. It was utilized in city street lighting and for department store displays, but it ultimately proved to be too bright for domestic use. The arc's intense, unstable spark lacked the adjustability of gas lighting.

Industry created a great need for efficient, cheap light. The relative efficiency of gas lighting transformed the natural rhythm of the day, enabling round-the-clock industrial production during the nineteenth century. But gas caused fires, explosions, poisoning and asphyxiation, and for a while, electric arc lighting seemed to be its natural successor. However, the introduction of electricity created new problems. The naked electric arc was as dangerous as the exposed flames of gas lights, and it lacked the advantages of a centralized system of efficient storage and distribution provided by gas companies. Electricity could only be produced on site by a steam engine or water wheel driving a dynamo, and it could not be piped to site from a central location, as was the case with gas.

Joseph Swan, an English chemist, solved the first problem. On December 18,

1878 he exhibited a carbon filament vacuum lamp at a meeting of Newcastle's Chemical Society. This incandescent light, a forerunner of the electric light bulb, removed the danger of fires and explosions, thanks to its enclosed filament. The filament, a carbonized thread of cotton, replaced the naked spark, but it was inefficient and burned out after a few hours. Thomas Edison modified Swan's cotton thread filament in his New Jersey workshops, and on October 21, 1879, he patented an electric incandescent lamp which used a filament of carbonized bamboo slivers. Charles Brush went further by solving the second problem in 1882, when he improved the design of storage batteries. Dynamos, driven by water wheels or steam engines, generated electricity - but there was no efficient way to store that power, until Brush's improvement. The ideal situation for industrial undertakings like the Linen Company would be to generate the power through the day and store it in batteries, ready to be tapped for night time illumination of the more efficient and easy-on-the-eye incandescent lamps. Each of these technological advances was tested in Willimantic by the Linen Company's President, Austin Cornelius Dunham.

Dunham was born in South Coventry, Connecticut in 1833. At the time of his father's death in 1877, he was a successful, energetic, talented businessman and engineer, and a personal friend of Thomas Edison. He took over the presidency of the Willimantic Linen Company at an important time. The aptly named "A. C." Dunham was intrigued by the promise of the emerging electrical technology, and in December, 1878, he instructed William Eliot Barrows to purchase one of Charles Brush's latest arc light systems to illuminate Mill Number Two's winding room. Barrows purchased Brush's "electric light machine" in January, 1879, and shipped it to Willimantic "for tests to light the mills."[1]

Several weeks later, Dunham and Barrows invited "a large number of distinguished gentlemen from various parts of the country" to witness a demonstration with two electric arc lights, which took "...the place of sixty gas burners." The arc lights were powered by a water wheel, which generated electricity by "revolving an iron wheel near the face of and between powerful magnets." In comparison, the gas lights in an adjacent room "shed their dingy and yellow rays." A local reporter described the new lighting process:

> From the machine the electricity is carried by simple wires to the lamps or burners. As long as the current is furnished with a good conductor, it flows along silent and invisible. But at the lamps it is led to two pieces of carbon, which is a poor conductor, and the resistance which they offer to the passage of the current instantly makes them of a glowing heat, and the result is a brilliant light...The electric light has no smell. It cannot explode, the wires never leak like gas pipes. These and other points of superiority will make the electric light popular when future

discoveries and improvements will have made it available and cheap. At present there are a very few of these lights in practical use throughout the country. Our citizens can see any evening what many persons last week came a long distance to examine.[2]

The invited guests consisted of state governors, military leaders, scientists and newspaper editors. They witnessed America's first demonstration of electric arc lighting applied to industry. After the exhibition, they were ushered to the Dunham Hall Library and treated to a sumptuous feast along with the obligatory speeches. It was a historic occasion, bringing to practical fruition the extensive research conducted by Messrs. Swan, Brush and Edison, and it created a foundation for further experimentation.

The Willimantic Linen Company bathed in the light of positive publicity, but good press is often accompanied by bad press. The Company's arc-lighted operatives were described as "White Slaves" forced to vote the Republican ticket. The charge was vigorously denied, and newspaper reporters were treated to a tour of the Company's winding room:

> We visited the White Slaves under the electric light the other evening. They seem to take their bondage quite cheerfully under the 10 hour system. We were told by one of the young ladies in the winding room, where the work is done by the dozen, that they earned about as much when they worked 11 hours. Said she, "I tell you, we work every minute now.[3]

The Willimantic Linen Company became highly skilled in the use of self-promotion. Newspaper reporters were warmly welcomed to Willimantic, resulting in much positive publicity. William Barrows believed that any publicity for the Linen Company was good publicity - and the Company's tinkerings in new technology attracted a great deal of it.

BATTLE FLAG DAY

A. C. Dunham had a sharp eye for publicity. He offered to light Hartford's State Capitol with his electric arc lights. September 17, 1879 marked the anniversary of the Civil War battle of Antietam. The Connecticut Legislature designated the date "Battle Flag Day." An impressive parade, made up of veterans, carried Civil War battle flags from the old Hartford arsenal to the State Capitol, where it was planned to display them permanently. Over 100,000 people attended, and some 30,000 remained in Bushnell Park to witness the illumination of the Capitol building after sunset.

The arc lights were transported by rail from Willimantic to Hartford and installed by six Willimantic Linen Company employees, supervised by an engineer from the Brush Electric Company. The arc lights were powered by a 10 hp engine borrowed from the nearby Colt Factory, and reflected through colored lenses around Bushnell Park and the city center. The crowd was amazed at this display - but it was nothing new to the blasé, world-weary people of Willimantic, who had been witnessing electric lighting experiments all summer long. The Linen Company mounted an electric arc light atop its spool shop chimney, and sparked it into power at sunset. Its intense, bright light was reflected into rays which were beamed across Willimantic with the aid of a "locomotive reflector." The light was none too bright on Main Street because the spool shop, the old Jillson mill, blocked the rays, but night was virtually turned into day in nearby North Windham, where people boasted that they could read the time on their pocket watches by the light of the arc's silvery spark.[4]

In December, 1879, the Willimantic Linen Company purchased a "new electric machine of 20 lights capacity " to illuminate Mill Number Two. The new Brush arc light system was installed in Mill Number Three to take advantage of its superior water power, and the electricity produced was "piped" to Mill Number Two, and lit 20 arc lamps. It was also announced at this time that the Willimantic Linen Company planned to construct a vast new single-story mill. The new technology played an important part in the new mill's unique design and construction.[5]

Five months later, Mill Number Three became the site of intense activity, after electrical engineers had installed more arc lights. The mill, which stood on Recreation Park, was in operation "day and night" to keep up with orders. It was noted that the Linen Company, "employed two sets of hands now that this factory is kept alight at night by the Brush electric light."[6]

A. C. Dunham, and fellow Linen Company directors Newton Case, C. B. Irwin, Henry Stanley and Morgan G. Bulkeley, shared an ardent interest in the emerging technology. In May, 1880, along with other industrial entrepreneurs, they organized the American Electric Company, and the Linen Company immediately became aware of any improvements or advancements in the new technology. The owners of New Hampshire's giant Amoskeag mills became intrigued by developments in Willimantic, and the American Electric Company installed arc lights there in August, 1881.[7]

Dunham and Bulkeley later became involved with the Hartford Electric Light Company (1882). Improvements in dynamos and the advantages of a central generating station, made possible by efficient storage batteries over portable, "single stations," were passed on to the Willimantic Linen Company's engineers. The Willimantic mills acted as experimental workshops for the new technology.[8]

WORLD'S FIRST

On September 7, 1880, William Barrows organized and conducted an experiment in the newly completed Mill Number Four to compare two types of electric arc lighting. The United States Electric Light Company, of New York City, tried to convince Dunham and Barrows that its "Maxime" light was far superior to the system they were currently employing. The Brush system lit six arc lamps, and the Maxime illuminated two arc lamps. The Companies were competing for a large contract to light the vast mill which Barrows and the Willimantic Linen Company's chief engineer, E. W. Thomas, had specifically designed to be illuminated by electricity. Mill Number Four was the world's first textile factory to be specifically designed and built to accommodate electric lighting. The belts driving the machinery and looms were installed underground so as not to interfere with the electric arc lighting system planned for the mill ceiling. This first demonstration of lighting in the new mill attracted much attention:

> The whole lower end of the vast room was brilliantly illuminated. The Company are fixing up the mill to look handsome. The roof and supporting pillars are painted in various harmonious shades all of which were clearly brought out by the strong illumination. The light green and other delicate shades being as bright as in the daytime...One end was as light as day, the other end was plunged in profound darkness. We can offer no opinion to the comparative merits of the two systems of lighting or the final effect when the lamps are placed in position permanently. This was an experiment only, but it would seem impossible to find any part of the room where any kind of work could not be performed, even in the shades of the pillars or the machinery.[9]

The staunchly Republican Willimantic Linen Company made no secret of its political allegiance. Eleven days after the experiments in Mill Number Four, it called upon its public relations expertise and organized a "grand social bash" for its operatives to celebrate the completion of the new state-of-the-art mill building.

Saturday, September 18, 1880 was "a perfect specimen of September weather - the most beautiful of the year." The 'bash' was a thinly disguised Republican mass meeting to inaugurate a "Garfield and Arthur Club." (James Garfield and Chester A. Arthur were the Republican nominees for President and Vice President at the 1880 election.)

A stand was erected in the center of the largest room in the new mill, big enough to hold 200 people. A choir, the Hartford Glee Club, and the Willimantic Band provided the entertainment. The opening speech was made by John T. Waite, the member of Congress for the Willimantic district. The crowd slowly grew, and was estimated at its height to be some 7,000 strong. They toured and admired the Willimantic Linen Company's grounds. But only 500 hardy souls surrounded the platform to listen to the haranguing from the political speakers. The Willimantic *Chronicle*, the town's Democratic newspaper explained that, "Gen. McCook, of New York, was introduced and delivered an hour and a half address brimful of bloody-shirt utterances, which disgusted the Democrats present, and most of the Republicans...the people began to get uneasy and move about, evidently more interested in the building than in what was being said."[10]

The politicking was over by six p. m., and the celebration got under way. The immense mill was lighted at dusk, end to end, by the electric light. The "intense white light" shining from the windows of the vast, illuminated building was distinguishable for miles. It was considered by all present to be a "splendid sight," inside and out, supplying light far superior to the "ordinary method of illumination."

A. C. Dunham recalled the success of his electric lights at Hartford the year before, and organized a "superior light show" to celebrate the opening of the largest textile mill in the world. Dunham instructed Barrows to construct a huge spray fountain near the new bridge over the Willimantic River, which connected Mills One and Two to the new mill. The spray was thirty feet high, and "cleverly illuminated" by a beam of light reflected through colored glass, emanating from a Brush electric light situated on the opposite bank of the Willimantic River near Mill Number Two:

> The ray of light (grew) broader as it crossed the river and struck the fountain, where it dissolved into all the colors of the rainbow. In the mill the scene was of a most animated character. Seven thousand tickets of admission had been printed and given away by the company, and hundreds were admitted without tickets. A large space was kept clear for dancing in the eastern half of the mill room by a rope stretched around it, and four hundred couples were seen to be dancing at once. Rollinson's Opera House Orchestra of twelve pieces furnished music for the dancers. The great crowd danced and promenaded back and forth across the great room until 10 o clock, when the evening's entertainment in the mill closed. There then followed a fine exhibition of fireworks from the railroad bank fronting the mill, and the people remained in the grounds until it was over. It was the greatest collection of people ever witnessed under one roof in the state. The mill would have held several times the number of those present.[11]

The innovations at the Willimantic Linen Company did not go unnoticed. William Barrows enjoyed his new role in presenting his Company's latest advances to scientists, engineers, politicians and students from across America and around the world. In 1881, the Chinese government made a flattering offer to E. W. Thomas, Mill Number Four's designer, to build a cotton mill in Shanghai. He decided to stay in Willimantic to assist in the intriguing experiments in electric lighting.[12]

This new technology had to be handled with care. Charles Smith, the engineer in charge of the Company's arc lights, was explaining their workings to a visitor, when he turned up the burner, which was "not working to his satisfaction," and looked at the lamp directly. He saw stars and awoke the next day, almost blind, but his sight slowly returned. The Willimantic Linen Company was greatly concerned as it had paid a lot for Mr. Smith's expertise, having just installed him in one of its new cottages at the "Oaks."[13]

FROM ARC TO INCANDESCENT

The Willimantic Linen Company began to have reservations about the Brush arc system. Because of the ever-present fear of fire, Barrows and Thomas did not use the arc lights in buildings where bleaching and dyeing processes were conducted. Also, the Brush machinery was reliant on the water wheels for its power. When the wheels stopped for repair, low water or ice, the lights went out. The "Wizard of Menlo Park," Thomas Edison, was busy perfecting an incandescent electric light in New Jersey, and "A. C" kept an eye on his progress. A suitable storage battery had yet to be designed, and the Linen Company retained gas burners for emergencies.

The Company dispensed with the Brush arc light system in 1882 and purchased Edison's newest invention, an "incandescent plant," which was installed in the winding room of Mill Number Two, to light 60 lamps. It was powered by steam, but the lights went out when the machinery stopped. Nevertheless, after early teething difficulties, Thomas A. Edison's system was adopted throughout the plant, gradually replacing the Brush system.[14]

In 1883, Barrows persuaded the Linen Company to develop a vast tract of its land into a "Fairgrounds," to house an annual agricultural fair to compete with the highly popular one in nearby Brooklyn, Connecticut. A massive amount of capital was invested, and a trotting and horse racing track was built in the area better known today as Recreation Park. Barrows announced his plans to stage an evening race meeting illuminated by the latest advancement in electric lighting technology. The "Brush-Swan" system boasted improved storage capabilities and incandescence, making the electric arc lights obsolete. The Linen Company's engineers constructed multi-celled storage batteries, and Barrows demonstrated them in the company store. The system was described as a "method of storing electricity in any quantity desired in a large electric battery composed of numerous cells, and from this one or more currents of the fluid may be taken at will...it is a great scientific triumph, and particularly so as the most eminent European scientists have asserted that the storage of electricity is impossible."[15]

On the evening of August 27, 1883, Barrows arranged a public demonstration of the new lighting system. The large audience included "a party of gentlemen from abroad." Barrows illuminated the store and library, and the second story of Mill Number Two. Everyone agreed that the new lamps were far superior to the original electric light, which had produced a "harsh, piercing, almost unbearable (light)." The new lamps had "a soft agreeable effect on the eye." The electricity was "accumulated in tanks" throughout the day. For 50 cents, this latest system of storage produced the equivalent to one thousand feet of gas, costing $2.50.[16] Despite these successes, the Linen Company retained its gas lighting system well into the twentieth century, and used it for emergency backup.

Several weeks later, the Linen Company demonstrated its new electric system to a committee from Bridgeport, which planned to employ it to light its city streets. They were accompanied by the nation's leading industrialists, and powerful figures from the U. S. Navy and Army. Willimantic was the place to be. The distinguished guests were welcomed by superintendent John Scott. William Barrows had resigned several days earlier, and was traveling to Chicago to work for railroad magnate George Pullman.

Scott demonstrated the Brush-Swan system to the VIPs at 5:30 pm on October 3, 1883, little suspecting that America's industrial development was to take a new course, instigated in this small, eastern Connecticut backwater. Scott took the party into the carding room of Mill Number Two where 200 Swan incandescent lamps were powered by stored electricity from the surplus water going over the Company dam during the day. Each battery was filled after eight hours, and supplied four hours of "a remarkably brilliant and steady light." The Brush Company boasted that the batteries would last for 20 years. It was now possible to turn out the lights by section or individually:

> It was an impressive sight. The great workroom was deserted by the operatives, the maze of belting and machinery was still, and the place as quiet as the grave, but the brilliant little globes made everything as light as day, not for an instant flickering or weakening, and the power all came from the batteries which had been stored hours before with only an appreciability loss of 10 per cent, in transmitting it from the dynamo...There were three or four scientific workmen present to answer questions.[17]

Everyone was pleased by Scott's demonstration, and impressed with his scientific grasp of the new technology. The Company served its eminent guests a sumptuous supper, and took them to the recently completed Fairgrounds to witness horse-trotting races taking place under electric floodlights. This race at the Willimantic track was one of the first sporting events ever viewed by electric incandescent floodlights. The generals, admirals and scientists left Willimantic that night dazzled by their experiences. The Linen Company continued to update its electrical machinery as soon as new developments became available. In 1884, it replaced its dynamos with an improved model, and installed 150 "Brush incandescent lamps" in its twisting room.[18]

Although the electric arc light was first demonstrated by an Englishman, Sir Humphrey Davy, in 1810, the efficient generation and storage of electric current was not perfected until the 1870s. Developments in electric arc lighting technology were made in Europe by Z. T. Gramme (ring armature generator) and Paul Jablochkoff (improvements in the arc lamp) in the mid 1870s. A Monsieur Menier lit his chocolate factories in France by electric arc-lamps in 1875, and a French railroad company, the Compagnie Chemin de Fer du Nord, lit its main parcel hall in Paris by arc-lights in 1876.[19] Charles Brush perfected his dynamo in 1875, and the United States quickly overtook its European rivals in the development and application of electric lighting, thanks to the experimentation that began in Willimantic's textile mills in 1879.

As a footnote to this history it must be mentioned that William Eliot Barrows, after being so closely involved in electric arc and incandescent lights in Willimantic up until 1883, was the first industrialist in America to manufacture gas mantles. The Welsbach Incandescent Gas Light Company's factory was based in Gloucester, New Jersey. Barrows was president from 1889 until his death in 1901. The venture was initially financed by Standard Oil and John Wanamaker, the Philadelphia store owner who is credited with the introduction of the large department stores which began to dominate American cities during the late nineteenth century.

It has been argued that the invention of the gas mantle, by Karl Auer in Welsbach, Austria in 1885, slowed down the progress of domestic and commercial electric lighting. The gas mantle increased the control and incandescence of gas light. Proof of this appeared in Willimantic. The gas mantle made its New England debut in April, 1889, when the owner of a Willimantic clothing store, H. E. Remington, illuminated his new Main Street premises with the Welsbach's gaslights:

> We doubt if there will be a handsomer clothing store in the state than this. A novel feature will be the lighting apparatus - the Welsbach incandescent gas burners - which is a new invention and the store will be brilliantly lit with 28 jets. This is the first store in New England to introduce this burner and the points of merit in it are that it consumes the ordinary illuminating coal gas in such a way as to make the incandescent electric light look positively yellow.[20]

Remington's new lights attracted visitors from across New England. Two weeks after the installation of the 28 gas mantle lamps in his store, the Welsbach incandescent gas burner was considered to be, "superior to the electric incandescent burner and they are being generally adopted here. H. E. Remington & Co, whose entire store is lighted with them are highly pleased and state that the consumption of gas is less than by the common gas jet."[21]

Be it developments in electric or gas lights, textile mill design, silk and cotton machinery, telephones or worker housing and education, Willimantic was often at the forefront during the late nineteenth century - proving that things sometimes do occur east of Connecticut River. For example, a Willimantic-based silk manufacturer installed one of Connecticut's first telephones in his Mansfield home, which neatly leads to the fact that Willimantic once boasted a thriving silk industry. This has generally been forgotten, as Willimantic silk has long lived in the giant shadow cast by the Cheney operation in nearby Manchester. However, the Willimantic-based workshops of W. G. & A. R. Morrison, Goodrich Holland and William Atwood, became the scene of several technological innovations in mechanical silk thread and cloth production. Research currently being undertaken at the Windham Textile & History Museum has revealed Willimantic's important contribution to the development of America's silk industry. The following chapters provide an outline of forgotten, but significant events in Connecticut silk history.

CHAPTER 5

Silk City 1860 - 1900

FIRST SILK MILL IN AMERICA. (Established in 1810.) Located at Hanks Hill, Mansfield, Conn.

"The First Silk Mill in America." This simple wood frame building is now located at Dearborn, Michigan. It is pictured here in 1905 on its original location in Mansfield, Connecticut.

Silk twist (thread), silk cloth and silk machinery were widely manufactured in Willimantic between the Civil War and World War II. The local silk industry's roots lay in nearby Mansfield, where mulberry trees and silkworms had been nurtured since colonial times. Mansfield pioneered the mechanized-loom production of silk thread in the early nineteenth century, at sites in Atwoodville, Chaffeeville, Conantville, Gurleyville and Hanks Hill. By 1845, Mansfield's silk industry was in a slow decline, thanks to European competition and a disease which destroyed mulberry crops. Nevertheless, five small Mansfield silk mills still gave work to 59 women and 17 men, who produced almost 8,000 lbs of silk thread during that year.[1] Silk continued to be manufactured in Mansfield until the early years of the twentieth century, but large scale production took off in Willimantic after the Civil War. The high quality of Willimantic silk was acclaimed nationwide - a fact often ignored by historians seduced by Manchester's more visible Cheney organization.

Rodney and Horatio Hanks pioneered the mechanized spinning and weaving of silk thread at Mansfield, Connecticut in 1810. Four years later, Harrison Holland and John Gilbert built a mill at nearby Gurleyville and produced silk twist. Alfred Lilly, Joseph Conant, William Fisk, William Atwood and Storrs Hovey took over Holland and Gilbert's abandoned mill in 1828, and formed the "Mansfield Silk Company." Englishman Edmund Golding, Mansfield's own Samuel Slater,[2] designed machinery for the winding, doubling and spinning of locally grown silk.[3] The Mansfield Silk Company operated until 1839. An 1876 account of it stated that: "Notwithstanding the misfortunes which closed their career, the Mansfield Silk Co. is fairly entitled to the credit of having built the first mill in this country in which the manufacture of silk was practically successful."[4]

A large number of entrepreneurs and industrialists tried their hand at silk cloth and thread manufacture in Mansfield before the Civil War. [5] Mansfield-based manufacturers such as Messrs. Bottum, Chaffee, Conant, Holland, Macfarlane and Turner, became synonymous with silk thread manufacture in Willimantic in the years after the Civil War. In 1843, Albert Conant, who organized the A. A. and H. E. Conant Silk Company in Willimantic in 1869, commenced the manufacture of sewing silk in the vacant Mansfield Company's mill. In 1853, Joseph Conant built a silk mill on the site partly occupied today by the East Brook shopping mall. In 1856 it was purchased by Charles L. Bottum, W. E. Williams and D. P. Conant.[6] Three years later, Bottum was joined by James and Goodrich Holland. This new Conantville venture profited greatly during the Civil War, and enabled the Hollands to build a brick, steam-powered silk mill in Willimantic.

Charles Bottum remained at Conantville. In 1869 he doubled the size of his mill, and by 1873, in partnership with G. A. Hammond and C. C. Knowlton, Bottum was manufacturing a very profitable line of silk thread called "patent machine twist brand." He opened sales offices in New York City and Willimantic, and in 1879, provided the capital for the J. S. Morgan Company to commence silk thread manufacture in South Coventry, Connecticut.[7]

Bottum moved on to Springfield, Massachusetts. In October, 1881, his vacant Conantville mill was purchased by Messrs. Gardner & Pearce, who met with little success despite the high quality of their silk thread. George Gardner sold the business to Hiram Conant in December, 1882, admitting that he couldn't compete with the larger manufacturers in the line.[8] Conant abandoned the mill soon afterwards, and it lay empty for many years.

In 1892, W. E. Williams, a Gurleyville silk manufacturer, leased the vacant Conantville mill, and the local press noted that, "...the pretty village will again be in accord with the active business life of the time."[9] But Williams' venture was destroyed by the financial panic of 1893, and Willimantic's Natchaug Silk Company purchased the vacant premises in 1894.

In the late 1840s, Joseph and William Conant built a silk mill on the Mount Hope River in Mansfield, at Atwoodville. They leased part of it to John Edwin Atwood, the son of William Atwood, a founder of the 1828 Mansfield Silk Company, who repaired and built silk machinery. In 1863, the Conants hired a young Scotsman, James Stewart Macfarlane. He arrived in Atwoodville having served a silk apprenticeship in Yonkers, New York. In 1865, Lewis D. Brown purchased the Mount Hope River mill and Macfarlane's services. In 1870, the L. D. Brown & Son Silk Company built a 32 x 30 foot extension, and dedicated it with a "grand ball in which none but the operatives participated." The mill's output quickly rose to 300 lbs of silk twist per week.[10]

Atwoodville's L. D. Brown & Son Silk Company almost relocated to Willimantic in 1871, but transferred operations to Middletown, Connecticut, instead. James S. Macfarlane took over Brown's vacant Atwoodville mill. As shown below, Lewis D. Brown did operate in Willimantic at the end of the nineteenth century. Silk entrepreneurs, such as Brown, were lured to urban areas like Willimantic and Middletown, where the workers were more 'industrialized,' and less controlled by the agricultural seasons.

Despite the exodus to the city, small scale silk production continued in the Mansfield countryside. The area's Fenton River, named in colonial times when a counterfeiter named Fenton escaped across it while being chased by the King's officers, joins Atwoodville's Mount Hope River at Mansfield Hollow. In 1870, the fast-flowing Fenton was driving 10 mills, three of which produced silk twist and cloth.[11] Steam engines became more efficient, and mill owners were able to build away from fast-flowing rivers like the Fenton, unfettered by seasonal ice, floods and droughts. Willimantic also beckoned the Mansfield silk men, because it provided a relatively stable pool of Irish and French Canadian millworkers unavailable in rural, agrarian Mansfield.

The earliest located reference to a Willimantic silk manufacturer is William B. Swift, a "son of Grant Swift of Mansfield," who operated a small one-story wood-framed mill on the northeast corner of Church Street and Valley Street, circa 1860. James and Goodrich Holland purchased Swift's mill in 1864, demolished it and built a "large new brick mill" on the site.[12] Swift moved into a small mill on nearby North Street, where he employed 20 women to manufacture silk machine twist with an annual market value of $35,000. The women earned $3 a week operating spoolers, winders and throwers, all driven by an 8 hp steam engine.[13] In 1866, E. B. Sumner built a wood-framed mill on North Street to manufacture silk twist.[14] Hiram E. and Albert A. Conant also moved from Mansfield and worked out of several small mills in Willimantic between 1870-1880, manufacturing about 13,000 lbs of silk thread annually, employing an average of 40 hands.[15]

THE HOLLAND SILK COMPANY

In 1864, John Atwood and Goodrich Holland designed and developed a machine which greatly improved the quality of silk machine twist. Their patented stretching machine was soon in use across the United States.[16] The following year, Goodrich and James Holland built a 100 x 40 foot silk mill on the northeast corner of Church Street and Valley Street. It was constructed of stone and brick, and its machinery was powered by a 40 horse power steam engine. This "fine looking, substantial structure," was replete with a 65-foot tall chimney, an engine house and a boiler house.[17] Silk production began there in January 1866, supplying employment for 50 hands. Subsequent profits financed the construction of a second mill on the adjacent corner of Church Street in 1873.

The Holland Silk Company, also referred to as the Holland Manufacturing Company, became one of the most well known manufacturers and suppliers of silk twist in America. It had sales offices in New York City, Philadelphia and Boston. The Hollands' sewing silks and twists, "acquired a national reputation for general excellence and purity," and in 1876, the Company occupied an impressive stand at the Centennial Exhibition in Philadelphia. By the late 1880s, the Holland Silk Company employed 200 men and women and produced 1000 lbs of silk thread each week.[18] Noting the advancements being made across town by the Willimantic Linen Company, the expanding Holland Company replaced its gas lamps with the latest in lighting technology: "150 incandescent Edison lights" were purchased and installed in its east and west mills at great expense.[19]

The Holland Silk Company performed consistently into the 20th century. It was 34 years old in 1900, and continued to produce high quality silk thread in Willimantic for the next 34 years. In 1929, on the eve of the Depression, it employed 210 hands on a 48-hour week, despite the silk sewing trade being considered "spotty."[20] The Depression hit the Company hard. Workers were laid off and part-time work was instituted. On October 20, 1932, Edward Kenney, the Company president, announced that plans were under way to transfer the operations to Stroudsburg, Pennsylvania. Kenney claimed his Company had been "discriminated against" in city tax assessments. Moreover, stock and machinery were not taxed in Pennsylvania. Stroudsburg offered a single, modern mill, better access to the Eastern silk market and a pool of skilled silk workers. The city of Willimantic responded by publishing figures which revealed that the Holland Company's taxes had been reduced from $264,778 in 1928 to $224,547 in 1931. The city fathers argued that it was a reduction far

Top: The Holland Silk Company's 1873 west mill looking south down Church Street towards the Chaffee silk mill.

Bottom: The Holland brothers' original 1865 mill, situated on the northeast corner of Valley Street and Church Street. In the right background is St. Mary's Church - before the 1938 hurricane destroyed its ornate twinned spires. *François Gamache.*

greater than those enjoyed by other local companies such as Rossie Velvet and Windham Silk.

The city refused to give the Company any further tax concessions, and the transfer of machinery and personnel began in March, 1933. By the following August some 85 of the Company's 155 employees and 60% of its spinning machinery were installed in Pennsylvania. The move was completed by early 1934, ending 68 continuous years of silk thread manufacture in Willimantic.[21]

THE O. S. CHAFFEE & SON SILK COMPANY

The Chaffee silk mill (1874-1895) stood on the southwest corner of Valley Street and Church Street. It is pictured above during the 1920s, when it housed the fish-line producing Chaffee Manufacturing Company (1896-1927). Situated at the rear of the Chaffee mill, facing onto Valley Street, is the Windham Silk Company's 1911 mill. *François Gamache*

The Chaffees were a long-established Mansfield family. Frederick Chaffee farmed there during the early years of the nineteenth-century. His son, Orwell S. Chaffee, was educated locally, but moved to Northampton, Massachusetts in 1838 to manufacture silk thread with his father-in-law, Joseph Conant. Orwell moved back to Mansfield in 1842, and manufactured silk at "Chaffeeville." A fire destroyed his mill in 1861, but with the help of Edwin Fitch, a well-known and accomplished builder and architect, Orwell built a large stone mill on the site in 1863, and subsequently formed the O. S. Chaffee & Son Company with his 16-year-old son, Joseph Dwight Chaffee.

After the Civil War, the Chaffees built a small silk mill in nearby Gurleyville, employing some 20 hands. Local rivalry was high. The Chaffees located near Emory Smith's Gurleyville silk mill. Smith boasted that he was producing more silk than the Chaffees with seven fewer hands.[22] Nevertheless, the Chaffees' profits soared in the early 1870s, enabling them to build a substantial stone dam, still partly extant, to increase the power at their Gurleyville mill.[23]

In 1874, the Chaffees took a controlling interest in the failing Paisley Silk and Thread Company, located in a mill on the corner of Willimantic's Church Street and Valley Street. The Paisley mill had been operating in Willimantic since 1871, employing an average of 100 hands and manufacturing some 5,000 lbs of silk annually. [24] The move to Willimantic brought problems that Chaffee had not experienced with his agrarian workforce at Chaffeeville, who left their looms only when reaping and sowing demanded. In 1880, 30 silk weavers marched around his Church Street mill demanding higher wages, "but not being taken notice of they went home." Work was resumed the following day.[25]

The Chaffees' Willimantic operations prospered, and the family was accepted into the town's social elite. In 1882, they installed Willimantic's first telephone, connecting their Chaffeeville mill to the Church Street mill. Later that year, a "vocal and instrumental" concert at H. E. Remington's Willimantic store, which contained the switchboard for the town's original 10 subscribers, was conveyed by telephone to the Mansfield home of Orwell's son, Joseph, who responded by conveying "exquisite solos" from the violin of his fellow Mansfield silk manufacturer, James Macfarlane.[26] In 1889, Joseph Dwight Chaffee purchased the most sought-after building site in Willimantic, and erected a magnificent residence on the northwest corner of North Street and Summit Street.

THE NATCHAUG SILK COMPANY

Orwell. S. Chaffee died in April, 1887, and Joseph, "the best businessman in these parts," took control of his father's business.[27] He resisted overtures to move to Michigan and entered into partnership with Charles Fenton,[28] overseer of the Chaffeeville mill, to form the Natchaug Silk Company. In August, 1888, Chaffee and Fenton purchased the looms of the bankrupt Willimantic Braid Company, and gave the W. G. & A. R. Morrison Machine Company the contract to build their new silk looms.[29]

The Morrisons built a new factory on North Street, Willimantic in 1888, and rented out space to the Natchaug Company. This "ornament to the business section" measured 150 x 48 feet and was constructed of brick and trimmed with granite. Its floors were built from "the best Georgia pine," maple, spruce and chestnut. It stood three stories high, and boasted an 80 foot tall tower. The Natchaug Company installed the silk ribbon and braid-producing O. S. Chaffee & Son Company on the second floor, enabling James S. Macfarlane, the Atwoodville silk manufacturer and violin soloist, to rent the vacant space in the old Chaffee mill on Church Street.[30]

The Natchaug Silk Company manufactured what many considered to be the

The Natchaug Company had a short, but interesting history. By the early 1890s, it was one of New England's premier producers of silk goods. Its ornate company logo, reproduced above, features engravings of its Willimantic sites, along with mulberry leaves, silkworms and rolls of silk cloth.

"finest silk cloth in America." It imported high quality raw silk from Japan, China and Italy, and manufactured it into fish lines, dress silks, silk linings, silk and mohair braids, watch guards, machine twist and sewing silk.[31] By 1892, the Company was riding the crest of a profitable wave. It increased office space in New York and Willimantic, opened a branch manufactory in Chicago, and leased out unused space in its mill to a Company manufacturing steel bobbins. It also absorbed the Willimantic branch of the O. S. Chaffee & Son Company, and installed 25 new braiding machines to meet the growing demand for its nationally known fishing lines.

The Natchaug Silk Company offered a purse of $50 in gold to the angler who hooked the largest pike with a Willimantic-manufactured line. In 1893, a Mr. H. Hildebrandt of Logansport, Indiana caught a 26-pound pike and claimed the prize. Hoping to expand into Michigan and "The West," Charles Fenton organized an elaborate and expensive display of silk weaving. It began a lengthy tour of the West in Detroit in November, 1892. The following year, the Natchaug Company's fish lines won numerous prizes at the World's Fair in Chicago.[32]

The Panic of 1893, and President Cleveland's intention to reduce the import tariffs on silk, cotton and wool products (The Wilson Tariff), caused the Natchaug Company to cut wages, lay workers off, close its dress silk weaving department and instigate a three-day work week. Full time work was resumed in February, 1894, but employees demanded that the 1893 wage cuts be withdrawn. Joseph Chaffee refused to meet a deputation of weavers, and more than 200 employees walked off the job. After a hurried meeting, Chaffee agreed to pay the weavers, twisters and warpers, all men, an extra 10% and they subsequently returned to work. The Company's women workers, employed as braiders, doublers, spinners, winders and dyers, accused Chaffee and Fenton of unjust discrimination, and picketed the mill for a day. Their protest was met with much derision by the men. They reminded the striking women that the Natchaug Company's female employees, despite recent reductions, were still the best paid in Willimantic, and the women returned to work the following day. Any sign of independent political or industrial action by women was greatly frowned upon at this time. The 19th Amendment, which guaranteed women the right to vote, was still a generation away.[33]

In May, 1894, Chaffee and Fenton installed two large dye vats in their North Street mill, and downtown Willimantic became plagued with noxious fumes. The dyeing operations also lowered the local water table during 1894's long, hot, drought-ridden summer. A massive petition persuaded the Company to close down its dyeing operations, and the following October it purchased the vacant silk mill in nearby Conantville, and transferred its dye vats and braiding machines there. The area situated near the East Brook Mall was blessed with copious amounts of spring water, a necessary component in silk dyeing. The move greatly lessened the burden upon Willimantic's city water.[34]

Joseph Chaffee and Charles Fenton had every reason to believe they would prosper as 1895 commenced. They had overcome the financial panic of 1893, pay cuts, short time, layoffs, strikes and petitions. However, on April 12, 1895, the Natchaug Silk Company's chief shareholder and director, 45-year-old Oliver H. K. Risley, suddenly died. His death set into motion a series of events from which Chaffee and Fenton would not recover.

Risley was well known about town. He was the secretary-treasurer of the local gas and electric companies, and the chief cashier of the First National Bank of Windham, the institution which financed much of the Natchaug Silk Company's operations. It was apparent something was seriously wrong when, a week after Risley's death, a Federal examiner closed the First National Bank pending an investigation.

It was subsequently revealed that Risley had embezzled hundreds of thousands of dollars. The bank's finances were in a complicated mess. On April 26, 1895, the Natchaug Silk Company was put into the hands of a receiver. Creditors panicked when they realized the Company's financial structure had collapsed with the bank, and they demanded immediate payment of outstanding debts. Chaffee and Fenton appointed a trustee, James Hayden, and closed their sales offices in New York, Boston, Chicago, Baltimore and St. Louis. They forestalled immediate closure by selling their existing stock for $90,000, which paid off a number of outstanding debts.[35]

James Hayden attempted to reduce manufacturing costs by hiring a weaver from Paterson, New Jersey, to "double-up" work on the Company's French looms. This practice, which entailed forcing weavers to operate two looms simultaneously, enraged the Company's 90 weavers and quillers. They walked out, forcing the mill to close. The men informed Hayden that they would not return until the Company agreed to re-institute the old working practices, and sack Barrett, the double-up "plant" from New Jersey. Hayden refused, but Chaffee and Fenton believed they had ridden out the storm, and persuaded Hayden to back down from the confrontation with the striking weavers. The "plant" was sacked, and old working practices were re-introduced, but Chaffee and Fenton had miscalculated. Their debts were too great. Risley had somehow managed to lose $295, 695 of the Natchaug Company stock.[36]

The demise of the Natchaug Company led to the birth of Willimantic's first ever bowling alley. The "New England Bowling Syndicate" rented the Company's vacant Valley Street dye house, refitted the interior and installed bowling lanes, "unequalled by any in Connecticut."[37] While avoiding the temptation to say the Natchaug Silk Company was bowled over by debt and controversy, its winding-up lingered on for the next five years in numerous court cases and accusations.[38]

The Natchaug Silk Company finally closed its doors on December 17, 1895, when receiver Hayden dismissed the remaining 70 operatives on the eve of the auction of the Company's stock and machinery.

The Natchaug's weaving room was purchased by the L. D. Brown & Son Silk Company of Middletown for $7,850. Its braiding plant was sold for $4,100 to the H. L. Stanton Company of Chicago. Joseph Dwight Chaffee purchased the Conantville braiding mill and his father's old Church Street mill, and organized the Chaffee Manufacturing Company, which manufactured fish lines there until 1927. Charles Fenton was appointed superintendent of the new L. D. Brown concern, which wove dress silks in Willimantic until 1899. The Stanton Company also began operations in the Natchaug's mill in early 1896. The three firms which rose from the Natchaug's ashes gave employment to 100 local hands.[39]

THE W. G. & A. R. MORRISON COMPANY

In 1873, Walter and Arthur Morrison opened a small machine shop, to repair silk looms, in the Paisley Silk and Thread Company mill. Seven years later the Morrisons had an annual turnover of $60,000, and employed 29 skilled machinists, fitters and laborers in large new premises located on the southeast corner of Valley Street and North Street. The Morrisons paid some of the best wages in town at the time - $2 per 10-hour-day for skilled mechanics.[40] The W. G. & A. R. Morrison Machine Company became internationally known for its silk-twisting machinery. Its down-twisters rattled away in silk mills around the world. The firm's success was credited to Walter Morrison's "mechanical genius and business ability," and Arthur Morrison's "conservative financial management."

In 1881, Willimantic's reputation as a leading manufacturer of silk machinery attracted China's Commissioner of Education, Woo Tsze Tang. American-made textiles had made great inroads into China's home market during the

This 1887 woodcut provides an excellent view, looking in a southeasterly direction down North Street, of the Morrison Machine Company's new factory. It also housed the mills of the newly formed Natchaug Silk Company. The structure at the left of the new building, facing onto Valley Street, was the Morrisons' original 1874 wood-frame workshop. It was demolished in 1911 by the Windham Silk Company and replaced with a modern brick structure. *WTHM.*

1880s. The U. S. Government wished to expand that trade, and it invited Woo Tsze Tang to view the country's textile industries. His appearance in Willimantic drew a great deal of attention. He was described as "...one of the most learned men in the Chinese Empire... dressed in an Oriental costume of dazzling silk and...a skull cap of black silk."[41] Woo Tsze Tang visited the Willimantic Linen Company's thread mills, the town's silk mills and the Morrisons' Valley Street manufactory. The Chinese diplomat was particularly interested in the Morrisons' latest silk machine innovations. No orders were forthcoming from Woo Tsze Tang's tour, but the Company did win a lucrative contract the following year.

Charles Bottum, whom we met earlier in this chapter, was an old acquaintance of the Morrisons. Bottum's Conantville-based silk business collapsed in 1880. Two years later, he was manufacturing silk thread in Springfield, Massachusetts, but he had not forgotten his old friends back in Willimantic:

> Mr. C. L. Bottum, who is so well and favorably known here, and who made and lost a fortune in the silk business at Conantville, again sees his way clear to enter into the manufacture of silk thread in company with a gentleman at Springfield. We hope he may be successful as he certainly deserves to be. The new inventions in machinery just perfected by W. G. & A. R. Morrison have been shipped to his mill.[42]

The W. G. & A. R. Morrison Company entered the export market in 1883, after securing a lucrative order to supply machinery to the Kerr Thread Company of Paisley, Scotland.[43] Its successes continued unabated. Silk mills across the nation installed Willimantic-manufactured products. The Morrisons' machinery found its way to the Merrick Brothers mill in Holyoke, Massachusetts; the Belden Brothers silk mill in Northampton, Massachusetts; Child's silk mill in Hillsboro Bridge, New Hampshire; Belding, Paiff & Co., of Montreal; and to the mills of the A. D. Warren Thread Company in Worcester and Ashland, Massachusetts.

In 1888, a number of Japanese industrialists came to Willimantic to inspect the Morrisons' silk machinery and work processes. The Tokyo-based businessmen had not been impressed with the silk machinery manufactured by the Atwood Company in Stonington, Connecticut, or by that built by a concern in Paterson, New Jersey. However, they found the Morrison machinery irresistible. The Japanese entrepreneurs left behind a Mr. Aari, who lived in Willimantic for more than four months, as the Morrisons taught him all they knew about the intricacies of silk machinery production - an investment subsequently repaid by a massive $40,000 order from Japan.[44]

The Morrisons' timber-framed workshops proved to be too small, and the Company extended down North Street, building a large brick factory partly financed by the newly-formed Natchaug Silk Company. It was officially opened on June 5, 1888. A concert was held on the third floor, with music provided by Weed's Band of Hartford, who serenaded the cream of Connecticut society. The guests consumed free lemonade, and danced until one hour after midnight in the factory's "dazzling electric light." [45]

The light of prosperity shone on the Morrisons for the next five years. It was extinguished by the financial panic of 1893. In March, 1894, a local iron foundry demanded that the Morrisons settle a $7,000 debt. Other creditors quickly followed suit, and the Morrisons unsuccessfully appointed a trustee to settle their outstanding accounts. The Company's demise was speeded when it was sued for patent infringement by the Draper Company of Hopedale, Rhode Island. The Draper brothers had purchased an Atwood spindle patent, and served an injunction on the Morrisons for manufacturing it without their consent. The W. G. & A. R. Morrison Machine Company was officially wound-up on April 28, 1894, with debts amounting to $53,492, and more than 100 skilled mechanics were thrown out of work.

Ironically, this local economic collapse occurred on the same day as the New England branch of Jacob Coxey's "army of the unemployed" arrived in Willimantic en route to Washington, DC. Coxey hoped to persuade President Cleveland to invest in a massive public works project to improve the nation's roads, and provide much-needed employment.[46]

Coxey's New England "troops" were lodged in the Willimantic town hall and fed with beef, ham, eggs, bread and cheese. An observer of the event expected to find a "gang of tramps." Instead, he discovered a group of unemployed workers: "composed of the ordinary working class of men, mostly English and Americans...merely demanding the right to work."[47] They were led by Mathew Murray, a weaver from Providence, Rhode Island.

Murray and his marchers arrived in a textile town suffering from economic degradation and extensive poverty, caused by the temporary collapse of the local silk and cotton industries. A local newspaper appealed for charity to ease Willimantic's "acute destitution." The article explained that Willimantic's unemployed millworkers were reduced to wearing scanty clothing, saving their money to purchase what small amounts of food they could afford. They were too proud to ask for town aid, and would spend the forthcoming winter without fire or fuel. Willimantic was compared with the deprived tenement districts of New York City. [48]

Mathew Murray and his men left Willimantic the following morning, and set out for Manchester, Connecticut. Jacob Coxey's industrial army marched across a country devastated by economic depression. During the winter of 1893/94, over 20% of America's industrial workforce was without jobs. The situation in Willimantic hardly improved during the difficult year of 1894. The financial plight of the W. G. & A. R. Morrison Company almost brought the demise of Arthur G. Turner, a local silk manufacturer, who owed the Morrisons more than $30,000 for the silk machinery in his Willimantic mill.

Turner survived, but the W. G. & A. R. Morrison Company, unable to pay its numerous creditors, finally closed its doors in February, 1895. The workshops' contents were auctioned off to help pay back some of the North Street factory's $36,700 mortgage. The Atwood Machine Company of nearby Stonington, and the Draper Silk Company of Hopedale, Rhode Island, picked up some excellent bargains. The Natchaug Company continued to occupy the building until its surprise collapse the following summer.

In 1896, Walter Morrison, the "W. G." part of the defunct company, obtained capital from his cousin, J. Henry Morrison, and briefly reinstituted the manufacture of silk machinery in Willimantic, albeit on a much smaller scale. The new Morrison enterprise succumbed in 1898, and was absorbed by the Atwood Machine Company. Walter Morrison had been apprenticed to John Atwood at Conantville in the late 1860s. Atwood, a highly skilled mechanic, made a living repairing silk weaving machinery for local mills. He originally worked in Atwoodville, but moved into larger premises in Conantville before the Civil War, when his repair business expanded into machine building. He subsequently outgrew Conantville, and built a three-story, 100 ft x 70 foot brick factory on Willimantic's Valley Street in 1870, and leased part of it to the A. A. & H. E. Conant Silk Company. Atwood won many lucrative orders to build silk looms. By 1873, his company was shipping carloads of silk machinery from Willimantic to all corners of the United States, including a massive order to a silk mill in Scranton, Pennsylvania.[49]

On Sunday morning, February 27, 1876, Willimantic's Starkweather grist and flock mill caught fire. John Atwood's factory was located next door and was destroyed in the resulting conflagration. The fire's intense heat, "curled the iron shutters on the windows like paper." Atwood lost over $5,000 worth of uninsured machinery. It was widely agreed that had it not been for the heavy snow on the roofs of surrounding buildings, the center of Willimantic would have been totally destroyed.[50]

The A. A. & H. E. Conant Silk Company remained in Willimantic, but Atwood moved his business to Stonington, Connecticut. Twenty-three years later, Atwood's ex-apprentice, Walter Morrison, joined him there and formed the Atwood-Morrison Machine Company. John Atwood died in 1903, aged 80, and his son, Eugene, took control. The small concern which had maintained and repaired silk machinery on the Mount Hope River in 1850, matured into one of the leading silk machinery manufacturers in the world. Eugene Atwood died at home in 1926. He had come a long way from Atwoodville, where he was born in 1856. How far? His 1926 abode was 300 Park Avenue, New York City.[51]

THE TURNERS

Arthur G. Turner was born in New York City in 1847. He came to Willimantic in 1886 from Mansfield, Connecticut, where he had been in partnership in a small silk mill.[52] Turner rented the basement and first floor of the Center Street Armory, and instituted a "raw silk mill" by installing a steam engine and silk throwing machinery. Workers flooded the basement of the Armory as they dug below the building's foundations. The excavations exposed several fresh water springs, and construction could not proceed without constant pumping. Turner's production was hampered by regular flooding, and, during the following year, he was forced to move the manufactory's steam engine from the basement, and install it in a purpose-built engine-house at the rear of the Armory.[53]

Arthur Turner had located in Willimantic because of the town's large French Canadian workforce. He had no wish to share his father's problems in nearby Turnerville where, as in Mansfield, it was difficult to find suitable labor. Phineas W. Turner was born in Coventry, Connecticut in 1819. He worked in the silk trade in New York City, Tolland and Mansfield Hollow, and by 1853 had acquired enough capital to purchase the water rights of the North Pond at Hebron, Connecticut, known today as Amston Lake. By the 1890s, 'Turnerville' had developed into a thriving silk producing community straddling the three Connecticut towns of Hebron, Lebanon and Colchester. It boasted its own railroad depot on the busy Air Line route between Boston and New York City.[54]

The Turner Silk Mill, built in 1889, stood on the southwest corner of Bank Street and Valley Street in Willimantic. This circa 1900 view looks north up Bank Street. Proprietor Arthur G. Turner went out of business in 1917. The mill was subsequently purchased by the Goyer Company to manufacture cables. It was extensively remodeled in 1928, and opened as the Willimantic Trade School. *François Gamache*

The transition from agricultural work to the more rigorous demands of industrial production was not an easy one. For example, silk workers in Hebron abandoned their looms at harvest time. In 1886, plagued by a continual shortage of suitable labor, Phineas hired a number of weavers from Switzerland to manufacture silk ribbons. Things went well. The Swiss workers were most conscientious, until Phineas hired a "Marlborough girl who wished to learn the silk trade." He ordered a Swiss woman to instruct her, but Turnerville's new Swiss community was outraged when it discovered that its trade secrets were being revealed to an outsider. The strict rules of the Swiss trade-guild demanded that the intricacies of silk ribbon weaving be passed on only to indentured apprentices or relatives. The Swiss weavers walked off the job. Turner demanded that they return to work immediately. Violence erupted, and several pistol-brandishing Swiss strikers chased Phineas out of town. He returned with the police, and the ringleaders were arrested and locked in a box car. They were subsequently fined $7 each for disturbing the peace. Turner locked the Swiss malcontents from his mill, stating that he would never give in to strikers.[55]

Meanwhile, back in Willimantic, Arthur G. Turner's Center Street silk mill in the town Armory became too small to fulfill his growing order book. In October, 1887, Turner resisted overtures to move to Colchester,[56] and searched Willimantic for new premises. An ideal spot was discovered on "Johnson Park" facing Valley Street and Bank Street, and plans were made to build a mill there.

After advising his son never to hire Swiss weavers, Phineas Turner supplied the necessary capital to build the new silk mill. The Turners quickly became embroiled in a nasty legal quarrel. They fought off attempts instigated by local silk industry rivals to preserve Johnson Park as a public common.[57] The Turners wisely decided to offer the contract to build their proposed mill's machinery to the W. G. & A. R. Morrison Company, and the Morrisons persuaded their friends at the Holland, Chaffee and Natchaug companies, to drop their petition.

The Turner silk mill was finished in 1889. Architecturally it compared with the textile mills which graced the Massachusetts manufacturing town of Fall River. It was four stories high with dimensions of 135 x 100 foot. Its looms were powered by a 150 hp steam engine, supplying employment for 75 hands. By 1892, Turner advertised extensively in New England newspapers for raw silk winders, tempting them with earnings of $6 a week.[58]

Arthur Turner's workforce eventually rose to over 100, but the Bank Street mill was hard hit by the 'Panic of 1893,' and Turner instituted short-time working. In August, 1893, an outstanding debt to the virtually defunct W. G. & A. R. Morrison Company almost led to liquidation. In an interview conducted at the time, Turner blamed his difficulties on the Wilson tariff legislation. Turner survived, and continued to manufacture high-quality silk products for the ensuing generation. The Turner mill went into receivership in 1915, and was wound-up in 1917. The mill's machinery was purchased by Joseph Bonneville, a Canadian manufacturer, who shipped it to his Montreal silk mills.[59]

Willimantic's postbellum prosperity was not wholly the creation of the Willimantic Linen Company's top grade cotton thread. The local economy was also fired by silk industry manufacturers such as Goodrich Holland, Arthur G. Turner, Orwell and Joseph Chaffee and Walter and Arthur Morrison. Willimantic had the advantages of being on the doorstep of the birthplace of American silk culture, having excellent railroad connections, and having access to an experienced industrial workforce drawn from its Irish, Polish and French Canadian families. The prosperity continued into the twentieth century, thanks to the foundations laid by the early entrepreneurs. The Windham Silk Company and the Willimantic Machine Company continued to build Willimantic's reputation as a silk center. By the early twentieth century, Willimantic was a relatively well-integrated, multi-ethnic, predominantly Roman Catholic community. However, one more ethnic/religious group moved into the area, and encounterd the prejudice which non-Yankees and Catholics had previously experienced. A large number became farmers. They also wrote Silk City's final chapter. In 1928, several Jewish entrepreneurs arrived from New York City and invested heavily in Willimantic's faltering silk economy.

CHAPTER 6

Silk City 1900 - 1940

As the twentieth century got under way, Willimantic's Board of Trade boasted of the young city's Arcadian milieu and pastoral countryside and farms, in an attempt to convince existing industries that it was an ideal setting to relocate to, and to persuade new businesses to set-up-shop in such pleasant surroundings, far from the madding crowds of Boston and New York. Agriculture had been dominant in the area surrounding Willimantic since colonial times, but it declined with the onset of the industrial revolution, and numerous farms were abandoned.

In 1910, Elisha Winter penned a letter to the local newspaper, congratulating Willimantic on its early twentieth century prosperity. Whilst he welcomed new industries to town, he was sad that Windham was abandoning its rich agricultural heritage. He recalled that the area once grew the best apples in the country, fine cedar and pine trees and top grade potatoes, but the old orchards and farms were now decaying. Winter appealed to local industrialists to regenerate the agricultural economy - but his agenda was two fold:

> We have fine gardens and can easily have more. Some of the same boom that is caring for our industrial enterprises should be extended to our agricultural possessions. The Hebrews see this and are taking advantage of the situation to the disadvantage of our resident population. Is this wise? Our farmers' sons should stay on the farm.[1]

Winter hoped that by redirecting some of the prosperity to the area's farms, the Jewish expansion there could be stemmed. Abandoned farms in and around Willimantic, in places such as Colchester, Bozrah and Hebron, had been revived by a recent influx of Jewish immigrants. If Elisha Winter had been around in 1928, he would have been shocked to discover that Hebrew immigration had penetrated local industry too. Jewish capital from New York City's garment district helped rejuvenate Willimantic's dying silk industries, creating much-needed employment for 900 local people at the height of the Depression.

The 'Panic of 1893', and some questionable financial dealings involving Joseph Dwight Chaffee and Joseph Fenton, caused insurmountable problems for Willimantic's silk industries during the nineteenth century's last decade. However, the Holland and Turner Silk Companies survived into the new century, and by 1905, Willimantic experienced what can only be described as a silk renaissance. The Morrison Company had been superseded in 1899 by the Willimantic Machine Company, and the controversial Natchaug Silk Company was replaced in 1901 by the Windham Silk Company.

Prosperity returned to 'Silk City,' and 1905 was a particularly good year. The Willimantic Machine Company declared a 10% dividend. The Turner silk mill, the Willimantic Cotton Company, the American Thread Company, and the Windham Manufacturing Company boasted full order books. The Chaffee Manufacturing Company made silk braid and fish lines in the old Church Street mill, and shared in the prosperity.[2]

The Willimantic Board of Trade, fired by this growth, produced a promotional pamphlet to attract further industry to the city. It boasted of the area's attractions, and pointed out that Willimantic was soon to be connected by trolley cars to Storrs, South Willington, Stafford Springs, Coventry, North Windham, Chaplin, Eastford and the Woodstocks. The prosperity of the local silk industry was also highlighted and Willimantic was defined as a "growing silk center."[3] The growth did not last long. Willimantic's silk industries, like its trolley cars, would disappear by the outbreak of the Second World War.

Understandably, there was much industrial activity in Willimantic during the 1920s, as the United States experienced unprecedented economic expansion. The Eastern Connecticut city did not exactly roar; the 1925 strike at American Thread caused numerous social and economic problems for Willimantic, but several small industries added to the city's prosperity during that decade. The Rossie Velvet Company abandoned its operations in the Center Street Armory and the New London-based R & J Waist Company, "manufacturers of silk and muslin underwear," moved its Colchester manufactory into the vacant space. The old Center Street Armory, built in 1880, had served as Arthur G. Turner's first Willimantic silk mill in 1886, and later became the home of the Franco American Social Club.

While R & J gave employment to 100 local "girls and women," it went into liquidation in 1928. The S. P. S. Silk Company operated out of the Natchaug Industrial Company's Wilson Street factory, yet it went into voluntary liquidation in 1928. The S. P. S. Company was replaced, in the vacant Wilson Street factory, by the Uncas Silk Company, an expansion of North Windham's L. M. Hartson Silk Company, which employed 25 hands. The Connecticut Braiding and Cordage Company operated out of the old Chaffee silk mill on Church Street, and also folded in the difficult year of 1928.

The Depression bit hard into Willimantic's fragile economy, and the local silk industry gasped for breath. But there had been an earlier fatality. The Turner silk mill went into receivership in 1915, and proprietor Arthur G. Turner died in Albany, Georgia during the winter of 1917, attempting to escape the New England winter and his deep financial problems. The Holland Company, the city's pioneer silk manufacturer, abandoned Willimantic in 1934, and the Windham Silk Company began to lay off workers in 1935. But there had been no reason, at the turn of the century, to suspect that Willimantic's industrial expansion would flounder, particularly in 1899, when local businessmen decided to reinstitute the local manufacture of silk spinning and weaving machinery.

THE WILLIMANTIC MACHINE COMPANY

The failure of the W. G. & A. R. Morrison Company in 1895 came as a great shock to all in Willimantic. The collapse created a large pool of unemployed skilled workers in town. A group of local entrepreneurs decided to invest in a new company to tap the town's rich vein of skilled machinists and fitters. On June 6, 1899, a charter was granted to Charles Leonard, E. H. Holmes and George Stiles, to incorporate the Willimantic Machine Company. A small workshop was prepared in the old Kingsbury Box Shop on Valley Street. The floors were strengthened and an engine and boiler were installed in a newly-built extension. Twenty-five men were given immediate employment, some of them returning from Stonington. In 1901, the Willimantic Machine Company and the newly-formed Windham Silk Company moved into the defunct Morrison Machine Company's 1888 North Street factory. The Willimantic Machine Company grew rapidly and soon employed 150 mechanics, providing stiff competition to the Atwood-Morrison Company in Stonington. Eugene Atwood quickly recognized the danger and by 1909, he had a controlling interest in the Willimantic Machine Company.

In 1910, the Windham Silk Company purchased the entire North Street factory, and gave the Willimantic Machine Company notice to quit. This caused great local concern. It was rumored that George Stiles, the Company's President, would take the route to Stonington traveled by John Atwood in 1876 and Walter Morrison in 1898, causing Willimantic to once again lose a prestigious and profitable manufacturing industry. Stiles announced business was excellent and assured the city fathers he had no intention of moving. Stiles and his Willimantic-based shareholders subsequently held a meeting in the Hooker House Hotel with the Atwood Company's directors. Sufficient capital was raised and the Willimantic Machine Company purchased a large tract of land known as the Moulton lot, located on Milk Street. Ground was broken on

May 3, 1910, by C. Morgan Williams, a Norwich building contractor who had recently built Willimantic's new model school on Windham Street.

The new factory, costing over $30,000, measured 50 x 226 feet, with a 18 x 40 foot boiler house connected to the rear. It was described as being of "substantial mill construction...three stories high...with two stories fronting on Milk Street...containing a regulation maple mill floor...with all partitions being of fireproof construction." The floors and walls were designed to support excessive weights. The back of the building faced the railroad tracks, and facilitated easy access for freight shipments.[4]

By 1916, the Willimantic Machine Company was one of America's premier manufacturers of silk and cotton machinery, and the Atwood Machine Company decided to take full control. The Milk Street-based Company became a branch of the Atwood Company and Eugene Atwood promised the Willimantic Machine Company's shareholders that, because of increased orders at his Stonington plant, he intended to double the local workforce to 150, and share production with Willimantic. Atwood forecast that he would be employing more than 250 local workers before the end of the year.[5]

The local manufacture of silk and cotton machinery continued in Willimantic throughout the 1920s, but the local branch of the Atwood Machine Company became an early victim of the Depression and the downturn in New England's textile industries. It closed its doors in 1931, and the vacant Milk Street factory was purchased by the Roselin Braiding Company in 1935.[6]

THE WINDHAM SILK COMPANY

After the L. D. Brown & Son Silk Company vacated the North Street factory in 1900, Superintendent Charles Fenton decided to stay in Willimantic and along with overseer Lyman Nichols and a group of local businessmen, led by Hugh Murray, instituted the Windham Silk Company on April 2, 1901. The new concern rented the space vacated by the Brown Company in the 12-year-old mill, and commenced the manufacture of silk linings, ribbons, hat bands and dress materials. By 1905, the Windham Silk Company employed 128 hands and had 135 looms in operation.

The Windham Silk Company's President Charles Fenton had organized the defunct Natchaug Silk Company with Joseph Chaffee in 1887. The new superintendent, Lyman A. Nichols, had learned his trade with the Haskell Silk Company of Westbrook, Maine. He was hired by Fenton in 1887, and retained by the Brown Company after it had purchased the defunct Natchaug Company's weaving department.

In 1910, a wealthy and successful Windham Silk Company purchased the North Street manufactory, and ejected the Willimantic Machine Company which had shared the premises since 1901. The Windham Silk Company tore down the wooden structure adjoining the mill facing onto Valley Street, a building originally erected by the W. G. & A. R. Morrison Machine Company in 1874 after its removal from the Paisley Silk Mill. In its place, the Windham Silk Company erected a three-story brick building with basement. The new extension, designed by P. F. Sheldon & Sons, architects and engineers of Providence, Rhode Island, was 119 feet 6 inches long, and 37 feet 8 inches wide with a saw tooth roof. A new floor was laid in the North Street mill, and its interior was completely repainted.

The new mill, which cost over $35,000 to build, was ready for occupation on April 1, 1911, in time to celebrate the Windham Silk Company's 10th anniversary. The Windham Silk Company's 140 hands had an extra 13,000 square feet of floor space in which to manufacture the high grade black silk goods for which it had become famous. Some of the extra space was rented to A. G. Turner, who installed silk quilling machinery in the basement, and to Harry Smith who had manufactured silk machinery supplies in various locations in Willimantic for many years.

The Windham Silk Company prospered throughout the 1920s, but the Depression and downturn in America's silk trade led to its eventual closure in 1937. Robert H. Fenton, the Windham Silk Company's President, son of founder Charles Fenton, called in a receiver, and Vice-President Lyman Nichols was given the task of supervising the liquidation and removal of machinery from the plant. It proved to be a demanding job for a 79-year-old, and Nichols collapsed and died of a heart attack in the Company offices on a cold January morning in 1938.

Nichols' tragic death brought the curtain down on silk manufacturing on Valley Street, a process launched on a large scale some 71 years previously by the Holland brothers. The North Street manufactory was purchased by the newly formed Windham Development Company, a group of "public spirited businessmen," in April, 1938, and they leased it to the Synchro-Flame Oil Burner Corporation of Hartford.[7]

CORN, KOBE & ALCORN

In 1928, the Domestic Silk Company of 162 Madison Avenue, New York, owned by Abraham Corn, Max Goldstein, Max Stein and Nathan Stein, closed its mills in Paterson, New Jersey. The three gentlemen transferred operations to Willimantic's vacant Bridge Street mills, where they subsequently formed three companies: Willimantic Silk, Corn Spinning, and Kobe Weaving.[8] Domestic Silk was lured to Willimantic by a $12,000 grant from the Willimantic Chamber of Commerce and the Rockville-Willimantic Lighting Company, to pay for the heating and lighting of the mills during the Company's first year of operation.

The newly-formed Willimantic Silk Company began the manufacture of broad silk cloth on November 1, 1928, employing 150 hands. Max Goldstein inaugurated the Kobe Silk Weaving Company in May, 1929, employing 25 hands, but he expected to increase production and employ 200 hands. During the last two weeks of May, 1929, the Willimantic Silk Company produced 64,000 yards of silk and paid out $5,500 in wages.[9] The Corn Spinning Company was organized soon afterwards to produce silk thread, providing more local employment. Willimantic's ancient cotton mills received a new lease on life. The interiors were repainted and renovated, and state-of-the-art Crompton-Knowles silk looms were installed. The local press reported that working conditions in the new silk mills were excellent. Albert Garneau worked there:

> I got a job at the Kobe Silk Mill on Bridge Street. Kobe was the furthest on Bridge street, close to Willimantic Silk. There were two other companies there. There was Corn, the newer building, which didn't do weaving, and there was Willimantic Silk. The mills on the east side were empty, but the old buildings were there. During the NRA, Willimantic Silk went on strike. I went to work there for a while, for a year. I worked in weaving. It was basically a sweat shop. We got paid by the number of picks your machine made. When I was there, they increased the number of picks your machine could make per minute. They cut down the wages to make Roosevelt's demand of $13. 50 a week. That was why the place went on strike, and it eventually went down South. There were no toilets. They had a bathtub to urinate in. There was no toilet paper. You knew you had to work under those conditions, because there were four or five people waiting for your job."[10]

The parent company, Domestic Silk, worked with a tight profit margin and produced silk cloth and thread strictly for order, not for stock. Its silk products were sold to firms operating in New York's garment district. The Company had its critics, but it provided employment for almost 1,000 local people at the height of the Depression. On November 5, 1932, the Company closed its plants, throwing almost 900 hands out of work, a disastrous blow to the city.

Max Stein claimed the closure was due to the unwelcome activities of the state labor department and high city taxes. Stein was aware that Willimantic was reeling from the shock of the threat of losing the lucrative Holland Silk Company, and he felt the time was ripe to obtain favorable tax concessions. He was right. After a successful meeting with Willimantic Mayor James Hurley in the Nathan Hale Hotel, the Bridge Street mills were quickly reopened.[11]

The following year, Domestic Silk ignored President Roosevelt's National Recovery Act (NRA), which instructed textile companies to reduce hours and work a 40 hour week, and pay a minimum wage of $13 a week. The Kobe Company reduced hours from 48 to 40, but increased the required work rate by 15%. Four hundred weavers walked off the job on July 20, 1933. A week later the remaining 400 went on strike. The mills were closed until the following September. Pressure from Washington D. C. persuaded the Company to meet the strikers' demands of $1.85 per 100,000 picks, a rate which satisfied the NRA's guidelines.[12]

Domestic Silk closed its Willimantic mills in 1937. Joseph and Abraham Corn remained in town and put together a financial package which enabled the mills to briefly re-open. In March, 1938, the newly formed Willimantic-Corn Company was employing a skeleton staff of 25. The following October, the Corns appealed to the Willimantic Chamber of Commerce to put together an application for a low interest loan from the New Deal's Reconstruction Finance Corporation (RFC), to enable the Willimantic-Corn Company to purchase the now idle Bridge Street mills and stock from owner Max Stein. The appeal, crafted by congressmen, consultants and local businessmen failed, and the mills closed soon afterwards.[13]

In February, 1939, Willimantic's city fathers appropriated $4,000 to persuade Alexander Rosin, the proprietor of the Alrose Manufacturing Company, to locate in the vacant Bridge Street mills. The money was used to pay for the transfer of machinery, and a new oil-fired heating system. Rosin took a two-year lease on the property and immediately employed 65 skilled weavers, promising immediate expansion. This was the city's last silk manufacturer. Rosin went over to rayon production before the enterprise closed in 1941.[14]

Early in 1938, Paul Hayden, of the Connecticut Light and Power Company, addressed the annual meeting of the Willimantic Chamber of Commerce. It was obvious to all present that evening that Willimantic's silk industries were in their death throes, and it was imperative that new industries be attracted to the city. Hayden stressed the good points about Willimantic: a low cost of living, excellent freight connections to New York and Boston, low wages, good labor relations and an excess of skilled silk workers, "which easily and quickly adapts itself to other types of industry."

He also outlined the city's bad points. Eastern Connecticut, he explained, was full (2.3 million square feet) of old-fashioned, abandoned textile mills, unsuited for modern day single-line production. Willimantic had its fair share of old abandoned mills such as these, thanks to the recent collapse of three local companies: Domestic Silk, Rossie Velvet and Windham Silk. "In spite of these handicaps," he concluded, "efforts should be made to sell the available plants to diversified industries rather than to textiles."[15]

Stanley J. Sumner, a member of the Chamber's industrial committee, followed Hayden onto the platform and explained that Willimantic's failure to attract diversified industries in the past had been because of lack of space. He was confident, however, that the city's vacant plants might attract suitable small industries. One year later the city allocated $5,000 to persuade a New York City manufacturer of electrical components to locate in Willimantic. In March,

1939, Electro Motive moved into the Rossie Velvet Company's old factory on South Street, and later occupied part of the old Bridge Street mills. Willimantic workers who had once woven and spun silk were now soldering components into radio receivers. Silk City was no more.

This brief tour of Willimantic's nineteenth and early twentieth century industries comes to a close. Gaps in this mostly forgotten chapter of Connecticut history continue to be filled. The business records of the town's largest industries remain to be discovered, along with the missing issues of the Willimantic *Public Medium* (1847 - 1861) and the Willimantic *Journal* (1866 - 1872). Until then the story continues as told by those who worked and lived in the mills and houses built by the area's silk and cotton manufacturers.

PART II

COMMUNITY

Part II

COMMUNITY

My mother lived on "Cork Alley" when she was young. That was Jackson Place, and everyone around her was Irish or of Irish descent. The families were Killoureys - they were undertakers. There were the Picketts. She often told me about the Irish funerals down there, which to me sounded like orgies! They were Irish wakes and they did strange things like putting a pipe into the corpses' mouths so they could have their last pipeful of tobacco, and she told me about their wailing and moaning over the corpse, and about the whisky and partying. My mother could imitate an Irish accent very easily. She always did it when she was telling me these stories about Cork Alley.

It wasn't that much Irish when I was growing up. I remember Italian and French families in that area down there. In later years, around the 1930s, there were Italian and Polish families down there. Most of the French and Polish were living down in what we called the lower village, or "Sodom." My mother's sister lived on Willowbrook Street then. The "WASPS" or Anglos lived predominantly on this side of the river. One of our neighbors was Eugene Boss Lewis who was an overseer at American Thread. He was named after an old agent who was in charge there for many years.

This part of Willimantic was known as the Fourth Ward, or as we used to say, the "Forgotten Fourth." It is a very quiet part of town. We had a blacksmith, a carriage painter, and the canoe club. There was also a sausage maker, a Mr Parent, who worked for a butcher. It was a terrible smell. I remember that when we moved into this house, there was no electricity. My uncle would not have it. The house was lit by kerosene lamps! Several of the houses around here would not have electricity when I was young, so there was still a demand for kerosene.

Excerpt of oral history interview with Gladys Bowman, conducted July 2, 1991.

CHAPTER 1

The 1979/80 Millworkers of Willimantic Oral History Project

The interviews featured in this chapter were conducted in 1979 and 1980 by students at the University of Connecticut, and complement the oral histories more recently conducted at the Windham Textile & History Museum (See chapters 2 through 14).

On the whole, the 1979 students did well. Oral history interviewing, transcription and analysis is a complex process. However, the students often failed to provide a context in which to place the information revealed by their questions. They posed few biographical or local history questions. For example, in the opening interview with the Dubinas, the reader fails to discover "Mr." Dubina's first name. Margaret Dubina was born in Hungary, but her date of birth or maiden name is not known. When did Mrs. Dubina first arrive in the United States from Hungary? What were the circumstances which led her family to leave their homeland? Why did they come to Willimantic? Nevertheless, despite its shortcomings, the interview provides some intriguing insights into the bitter 1925 strike at Willimantic's American Thread Company (ATCO), a dispute which divided the community for many generations.

Leona Delude and Lil Despathy offer differing views of their working life in the mill. Isabelle Moran's interview reveals that, in her youth, Willimantic's well-established Irish community considered themselves to be a cut above the ethnic groups replacing them as mill labor. Isabelle spent a virtual lifetime at ATCO, but she was under no illusion that the community's major employer was a workers' paradise. Isabelle's attitudes stand in stark comparison to those of Charles Hill. A company man through-and-through, Hill spent most of his working life in ATCO's Willimantic mills. Mary Benoit and Daniel Gallagher offer some insights to unionization in the mills, and the chapter closes with an autobiographical piece by Alice Stabile, who was employed at ATCO between 1927 and 1935.

MARGARET DUBINA

Margaret Dubina lied about her age, and began work at the Turner silk mill on Valley Street, Willimantic, circa 1914. She was thirteen, but looked older. Her family needed the extra wage. She was employed on silk thread reeling and winding from 6: 00 a. m. to 6: 00 p. m., Monday to Friday, and from 6: 00 a.m. until noon on Saturdays. Her lack of inches and years forced her to wear high heels so she could operate the machinery, and look 16- years-old, which was the legal minimum age at which children could be employed in the textile industry. "I had to comb my hair like a big girl...bobs and everything...I got away with murder." A. G. Turner, the silk mill's proprietor, asked for her birth certificate. Margaret explained that she did not have one because she was born in Hungary. Margaret's workmates at the Turner silk mill were mainly female Italian and Poles.

The Turner silk mill closed down two years after Margaret began working there, and she subsequently found employment in ATCO's packing depart- ment. Her recollections of this part of her life reveal the tough conditions endured by immigrant textile workers. She recalled that the physical working conditions at ATCO were better in her early days, when she packed boxes of colored cotton thread for piecework. The machinery and walls were washed constantly, and everyone was "friendly." However, as the interview continues, Margaret's nostalgia wears thin, particularly when she recalls ATCO's disturb- ing "foghorn," heard across the Windhams, Mansfield and Lebanon when the wind was in the right direction. It beckoned workers to the mill every morning. If late, their pay was docked, and if a worker was regularly late, they were dismissed.

ATCO's hours were not as long as Turner's. Margaret worked from 7: 00 a.m. to 5: 00 p. m., with a "nooning" hour for lunch, and from 7: 00 a.m. until noon on Saturdays. The packing of thread was highly competitive. More boxes packed meant more wages, so the women raced around the department. Mistakes were often made. Wrong colors had to be retrieved, and boxes short of the correct number of bobbins had to be refilled. Margaret was fast. She made good money - but her overseer, George Easterbrook, made life difficult for her.

According to Margaret, Easterbrook hated 'Polacks'. "He was a devil...he always called me a Polack...I wasn't no Polack. I wouldn't mind if I was." Margaret admits that her speed forced mistakes, but no more than anyone else. A male colleague warned her that Easterbrook was switching the colors in her packed boxes to get her into trouble. Margaret was very upset, but powerless to do anything about it. "He hurt my feelings all the time. I never said nothing to him. He mixed my boxes and numbers...he'd be so glad and he talked to himself,

'I got that Polack.' He was crazy."

Margaret's mistakes led to a three-day suspension - despite her protestations of innocence. The "boss," a Mr. Branch, accused her of working too fast. Easterbrook, seeing that Margaret was no longer on the job, thought she had been fired. When she returned to work on the completion of her suspension, her overseer "...had ten fits, and was pacing up and down saying, 'That goddamned Polack. She had to come back. How did she get back!?' He was a Yankee. He was a skunk. I hated him." Margaret often caught Easterbrook mixing up her packed boxes, but when challenged he claimed he was correcting her mistakes. Easterbrook's xenophobia was matched by ATCO's cruel practise of 'speed-up'. When Margaret and her coworkers achieved the piecework maximum, around 48 - 50 boxes of packed thread per hour, ATCO's management claimed it was too low, "...so you had to pack 60 per hour for the same dollars."

Margaret worked in packing for about five years, then left to get married and have a family. Getting full-time babysitters was difficult, so she returned to ATCO in the early 1920s and worked part-time in Mill Number Two on a spinning operation. This period, directly before the 1925 strike, seemed to be the happiest. She earned good money, and was reluctant to strike after ATCO announced a large wage reduction in January, 1925. She was puzzled by the workers' attitude: "I could not see why they wanted a strike...they'd been making good money." ATCO's management tried to persuade Margaret to work through the walk-out, but she "hated to go against the people." ATCO's large Willimantic plant was mainly non-union and had resisted the formation of locals since 1912, when the I. W. W. had held a successful strike there. Margaret believed that unions caused strikes: "The only time we got into the union is when we went out on strike."

Three thousand workers walked out of ATCO's Willimantic mills on a cold March morning in 1925. The Polish employees were a major force behind the strike. Many of Margaret's best friends at the mill were Polish. Her experiences in the packing department illustrate the presence of ethnic discrimination. It can be supposed that discrimination also played a part in the 1925 dispute. Indeed, Margaret, who stayed loyal to the strike, recalled that the first strikers to return to work were mainly Americans who worked in ATCO's Number Five and Six Mills, where few Polish workers were employed.

The Polish could speak little English, but Margaret spoke Polish, so the strike organizers elected her to serve on the strike committee as an interpreter. Most Willimantic people thought the 1925 strike would be over in a matter of days, but both sides became entrenched. ATCO was confident it could control its labor force because of the lifting of war-time restrictions on employers. The employees, empowered by advances in wages and stature during World War One, were equally confident of victory - the withdrawal of a 10% paycut.

The strike committee regularly met to keep up morale. They held regular meetings in Main Street's Franklin Hall, or in the larger Loomer Opera House if a particularly important speaker was engaged to rally the strikers. ATCO invited state troopers to town, and lodged them in its 'Elms' boarding house. The state troopers escorted the 'scabs' to work. Margaret claimed that Willimantic never wholly recovered from the bitterness created by the 1925 strike: "When we saw our local people on the street who were 'scabbin'', we didn't look at each other, and some strikers spat upon the pavement when the 'scabs' walked by."

Some 40 years later, whilst Margaret was working at Electric Boat in Groton, she recognized two women during a lunch break, and remembered that they had scabbed in the 1925 strike. She turned to a colleague, and making sure the two women could hear her, Margaret loudly proclaimed: "Darn old scabs. They were no good. They took our jobs." The two women, still guilty about their betrayal of the strike, did not respond. According to Margaret, they "...didn't say a word, they got red in the face."

Although the Polish workers formed the greater part of the grass roots struggle against ATCO during the 1925 strike, its organizers were French, Irish and Yankee. Margaret refers to a photograph of the strike committee, and identifies the leaders by gender and ethnicity. Mary Kelleher is the only one actually named - she was an Irish labor organizer from Scranton, Pennsylvania. The remaining seven consist of four men and three women, three Irish, three French and one Yankee. Margaret passed on the committee's decisions to the Polish strikers. The reports revealed how many strikers were returning to work, and how the committee was distributing strike funds.

Margaret often visited Mary Kelleher in her Hotel Hooker room to keep abreast of the strike news. Kelleher persuaded her to stay involved in the strike, but Margaret's resolve slowly weakened. She became disillusioned. Why should she sacrifice and suffer for the ungrateful strikers returning to work? But her loyalty to the strike remained, even though she felt that "...a lot of people that didn't need no money got it."

The strike committee organized the distribution of strike funds according to individual and family hardships. Margaret received no assistance because her husband worked. Mr. Dubina cleaned machines in ATCO's Mill Number Two. When the strike began he worked as a weaver at the Rossie velvet mill. Margaret asked the strike committee for $5 a week, but she was refused. "I was out two years on strike. Didn't get a cent from the union." Even so, she traveled widely around New England on fund raising missions with Mary Kelleher and a local organizer, Amy Hooker, "...a country girl from Hebron...who lived in Willimantic and worked in ATCO's Number Six Mill."

Dubina, Kelleher and Hooker traveled to ATCO's sister mills in Massachusetts at Fall River and Holyoke. The workers there generously supported their Willimantic colleagues, but they refused to join the strike. Margaret also traveled across Connecticut selling flowers to raise strike funds. She remembered the excellent support gained from the hatter's union in Danbury, and the solid support from various union locals in Willimantic, particularly the carpenters' union.

During the early weeks of the strike, Willimantic was visited by communist party organizers. The interviewer asks Margaret if she remembered them. She denied it and declared that communists were not involved, but she admits that some strikers may have had leanings towards the left: "Maybe they called me a communist because I told the strikers to go out and fight and win the strike." Margaret Dubina's frustrations, 54 years after the event, are aimed at "union leaders" who "did nothing." She believed that the strike committee's guidance to avoid violence and name calling at all costs may have been wrong. The strikers were too passive.

The strike lingered on. In June, 1925, ATCO announced that all strikers not returning to work would be instantly dismissed, and those living in company houses should vacate them so incoming workers could be housed. Margaret remembered that ATCO paid the "scabs" higher wages and financed their traveling and moving expenses to Connecticut from New Hampshire and Massachusetts. The replacement workers caused tremendous splits in the city. Many of the strikers thrown out of ATCO's houses and tenements were forced to live in tents on Route 6, just over the city border, in a community which became known locally as "Tent City."

Margaret recalled the intense bitterness between the French Canadians loyal to the strike, and those imported by ATCO. The bad feeling was "smoothed out" by the priest at St. Mary's, who told the strikers to be friendly with those workers coming into town. Many of the striking "Polish and Russian" workers left Willimantic after ATCO's ultimatum, and found work in Ansonia, Shelton, New Haven and Waterbury. The strike lingered on. The strikers were ignored and it was business as usual for ATCO. Margaret decided the fight was lost in 1927, and she began work in the Holland silk mill on Valley Street.

The preceding oral history is significant inasmuch as it demonstrates the social and economic impact of the 1925 strike at ATCO - one of the textile industry's largest strikes in the post-World War One period, and Margaret Dubina played an integral part in it. The interview also provides a brief insight into the racial tensions fired by the dispute. Margaret Dubina was asked about ethnic discrimination:

> There was discrimination then, and there is discrimination now...Yes, you've got a foreign name....it's because you're a foreigner. It's same for the Puerto Ricans and niggers today. Same thing then. You could not get a job in Number Five or Number Six mill if your name ended in "ski" You're a Polack. That's the way it was. Nobody cared like today

(1979). We would never think of marching around like Puerto Ricans. We never did that. We were quiet about it. We got a job."

Trade unionism in ATCO's Willimantic mills was virtually wiped out after the crushing of the 1925 strike. The Textile Workers Union of America, and activists like Margaret Dubina, made brave attempts to organize ATCO's mainly un-unionized workforce, but unionism nationwide went into decline as the country enjoyed its national prosperity prior to the 1929 stock market collapse. Unionism in Willimantic made a recovery during the late 1930's thanks to the Depression and Roosevelt's New Deal.

LEONA DELUDE

Leona Delude was born in Willimantic in 1915, and began work at ATCO in 1946, aged 31. Leona lived on Quarry Street, and walked to and from the mills in the east end of town everyday, until learning how to drive at age 54. She worked at ATCO for 26 years, until being unceremoniously laid off in 1972, aged 57. Leona was still bitter, seven years after the event, and held ATCO in contempt: "They know what they done to me. All those bosses, when I see them shopping somewhere, they don't dare to look at me."

Leona was employed on "single winding and bobbin cone," which demanded constant attention, and required her to be on her feet all day. Leona watched 90 ends. She claimed that much of the work was "junk." Poor quality yarn, with knots and twists, required extra attention and slowed the job down. This reduced Leona's chances to earn a good wage, as she was paid by piecework. As far as Leona was concerned, "...the favorites got the best work."

Margaret Dubina had an unpleasant Yankee boss. Leona's supervisor, however, was Polish, and she still retained strong opinions about him: "I had a boss. He was Polish. Oh my God, wasn't he a son-of-a-gun of a Polish fellow. He was terrible! He complained when we went to the ladies room, but the union allowed us between five to ten minutes a hour to go to the ladies room." Another foreman constantly accused Leona of talking too much.

Leona recalled constant intimidation by ATCO's management, who demanded that the workers stayed at the job constantly, which meant that they had to eat as they worked, taking a bite of a sandwich, and putting it in their pockets until the opportunity arose to take another bite. She thought this was a very unhealthy practise, but the workers had no choice. Leona worked the morning shift, from 6: 00 a. m. until 2: 00 p. m. All the workers keenly looked forward to the end of the working day, "...we were on our feet all day...we were right near the door when the whistle blew, and out we'd go!" Leona's original job, in Mill Number Four, was transferred down south, and she was regularly moved between departments until finally ending up in the box shop.

The monotonous working day was relieved by visits to the ladies room or medical center. Leona enjoyed those occasions. Her hands and fingers were often pierced by slivers of wood or metal, and she walked to the medical center to have them removed - the perfect opportunity to have a rest, and a chat with the nurse. The breaking down of machinery, and the arrival of the fixer gave her another opportunity to break the tedium.

Leona worked at Electro Motive during the war. She took the job at ATCO in 1946 for a "better deal," but maintained that it was a terrible mistake. Electro Motive paid their workers a bonus at Christmas. ATCO's workers received no such bonus, but a Christmas card instead - a card manufactured in its print shop. Margaret recalled that the "cheapskates" at ATCO did not even mail them out. They handed them to the employees with their pay packets.

ATCO's female workers had little chance for advancement, unless, according to Leona, they went ten pin bowling - a pastime exclusively reserved for the "girls in the office," as "mill girls" worked the first shift, and had to be in bed early. The "mill girls" also worked the second and third shifts, and could not visit the bowling alley.

Leona Delude thought that ATCO treated their workers poorly. She had an almost perfect attendance record over 26 years, and lost only three days by attending the funerals of near relatives. She felt her loyalty was not recognized and believed that the Puerto Ricans were favored much more: "They killed everything. They cut everybody's throat you know, them Puerto Ricans...they pushed us out... ATCO favored them...We were born and brought up in Willimantic and we were working here. It seems that we should get a better job than those Puerto Ricans."

The working conditions in ATCO's mills were dreadful. The noise was unbearable, "...it went bang, bang, bang...it was awful loud, very loud...we came out with our ears buzzing. You talked, and you couldn't even hear yourself." Leona recalled the steamy summers: "...it was awfully hot in the summer. We went in at 6: 00 a. m. We were in there half-an-hour, and we were all wet, ready to come home." She recalled sex discrimination: "...men were better paid than us...we worked twice as hard as the men...they would smoke in the men's room for half an hour." Her 26 year stint in the thread mills was not wholly enjoyable.

Leona believed she was laid off in 1972 because of favoritism. She worried that no one would want to employ a 57-year-old woman, but she got a job at the Electro Motive Company - but it closed down several months later. Leona eventually found job satisfaction in caring for the elderly, and in a local meals-on-wheels program.

Scenes from a Strike. The 1925 strike at the American Thread Company tore Willimantic apart. Feelings ran high in the community for generations to follow. Connecticut State Policemen took a series of surveillance photographs, particularly when pickets confronted the "scab" labor being escorted into the plant. Top left. State troopers guard the main entrance to the American Thread Company's Willimantic plant. Far left. A car drives by, and a police photographer within takes a photograph of pickets assembled on the sidewalk opposite the entrance to Mill Number Two. Above top. Replacement workers are escorted from Mill Number Two. A remark, or sharp noise, attracts everyone's attention, and the police and scabs glance back at the assembled pickets. Above. A picket is escorted away from the scene of the strike. *Roger Morgan.*

LIL DESPATHY

Leona hated it, but Lil loved it. Lil Despathy was born in Willimantic in 1902. She began work as a winder at ATCO in 1919, and remained there until 1967, save for a two year period after the 1925 strike, when she was dismissed, and a brief period during the 1930s, when she was laid off. Lil returned in 1927, when ATCO declared an open house, a pardon, for those who stayed out on strike and were subsequently sacked. Lil was against the 1925 strike, but she recalled that she, "... could not go back to work because my husband was a union man." Was the 1925 strike justified? "I can't remember what the strike was about." Were the strikers cruelly evicted onto the streets? "No. The workers did not get kicked out, they had to get out. They wouldn't work so they had to get out." Was it tough in the depression? "I was laid off during the depression, but did housework. We got by."

According to Lil, life in ATCO's mills was almost idyllic. She had been retired for 12 years at the time of the interview, but she still badly missed the place. "I always enjoyed my work. I just loved it." Were there any nasty overseers? "I had wonderful bosses." Great work. Great bosses. But what about foreigners? "The Polish were good workers. They'd never loaf...I hear that the Puerto Ricans are also good workers." OK, Lil. A great place to work, but a lot of people have complained about the unsafe and dirty working conditions. Were the working conditions bad? "No. People fell down and hurt their backs because the floor was oily. Nothing serious."

The Despathy interview provides an example of how an individual interview can deceive. It is a specific point of view which has to be juxtaposed against other interviews. Lil perceived the mill to be her whole life, and seemed incapable of saying anything negative about the company. Her uncritical view is revealed in the last response about working conditions. A textile mill was an unpleasant and dangerous place at the best of times. But according to Lil, workers who were injured had only themselves to blame for being so clumsy. Lil Despathy's recollections about ATCO differ greatly from those of Isabelle Moran, who was badly injured at work and refused to sign an agreement lifting any blame from ATCO.

ISABELLE MORAN

Isabelle Moran's grandparents were born in Norwich, Connecticut. They were of Irish extract, but she had no idea why they came to Willimantic. "When they arrived, there was nothing here, only Main Street." Her father was born in Willimantic in 1853. He was a councilman when Willimantic became a city in 1893, the year she was born. He originally worked in the Willimantic steam engine roundhouse near the railroad depot, which turned locomotives around for travel in the correct direction. She was taken there as a child by her father.

She explained that the roundhouse turned the railroad engines around so they could travel back to Boston. Isabelle's parents never worked in Willimantic's textile mills, but she remembered that her aunts and relatives worked in "the mills on Bridge Street." "I wouldn't work in the Bridge Street cotton mills, that was out...it was dirty, and it was awful noisy. They made cloth there. American Thread was the best place to work when you were young."

Isabelle Moran began work in ATCO's inspection room in 1909. She was 16. Two years later she went into the office of the carding room in Mill Number Four where, for $9 a week, she checked, weighed and tested raw cotton. Isabelle had a good head for figures, and enjoyed working with the payroll. She costed jobs "according to the speed of the carding machines and the kind of cotton suitable for skeins...We had to know every kind of cotton...Egyptian cotton was the best." The cotton bales from Egypt arrived by ship at Norwich, and were transported to Willimantic by rail. Isabelle remained there until she retired. "In all the years I worked there, I never earned a dollar a hour."

The job was tough. Isabelle recalled the constant danger of fire. The combed cotton often caught fire, filling the inspection rooms with smoke. The cotton-combing process often missed the odd seed, which ignited the clean cotton as it went into the twisting machine. Fires occurred about once a month, and the area was immediately sealed. "And what they did was very mean. The smoke was terrible..." The area was sealed to stop the spread of fire. Also, Mill Number Four's windows consisted of large, sealed glass blocks. "It was something to do with the humidity." Isabelle explained that the mill ceiling contained "big machines" which constantly sprayed water. "They had to keep a certain humidity in there, or the cotton would break going through the machines." The combination of smoke and extreme humidity created an unpleasant working environment. Isabelle also explained that "French and Polish women" often cleaned out the carding machines as they were in motion. One woman was too slow. "She lost all her fingers." The majority of Isabelle's workmates were "a certain class" of French and Polish. They were "good people," but "not very educated...let's say very primitive...very down to earth...I found them very vulgar at times...I don't know how to put it. French people are very crude...they got drunk."

Isabelle was most offended on one occasion as she empathized with a French Canadian woman whose drunken husband had come home, and broken all the dishes, and knocked the stovepipe down. "I asked her why she lived with him, and she replied that if she left she wouldn't have a husband and be an old maid like me! That finished me. I said don't tell me anymore." Isabelle liked the women who worked on the mill floor. She felt sorry for them, and often helped them out. "I'd go out and talk to them. I'd go to the cafeteria with them. So I got to know them better, but I never associated with them after work...They asked me to go to a tavern. I never went to a tavern in my life. They always went to taverns and ended up fighting."

One of Isabelle's working companions in the office hated the women mill workers, and never mixed with them at work or socially. Isabelle reckoned it was because she thought she was much better educated than they were. Isabelle explained that the women mill workers were always covered in "muck-grease." "Sometimes their hands were not too clean. I wouldn't eat anything they gave to me...They couldn't go and wash their hands, they didn't have the time. They'd eat their own lunch with paper, so all the black grease wouldn't get onto the sandwich.",

Isabelle continued to fraternize with the workers, but that ended when a new overseer forbade the office staff to communicate with the "help." The French and Polish "help" had no education. Isabelle recalled that most of them could not speak English. She mastered the Polish language, and often acted as an interpreter, but she was never able to understand the French Canadians.

Despite her fraternization with, and affection for, the immigrant workforce, Isabelle identified with the management, the superintendent and the foremen. "I was part of their class. That's why we got along so well." However, Isabelle sided with the union during the 1925 strike. She refused to leave the office and work the machinery. ATCO fired her, and she worked in Hartford for a year, at Aetna. "I was not in the union, we were not in unions in the office, but I would not break the strike."

The strike did not surprise her. She explained how horrendous the working conditions were, and that the workers were poorly paid. Isabelle's detested the "French people" brought to Willimantic to replace the strikers. This strengthened Isabelle's ethnic identity: "The Irish were better educated, were better people, not because I'm Irish. The French...never went to school. Why, none of them ever went to the fourth grade...they have no background." Isabelle was reluctant to discuss the 1925 strike. She lived in Hartford for its duration. The interviewer forces the subject, and she recalled how degrading it was for those on strike. Her brother, Tom, was a pipe fitter at ATCO, and during the strike he had to go out, door to door, selling bookends. He told his sister that she should always be polite to salesmen who come to the door, because she had no idea how demeaning it was to have the door slammed in your face, and be called a bum. Isabelle's father made sure that all his children were educated. Each of his sons had a trade, and one daughter gained a teaching degree from NYU. Isabelle explained that bitterness about the strike still lingered in the town. Many strikebreakers came to Willimantic from Lowell, and were still referred to as scabs.

An Irish friend of the family, who had worked in the finishing department, committed suicide by jumping into the Willimantic River. Her husband had died and she and her child were starving. Isabelle's mother fed her, but she was Irish, and too proud to ask the city for assistance. "Towards the end there were very few Irish in the mill. Second generation Irish were all very well educated." ATCO raised the workload for each hand after the strike, as revenge. "When I first went in that office, they had 10 men to run 10 cards, then they put 20, then 30 cards on each man and then they had two men running 100 machines!"

Isabelle's mother fed a lot of people during the strike. "We didn't have much money...there were seven kids...but she always had something for someone that was hungry. I had a very good childhood. We never went hungry. Now, my grandnieces expect everything."

Isabelle's family lived in the "Oaks." She explained that there were no French in the "Oaks." Her neighbors were "superintendents and bosses...everybody had their own phone. We got over there because my father was maintenance. Ordinary mill folk could not get a house in the Oaks." However, during the strike, the Moran family was ejected and moved into a tenement. Isabelle recalled that the "Oaks" houses were well maintained. "(ATCO) had a fleet of paperhangers and painters, and every year they did your house, one or two rooms at a time." The rent was a $1. 50 a week, taken out of the pay.

Isabelle believed that things improved at ATCO once the union became established. While walking to work in 1944, she slipped on the railroad tracks in ATCO's yard and broke her neck. She was in a plaster cast for a year. She refused to sign a waiver, and was paid in full. Another worker fell on the same day and broke her arm, signed a waiver, and received $300.

Isabelle moved to Jackson Street in 1941, on the day after Pearl Harbor was bombed. She related how Jackson Street was long considered to be the "low part of the town," but Isabelle carefully separates "lower and upper Jackson Street." Lower Jackson Street between Valley Street and Main Street housed "the saloons and the Knights of Columbus and all that," but upper Jackson Street was always "more residential." Isabelle Moran retired from American Thread in 1955, and worked in the children's library on Prospect Street.

According to Isabelle, the French and the Polish lived in the part of town once occupied by Isabelle's grandparents. The area is referred to as the "New Village, Sodom and Cork Alley." She also explained that the various ethnic groups rarely mixed socially. "They lived together and associated together." Being Irish, the Morans closely identified with St. Joseph's Church. She was still bitter that "the French people" had left the "mother" church, and instituted St. Mary's in 1903. Isabelle's grandfather had helped build the basement of St. Joseph's in 1872, without payment, and she didn't think that St. Joseph's should continue to pay for the education of French children, and she didn't like the fact that St. Joseph's old school was being used to educate "dropouts." It annoyed her that French kids at St. Mary's were taught only in French. "Now, if they want to learn French, the kids should have to go to an extra hour, just like the Jewish kids go up to the synagogue to learn Hebrew."

The Polish community remained a part of St. Joseph's, and that may explain

Isabelle's preference to them over the French - but she disliked the Italians in St. Joseph's. "There are very few Irish left in Willimantic. They've all inter-mingled or they've gone out of town. I haven't got one relative in Willimantic now. They're in Florida, in California, in Maine, in Pennsylvania."

Isabelle's interview reveals much about the upward social mobility of the Irish, and ever-present ethnic and class differences in an early twentieth-century New England mill town. Charles Hill had no worries about social mobility. He was a Yankee, and "management."

CHARLES HILL

Charles Hill was one of the most well known men in Willimantic. He was 92 when interviewed by Lynn MacDonald and Nancy Leonard. Hill was born in Rhode Island in 1887. His parents moved to the Willimantic area in 1905 to care for his father's elderly parents, who lived in Mansfield Center, and eighteen-year-old Hill left his job with the Providence Telephone Company.

Charlie's father, Wallace G. Hill, was also a well-known local figure. He was born in Farmington, Connecticut in 1860, and shortly after arriving in Mansfield in 1905, he was hired by ATCO to take care of their boarding house for women, the "Elms," on Main Street, opposite Mill Number Two. Wallace was an aficionado of harness racing, which drew thousands of spectators to Willimantic's Fairgrounds at the turn-of-the-century. He died in Willimantic in 1942.

Charlie Hill was persuaded by his mother to apply for a job in Willimantic with an old family friend, a "canny Scotsman." This was H. C. Murray, who built the "finest department store east of Hartford" in Willimantic in 1894.[1] Murray was waiting in a horse-and-buggy when Hill arrived at the Willimantic railroad depot, and took him, not to his department store, but down to ATCO's mills for an interview with "General Boss." Hill was hired in a clerical position at $7 a week, $3 a week less than his Providence job. He remained at ATCO for the next 51 years, and held a wide ranging number of clerical and managerial positions.

Hill refers to himself as an "outsider" during the interview. It was custom and practice for the textile mills to hire family members. Labor shortage was not a problem for ATCO in those days. Waiting lists for employment were long - and a family member or friend in the mill helped prospective employees to climb up the list. Charles Hill was sure that if not for Boss' intervention, an outsider like himself would have stood no chance. He claimed to be the first ever office employee from outside Willimantic, and the first not related to a mill executive or overseer. "I was as welcome as a skunk at a lawn party." Nevertheless, he attained quick promotion within the mill and local community:

I was a pusher and a fighter, and I was able to advance quite rapidly. At 27, I was assistant superintendent of the finishing department...There was always something about me...the older men associated with me. Fred Jordan, who built the Jordan building...was 25 years my senior...he got me on the building committee of the Natchaug School. George Taylor, of Hillhouse & Taylor, was 35 years older than I. He was chairman of the hospital committee...he got me on the building committee of the hospital.

In a margin of the interview transcript, it is noted that Mr. Hill was perhaps, "a little swell headed." Even so, Hill is self-conscious of the fact that he held no qualifications beyond high school. He answers a question concerning his education with a lengthy epistle about how easily he figured out a spinning average for a top official from New York, a question which had stumped all the brains in the Willimantic mills.

Charlie Hill was sent to New York and ATCO's Kerr mills in Fall River during the 1925 strike. He believed the dispute was an aberration, an exception to the rule of perfect worker-management relationships in the Willimantic mills. Hill was a management man, but he retained good relationships with the millworkers. He was on their bowling team, their basketball team and President of their Athletic Association. The American Thread Athletic Association (ATAA) was formed in 1912, and by 1925 it had more than 1,700 members. It published a lively monthly magazine called the *Atco Star*, and Charlie Hill edited it. The *Star* featured company editorials, articles, sports, biographies, departmental news, marriages, information about works entertainment programs, and published a list of journals subscribed to by the Dunham Hall Library. The January, 1925 edition features two articles penned by Charlie Hill. The first focuses upon ATCO's new plant in Dalton, Georgia. The second, entitled "A City Within a City," gives a detailed description of ATCO's extensive company housing, destined to be the scene of controversy and heartache several months later when ATCO conducted a mass eviction of all striking workers. Hill's *Star* article reveals that in 1925, ATCO rented out 180 houses in Willimantic, containing 266 men, 358 women and 358 children.

ATCO nominated Hill to negotiate with the strikers, when their committee voted that the ATAA's funds be turned over to the strike fund. Hill recalled that the ATAA treasury held over $8,000, and that the ATAA's Vice President was a "union man." The union asserted that the money belonged to them. According to Hill, he officiated at the meeting and persuaded the strikers to elect someone neutral to allocate the money. He argued that if the strike was of short duration, and the money was in the strike funds, it would sound the death knell of the workers' much beloved Athletic Association, and the strikers' committee gave Hill the job to distribute the money.

An individual's memory or perception can be checked against recorded documentation. The meeting to which Hill is referring took place on March 16, 1925, and differs from Hill's account of it on a couple of points. It was reported in the following day's *Chronicle* that the ATAA's treasury stood at $3,300, not $8,000, plus some perishable items in the works canteen. The funds did stay in the ATAA's coffers, but Hill did not distribute them. This was done by a 12-strong committee of strikers, consisting of three representatives from each city ward. They met each week, and listened to the neediest of cases. The ATAA gave the money, as needed, to the committee for distribution. The perishable goods were retrieved from the works canteen by members of Willimantic's Ancient Order of Hibernians, and auctioned at the St. Patrick's Day celebration at the Gem Theater. The proceeds went to the strikers' fund.

Hill recalled the origins of the strike. It began when New England's textile manufacturers forced a 10% pay cut. The union at ATCO's Willimantic mills consisted of only a few dyers and swift spoolers, who held little influence. The strike was a 'grass roots' walk out, later organized by area officials of the Textile Workers Union of America. Hill's loyalty was with ATCO. In his eyes, the union was the villain of the piece. He made no mention of ATCO's massive paycuts after World War One, but explains that ATCO offered to reduce the cut to 5% after the workers had been out for two months. The "union" refused and ATCO sacked the strikers. Unfortunately, Hill is asked no further questions about the strike.

ATCO ran on short time during the Depression. Hill claimed that ATCO would have closed, had it not been for the New Deal's National Industrial Recovery Act (NIRA). "When (ATCO) had the NIRA, we did what Roosevelt asked for...ran two shifts with no orders and no business coming in...we complied with all the government regulations." Hill was asked if wages dropped in the 1930s. He replied that they did, and unwittingly responds to Leona Delude's critique of ATCO's tradition of distributing cheap Christmas cards, instead of bonuses, to the workers. "There were no bonuses. In the textile business you run with a very close profit, and you don't have too much money for bonuses and pensions and things like that."

When asked if there was any social interaction between ATCO's management and workers, Hill responded with an emphatic "No," explaining that there were two distinct groups. "The management lived their life and the workers lived theirs." But he remembered that the management did hold clambakes and outings for the workers in his early days with the company.

Charlie Hill was held in great respect by the "millgirls." He always tipped his hat to them when he walked through the mill, a habit taught to him by his grandmother. One veteran female millworker told him that in all the time she had spent in textile mills in Willimantic and Woonsocket, he was the only official to raise his hat to women as he passed through the mill.

Hill had nothing but repeated praise for ATCO, "a high class concern." He recalled its "top quality" managers and agents, such as Eugene Boss, Don Curtis, David Moxon, E. Burton Shaw, and a "real high class individual, John Love, who graduated from MIT."[2] Hill believed that the management was held in respect by the workers because the managers had worked through the mill and knew the different work processes. Hill named an agent not easily fooled by the union: "E. B. Shaw was one of the best manufacturing men in New England...if the union said a specific number of spindles could not be run, he'd face them right down with, 'what the hell are you talking about...I'll go right over and run them for you.' That's why ATCO is successful. They've had men who were in the mill. They know what it is, and they know how to handle the help." Hill ends the interview with his recipe for success in an industrial concern, and in America:

> If you're an alien and you come in here and you expect to climb to the top, you've got to change your clothes. You've got to change your haircut. You've got to adapt yourself to the United States' way of doing business. You can't go into any organization and have something that belongs in Hungary or Greece sticking out all over you. If you do, it won't do you any good. But, if you go in and apply yourself there's no reason anybody can't get anywhere.

Hill was a management man. The following interview, which also reveals some interesting details about the 1925 strike, gives the view from a union angle.

ROMEO AND MARY BENOIT

Romeo and Mary Benoit were interviewed together. Romeo Benoit was the first local president of the new CIO textile workers' union in 1942. Romeo and Mary were born in 1898. Very little is revealed about their early lives. Romeo was a Western Union telegraph operator on the railroads up until 1929, when he began work in ATCO's dye house. His wife started at ATCO in 1913 as a bookkeeper in the shipping department in Mill Number Six: "I had one of those pneumatic things...and sent messages." She was dismissed for not returning to work when ATCO declared the strike was over in the summer of 1925.

Romeo Benoit was a little confused by the questioning, and his wife completed the interview. She explained that the 1925 strike was badly organized. "We had a dope for a president...Amy Hooker...she was really an antagonist." The leaders "...did not know one thing about how to conduct a strike." Vague accusations suggest that the strike leaders were lining their own pockets from strike funds. She recalled that the strikers were ejected from the company houses, including Romeo's brother, Oliver Benoit. "People in the company houses had to get out and look for another apartment. The biggest part of them went to Hartford. They went to Royal Typewriter, different places. They got twice the money in Hartford...ATCO paid very little." Oliver Benoit, who had worked at ATCO since 1907, saw his wages in Hartford rise to "thirty some odd dollars a week" from $16 a week in ATCO's spinning room, but ATCO's relatively low wages were welcomed by the long term unemployed millworkers imported from "New Bedford...and New Hampshire."

Romeo Benoit's contributions to the interview are merely interjections, so little is discovered about the CIO's attempts at unionization in ATCO's Willimantic mills during the New Deal. But Mary does say that, "...while Romeo was president... there were no strikes or anything. He's a honest, peace loving guy. He went into arbitration, and took the big shots in with him, because there was a lot of friction in the American Thread." The friction was caused by the splits generated by the 1925 strike. Romeo did recall the poor working conditions at ATCO. He went into the carding room in Mill Number Four on union business, and his best clothes turned white because of the cotton dust in the atmosphere.

By the early 1940s, Mary was employed at the Windham Hospital as a cook. One day, while out for lunch, she looked upwards and saw a plane trailing a large banner across the sky above Willimantic which read: "Vote CIO, Romeo Benoit for President." Mary was shocked because of her ambivalent attitude towards unions at that time. She felt they had caused the 1925 strike, and was uneasy that Romeo held union meetings in their home. "The strike ruined Willimantic...it was a nice town, a good town...until they let those different people in. Give me the good old Willimantic."

Because of Romeo Benoit's failing memory, the opportunity to discover more about the workings of the CIO at ATCO was lost. Fortunately, the interview with Dan Gallagher fills some of the gap regarding unionization in ATCO's mills.

DANIEL GALLAGHER

Daniel Gallagher was Joint Board Manager of all local Willimantic textile unions from 1943 until 1965. He was interviewed by William Knox in Norwich, Connecticut, in November, 1979. Gallagher had worked in several textile mills in Massachusetts during the 1930s, when jobs were particularly scarce. He first worked in a bleaching unit. Soon after, in 1938, the Congress of Industrial Organizations (CIO) was formed, and undertook the immense task of organizing unskilled workers in America's major industries. Someone asked Gallagher to attend a CIO meeting. He joined the new union and was appointed president of the local soon after. Several years later he was hired full-time by the CIO, and worked as a union organizer in textile mills in Salem and

Holyoke, Massachusetts. In 1943 Gallagher was appointed by the General President of the Textile Workers Union, and organized a joint board in eastern Connecticut's textile mills, to centralize the numerous, small, separate union locals which had sprung up during the New Deal years.

Gallagher gave two local examples of the importance of central organization. The Max Pollack Company operated in an old silk mill in Conantville, employing 50 people - ATCO, employed 1500 people. With a Joint Board Manager, the voice of the workers at the Max Pollack Company was as loud as those employed by ATCO. Gallagher also organized millworkers in Jewett City, Danielson, Taftville, Putnam and Norwich.

Gallagher admitted that union organization at ATCO's Willimantic mills was not easy. The storm clouds of 1925 shielded more than half of ATCO's workers from any trade union sunlight. He had to deal with propaganda which clothed the CIO in communist garb. He also had the difficult task of organizing several hundred workers who were originally brought to Willimantic as strikebreakers. Gallagher was resisted. ATCO's workers could not grasp such alien concepts as insurance, paid vacations and grievance procedures. Gradually, shop stewards were elected in each of ATCO's department to take up grievances such as workloads, seniority and changes in materials. The whole plant voted for the union's President, Vice President and Secretary. The management and senior union officials met to settle differences which could not be settled departmentally. The next stage was arbitration. In extreme cases, the union was empowered to hire attorneys to fight for controversial issues like worker compensation.

Gallagher felt that great strides were taken in the first few years at ATCO, but progress was impaired somewhat by the Taft-Hartley Act of 1947, an amendment to the original 1935 Act, which limited "unfair practices" by labor. ATCO's management could persuade workers not to join the union, but the vast majority were already signed up. This was an achievement, considering the deep distrust of trade-unionism at a textile mill traditionally consisting of un-unionized labor.

Gallagher remembered that 50% of ATCO's Willimantic workforce was made up of women. He and the union ensured they were not discriminated against. Women were not allowed to lift more than a certain amount of weight and chairs were supplied for them. They could not be employed in the dye house, because of the dangerous nature of the job. ATCO's female workforce found employment on shuttle bobbins, and in the card room. Gallagher thought they made excellent shop stewards. He was slightly concerned that he could never convince the women to take lunch breaks. They preferred to eat on the job, so they could get home earlier, but he remembered that the union won them the right to leave the job to smoke a cigarette in a designated smoking area.

Looking back at his time as Joint Board Manager, Gallagher believed that the union made advancements in establishing seniority rules. No longer could the bosses pick and choose who they wanted to work. He remembered his early days in the industry when workers collected every morning in the mill yard to wait and see if there was any work that day. Those not chosen had to trudge home, many having traveled several miles by trolley car, bicycle, or on foot. Seniority cut down on favoritism. The union also fought for "reporting pay," where employees were guaranteed four hours pay, or four hours labor, if they turned up at work. The company had to inform the worker the night before if there was no work for them the following day. This forced the textile companies to plan and organize their workloads with more efficiency.

Gallagher's personal experience with ATCO's management was positive. He recalled that they almost always filled their contractual obligations. There had been one brief strike sometime around 1964, when contracts were not signed. Gallagher felt that ATCO's biggest problem lay in its great turnover and constant shortage of labor. When asked about the ethnicity in the Willimantic mills, he remembered that the carding room in Mill Number Four consisted mainly of Polish labor, and the shuttle bobbins were manned by French workers. He remembered a sprinkling of Irish and British labor, but the majority of those worked in the Cheney mills in Manchester.

Gallagher's reign took in the decline of the textile industry in eastern Connecticut. Many mills had closed or gone south by the time he left his post in 1965, to become a state mediator. He estimated that over 10,000 jobs were lost in the textile industry, but many of those workers found work with Electric Boat and Pratt & Whitney.

ALICE STABILE

The actual interview with Alice Stabile reveals very little, but Mrs. Stabile also contributed an autobiographical piece. She was born in 1911, but there are no details regarding Alice's family, other than that she worked on her parent's 87 acre farm on Hennequin Road, Columbia, until her father sold it for $1,500 in 1927 - the year Alice found employment at the American Thread plant in Willimantic. The interviewing students concentrated upon Alice's experiences in the mill. When asked about company-sponsored social activities, Alice replied: "You did your days work and that was it ya know." On ethnic tensions: "Everybody got along. No arguing, no nothing." On relations with management: "You had to keep busy...They expected a days work...You answered the boss." On employment eligibility at American Thread: "If you breathed, had two arms and two legs you were in." Alice's essay is reproduced unedited in its original form, and provides an ideal conclusion to the interviews undertaken by Dr. Bruce M. Stave's students at the University of Connecticut in 1979.

How fast we travel through life, and one day we awake a senior citizen. Life is just as interesting as it was in the beginning. On a nice spring day in 1927 I wandered into the employment office of the American Thread in Willimantic. After the interview, an employee escorted me across the street to number six gate, and to the tube and cone winding department, where I met my boss, Mr. William Higgins, who said for me to start work the next day. He was a short stocky man who walked with a limp. A good boss if one did their job, but a hard task master if one was caught loafing. Later on I was to work for his son, Mr. Ernest Higgins, who was much more gentile mannered.

My job was to run a machine winding shoe thread. There were six spindles on a machine and each girl had to run two machines or 12 spindles in all. Being heavy thread it would fill the pound tubes real quick and we had to be fast to keep the machines going. We started work when the whistle blew. People in the city set their clocks by that whistle.

Our day started at seven in the morning to a quarter of five in the afternoon every day for five days, and on Saturday we worked until noon and received $17.50 a week for labor. At noon on Saturday all the big white shades on the street side were pulled way down in the windows. Apparently, someone thought it looked nice. Later on I was promoted to inspector to the tube and cone inspection. We watched for mixed threads; work that was not neat or soiled was handed back to be rewound, and how the operators of the machines would get mad.

The girls would have as many as six or eight machines to run and the inspector examined the work of between 10 and 12 girls. The work was examined, then it was sent to the basement where the packing room was and it would be boxed for shipping. Our initials were on the order slip when it went down to the packing room and woe to the girl who let shoddy work go through. It was the one time the employees were allowed to go down the shop elevator.

We had no time clock to ring in. A section foreman would check to see if we were in and to take care of our time. There was no pension plan or paid vacation, no cafeteria and the floors were plain rough boards. All workers who did not go home for lunch had to carry their own lunch to work. It was hard times in those days. Little did we dream that we were headed for the great depression. If anyone had a job they took good care of it, and the boss was respected. No pet names for him. He was King. People wore clothes that were old, but clean. No one tried to keep in style.

There were many nationalities all working together and all getting along in our struggle to make a living. The Poles worked right up until the whistle blew and were very dedicated to their job. Then there was Jessie, a little Scottish lassie, who each day spoke of when she would meet the Scottish mon. She hadn't met him when I left. There was Sal, an Italian who loved garlic so much he even had it on bread for lunch and we smelled him ten feet away. The French Canadians were really good workers and the girls would lay their pay on the table at home and their parents would give them a couple of dollars for the week. They said when they would marry, they would have a big wedding. And my how they would work.

My sister and I were the only France French on the floor and like the others we gave the boss a good day's work. It was interesting listening to the little French Canadian girls talk among themselves. The difference would be like listening to English and Irish, many words were the same.

And of course I remember Mabel, the spinster, who inherited my job. She was so slow I often wondered how long she was there. There were so many it would be impossible to remember them all. Miss Mack, our mill nurse, tended strictly to business. She was a tall, stocky woman who would struggle out of her desk chair and dispense with some aspirin for our headache or take care of our minor injuries. The first aid consisted of one hospital bed, a few chairs, a medicine cabinet, and Miss Mack's desk. No one loitered in her department for long.

I worked on the sixth floor, and we all used the stairs. They were all covered with tin throughout the shop. One night I caught my heel on a broken tin and went all the way down, tumbling all the way. I was home for all of a week and was told to report to the superintendent's office when I returned to work. His name was Mr. Charles Hill. He said he would pay me my week's pay for my injuries. "A week's pay," I said. "I didn't suffer for eight hours, I suffered around the clock." He made it right with two weeks pay. The most money I had seen in months. He was a nice man. Once the mill was on strike and the workers who wanted to smoke were allowed to use his waiting room. The poor man would enter and the room was blue with smoke.

I lived with my sister, Juliette Brosseau, for a while in a mill house. It consisted of three bedrooms, a kitchen, living room and a dining room. It had one cold water faucet in a black cast iron sink in the kitchen and a toilet in the cellar. My brother, Lucene Hennequin, had a mill house too with the very same convenience. What a project to take a bath. The house was heated with a wood or coal furnace and the tenants supplied their own fuel. They had a man who went around the mill houses to see they were kept clean. The rent was deducted from the employee's pay. One time when work was slow and the rent was deducted, my sister received a five cent check from the company. That was all that was due to her that week. Our boss, Mr. Ernest Higgins, bought the check from her!

Later on I married and went into our own rented apartment that was not associated with the mill. We rented from Mary Gavigan at 15 Fairview Street and had four large rooms, front and back entrance, hot and cold water and white sinks and bath. What a luxury. We paid seven dollars a week which included heat and electric. It maybe was expensive at $17. 50 a week for pay, but we enjoyed it.

Time passed and one day in slow time my boss Mr. Ernest Higgins said he was giving me my time as I had a husband to support me, and the spinster they hired needed the job. If it was today the Labor Department would have heard about it. That was in 1935. I took my pay and never went back.

They had a mill truck that ran errands with a funny horn that went tweet tweet. My how the young folks would like to have it for their cars now. They also had a small train that ran through the mill yard to number four and back and was owned by the company.

In the attic of our mind we store our memories. Looking back I would say the work wasn't too hard. We had to stand up most of the day and that seemed the hardest. There were very few sitting down jobs. Even now the old mill stream flows by the box shop and the whistle still calls them to work. Times have changed and I was glad that I was part of that era.

The remaining chapters in this section are reproduced from the files of the Windham Textile & History Museum's Oral History Institute. The interviews were undertaken between March, 1990 and November, 1992. The subject matter expands the 1979 American Thread Company focus of Bruce Stave's project, by an investigation of social and cultural life in Willimantic during the first half of the twentieth century. A full list of the Institute's interviews is included in the Finders Guide.

CHAPTER 2

We're Going to Teach You
the Business

John Love, interviewed December 11, 1991

American Thread

I was born in Baltimore, Maryland, June 1, 1925, the eldest of five children. My father died of a heart attack when I was 12. He owned two liquor stores and died when he was drying out from one of his alcoholic bouts. I went to public schools in Baltimore up until my father died, when my mother had to run the business during the day. Because she was now running the business, she switched me from a day to a boarding school for one year. From there I went to a Jesuit high school, and finally on to Loyola College, also a Jesuit school.

I was 17, a senior in high school, when the Japanese attacked Pearl Harbor. Then I started college. During that year, you could sign up in either the navy's V12 program or the army's ASTP program. They were sort of like ROTC where the navy paid for you to go to a certain school, taking regular courses as well as naval courses. The difference was that they assigned you to the college. I joined the V12 program, at first being sent to Villanova, where I was found to have a double hernia and was discharged for four months. After the four months were up, I was called back and sent to Harvard, where I stayed from March 1944 to March 1945.

In March of 1945, because of a decree that anyone with a major connected with business was to go to midshipman's school to become a supply officer, I ended up in a big base in New Jersey, where I, and 1,200 others, went through a three-hour interview. Four days later, 60 of us were chosen to leave at eight o'clock in the morning, not knowing where we were going or why. It turned out I was going back to Harvard, to the Harvard Business School.

We took Harvard Business School courses and a few navy courses, the aim being that in the end we would be able to renegotiate naval contracts with certain companies. When the war ended, we were given a choice of whether or not to continue, but if we continued, we would have to serve four years active duty. I wanted no part of that. We were shipped to the 90-day midshipman's school. Then I went to a destroyer. While on the destroyer, I wrote to Harvard College saying that I had a certain number of credits from there and a certain number of credits from Loyola, and I did the same thing for Loyola. Since Loyola was a Catholic school and Harvard wasn't, not all the credits were accepted, so I would have had to stay two terms and write a thesis in order to get a degree, even though I had enough numerical credits to qualify for a college degree. I had $1,350 and the G. I. Bill, which I figured would get me through a year of college. I wrote to the Harvard Business School telling them the situation and explaining that I had been there and had gotten good marks. I asked if they would accept me without a college degree. They did. To my knowledge, I'm the only guy to ever go to Harvard Business School without a college degree. I was there from October, 1946 to September, 1947. I got my MBA and after that, joined American Thread.

There was a very effective placement office at the Harvard Business School. American Thread had an interview there, and I talked to the vice president of personnel at the Stappler Hotel in Boston, where he was staying. I was invited to go to New York, which I did. It was 1947. I was very interested in personnel and human resources. That's what I wanted to do. I must have struck a sympathetic ear with the guy. American Thread's directors had decided that they ought to have somebody from the Harvard Business School and it turned out to be me. I signed up for Clover, South Carolina, but while visiting my now present wife, Pierce Weleton, the Vice President of Personnel, called me and asked if I was set on it, because he had a bigger plant in Willimantic, not far from where I was, in New Britain. Had I heard of that? I said No. He told me where it was and to go talk to the agent there named Shaw.

I questioned the term "agent," explaining that my interest was human resources, not purchasing. He explained the term "agent" in textile terms. The agent was the guy who managed the plant. I went and had a discussion with Bert Shaw. I was supposed to show up for work on October 13. Kevin Coley, the Personnel Manager, did not tell me that October 13 was a holiday. So, I showed up my first day and the place was empty! I found one guy in Mill Number Two. He said to me, "No, it can't be today. Today's a holiday." So I spent the rest of the day, disillusioned, walking around Willimantic because I didn't own a car. My father-in-law had driven me from New Britain. I thought Main Street in Willimantic looked OK. The plant looked OK. The buildings were old. I knew I wasn't going into some virgin industry. I guess my overall impression was nothing. I didn't get to see very much of it. I just wandered around, stopped and ate lunch, then went back to my hotel and waited for the next morning. This was on Columbus Day. As an aside, when I got into the union negotiations we ended up swapping Columbus Day for Good Friday. We wanted Good Friday because it was Polish tradition that on Good Friday the priest came around and blessed the Easter ham. At least 25% were of Polish extraction, so almost all of our employees would stay home anyway.

It had been decided, because I was an experiment and because I was the only college-trained management trainee in the whole of American Thread, that I would work in each department, in work clothes, so that when I went to work in personnel, I'd know what I was talking about. It was a union shop, and had been since 1939, I believe. At the end of each week, I prepared a report and gave it to Bert Shaw. Years later, Bert Shaw told me he had been flabbergasted by these reports, because, in his point of view, their purpose was to report what I had learned, not to report what I thought didn't look right in the plant.

In the spring, while I was at Ocean Beach with my wife, Bert Shaw called to say that the president of the company was in Willimantic and wanted to see me. So I went up there, and we talked. He told me that if I really meant what I had said - that I wanted to become president of the company - then he wanted to tell me I'd never do it through personnel. He said that I should go into sales or manufacturing if that's what I wanted to do. I went into manufacturing. I worked with a fixer and a card tender.

There was a company golf tournament each year. This was the only occasion when the Southern manufacturing people ever saw the Northern manufacturing people. At one of these, I met the vice-president of the Southern plants, whom I discovered two things from. (A) He was a real sneak, a phony, and (B) there was a plan that had been approved to shut down all the New England plants and move them to the South. In 1949, Daughdiral and Bert Shaw were going to England on a luxury liner, and before he left, Bert Shaw called me into his office. He sat me down at a desk and said "From now on, that's your chair. This is your office. We're going to teach you the business." He instructed me that I was to run it during the four weeks he was gone. Previous to this, I had been promoted to supervisor of the single line department after Bert had fired a guy named Pop Morriset. Pop was popular but he'd never discipline anybody. I was 24 at the time Bert went to England, and promoted me as his protegé.

About a week after he left, we had our first strike. The spinning people, I think, walked out. That brought manufacturing to a halt. The strike occurred during a 30-day trial period of new wage rates and working conditions that had started before Bert Shaw left. The only name I can remember from the union was George Peterson. He was president of the local at the time. He was a carpenter. The girls were finding faults with the conditions, but the ultimate aim was to get the company to make certain concessions because whatever had been changed was going to make a new set of piece-work rates. Under the union contract, at any time during the trial period, the company had the right to have, say, only 30 people run the whole department. All of the machines running at once. The workers' protection was that he or she got the average pay no matter what happened during the 30 days. It affected the whole plant, but this particular one was in Mill Number Two. There was a concrete building, just after you come over the bridge from Mill Number Four, that was used for storage. There was a loading platform that was where they brought the stuff by train from Number Four to Number Two. On this day, you couldn't unload the stuff because of the walkout. We made a compromise to wait until Bert Shaw got back.

In 1925 there was a strike that, in 1947, people still remembered. The plant shut down for eight or nine months. Everyone felt it. People didn't have credit in the store; people were losing their homes. It was confined to Willimantic. French Canadians were brought in as strike busters. In 1934, the entire textile industry in New England went on strike except for one plant, the one in Willimantic.

Bert Shaw was a native of Fall River. His father, Edwin B. Shaw, carried the title of General Supervisor of Finishing in the American Thread finishing plants, which in those days was situated in East Hampton, Fall River, and Willimantic. They weren't all there, but just a portion of them. Bert started his career in Fall River before becoming supervisor at Willimantic. He didn't get along with the guy he was supervising for, so he left. He took, then later taught, courses in textiles at a technical school. He went to Dalton, Georgia, to run the plant there. I think Bert became agent in Willimantic in the 1930s, I'm not sure of the year. He was the smartest manufacturing man I have ever seen.

In 1952, Bert was made general superintendent of New England plants, in January. The only two remaining plants in New England were in Willimantic and Fall River. Between 1947 and 1952 they closed down East Hampton, which had a small finishing plant, Holyoke, which had the shell bottoms and other departments, and they had closed down the yarn manufacturing plant in Fall River. There was just a small finishing plant left there. Bert's real responsibility was to finish closing Fall River which was replaced by Sevier, North Carolina. Sevier took the place of two plants: the Fall River finishing plant and another plant in Bristol, Tennessee. Sevier was a huge finishing plant. Nothing had been closed when I got there.

We had a spool mill up in Milo, Maine. The reason we had a spool mill there was because in those days all the spools were made of wood, and that wood had to be birch. If you used anything but birch, when the thread was put in, it would break off. The average age of the work force in Maine was 73!

Bert was finally made Vice President of Manufacturing and went to New York, on July 4, 1952. I, at that point, had been running Willimantic and was expected to run Willimantic, but I was too young to be given the title. I was 27. They were going to bring down a guy named Arthur Stewart, who had run the Holyoke plant. He had graduated from college, and had spent his whole career in American Thread. He had worked his way up to agent at the Holyoke plant. He didn't like unions and had never met with one, so I was to handle that part. I used to hold supervisory meetings in the library every three weeks. He never once asked me what went on in them!

There was a management committee, located at the headquarters at 260 West Broadway in New York City, which was made up of the chief executive officer, the vice president of Industrial Sales, the vice president of Consumer Sales, the chief financial officer, the executive vice president, who was Henry Roe, and the head of personnel. It met once a year. Bert presided over some of the meetings. They would call, without fail, Willimantic at every meeting.

The headquarters at 260 West Broadway was a 10-story building purchased in 1898. It was moved to 90 Park Avenue in 1965. I had persuaded Bert to move it, for a number of reasons. The Park Avenue building was about two blocks from Grand Central Station and was brand new in 1965. The old place was sold for $100,000. Nobody had wanted it. It was not a nice part of town. The welfare office was a few blocks away and there was a place we thought was used for laundering money for the mafia. The female workers at American Thread were afraid to go to the subway when they left work.

Stewart retired in 1961, so it was then that I took over the plant as general manager. I took Bert's son, Ted, as my assistant general manager. He had been working in manufacturing and I moved him to finishing. He didn't know anything about finishing. My assistant before him, who was named Johnson, knew about finishing, but not manufacturing. He was there one year before they moved him to Sevier in North Carolina.

When I got promoted in 1963, and was based in New York, Bert told me I would have to run Willimantic on the side, because Ted wasn't prepared to run it yet. My duties were research, purchasing, and personnel in addition. I was also going to be Bert's assistant, though that wasn't in my title. It was an understanding between Bert and I. 1963 was also the year I moved to Westport, to the house I live in now. I was at headquarters from 1963 until I left American Thread in 1979.

If We Could Have Had a Modern Facility in Willimantic, We Would Have Been in Clover

Charles Johnson, interviewed November 6, 1992

Fran Funk

My name is Charles Senter Johnson. I was born April 23, 1920, in Derry, New Hampshire. My father, Charles Sumner Johnson, was a Methodist minister and served the Methodist Church for almost 50 years in every state across New England. Methodist ministers usually stayed in one place for up to four years, then moved on. I have four brothers and one sister, and I'm the oldest. My sister was born in Vermont, one brother in Rhode Island, two in Massachusetts and one was born in Rockville, Connecticut. My father served as pastor of the Willimantic Methodist Church from 1936 until 1941, and that is how I came to live in Willimantic. I was 16. I think that having a minister for a father played an important part in my life. Later on, when we lived in Windham Center, I was on the board of trustees and a deacon at the Congregational Church, and a superintendent of Sunday school.

I met my wife Lynn in 1944, when I was home on leave. She's from Manchester, Connecticut. We were married on January 16, 1945. All my children, two boys and two girls, were born in Hartford, Connecticut. I have a daughter, Candy, who lives in New York State, just above Albany. She is a teacher. My other daughter, Debbie is also a teacher and lives in North Carolina. My son Timothy, Tim, is in business with his brother, and lives in a little town in Sussex county, England. He has a lovely manor house over there. And then, of course, there's Brook, who lives in Greenwich, Connecticut. Both boys went to Windham High School, but they did not graduate from there. Brook just made a run for the national Senate here in Connecticut, and did very well. We did not expect to win, but he came away with 562,000 votes, and 97% recognition in the state. You have not seen the last of him. He has a very good sized business, and has certainly lived the American Dream. He felt strongly that he had to get into politics, but my advice to him was not to do it, but he did not take my advice! He wanted to make sure that a lot of other children coming after him would have the chance to do what he had done.

Before coming to Willimantic, my family had been knocking around all New England, and I went from one school to another school, and of course I had to go to Sunday school and church. My father was a minister in Georgia, Vermont; Sanbornville, New Hampshire; North Deighton, Massachusetts; Middlefield and Warren, Rhode Island; Rockville, Willimantic, East Hartford and Moosup, Connecticut.

My father and mother never thought that any of their four boys would be a minister. One went into business school and got his MBA, and another went into engineering, but they both went back to divinity school and became ministers. One is a minister up in Massachusetts, and another is now the head chaplin at a veteran's hospital in California - I was the black sheep of the family - but we all served in the forces during the war. In fact my father was a Chaplain in troop ships crossing the Atlantic to England, and to campaigns in Italy and North Africa.

My father was transferred to Willimantic from Rockville, Connecticut. I moved into the Windham High School as a junior, and graduated from there in 1938. We lived in the Methodist parsonage up on the corner of Prospect Street and Bellevue Street. That building is no longer there. They knocked it down and built a new one. They also knocked the old Methodist church down which stood on Church Street, and built a lovely new church out in Mansfield. And of course, there is the Methodist campground in Willimantic. I was very familiar with the campground because I went to all the services there with my parents. At that time, being a 16-year-old, I was part of the youth group in the church. We went to the service and the fellas and the girls sneaked off to a little spot over there, which is still there by the way, called "sunset rock." My dad would look around the meeting and see that there was a lot of faces missing! So he would go out on a patrol to see if he could round up the lost sheep. My mother still has a place over at the campground.

Things were tough in Willimantic in those days. Jobs were very hard to come by. The major industry in town was the American Thread Company. During those depression years, the mill was working sometime three days, sometimes four days and if ever it was good they worked all week. There was not much other industry here at that time. There was the Holland silk mill, but that was a very small mill. There were several small establishments in town. The old mills on Bridge Street were closed down and empty in those days.

I was at high school, and money was hard to come by. I worked after school at the Church & Reed clothing store, which was on the corner of Main Street and Church Street. And on Saturdays I worked in Spellman's market, which was on Church Street almost directly across from the old Methodist church. As soon as I could get a license, I delivered groceries. I filled all the grocery baskets, put them in the truck and roamed around Willimantic delivering them and collecting the money. I did that up until I graduated high school in 1938.

After high school I went off to Boston to Wentworth Institute to engineering school. It seemed like a good idea at the time. I did that for a year, then left. I came back to Willimantic and was not sure what I wanted to do, so I went to the American Thread Company to look for a job. At that time, they still had what they called an agent. The last agent was David Moxon, an Englishman. Of course, American Thread was an English company, owned by the English Sewing Cotton Company of Manchester, England. I knew Mr. Moxon, because his daughter was in high school with me.

At that time, a very prominent individual in town was a fellow by the name of Charlie Hill. He was an institution in Willimantic, and had spent a lifetime working at American Thread. He was a production manager, then the assistant manager. I met him often, as he ate in the same restaurant as me on North Street, the Clark House, and he also had a daughter who went to Windham High School the same time as me. I also knew him through church. You got to know a lot of people with your father being a minister. Moxon and Hill decided to give me a job. The first job I had was in the audit department in the little stone building in front of Mill Number Two.

My first wage was $12 a week. At that time, they had social security, and they took a penny for every dollar, so they took out 12 cents, and I ended up with $11. 88 for a 40 hour-plus working week. It was less than 30 cents a hour. That was a good wage and a good job for a 19-year-old. I came to work dressed and worked in an office behind a desk. The job entailed checking the audits from the thread which had been sold. The thread was either drawn from inventory, stock, or was processed through the plant. So I wrote the orders for replenishing the inventory, or for special orders. Some orders were not on stock, of course, and had to be manufactured separately. Special orders usually consisted of new colors of thread.

I worked in that department for a fellow named Harry Larkin. He was a nice guy, but he was a grouch. He never had a smile on his face. I don't think I ever saw him smile. He ruled with an iron hand. I did not pay a lot of attention to him. I got along with him. Also at that time in that stone building was a fellow by the name of E. Burton Shaw. He had been the superintendent of the Dalton mill in Georgia, and was transferred back to Willimantic as superintendent of manufacturing. Bert Shaw took a liking to me, which was very fortunate for me. He decided that I had potential, so he took me out of the audit department and sent me into manufacturing in the mill onto some of the dirtiest jobs going, such as cleaning cards, about the dirtiest job you can get in Mill Number Four.

I did it because I was interested in going some place. I then got into quality control, spinning and they eventually let me run the night-shift as a foreman. Mill Number Four was the place you went through from picking all the way through to winding. The transportation for the product in those days, no matter what it was - coal to the boilers in the turbine room or thread from one mill to another, was carried out by by steam train.

I worked in all kinds of positions at American Thread through to 1941. The war started, and I didn't want to get drafted, so I joined the air force right after Pearl Harbor in early 1942. I wanted to get into their cadet program. I wanted to be one of those fly-boys! I went through the cadet program in Helena, Arkansas and Coral Gables and Homestead airbase in Florida doing training courses. Eventually, I was very fortunate, because after I graduated I was assigned to the Air Transport Command. Their primary function was delivering airplanes all over the world. I then had the experience of going everywhere. I delivered airplanes to England and India, and to Alaska where the Russians picked them up. I was eventually based in New Delhi, India, where we delivered aircraft to Kun Ming in China, so they could fight the Japanese. My oldest son, Tim, was born while I was in India.

By this time, I was a captain in Air Transport, and due for promotion to major, but I had enough service and combat points to get out of the air force. We had some close calls. We delivered a lot of airplanes to the British Isles from Casablanca up the coast of occupied France. One time a German submarine took a shot at the B-25 I was flying, and a shell went right through the plane without exploding! I came back and I had to wrestle with the decision to stay in or come out. Back in those days, being a major in the air force was a pretty good deal. You had a good life. But I made the decision to leave, and came back to Willimantic in 1946. Lynn and I located in Coventry, Connecticut, up by the lake. I needed a job, so I walked into Mr. Shaw's office at American Thread. Being a captain with a lot of experience, I thought I'd take his job, but it didn't work out that way! I marched into his office dressed in my captain's uniform, and he said to me, "Just because you're a captain, you're not ready for my job yet. You've got to get out there in the mill and learn this job!" I said, "I understand." We then moved to Willimantic, and lived in some new housing, which in those days was public housing, on Terry Court off Ash Street. We eventually settled in Windham Center.

I went all the way through the jobs in Mill Number Four in a rapid fashion, then I spent some time in Mill Number Two to get some twisting and reeling experience. I ran the second shift there for a couple of years, before moving into finishing in Mill Number Six. I spent some time in research there. Sometime around 1949, American Thread decided to move the shuttle bobbin department from their mill in Holyoke, Massachusetts to Willimantic. It was my job to oversee the transfer, as it was planned that I should take care of the department when it was finally established in Willimantic. I trained all the help.

In 1953 I was promoted to assistant-superintendent of finishing, which included all processes after the dye house operations. At that time we ran our own box making, and our own print shop. I was then promoted to superintendent of finishing. That was around 1958. Our general manager, Bert Shaw was then made President of American Thread, and moved to the office in New York City down in the garment district. Mr. Shaw's personal assistant, John Love, became the assistant general manager of the Willimantic plant. The new general manager, Arthur Stewart, came from Holyoke. When he retired, John Love became the general manager, and I became his assistant. That was 1961.

The following summer, Mr. Shaw came down from New York. I was sitting in my office in the building which now houses the Windham Textile & History Museum, and Mr. Shaw says to me, "How would you like to go South?" I said, "Yeah, I'd like to go South." He told me that he wanted me to take over American Thread's Sevier finishing plant in North Carolina. That was a new plant, situated in the Blue Ridge Mountains. It was a big plant. I had some friends down there, so I went home and talked to Lynn. It was a difficult time to move. Our son Tim was already a senior at Windham High School, but we made the move at Thanksgiving in 1962. It was a tough move, as I was heavily involved in the local community. I was the president of the Windham Center Parent Teacher's Group, and had been involved in the local church. And I had been the president of the Willimantic Lions Club. I was also involved with the Boy Scouts, the YMCA, the Chamber of Commerce and the Windham Hospital. It was certainly traumatic leaving all that. But we made the move.

The Sevier plant had been built in 1952 to replace an older facility, located at Bristol, Tennessee. It was 600,000 square feet all on the one floor, and a straight-line operation which employed about a thousand people. When they built it there, the housing situation was bad. It was in the boonies, so American Thread built a small village, like they had in Willimantic many years before. The general manager's house was the biggest house in the village, standing on a hill. So we got the biggest house in the village, and we had a lady who helped with the cleaning and cooking as part of the deal. That helped to soothe the move to the South!

I'm a pretty outgoing person, so I had no difficulties. They didn't mind that I was a Yankee, but I suppose they were a little apprehensive of me. But I soon began to apply my management principles and policies, and became accepted. We were the major finishing plant for all cotton thread produced in the south. It was unlike the Willimantic operation, which was an integrated mill that did all the processes from manufacturing through finishing. There was also a finishing mill in Tennessee and manufacturing plants in Troutman and Clover in South Carolina, and in Dalton and Tallapoosa, Georgia. They fed their products into our finishing.

Our labor force down there was made up mainly of local people. It was mainly WASP, white people with English ancestry. There were very few blacks. Several plants in the South were union mills, but Sevier was not one of them. The union always came after me. They hit me before I got my bags unpacked. They knew I was from a union plant in the North. But I resisted them. I didn't want them in, although I had never had any problems with the unions in Willimantic. The union never broke any of my mills in the South. The unions were a lot of aggravation, and made my job a lot more difficult. Moreover, the people would not get anything more than they were getting already. All they would do was pay dues to the union, but the policies I organized meant that Sevier paid as well, if not better, than union plants. Job benefits were better too, so they could get nothing more by being members of the union.

I started a scheme in the plant there, which I believe is still operating. I started a program which I called "Birthday Parties." We operated three shifts, and each week I organized a birthday party on each shift. I invited into my office or conference room, depending upon the size of the group, all those people who had birthdays that week. I invited them in for a catered meal and a birthday cake. This was a means of communicating with the people. It was not a one-way street. Those people soon learned that they could ask me anything. I gave them an honest answer, but this did not always mean that they liked all my answers. They were not afraid. They asked me anything, so I had a wonderful relationship with them. The program was so successful that they're still doing it today and I've been retired for 12 years. I was the chief honcho, but I spent all kinds of time on the floor. They never knew when I was going to be there. I went in on every shift, and people flagged me down to talk.

Union organizers were in there all the time, but they could never generate enough interest on the shopfloor. One of the biggest union people from Willimantic was Betty Tianti who went on, and I give her a lot of credit, to become Connecticut's Labor Commissioner. She was a great girl. First thing she did was to go to the South and try and organize me! She was a good friend of mine. I always had a good relationship with the union in Willimantic.

In 1965 I was promoted to a new post as general manager of all American Thread's Southern plants. I was in charge of their plants in Sevier and Rosman, North Carolina; Clover, South Carolina; Tallapoosa and Dalton, Georgia. I made my HQ in Sevier, and my place at the Sevier mill was taken by William McBee, who had learned the trade in the thread mills at Willington, Connecticut.

I came back to Connecticut in 1970, and took a post as vice-president of manufacturing for the whole country. We lived in Ridgefield, and I commuted to New York to our offices at 90 Park Avenue. Soon after, the corporate offices were moved from New York to Stamford, Connecticut - so that relieved me of that murderous commute to New York, two hours out and two hours back. We then moved nearer to Stamford, to Easton, Connecticut in Fairfield County. Soon after, the kids had left home, and Lynn and I moved into a condominium in Stratford, Connecticut, right up the hill from Sikorsky.

I was in the corporate office until 1980, and retired when I was 60. There was a lot of changes at this time. American Thread's corporate offices are now located in Charlotte, North Carolina. Roger Cothran is in charge - a guy I hired right out of Clemson. He's doing a very good job. There's been a lot of changes in the industry, and American Thread is now known as Coats-American. American Thread started out as part of the English Sewing Company, and then English Sewing got a hold on Calico Printers, and it became English-Calico. They were then taken over by Tootal. Veyella took over Coats, and became Coats-Veyella. Before Veyella took over Coats, they made a lot of passes at Tootal, but they eventually managed to take it over.

Some of the old managers at American Thread would turn over in their graves if they knew about the merger with Coats! American Thread was strong in industrial threads, but weaker in domestic and consumer products, whereas Coats was strong in domestics and weaker in industrial, so really, it made a very good marriage. Coats were smart enough to dump all their management and keep American Thread's management to run the industrial. So Coats-American is now the number one producer of industrial thread in the world.

In the 1960s, American Thread rationalized by closing some of the older plants in the South and opening two new plants in North Carolina at Rosman (The Sylvan plant), and Marble (The Murphy plant) in 1965 and 1967. It has been argued that the mills in the Northeast, like Willimantic, closed down as labor and production costs were cheaper in the South, because the Southern plants were un-unionized. This was not true, because the wages and fringes were the same in the North and the South. The reason the Northeast declined was because it did not make sense to build new facilities in the North, because the costs were too high. The old nineteenth-century facilities, like Willimantic, made production difficult because they usually existed on several stories and the movement of materials and machinery up and down elevators made the job more expensive and difficult. In the South, the new facilities were built all on one level. You dropped off the bales at one end of the plant and ran them quickly through straight line modern equipment out of the other end, finished and gone. It had nothing to do with labor costs. If we could have had a modern facility in this area, with the good, experienced labor in Willimantic, we would have been in clover.

Well, Lynn and I planned for retirement, and we now spend the winters in Florida, and the summers in the Blue Ridge mountains in North Carolina, because its nice and cool there in the summer. But it has certainly been nice coming back to Willimantic. It has brought back a lot of happy memories.

CHAPTER 4

I Was the First Woman President of the Union.
American Thread Did Not Know What to do With Me

Betty Tianti, interviewed March 25, 1992

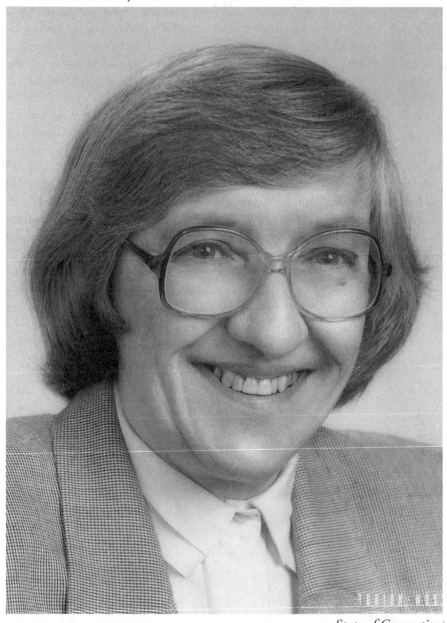

State of Connecticut

I was born in Plainfield, Connecticut, in August, 1929, in the year of the Wall Street Crash. I was brought up and went to school in the general area of Eastern Connecticut. My parents were both millworkers, and worked in textile mills in places such as Sterling and Moosup. We lived in company millhouses. My mom and dad separated when I was about seven-years-old. I had three brothers, two older and one younger, and my mom brought the four of us up by herself. My maiden name was Mathieu. My mother was German and French, and my father was French Canadian. I suppose I'm three quarters French and a quarter German!

They were tough days. It was the Depression. When my father was out of work, he would go down to the mill, to stand around, and wait to be chosen to work. Maybe he got five hours of work a week. We grew our own vegetables, and had a cow, a pig and chickens. We got by. As soon as my two elder brothers were old enough, at 16, they quit school and went to work, getting jobs in the mills. I was the first in the family to go on and finish high school. That was Plainfield High in 1946. I was 17. My parents pushed me to go on to college. I did quite well at school, and went to the University of Connecticut, but lasted for only one semester. I quit and went to work. I didn't really want to leave college, but none of my friends had gone on to university. In those days, you just did not go. I think only 10% of the class that graduated high school that year went on to college, about 40 kids. It was at the end of the war, and the guys signed up for the forces when they became seniors.

I found work at the Ashland mills in Jewett City, and the Cranska linen mills in Moosup. After that I went with a friend to Winchendon, Massachusetts where this New York leather goods concern was making pocket books. It was a novelty item. They were made out of small wooden buckets, with leather straps. After that fad was over, they moved the balance of the company back to their HQ at West 34th Street in New York City. I was around 20 or 21 years-of-age and had worked there for about three years.

I met my husband in New York in the early 1950s. He was in the Air Force reserves, and was called up when China bombarded the islands of Quemoy and Matsu in 1954. He was overseas when my daughter was born in October, 1954. I came back to Danielson, Connecticut, and stayed with my mother. Soon after my husband and I separated and divorced.

In 1955 I began work with the American Thread Company in Willimantic. I worked in Number Six Mill in the shuttle bobbin department. My first wage was a dollar and three cents a hour. My mother worked the first shift, so I worked the second shift while she looked after my daughter. It was about a 40 minute drive to Willimantic from Danielson, but several of us traveled together. There were close to 2,000 people working at American Thread when I arrived there.

In 1956 they hired a lot of Hungarian refugees who came here after the failed uprising against the Soviet Union. Many had relatives here already, as some

Hungarians came to Willimantic as Displaced Persons to work after the Second World War. The majority of my workmates were French Canadians, followed by Polish and Ukranian, but Willimantic was basically a French community. There were a few old Yankee families, like the Motts. Also at this time in the 1950s, there was a large contingency of Greeks, who came to Willimantic from Danielson, when the mills there began to close. Some of them had come straight over from Greece as their families were already here. There was something like a 10 to 15% turnover per year of labor, but that was not too bad when you consider the size of the mill. A labor shortage hit the American Thread hard in the late 1950s and early 1960s, and they began recruiting Puerto Ricans. Once an ethnic group became established in the community, they brought in others. There were several English families who had been in Willimantic quite a while, because of their mechanical skills. There were a few Irish, but they had become mainly assimilated by the 50s.

Willimantic was a typical, small textile city. I never actually lived there, but I got to know the place pretty well. It went through many of the agonies that many urban areas have gone through in the United States. There was a move to the suburbs by the middle classes, and the downtown area became deserted and developed problems in microcosm of the big cities where the minorities live in the old urban area, where there are urgent educational and housing needs. Willimantic suffered because of the divide between the suburban, wealthy Windhams and the poverty stricken urban core, abandoned by the periphery. I witnessed the urban blight in the 1960s and 1970s, and I remember urban redevelopment. The area of Willimantic eventually demolished was not that bad when I arrived in the 1950s. There were stores and small businesses and tenements. I did a lot of shopping in Willimantic, but those businesses died, because they could not compete with the massive supermarkets and the malls.

I guess you do not see the warts when you are in a place for a long time. I was at a union meeting in Willimantic, when Joe Rourke, the first treasurer-secretary of the merged AFL and CIO, came to Willimantic to speak to us. Urban renewal was the big response to problems at this time. I recall they tore up all of downtown New Haven. Anyway, he came in and he said something like, "Boy, driving down this Main Street, I can see it badly needs urban renewal." You could almost feel the people in the room stiffening, as if to say, "What's the matter with our town?" But, when I left the meeting I could see the city was really run down. People who lived there did not notice, I suppose.

I had not been working in Willimantic for too long, when I became annoyed by how the piece-work rates were being calculated. I asked the shop steward in the department to explain how it was worked out. He did not know, so he asked the boss. The boss came over to me and asked what my problem was. I said that I did not have a problem, and that I'd asked for some information from the steward. I was a little annoyed at the steward, because if I had wanted to have asked the boss about it, I would have asked him directly. So I shot my mouth off to everybody and anybody about what a lousy job he was doing. A lot of people agreed with me, and in essence what they said was put your money where your mouth is, and run to become the steward, so I did!

I was elected. I beat this guy, his name was Fred, and became a shift shop steward for the Textile Workers Union of America, AFL-CIO. But that was no big deal. It was difficult to get stewards. It was a thankless job. You do not get paid for it. It digs into your piece-work earnings. Many stewards had the job by default, because no one else wanted to do it! This was 1956, and there was certainly a weakness within the union structure. Joe Dumas was the president of the local at the time. He and a guy called Romeo Benoit battled each other for the position every two years. The secretary-treasurer was Susan Mott. She was a staunch trade-unionist and a dedicated worker - but she lacked diplomacy and became unpopular in certain quarters.

Dumas and Benoit approached me and asked me to run against her, even though I'd only been the steward for a very short time. I didn't really want to, but I was becoming interested in the union. I'd been to a few meetings and I wanted to learn more. I ran against her, and won. Not because I was something special, more because she was unpopular. There are no ifs and buts about it. I was elected on Dumas' and Benoit's coat-tails. They were working for me. I think that was in 1957. I was new and a little green, and Susan Mott defeated me in an election soon after to become a delegate to the international union. But I began to learn quickly.

This secretary-treasurer's job was a part-time position. I still worked full time on the shuttle bobbins, and fixing. I received something like $50 a month to do the union duties, but the work dug into your piece-work earnings, so you can understand why it was such an unpopular job. After shuttle bobbins, I worked as a machine fixer. I think I was one of the first women ever to be a machine fixer. This had been strictly a male domain, but I needed the pay. Anyway, the women were usually more knowledgeable about the machinery, because they had been operating it for the longest time, so they were qualified. I had soon worked out how to change the pulleys, without calling a fixer. I knew how to block the pulleys up with the wrenches to take the weight. It was no big deal, but when you were a fixer, the pay was double! OK you got your hands dirty, but it came off with soap and water, and you were not working any harder than when you were as an operator!

The company knew that they could not refuse me the job, because the Equal Rights Amendment had just been passed. They knew that if they had refused me, I would have brought in a sex discrimination case against them. So American Thread gave me the job as fixer, and it worked out until I became president of the local. Even so, some of the guys who were teaching me how to be a fixer did not like the idea. I could not keep the fixing job up when I had more union duties, it was not fair on my partner, so I took a job down the other end of Mill Number Six, where I helped to distribute the work by getting the boxes ready for the packers, and getting all the equipment ready which was needed. This job gave me a little bit more freedom to pursue union duties. I was able to travel to different parts of the plant to do that job, so I kept a finger on the pulse!

I had some excellent support from my workmates and the union. The president's job was different. You were allowed one day a week to go around the mill and check out any grievances. It was time consuming. My daughter practically grew up in the union hall. We met in the hall on the third floor above the theater on Main Street, across from the Hotel Hooker. We rented those premises, but the union later moved onto Jackson Street. I was on the purchasing committee of the Joint Board when we bought the Jackson Street building.

The days as shop steward and secretary-treasurer taught me a lot. I attended summer school at UConn, and several textile union courses up at UMass, and I attended conferences, so I was picking stuff up all the time. I got a leave of absence from the American Thread in 1962, to work as a union organizer in the South. I was very interested in this type of thing; and the money was a lot better! I didn't actually move down there. I lived out of motels. We started with the J. P. Stevens Company, whose mills were all unorganized. I worked in Roanoke Rapids, North Carolina. It took a long time for the union to get established at J. P. Stevens, about 19 years. It was unbelievable. They fired several hundred people from their mills, wherever we campaigned. They pulled a lot of dirty tricks. It was a bitter, bitter campaign. They even fired a girl for testifying in Congress.

It was certainly tough in the South. We also worked with the UAW, who were attempting to get Southern auto works unionized. We supported them on the picket lines, and were often confronted by goons with baseball bats. They slashed the tires of our Buick, and we had to drive miles out of town with the tires cut, because the gas stations and garages were frightened to change them in case of repercussions from the company. It was difficult for Northerners down there, and most of the union organizers were Northerners.

I was down there about a year. My daughter stayed with my mother. I came back to Connecticut because of problems at the national level of the Textile Workers Union at this time. There were splits at both the national and local level. The Joint Board Manager in Eastern Connecticut, Dan Gallagher, and I were on opposite sides. The general president wanted me back in Connecticut because there was an election coming up.

Emil Rieve was the first President of the Textile Workers Union of America (TWUA), which was mostly composed of local unions organized by the Congress of Industrial Organizations (CIO) organizing committee. This effort was supported by seed money provided by the clothing workers, the ILGWU, I think. The CIO-backed TWUA grew quickly and attracted locals of the American Federation of Labor (AFL) United Textile Workers, but a total merger never took place. Within the TWUA, factions polarized around the old AFL and new CIO unions. A schism developed and sometime in the late 1950s, Emil Rieve stepped down and became president emeritus. Bill Pollack, Rieve's secretary-treasurer, became president, and John Chupka became secretary-treasurer. The schism festered even after the AFL and CIO merged in 1955. The textile unions never totally merged. I believe there are still some UTW locals still in existence within the AFL-CIO. The factional fight for control of the union finally came to a head at the union conference in New York in 1964. Bill Pollack defeated the opposition, so all his people went into senior posts, and those opposed to him were dismissed or left.

Dan Gallagher went soon after this. He had been a Joint Board Manager since the 1940s. Dan backed my opponent, Frank Czanski, when I ran for the position of president at the American Thread local in Willimantic, even though there was a doubt that Frank qualified to run for president. He had been a shop steward for less than a year. That reflected the divisions, right down to the local level. Gallagher had done some excellent work in Eastern Connecticut. He was in his early sixties when he left in 1965, and became a mediator at the Connecticut Department of Labor. He was a very intelligent guy, very well read and educated.

Frank Czanski beat me by one vote. There was some confusion at the election, however. A young Puerto Rican guy, who couldn't speak English very well, had wanted to vote for me, but he voted for Czanski, after a Czanski worker assured him that Czanski was the name of the woman standing for election. I filed a complaint and a re-run was ordered. Czanski, with Dan Gallagher's support, appealed to the Joint Board to stop the re-run, and I countered by appealing at the national level, claiming that Dan Gallagher was prejudiced. The Puerto Rican guy, Jesús, was questioned. An interpreter came down from UConn, and Jesús explained what happened. The re-run went ahead and I became president by about a dozen votes, but the number who voted was double the previous election, as we covered all three shifts. We'd previously voted on a Sunday, so those wanting to vote had to make a special trip into town. I finally won all my appeals and took office. This was January, 1965 so my first year as president got going with a bang!

I was the first woman president of the union, and American Thread did not know what to do with me. They often promoted the men who became president, as they displayed leadership qualities, and the company could use them. But these were the days before sexual equality and equal rights legislation for women had spread into executive jobs. There were no women bosses in American Thread, so I could not be promoted out of the way. But they were not beaten. American Thread had just started a credit union, and they asked me to become the head of that even though I had no skills whatsoever for the job. I refused, and they did everything they could to cut me off from the people. Even so, I got on well with the management. I dealt a lot with John Love and James Service. John Love was the boss. He was tough, but very honest. He was smart.

The company tried to handcuff me, and sent a memorandum around to all departmental heads that when I toured the plant, I would not be able to confer with anyone but the steward. But I got around that. I had not been president long when a heavy snow storm hit soon after a holiday. Something like 90 workers could not make it to work, or were late after struggling through the storm, so the management refused to pay them for the holiday. We grieved, and won 89 of the 90 cases. We only lost one case, and this guy was ready to be promoted to management, so I did not push that one. Some of them were classics. One guy had been working at American Thread for three years, never been late, never missed a day. He was one hour late, and he lost his holiday pay. Another guy had car trouble. He even showed the company the bill for repairs and the tow truck. He lost his pay. We went through each case with John Love, and he said, pay them, pay them. That made me look so much better. My early differences with management were overcome, and we worked together and did pretty good for the members.

The American Thread Company was by far the biggest concern in Willimantic at that time. There were other industries. I remember the Brand Rex Company, the Rogers Corporation, the Electro Motive Company and the Rosenstein ribbon factory. American Thread did not desire too much competition. Rumor had it that they kept other industries out of town. There's no doubt in my mind about that, but I can't prove it. They dominated the economy of the area. Since they had trouble getting help, they did not want anyone else in town paying a higher wage.

We negotiated some good contracts. American Thread in Willimantic was just about the largest textile concern in New England by the early 1960s, so we began to set the pattern for contract negotiations. Just previous to this, other firms in Maine and Massachusetts had driven contracts. The firm who drives the contract negotiations always does a little better than the other firms, so we did pretty well.

We were aware, however, that the American Thread Company was slowly running down the Willimantic mills. They were suffering from an acute shortage of labor at this time, and began a recruiting drive in Puerto Rico. They brought plane loads into Connecticut, about 50 to 60 at a time. It got to the point that in some departments they spoke Spanish only. Only one or two could speak English. There were problems, because I felt that the Puerto Ricans did not always get what they should have had. I arranged some English classes up at the union hall, in an attempt to make more of them bilingual, so more of them could qualify to become departmental shop stewards, and be better able to represent the Spanish speaking workers. We organized translations into Spanish of some of the key points of the contracts. There was also a large contingency of Greeks in the mill, so this caused double problems as most of them could not speak English either.

I detected some social unrest. It was not as overt as it became later, but you could see the beginnings of it. They were very much in a minority when they first arrived. There were no Latinos whatsoever in Willimantic before American Thread began recruiting. The second generation of Latinos, who were educated here, and who learned how to speak English, began to greatly resent the bigotry against them and their families. I had good relations with the Latino community, even if I could not speak their language. I managed to communicate somehow with them, and arranged to have interpreters with me when I visited their social clubs. If any of them were out ill, I tried to visit them at home, to see if the union could help in any way.

It was clear that a tense situation was developing within the community. This was the time when American Thread was closing departments. In 1966, ATCO contacted us at our Convention in Montreal and told us that they intended closing the spinning room. It was obvious that things were moving away. This was a Catch 22 as many of the Latinos were not skilled. The Company kept the more skilled work, like shuttle bobbins, dye shop work and synthetics in Willimantic, which the Latinos were not trained to do. In many of these instances, the job required that you read and write in English. So this was a factor. The shortage of skilled labor helped to quicken the exodus of American Thread. Also, the Company were not paying enough to attract younger people to the job. American Thread existed in Willimantic in the later years thanks to the loyalty of the older workers in the city who were comfortable in Willimantic. I remember one year that our negotiating committee of 10 had a total of over 200 years service to the Company. There were some long servers there. There were few middle level people there, just old timers, and the new Latino workers. Gradually, the middle level left. They could see the handwriting on the wall. They left to get more stable employment, or better paid employment in town or at Pratt & Whitney in Hartford, or at Electric Boat in Groton.

The major problem within the textile industry in Willimantic, New England, or the South, was that the textile workers never really organized properly. In the New Deal years, the difference in pay between the autoworkers, the steelworkers and the textile workers, was pennies. The average hourly wage was something like 27 cents for them all. But the steel workers and auto workers became organized across the country, and their wages shot ahead, but the textile industry could not get organized in the South, so this held them back. There was some vicious fighting in the South in the 1930s. The troops were brought out. They were stationed on the roofs of the mills with machine guns. This damaged the industry's labor unity, so their wage rates fell behind.

There was a big strike at American Thread in Willimantic in 1925, and that was ruthlessly crushed. Susan Mott was here at the time, and she told me that the strikers were evicted from their homes, and had to live in tents outside of town. The strikers sent their children out of town because they expected trouble. But the strike was ultimately broken by the importation of French Canadian millworkers from mills in Massachusetts and Maine. The old timers never forgave them. By the time I got there in the mid 1950s, the majority of old timers had gone. The majority of them were never taken back by American Thread. Joe Dumas, later the president of the local, was one of the scabs, but people like Susan Mott never forgave him. The feelings still ran high some 30 years after the event. When any disputes arose while I was there, you could bet that the strike was always brought up, right into the 1960s. People were still identified by whether their parents had, or had not been scabs during the 1925 strike! The demographics of the town were changed. Prior to the strike, there were many Connecticut Yankees, English and Irish in town, but they left and were replaced by French Canadians.

We had no strikes in the years I was there, well, maybe one. We voted to strike. We had a horrible expiration date for the contracts. I think it was on an Easter Sunday. The Company knew that we would not hold a strike meeting, or a union meeting over Easter. This was 1964, I think, and we called a strike on the Thursday before Easter, but the company settled over the holiday and only one shift lost pay. We also managed to get the expiration date changed. We set up pickets and frightened them a little, I think.

I was president of the Willimantic union until 1968. That's the year I left to work for the union at the national level, based in Boston. I was very interested in organizing, and in the political aspects of union work. I had become very active politically, as a result of my union activities, and so this was a chance to move ahead. Boston was not too far from home.

One of the first assignments I had was down in Warwick, Rhode Island, where there was an independent textile workers' union for the whole town. They were losing membership, and made approaches to the AFL-CIO Textile Workers Union for support, so I helped to organize the mills there, and also in Bristol, Rhode Island.

In the fall of 1969, I think it was, John Driscoll, the head of the state AFL-CIO, called me to see if I wanted to work at the Labor Department in Connecticut. I accepted, and started work there in February, 1970, as assistant agent for the State Board of Labor Relations, which is in essence the state level of the National Labor Relations Board. The major portion of my responsibilities lay in the public sector, in such things as municipal work, the police, fire, clerical and maintenance workers, hospitals, and small businesses, like garages and bakeries; investigating unfair labor practices; conducting elections and reporting back to the Board. If the parties could not negotiate an agreement, the parameters of an election, or the resolution of a complaint, the State Board held hearings. I did that job, as investigator, for four years. It was very interesting and rewarding, but the workload was very heavy as there were only two of us.

In 1974 the Committee on Political Education (COPE) job became open for the state AFL-CIO, and I began work as the political director. That was the year Ella Grasso became Governor. I did that job for two years, and then became secretary-treasurer for the state AFL-CIO, and then the president until 1988, so a lot of my time was spent at the Capitol as a lobbyist. That's when I became very active politically, at the state level. We did collectively for the unions things which they could not do as well by themselves, such as coordinating social, educational and community services for them. We worked with the Democratic Party, but we did have a few contacts with the Republicans. Philosophically, labor does not have that much in common with the Republicans. In 1988, I was appointed as State Commissioner of Labor by the Governor, Bill O'Neill. My main duty was to enforce the State's labor laws in such areas as unemployment compensation, wages, hours, OSHA and other protective legislation. Once enacted, those laws had to be enforced, so I oversaw that they were. The position is pro-labor because of its very nature. There was some opposition when I was appointed, because it was thought I was too pro-labor, but the Department of Labor's charge is to enforce the laws that are on the books. I cannot introduce any new ones. If laws are enacted that some people do not want enforcing, then that's not my fault! If I was too pro-labor, logically, I should be removed, and then I could have worked to change the laws, to make them better. I could not do that as Commissioner!

I have had an interesting career when I look back, from a shuttle bobbin operator, to State Commissioner of Labor. I enjoyed what I did, and I got paid for it. Not too many people can say that. I don't think I ever became jaded, because of this. I know that I owe a lot to the union. I think I still perceive myself as blue collar, as working class, but I suppose I'm now middle class! I made a decent and enjoyable living, and now I am enjoying retirement.

CHAPTER 5

I Still Miss England

Edith Blackburn, interviewed April 6 and 13, 1990

Tom Beardsley

My maiden name is Edith May Hartley and I was born May 16, 1908, in Summit, Lancashire, England, which is just outside Rochdale, and I still miss England after all these years! Summit was a milltown. Almost everyone I remember worked at the mill. It was only a little village. There were also some mills in the next village, Littleborough. It wasn't an easy life by any means. In those days you obeyed your parents. My mother was very strict. I went to work, came home, and had to work in the home. In those days you had to wash the windows inside and out because of the smog and the fog from the factory chimneys. We also had to stone the sidewalk outside the house and polish up the door knob and the garden gate.

My father worked at the mill, my mother didn't. But before my father went to the mill, he was a carter, that's better known over here as a teamster. He used to cart something in barrels from Walsden. He had his own horse and cart, but worked for someone else. Then he left to work in the Sladen mill. He had to work the correct shifts to look after my mother who had bad asthma. But we got by, we had enough to live on, probably because my mother was so frugal. We never used to waste anything, and we used to save up to go to Blackpool for one week during the summer when all the mills closed down.

I remember starting school, baby school as we used to call it, not kindergarten, when I was five-years-old. The school was very strict, we used to get caned. We learned writing, reading, arithmetic and geography, and the boys used to do woodwork in the winter and gardening in the summer. I left school, in 1920, when I was 12 and worked at the mill, Fothergill and Harvey's. My first job was carrying yarn, or cops as we used to call them. Cops were like bobbins which fitted onto the spindle, and I used to carry them from the spinning room. A cop was like a tube which fitted onto the spindle. They were a bit simpler than bobbins.

We started at six o' clock in the morning and finished at five-thirty at night, and we worked half a day on a Saturday. We walked to and from work in our clogs and shawls. You only wore shoes on a Sunday. The clogs were wooden soles with iron tips and leather tops and very hard wearing. I made 10 shillings a week, and I used to hand it all over to my mother. I did that until I was 21. She bought all my clothes and I could only wear them when she said so. She was very strict. She had been a widower. My father was her second husband. I have a half brother who was born after his father died, and he came over here to work. George was seven years older than me.

I came to America, for the first time, when I was only three-years-old. That was in 1911, but we went back home in 1913. My mother came over because she had a brother over here, at Central Falls, Rhode Island, and some friends in Connecticut, the Dawsons. My father came to Willimantic to work, I think he worked at Mill Number Three which was down near the Recreation Park. It was a granite mill, the stone was the same color as Mill Number Two. We used to live on Grove Place. We were there when the *Titanic* went down. Grove Place was down near the railroad station, where the footbridge is. There was a little paper shop down there, and my brother can remember reading the headlines when the *Titanic* sank. That was in 1912. We went back to England in 1913, but I don't remember why. It was something to do with my mother. But when we got back, my mother wanted to come back to America, but we couldn't because of World War One. We went to live in our hometown, Summit. We didn't come back to America until well after the War was over, that was in 1923. My mother never worked at the mill, she used to work hard at home, as well, but she also worked in a pub as a waitress.

I have happy memories of my youth in England. I was at school and worked in the mill. They were happy days. I was in the mill from 1920 to 1923. We were not allowed to have boyfriends and had to sneak out. We went over to Hollingworth Lake where all the boys and girls met, then we would catch the last trolley bus home. That was nine o' clock. This was on a Sunday and we were supposed to have been out at church! We had to be sneaky! I was only 15 when we eventually left for America. I remember landing here, it was on Labor Day, 1923.

We came back to America because of my mother's asthma. The doctor said that she should move to a warmer climate and he recommended the South of England, but my mother lied to my dad and told him that the doctor recommended America. I know my father said that he would never leave England until after his mother died, but my mother got her way, and my grandmother died when we were at Pawtucket during the strike of 1925. But my mother wanted to come here because my brother was here. He had left for Canada in 1922, and came eventually to work in Willimantic. Somehow, he managed to have a Company house ready for us up in the Oaks at Quercus Avenue — number 75. I remember that first night in the house at Quercus Avenue, my father broke down and cried, because he had left his mother alone in England. I remember a song on the radio which caused him to break down and cry, it was called, "When You Come to the End of a Perfect Day." It was the first time I ever saw him cry. His mother had been sick.

I remember that for some reason I had to go and take a test up at the Normal School in Willimantic, and I found that my schooling in England equaled the second year of high school here, but at school in England, we never learned anything about this country. We were only told about Canada. The only parts of America I knew about were Connecticut and Rhode Island. Maybe the test had something to do with immigration. I know that we had to wait a few years for our number to come up, so we could come over.

My father was a washer at American Thread, then he went into the card room and carried yarn to the spooling room. I always used to work with my father. I remember the working day. In the beginning, in 1923, we used to have an hour's nooning, which was a noon hour, you see. We came out at noon and went back to work at one in the afternoon. I used to walk home for lunch to our house in Quercus Avenue. There used to be a blower, a hooter, at the mill, which would go off at noon, and one hour later, to let you know lunch was over.

You know, it was beautiful at American Thread. All on the window sills there would be boxes of flowers, and they scrubbed the floors every week. And if a carnival, or a circus came to town, they would let you go to the windows to see the parade go up Main Street - although you couldn't see too much from Number Four Mill where I worked. If the temperature got up to 90 degrees, the mill would shut down because it was too hot to work. But nowadays they wouldn't shut down.

And when I first came we had 24 ends and we had a seat at each end of the frame where the yarn ran out, and we could tie it. When I left American Thread they were running 74 ends. But in those early days the working day was only eight hours, and we used to stop in the middle of the morning and the middle of the afternoon to clean up the machine. At weekends you were shut for one and a half hours and everything came off so you could clean that machine. As I say, there were 74 ends when I left in 1952. The mill ran for three shifts. It never shut down. It run continually. You tied this end up and when you got to the next end, the last end would be down again. Non-stop work and there was no longer any noon hour.

You took your own lunch and ate it as you were working. You couldn't afford to stop because you were on piece-work. Then they started with the wool, but when I first came here it was all thread, cotton thread and shoe thread. The job was very similar to the one I was doing in the mill in Lancashire. I worked in Mill Number Four, the red brick mill, the only difference was that in Lancashire I worked cops, but here they were spools. It was in Number Four where all the raw cotton came in from the railroad, which ran at the back of Number Four. The raw cotton came in direct from India, it would be chopped up and carded and from there it would go to the spinning room, and from there to the spooling room.

When I first came I didn't know anyone, I didn't bother with anyone. I was lost, I stayed with my family, and just sat on the porch at night. Everyone spoke different languages, there were Polish and French and one or two Jews, a few Italians, Russians, and the Americans, of course. They would talk all together in their own languages across the machines, and all I had ever heard before was English, or Lancashire. And, of course, I had never ever seen a colored guy before, but none worked in the mill. There were only three colored families in Willimantic for the longest time.

When the big strike began in 1925 we left Willimantic and my father and I found work at the mills in Central Falls, where my uncle worked. There were no unions in 1925. That was the trouble, you see. They were trying to get unions in and American Thread didn't like it, so they brought in all those French people when the strike began. But we left and went to Central Falls. My father had a family to support. We used to live in a tenement, on the third floor, in School Street, Central Falls. We worked at a mill owned by J. P. Coates. We were there for two years - on the third floor, and that was when I became scared of thunderstorms.

The weather is extreme here. The snow lasts longer and the heat gets into the 90s, and when it's hot, it's humid, it's terrible, Oh Lord! In 1937 my mother and I went back to England for a holiday, and my cousins asked me about the weather, but they didn't believe me when I told them it got into the 90s. They said I wouldn't be here if it had been as hot as that! Those thunderstorms scared me, I'm still petrified of them. Anyway, we moved back to Willimantic in 1927. Mr. Moxon told us there would be a job and a house for us if we came back - probably because we were English.

I worked at that same job right through till 1952. I was a spooler for 27 years. I did the same job for all that time, there was little chance of promotion in those days. There was the overseer and the boss, but we couldn't get any higher. My father got a job in the card room, but I can't remember what it was.

There was some bitterness in town against the scabs, but people got used to them because they stayed. They were French who came here from Maine and Massachusetts. Many of my workmates spoke in the French language. My son's mother-in-law was one of those brought in. She was only 14, and was one of a large family who all came to work.

I had a Syrian boyfriend before I met my husband. His name was Tom Skaff. We used to go to the square dances at Bolton. Tom had a car, but they were open in those days, so you had to wear a rug around you. He wanted to marry me at 18, but my mother would not allow it. Then I met my future husband, Meryl Lewis Griffin. He was a baseball player, and I hated baseball. I still do. We went out together for five years, but we courted over the telephone. We were married on December 24, 1932. Griffin did not work at American Thread, he worked on the farm. I got him a job at American Thread in 1932, for $12 a week, but he only lasted for three weeks. He got his hand caught and that was the end of that!

This was the time of the Depression and times were bad. We lived with our parents after we were married. I'd never do that again! Griffin had a variety of jobs in the 1930s. He worked for the telephone company, driving a truck, but some weeks they didn't pay him, so he quit; then he got a job pumping gas; then he worked for Pratt and Whitney where he got a bad oil rash from the degreasers. He lost all his hair and was out of work for three months. We didn't have a cent coming in as I was pregnant and off work. After that he began work for the town of Windham, then the City of Willimantic; a job he had for 13 years. We lived with my parents for four years, 1932-1936, because the times were so hard. This was on John Street. We then lived on Lewiston Avenue.

You didn't see much of the big bosses at American Thread. There was Mr. Moxon, and then Mr. Clark, Bert Shaw, Joe Atkinson, an Englishman, he came from Bolton, Lancashire. There was Percy Wilmot, he was from Bolton too, but you saw the overseer everyday, he walked around the machine to see that the job was going OK. I worked in the spool shop and they were nearly all women. The only guys were the fixers, the guys who mended the machines. There were also "spotters" who'd come round and stand behind you and clock you to see how long it would take you to do this and to do that, and the next thing you knew there was something on the billboard and you were supposed to do so much in so much time.

They used to make me nervous, especially when we were on the new machines, you had to work faster, and you had no time to clean them down, and they were always breaking down, and the thread was breaking. The fixers were there all the time. You had to keep going for all the eight hours.

There wasn't a union, that was one of the reasons why they went out on strike. They got a union before I left, but I never joined. No one ever asked me to join. I know a few people who used to have meetings. I wasn't interested in the union. If you would lose one week's pay, you could never make it up, and what you get extra after being out on strike will never bring you back what you lost. But the union was OK when it reduced the hours, but what's the use of getting a raise when you're never any better off, and your union dues go up all the time, so what do you gain, only the ones at the head of the union get the gains, the workers do not. I do not believe in unions.

When I left in 1952, many displaced persons worked at American Thread. They'd come to America after the war. They were very, very good. They worked damn hard, not like the Puerto Ricans who lived on just potatoes! Some of the displaced persons had been doctors in their own country. They never bothered anybody. One woman still had the number tattooed on her arm from the concentration camp. They worked in the spool room, the card room and the finishing end.

American Thread put on concerts and square dances at the Armory. I didn't go to many functions. My mother kept me between her finger and thumb until the day she died!

I also worked at Electro Motive after my first husband died. That used to be a velvet mill, you know. There also used to be a silk mill on Valley Street, but American Thread was dominant. I worked at the school and eventually retired in 1977 when I was 69.

Willimantic used to be a nice friendly little town. In those days you could walk all around Willimantic day and night, I would not dare do it now. There used to be cotton mills where the Bridge Street Plaza is now. Across the street where the *Dairy Queen* and *Benny's* are now, there were all houses there. Also, from

Memorial Park right up to Mansfield Avenue, was all spare land, right up to where the VFW now is. Valley Street ended up near Mansfield Avenue. There was also a workhouse up by the VFW. During the war, they had temporary housing up there.

I can also remember the trolley cars. They ran to South Coventry and New London. You could also go boating on the Willimantic River. A lot of things used to happen at Recreation Park. There was baseball, trotting and the circuses set up down there too. The area down by the American Thread mills was known as Sodom. They were all mill houses. They sold all those houses, I think the highest price they got for one was $800. There were no toilets on the inside, the toilets were on the outside in a woodshed which was in the back garden. All that land in the garden was sold with the house. We lived up in the Oaks, even when we came back to Willimantic after the strike. We lived on the corner of Crescent and Quercus. It was a big house with dining room and a kitchen and three bedrooms. We lived next door to the Superintendent of the Mill, David Moxon. He still lived in the Oaks in 1927, before he moved to Windham Road. He was a nice man, an Englishman you know, from Yorkshire.

Yes, Willimantic has changed a lot. There used to be a big hotel on the corner of Valley Street and Bank Street. It was called the Central Hotel. They pulled down Temple Street and Center Street. That area is a green now. Railroad Street was a nice street, it was on each side of the footbridge. There was a hardware store there, a saloon and a paper shop. There was a French club somewhere down there too, where the cinemas are today. Jackson Street has changed, there were stores and a barber's shop. They also knocked the railway station down. We used to travel into Hartford by train, but if you have not got a car today, it's difficult to get there. There's only two buses a day which travel into Hartford. In those days you could travel all over the place. I remember taking the train down to Atlantic City with my mother and father, and walking down the seven mile boardwalk. We saw Rudy Vallee that week.

CHAPTER 6

Every Village Around Us in Poland Was Getting Mail From America Saying There Was Plenty of Work

Frank Klosowski interviewed September 20, 1990

Tom Beardsley

I was born on May 2, 1904 in Galicia, Poland. My father was a master tailor, a job which required a five year apprenticeship. He was drafted into the Austrian army, under Franz Joseph, at age 18 until he was 21. He was born in 1884, and died in 1962. I had three years of schooling in Poland, from age six to age nine. We were taught Polish in the first grade, Polish and Russian in the second grade, and German in the third grade. When I got here I had to go back into the first grade because I didn't know any English.

Galicia was near to a large river which marked the border with Russia. Poland was under the rule of Austria-Hungary then. They divided Poland between Russia, Austria and Germany. That's why I learned the different languages. I can still read and write in Polish, but I've completely forgotten Russian, and I only had German for a short period of time before we left to come here.

Galicia had a large Jewish population. Everyone was in business of some kind or another. On Fridays at sunset, an old Jewish Rabbi with a tall black hat, a beard down to here, and a little mallet would knock on the doors of the Jewish business establishments. That meant that nothing could be sold and you couldn't light any fire. But on a Sunday morning the businesses opened, and Catholics patronized them. They shopped for such things as salt, sugar and alcohol. My father would pick up a little cup and fill it with 200 proof alcohol and pour it into his bottle. When he got home he made twice as much by cutting it down to 100 proof. I remember in Poland they had very good beer, which my father also used to drink.

It seemed that every village around us in Poland was getting mail from America saying there was plenty of work. There was no work in Poland. My mother worked in the field weeding for 30 cents a day, from sunup to sundown. My father heard from Polish tailors in America that there was plenty of work, so he came over to check things out. My father landed in Willimantic at six in the morning and by noon he was working. He walked into a tailor shop, showed his diploma and sat down to work. The owner of the tailor shop was A. Butleman. He was Polish and Jewish.

My father was here for between two and three years, working for other tailors. He sent money back to Poland to support his family. He eventually sent us passes to come over. I think he had some feeling that the war wasn't too far off. I came to America in 1913. Our people were brave enough, a year after the *Titanic* sank, to take a chance to cross the ocean. We traveled from Galicia by train to Bremen, Germany, the port where our ship the *George Washington* was tied up. The crowds pushed us up the gang plank and some of the people, when they saw what a giant ship it was, went back on the train and went home, even though there was a band there playing to cheer them up.

We traveled third class. Our bed was table level. On the next layer was a family of gypsies. It was like a chicken coop; we all slept in this one little compartment all wired up. I knew everyone down in the baggage department. There was a third, a second, and a first class. The people in first class threw coins to us. I tried to pick something up, but there was such a rush. I was always up on the main deck watching the ships going by. They looked like little tiny boats. A smaller ship with one stack, left the day before us. Our ship had two stacks. We passed the ship with one stack on the following day. I remember that very well. I also remember looking through at the anchor and seeing the ship cutting water. I was nine-years-old.

The journey took seven days. I saw the Statue of Liberty when it was really small, and I didn't know what it was because it was in the distance. There were one or two days that I missed the upper deck, because the weather was too bad. It was fall, because we landed around the end of September, in 1913. The war broke out the next spring.

We came through Ellis Island. There were walls and walls of people. The doctors wore black or brown derbies and they checked your eyes and your skin for rashes. Then we climbed the stairs and got a train that took us to 14th street in New York City. New York had elevated railways, sky high buildings, and I'm pretty sure we went by Yankee Stadium, even though I didn't know anything about baseball then of course, but the car we were taking to the boat was filled with baseball fans. The World Series was on. There we got on another small boat that took us to New London. We slept overnight on this boat and early the next morning at five o'clock we were in New London.

We got off the boat, and crossed the tracks into the New London station. The train pulled up and took us to Willimantic. We got to Willimantic at six in the morning. My father and his partner were there to greet us. They took our baggage and put it on a buggy. Even at that time in the morning, people were on Main Street. American Thread was operating from seven in the morning. They paid a dollar a day. When we came over, my mother wanted to work there, but my father said no, as he could make enough. So she was a housekeeper.

There were not too many automobiles in town — maybe I saw half a dozen a day. Auto owners had a nine month car registration and they jacked up their cars for the winter season until April. Cadillac, Ford and Chevrolet were the only cars sold then.

I remember people going to work in the morning, in the winter time in deep snow, with a one horse plow. The roads were never cleared of snow because everyone who had a horse also had a sleigh. A two horse sleigh was a Christian. A one horse sleigh or wagon was Jewish. A man stood on the plow and guided the horse to make a path so people could get to work at the mill on time. Walking to school was fun in the winter; sidewalk slides 25-feet-long and hopping a sleigh for a ride. Many times I got a ride to school, because my neighbor would give all the children about a half mile ride to school. Sled coasting after school, and again until ten at night, was done on one of eight Willimantic hills. The most popular hill was Lewiston Ave.

I went to St. Joseph's Parochial School. That's when my father made a mistake. Instead of going with me and registering me the right way, he had me follow a boy to school who was in the first grade and that's where they kept me. I went until fifth grade. My sisters were luckier; they graduated from grammar school, high school, normal school and teacher's college. I have three sisters, Marie, Helen and Ann, and a brother, Fred. I am the oldest.

I was a paperboy when I was ten. I was still in school. I was a paper boy for the mayor of Willimantic, Danny Dunn, who was a great sportsman. He had a shop on Railroad Street and was able to pick up the latest baseball scores from the telegraph at the railroad depot, and I took turns answering the telephone to tell people the latest scores. I bought newspapers at a nickel for four copies and sold them for two cents each, and made a profit of three cents for every four papers sold. At that time, there were too many paperboys in town. They all had their corners picked. About 15 paperboys picked up their papers and turned back what they didn't sell. I sold the *Boston American* on Main Street. I yelled my head off. At that time Main Street was like Broadway. You could touch almost every person who was walking because there were no cars and everybody had to walk.

On Sundays over one hundred baseball fans could get instant scores as they stood on the platform of the railroad station telegraph office. About every five minutes the scores came over the wires, and were shouted out the window to the fans. For fans who had time and money it was easy to watch the games in Boston. I'd take the train at nine-thirty in the morning to go to Boston and be there by around noontime to go to Fenway Park. It came to about five dollars for the day; including hotdogs and entrance fee. I'd get back to Willimantic at eight-thirty at night.

I was also a baggage smasher. People used to get off the trolley cars with heavy suitcases. At first I carried the baggage, but I later got a wagon and for ten cents I took them to the railroad station, and from there they continued their journey. Trolley cars ran along Main Street. Many times I took that five or ten cent ride to Coventry Lake in the summertime. I went to Ocean Beach one time. I got on the Norwich trolley, which was at the foot of Jackson Street. In Norwich I got on the trolley to New London. All this was for no more than a dollar.

I also worked for a fruit store delivering fruit to people on the hill. After school, when I reached 14, I got a job for $15 a week, sweeping at American Thread, so I gave up the paper route and baggage smashing. You had to be 14 to get a working permit. I graduated the fifth grade and never went back. That was the time there was a shortage of manpower because the war was going on. I had no trouble getting a job. I just had to show them my birth certificate and they put me in the spinning department sweeping the cotton in Mill Number Four. I was there for about a year, or a little more. If I missed the paymaster, I went to the building which now houses the Museum. You'd show him a ticket

Main St., looking East,
Willimantic, Conn.

The thriving textile producing community of Willimantic as it appeared when Frank Klosowski arrived from Poland. The trolley car tracks turn right into Lower Main Street, past Lincoln Square, and head towards the thread mills of The American Thread Company, before turning off towards South Windham. *François Gamache*

and you would get your pay. I used to go to the library upstairs. The offices of the American Thread were on the two lower levels and the library was on the top floor.

The very first time I went to the American Thread library, the woman picked out a book for me. It was about a boy who ran away from home and joined the circus. That reminds me of when we lived at Jackson Place. The circus was parked right out the door, that's where the railroad track was. Every morning at five, you'd hear the animals wanting their breakfast. That's where they were unloading and taking all the carts by draft horse to Bacon's lot on Natchaug Street, where the old Elm Market lot is now. At that time the Bacon's had a coal yard, a furniture parlor, and a grocery business. They were French Canadians. Mrs. Bacon was pretty well off. She ran a furniture business with her husband.

I'd go down to Bacon's lot and carry the pails of water for the circus, and get a free pass. It was 25 cents extra for the Wild West Show. It was hair-raising when the Indians on horseback attacked a pioneer group and burned their covered wagons. Then Tom Mix and the cowboys rode in and killed all the Indians. And then the cowboys did a lot of target shooting and fancy roping for good measure.

When I was cleaning in Mill Number Four, I remember that each woman had to work at least six or eight frames. When the bobbins were filled the doffers came in and took them away. I used to clean after a day's spinning. The cotton would fly so you couldn't see any part of the machinery and we would brush it out. There were six sweepers and we each had at least 30 frames to take care of.

That Number Four Mill was big. That's where my mother-in-law, Frances Curol, worked. She worked at American Thread for almost 60 years. She immigrated from Poland in about 1910. She took a job at American Thread at about that time. She married in about 1912. The Poles that came here were lonesome, so they married. There was a wedding every Saturday. She raised three children, Helen, Isabel and Rose. They were all educated, except my wife, Helen. She left school in the seventh grade because her mother needed help. She worked right through until about 1970, before she retired. She also organized the Saint Joseph's Polish Society Local 1169 of the American Roman-Catholic Union. That's an insurance organization in Chicago. She signed up at least 300 members and collected the dues. She had a daughter who became a nurse. Too bad she didn't have a son - he could have been Dr. Curol.

I remember the strike at American Thread in 1925. They had a parade. That was a big mistake. They could not wait for a raise. I'm sure that as time went on American Thread would have added something to their wages. They wanted a small raise and never got it, and were thrown out of the company houses. Many of them lived in tents out near the Natchaug River. Their furniture was actually put on the sidewalk because they didn't go back to work. Most of them were on welfare. Half of Willimantic had to move away. We had a poor farm where they raised good apples and potatoes. They used to donate to the ones that were on the strike. When they offered to my mother-in-law, she was ashamed to take anything from welfare.

I had two wives. I married in 1937, and 1958. I have two sons and a daughter. My son Tom teaches in Montville. Frank Junior is with the welfare department in Hartford. Kathy, my daughter, teaches seventh and eighth grade in South Willington. My first wife was born in America in 1913. We had a Polish hall on Ives Street and we'd have dances every Saturday. I met her there. Mr. Willard at the lumberyard built that building for $11,000 in 1933. My friend, a bricklayer, was paid 35 cents an hour to help build it. Before that we were down on lower Main Street, near Elm Street where the Moose Club is now. The Polish Club has a beautiful stage, dance floor, beautiful downstairs kitchen and lounge. There were a lot of members at one time, now they're dropping out; too many used to buy double shots and they've passed away early. My second wife worked in a silk mill at ten cents an hour, five dollars a week. She walked all the way to the silk mill in the winter time. On one side of Bridge Street was the Quidnick Mill where they used to make cotton sheets. On the opposite side the Jewish people took over. I think it was called the Corn Silk Company. My wife told me that when you bent down to tie your shoe, they warned you not to take time and to watch your machine. Both wives also helped me in the tailor shop.

There were different nationalities here before the Polish people arrived. First it was the Irish, then the French, who had all the company houses on the front of Main Street. There were also some Italians, some Jewish people, and maybe two or three colored families, and some Syrians. The first house we lived in was rented from a Syrian, Haddad. All the Syrians were in the clothing business and sold blue serge suits and brought them in for alterations, such as shortening the sleeves or finishing off the hem or cuffs.

When the Poles first came they had to rent rooms in the back of company houses. The rents, one or two dollars a week, were taken out of the paycheck, The first Poles came here sometime around around 1900. Somebody started it, they had some education and read the papers. Once somebody went and wrote back how pleased he was - work galore here, no problem - and as each one came others followed him.

After American Thread I got a job in the SCS Box Company making paper cartons, and worked there for about a year. My third job was for Windham Silk on Church Street. I remember the silk lining people used to buy to line overcoats.

My father and a partner, Mr. Kinczyk, opened a tailor shop in 1911. At that time we had 11 tailor shops in Willimantic, and about 12 cobblers. Today we have one or two cobblers and filling stations instead. He bought property on Jackson Street and built his own shop, so he didn't have to pay rent. We were number 57 Jackson Street. The name of the firm was Kinczyk and Klosowski. That's where we were until the cranes came and took it all away.

One day my father gave me an ultimatum. He said, "You either go back to school or come in my shop and I'll teach you tailoring." I was ashamed to go back to school, so I went to the tailor shop. I worked there until redevelopment put us out of business and broke up our shop. Around 1927, my father's partner didn't think we needed any extra help, and one afternoon they got into an argument about it. Mr. Kinczyk, pointed to me and said, "He's your partner, now. I want out!" So my father pointed to me and said, "Get your bank book and go to the bank and draw out $350." They took inventory right there and the whole shop was worth $700; two sewing machines, cutting tables and other tools and cloths. So I had to draw out $350 and hand it over to Mr. Kinczyk. He opened his own business on Union Street and he was doing better than we were. That's when I became not quite a full partner. My first wage at my father's shop was 50 cents a day. In Poland you had to pay the master tailor to teach you the trade for three years. The next two or three years you would be paid very little wages and then you finally got your diploma. I had to work another ten years before my father divided the profits. We had a tailoring department, and in 1937 I opened a cleaners - that kept me busy. My father died in 1962, and I was left with the shop, but I already knew the ropes pretty well.

My brother joined us after the war. He went to high school and UConn. While he was at UConn he had to leave to go to the service in the Second World War. He came back and finished school and got a job with the Aetna Insurance Company. They wanted to ship him out to St. Louis, but he didn't want to leave home, so we took him into the tailor shop. He took care of all the bookkeeping and he stayed with us until the redevelopment in 1974. Now he has a desk job at the hospital in charge of the supply department. He's 20 years younger than I am. I kept up the business when my father passed away. I had as many as eight or nine people working for me at one time - four in the cleaning department and four in the tailor shop.

One of my earliest memories is seeing cans of tomato soup in the stores. The stores were so different then. They cut your pork chops at the chopping block. Everybody had a little book, and the grocer wrote down how much you bought that day. When it came Friday, and you had your paycheck, you paid your bill. You could live on about six dollars a week for meat and groceries. If you paid up on time, they gave you a premium, like an alarm clock, to keep you as a customer. They also delivered. The grocer would ride around the streets and pick up the orders in the morning and deliver in the afternoon. Very few had telephones in those days.

We drank beer here too. There were three saloons on Jackson Street. Every Saturday the saloon people, they had a horse and wagon, delivered cases of beer to different homes. One saloon was Polish, another was Irish, "Murphy's." At that time there was a saloon on every other street in Willimantic. There were about 50 saloons and 48 grocery stores!

I lived all over Willimantic. Valley Street to begin with, and Jackson Place, where we lived up in the attic. My father bought his first property in Sodom on Willowbrook Street. There were two houses there. Mr. Kinczyk took one and my father took the other. The two houses, at that time, cost $3,500. It cost them $1,750 each, but they had to peddle a bicycle to Jackson Street and it got the best of them. After five years they sold out and bought right next to the shop. I bought this house in Hewitt Street in 1940 for $3,000.

It was nicer in Willimantic in those days. There were trains coming in every half hour, the trolley going back and forth to Coventry, people on the streets, a candy shop and and an ice cream shop. Every person who came to shop, had their ice cream money. There were also shoe shops, clothing stores, hatmaking shops. There were four theaters and I used to skip in. I never had to pay. I'd stand next to a woman with a long skirt and hold on to her skirt and walk in with her. I think the owner figured there are plenty of empty seats. The *Bijou* stood where Rosen's department store most recently stood, the *Gem* where the Y.M.C.A. is, the *Scenic* was on Bank Street, next to the firehouse, and the Loomer Opera House stood where *Nassiff's* is. An old man sold the tickets at the *Bijou.* I used to look at the posters and all of a sudden I would see he was asleep. He'd shut his eyes just to let me in. There were variety shows at the *Bijou* and the Loomer Opera House. Stock companies would come and play for a whole week with New York stars.

Mr. Loomer had the Opera House built. It had an orchestra, with three levels.

They called the top one, which was benches, "nigger heaven." We had fun up there. We used to make airplanes and fly them down on the audience. That's where we would slip in because we knew the city sheriff was a Knight of Columbus, and he'd let us in. I can't remember the exact year when the movies first came to town, but I saw something at the *Bijou* about a boxcar and a woman riding on it, and they showed colored people from Africa. At the Loomer Opera House I saw the stock companies plus the movies. One movie was *Jack and the Beanstalk.* They were all silent movies. They had cowboy and Indian pictures at the *Scenic,* and a woman playing the piano. She'd be rattling off on that piano while the film was on. The most memorable movies were the *Perils of Pauline* and *Birth of a Nation.* There were also Charlie Chaplin and the Keystone Cops.

The armory was more for dancing. American Thread put on a meal once a year and if you worked there you got a free ticket. There was roller skating at the Center Street armory. The new armory on Pleasant Street was built about 1912. I can remember men leaving their work and reporting to the new armory. They paraded around to Main Street and got on the train and off they went. They went to Hartford to join the rest of the soldiers, and travel on to Mexico to fight Pancho Villa. Otherwise the new armory was used for dances and there was a shooting gallery in the basement. Local guards went in there to practice every week. I remember when the Elks Club was built on Pleasant Street, across from the new armory, in 1927. When we were kids we used to play cowboys and Indians in the thick woods which were there before the Elks club was built. The Elks were organized about 1914. They had a building on Main Street. When I joined the Elks they already had their new club on Pleasant Street. Willimantic is not as nice as it used to be, but I still think it's a fine town.

CHAPTER 7

I Was Always For the Union When It Started. I'm Not Afraid to Say It

Rose Deshaies, interviewed June 29, 1990

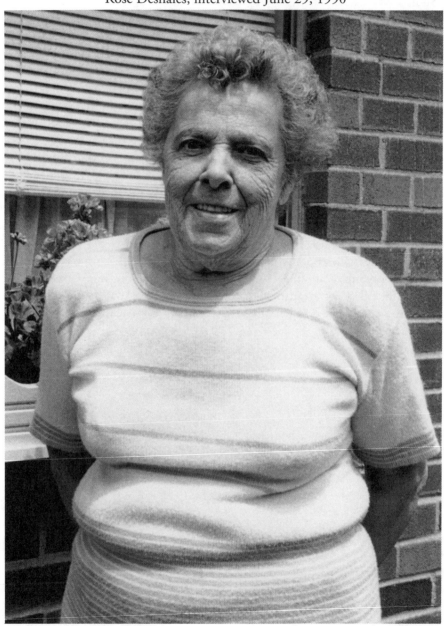

Tom Beardsley

I was born Rose Veilleux in St. Ephrem, Quebec, Canada, in 1916. I came to the United States when I was about three-years-old, around 1919. My mother was a U. S. citizen. She was born in Maine. Her maiden name was Lambert. My father was born in Canada. My mother went to school in Canada after her mother died. Her father remarried and my mother went with him up to Canada. The woman he married wanted nothing to do with his kids, so at the age of 12 she left school and went to do housework anywhere she could. She had gone to a convent in Canada, and it was there she had met my father and they got married when she was very young.

They worked on a farm for quite a few years, then they worked in textiles in Manchester, New Hampshire. They then worked here in Willimantic. American Thread came and fetched us as their workers were on strike. My mother worked in the spinning room and my father worked in the carding room. I remember that when we came here, the other kids chased us. They didn't like us because their parents were out of work. I remember we were always in fights. In school the other kids would gang up, and call us scabs and all that kind of thing. What did I know about a strike? I didn't know nothing about a strike! We were chased by the kids whose parents were on strike. I didn't know anything about it. Everytime we went out there would be a gang of kids waiting for us, calling us all kinds of names. They had been living in the American Thread housing and had to leave, they'd been thrown out. The strike kind of wore out.

I attended St. Mary's school and was married at St. Mary's Church. When we first arrived here in Willimantic from New Hampshire, we lived in the back of the second house on High Street. We were living upstairs. We later moved into the American Thread housing on Main Street. We lived downstairs in a tenement house, that one next door to the "Elms," the hotel owned by American Thread. We stayed there right up until the company sold that housing. Anybody who had the money could buy a house cheap enough, but we didn't have that kind of money to buy, and my parents were older and no longer working at American Thread. We couldn't afford to rent anything else so we had to move in with one of my sisters, and I wasn't old enough to work then.

I started work in 1932, when I was 16- years-old, down at American Thread. I went to work to help my parents survive. My parents had come down from New Hampshire to work during the strike, so American Thread said they would find us work as long as we wanted to work. My mother talked to Charlie Hill. I think he was the agent or one of the managers, and he got me in right away. The day I was 16 I got the job. You had to be 16 in order to work. My mother did not want me in the spinning room, she knew how dirty it was down there. You would get cotton all over you, so they put me in Mill Number Six, where it was much better. The cotton down in spinning would get in your lungs. It wasn't good. So I started in the finishing end, and my job on the shoe thread was a nice easy job, it was the best I ever had - two machines with six ends on each machine.

My parents did not work long at American Thread. They were getting old when they arrived here in 1925, and maybe they worked only for 10 to 15 years before they retired. I had two sisters and a brother who all worked at American Thread eventually.

My first job was cone winding in Mill Number Six. I was always in Mill Number Six. I was there for all those years, going on for 46 years, from 1932 to when I retired at age 64. But I had a year off when I had my last baby. The workers were not all French people, there were some Polish people and all kinds of nationalities. I remember that some of those strikers got back in at American Thread. Nationality did not mean nothing to me then. It didn't matter whether they were Polish or French if I got along with them. Communication was never a problem. I went to school here and learnt English, but I never lost my French.

The wages at American Thread, when I started there, were low, very low. I made $12. 50 for a 50 hour week. We worked Saturdays until noon. In the week we worked from seven in the morning with a hour off for dinner, then we went back and finished at five in the afternoon. The work wasn't that hard though, but it got harder and harder as the years passed by. They wanted more and more production, but when I went in it wasn't too bad. It wasn't piece-work then. All they were bothered about then was good work, but when it was introduced I worked piece-work for the rest of my life.

When they started to work piece-work, I wanted it too, because you could earn more than $12. 45. You could make more money! Then the NRA came and we got more money. The wages were still low, but everything was cheap. You could buy a pair of shoes for $1. 50 and milk for 10 cents, bread for five cents. The cost of living was cheap and you got a lot for your money. Today it costs you $50 for a bag of groceries. In those days you could eat all week for $10!

About 10 or 12 years ago, I was talking to a woman who had worked with me at American Thread for many years. She had saved all the wage packets from those early years and I found it hard to believe that we were paid so badly in those early days. They paid us weekly in small brown envelopes with the amount printed on them. The paymaster would come around the mill and hand our wages to us.

I was cone winding at first. Some were small cones. It depended; there were different types. We were running four machines when I first started on cones. There were various jobs in the different sections in Number Six Mill, and as I was working, I would watch the other jobs to see how they were done, and when an opening came along, I would apply to transfer to a new job, and any chance that came up, I would take it. After the cones, I worked on spools, then I got to work on shoe thread — that was a good job. I worked on 12 ends, two machines, that wasn't much, two machines for shoe thread. I worked on that for a long, long time. I don't remember exactly for how many years, but it was for a long time. I was making good money. Then the shoe thread went out and I went onto spools, and I stayed on spools until I retired, except for one summer when I hurt my wrist, so I was transferred to the woolen department in Mill Number Two, but when my wrist got better I wanted my old job back.

I was always for the union when it started there. I'm not afraid to say it. There were a lot of things I saw there that weren't right and it was the union that could correct them things. I voted for the union and it came in. Everybody had to join a union then. You couldn't work at American Thread if you were not in the union. This was when the NRA came here as part of the New Deal in the 1930s. I used to get the women who worked around me to sign up for the union, to sign a card before the union came in. That was not allowed and I could have got into trouble, so I used to get them to sign when they went into the ladies room, if they wanted to. When there was enough cards signed, the union decided that they would begin meetings. I did that for the union, but I was not bothered about being one of the leaders. I just wanted to belong and that's it.

When the union came in, Walter Taylor, my boss came up to me and told me that I was wanted in the Main Office. There was a union meeting there that day, but I didn't go. They wanted me down there, but I told him, I'm not going down there. Sure! I got people to sign for the union, but that didn't mean I wanted to be a leader. I didn't go so I don't know what happened over there, but it was better with the union in there. We didn't get any trouble. The union would negotiate new pay contracts, and they always went in, they always passed.

Three years or so after I got in there, there was another strike. It wasn't a strike from here, it was from other thread mills, and they came here to try and get us to come out on strike to support them. At this time, my boss sent me from the mill and sent me up to work at the "Elms" up on Main Street. The place was full of State Police, and they would turn away the people who came here to try and get us to go out on strike. I used to serve the tables and wash the dishes. I was getting the same pay there as I was getting in the mill. We had our meals there, and I was there for about a month. After that we went back to our jobs and the State Police all went away. They slept in the "Elms." I was living on Center Street at that time, and I had to walk to the "Elms" at five in the morning to get things ready. I would work there all day. There were three of us girls taken out of the mill to work over there. We were all young and single. I guess that's why they took us over there. I'd never done that kind of work, as a waitress, but it didn't make any difference to them. But I wasn't forced to go. It was OK. It made a change.

I was accompanied to work every morning by a state policeman to make sure nobody would hurt me. But the people here kept working. I don't know why these other people were trying to get us to come out. But believe me them State Police were treated well. They ate well and they were given cigarettes. They slept there and were not allowed to leave at night, but at night some of them went out.

The Willimantic Linen Company's boarding house for women was built in 1864. The American Thread Company officially named it "The Elms" in 1917 because of the numerous elm trees which stood along lower Main Street. *WTHM*

They sneaked out by throwing rope ladders out of the windows. Charlie Hill's father ran that place then, and they didn't want him to know they were going out on the town. They were state policeman, they were wise. I suppose they wanted to go out on dates or go to bars, a lot of them were only young.

I met my husband, Jules Deshaies, in Willimantic. He was a silk worker, a weaver, and he hadn't been working steady. The silk mill was always on strike, and if they were not out on strike, they were always closing. He worked all over where there was a silk mill, and finally there were no more, so he was out of work for quite a while. Then, in 1938 when we were married, he got a job in American Thread and worked there until he was 65. He was a carder. He was from Canada. His family came down from Canada and worked in Northampton, Massachusetts, before coming to Willimantic. This was when the silk mills were closing, and they went wherever there was a silk mill. They came here and they all worked in the Holland silk mill. We got married in the same year as the hurricane (1938). We were married in July and the hurricane came very early in September.

We lived on the top of Carey Hill. We could have bought one of those houses, the Thread Company sold them very cheap, but for us it was a lot of money. It was the Depression, and that was the year that American Thread got rid of all their houses.

I lived for a time in the "Oaks." My sister lived there on Quercus Avenue, and my father and mother and me went to live with my sister and her husband. I used to walk to work from there. My sister moved to Jackson Street, and we moved there too. That house has been torn down. They were hard times, it was the Depression, and many people were out of work, but I managed to work right through it, I never got laid off.

Everybody had to join the union, it was a closed shop. A lot of them did not want to sign the union card, and I said to them that they were not going to work next to me. A lot of them did not want to join because they remembered the problems their parents had during the 1925 strike. They blamed the union for that strike. I had a hell of a time with one girl. She did not want to sign the card, but I told her that if the union got in, she would have to get out. Everybody would have to be in the union to get a job at American Thread. So she signed it and stayed. She used to tell me how her family had had to make tents across from the bridge on Route 6, near the river, after they had been thrown out of their houses. I remember that we had our windows broken in 1925. The kids used to throw stones, and we were chased when we went outside and when we went to school. We were just as bad as them, though. We fought back.

I had two good jobs there on shoe thread and tube spools. Two jobs where I got good money. We managed to buy a house. I sold it two years ago when my husband passed away. It was on Jackson Street. We managed to pay for it by working at American Thread. The wages were good enough to live on and to save a little of money. I had three children, but my job was always waiting for me when I went back. They were satisfied with my work. I was a fast worker and I could produce.

Whenever the management wanted to cut wages, I was always the one who was cut first because I earned the most on piece-work. Time study used to stand next to me when they wanted to put a lower price on the job! I used to slow down, but you could not fool them. They knew when we were sleeping on the job. I could keep those 12 ends going, and that was fast work on coarse shoe thread. I used to like to work fast. I liked it very much. They cut our wages regularly. The only time we got a raise was when the union negotiated a new contract with the Company. They used to sign them every two or three years.

As the years went by the Company increased your workload. When I started on the cones in 1932, I worked four machines, but after a while it was 12 machines. And then on tube spool, we had six machines when I started, and by the end we were up to eight machines. They were always giving you more machines. I retired in 1980, but I didn't know that the mill was going to shut. I retired right on time! I had no idea they were going to close. I got some long service years for 10, 15 and 25 years. My husband has them as well. He's got a plaque downstairs for working 10 years without a day off. He often used to work 80 hours a week. Every year they would give him a sticker to put on the plaque for working steady. Me? I took a lot of time off work. It's hard work when you have three children, but they always kept my job open for me. I was not one to keep changing jobs. The more and more you do the same job, the easier it becomes. American Thread was good to me. I could smoke any time I wanted to. But I did not smoke too much because I was on piece work, and they never accused me of going to the ladies' room too often.

The overseers were nice. They were all OK. The bosses were nice too. When I first started there, I worked for Ernest Higgins. He was my first boss. He was OK, and after he passed away, seven or eight years later, Walter Taylor took his place. He was there for many, many years up to retiring, then Reginald Belrose took over the place, and finally Jules DeRosier. I was there under four different bosses.

I didn't know then that American Thread was a British company. Although I remember that English people, who had mills all across England, had shares in the company. Once in a while they would come here to have a look around and the management would tell us to clean the machinery and sweep the floor, and then those tall men would come around the mill.

We often went dancing over to the armory on Pleasant Street which was owned by the American Thread. They held parties once a year for the workers, and the meals and drinking was all free for those who worked there, and the bosses and the overseers would dance with the workers.

Willimantic has changed. It has changed for the worse. They took those streets down - Center Street and two or three other streets. There used to be a lot of stores downtown, but there's nothing there today. The stores are in the mall now. I've never seen a place like Willimantic. They're letting everything go, the roads - the taxes are going up but they're not fixing the roads. I can't remember the last time I saw them put that black tar down. I used to like the smell of it. Yes! It has changed. They're not doing anything to the city nowadays. I wonder what they do with all the money they get out of taxes? I used to pay over $1,500 a year on taxes on my house, and that does not include the water. They didn't do nothing up at my house. I used to plow my own sidewalk. It has changed a lot. I think I liked it the old way.

CHAPTER 8

There Were Policemen in the Trees with Drawn Guns

Rose Dunham, interviewed March 21, 1990

Tom Beardsley

My father's name was Michael Walsh. He was born in Ireland sometime during the 1880s and came to Willimantic as a boy with his parents from Colchester, Connecticut. When I was a young girl, he was in charge of the dam at the American Thread works in Willimantic. He met my mother at a dance held in the basement of St. Joseph's Church. They were soon married and my mother had four children. The first was a boy, a very ill baby, but the next baby was healthy. He weighed 18 pounds at birth, and my mother was laid up for quite a time after that! The next child was a little biddy thing, a girl, and I was the last one. I was born on July 23, 1906, and I've been called "Babe Rose" all my life, as I was the youngest of the family.

My mother was a wonderful cook and baker. We had more cookbooks, all kinds of cookbooks - she was very critical of other cooks. She baked beautiful things. I remember going out and picking strawberries for her shortcake. She was a natural born cook, but also made all our clothes as well.

She was born in County Kerry, Ireland and came to the United States by herself, aged 11. She came over the ocean in the galley of the boat. She stayed there for the entire journey. The cooks looked after her as she was only a child. There was somebody waiting for her at New York and they put her on the train to New London. There was also someone waiting for her there, and they put her on the trolley to Willimantic. She was afraid on this branch of the journey, as the track was surrounded by thick woods and forest, and she'd been reading stories about the Red Indians. She was terrified. She thought that the Indians would attack at any time!

When she arrived at Willimantic, her relations were waiting for her - but she would have nothing to do with them because they wore headshawls. People who owned property in Ireland would never dream of covering their heads with shawls! Can you imagine? But she soon adapted to the American way of life. She was a marvelous mother to us. As strict as could be, mind you, but very warm and loving.

Mama would always have guests at our house, talking, over a cup of tea and a piece of cake, when she lived down on Jackson Street, and after she came to live up here after my father died. But my mother remarried, a Mr. Healey. We all liked him. He was very nice. He died, then my mother was sick for a long time. She bought this house on Hewitt Street, and lived upstairs when my brother, a railroad engineer, and his wife came back to Willimantic to live. They lived in New York City, but his wife hated New York. They came back to Willimantic on weekends. But my other brother, Paul, worked and lived on Long Island. He and his wife liked New York.

My mother was not keen when I went to New York City to work and live, in the early 1930s. She let me go though. I used to send her a check every week. She was strict, but when she came to New York to visit me, everyone fell in love with her. She told funny stories but would not allow any dirty words! She never worked. She looked after a family of kids. Her job was being a mother. In those days, if women had families, they didn't work. Some women did work in factories, of course, but they usually did not have families.

Mama despised American Thread because they were British. They were not only British, they were rotten to their people. My father had his own office. He looked after the turbines which were driven by the waterfall. It was not an office, but he called it an office. It was almost under the bridge which carries Route 32, but he did not have anything to do with anybody. He only dealt with the man who came in from New York, who only knew one tenth of what my father was doing. He was very good to him.

My father was blown up and killed when a leaking gas main exploded beneath him on Jackson Street as he lit his pipe. It was all very tragic. But back to my mother, she had lots of British friends despite the fact that she hated American Thread. There was an old Englishwoman who lived down the street from us, who used to visit my mother. I loved her accent (See, 'Community', chapter 5. This Englishwoman, Mrs. Hartley, was Edith Blackburn's mother).

I worked at American Thread one summer in the 1920s. I dare not let my mother know! She'd gone home to Ireland for a holiday. I had a royal time there. The bosses hated me. I worked in the packing room, I used to pack six spools of thread, put them in a box, put a stamp on it and seal it up. I used to work up in the back by myself because I was always singing songs and composing words for songs. I had a wild time that summer. I made many friends, people who I'd never known, but when I found out my mother was on her way back from Ireland, I left and went back to school. I think it was in 1923, I was 17 or 18. I graduated as a teacher in 1926.

I remember the 1925 strike at American Thread. A lot of my friends worked down there, and I remember taking a day off school to join them in the picket line. It was horrible down there. There were policemen in the trees with drawn guns - not handguns, but those short shotguns - and there were people marching up and down the street. The policemen were from Hartford, I think. It is kind of vague now, it was a long time ago, but I remember it was wild. American Thread just waited for the strike to break. They opened the great big gates down there, and there was one girl, a Russian girl, walked through. We used to like this girl, we played with her, we skated with her, but nobody would have anything to do with her after that, boy, did she get ruined. Everybody screamed and yelled at her, but I went home. It was a terrible thing to do to the people.

A lot of people lost their jobs. There were two women who used to live in that big house next door. They had to go to Hartford to work. It was awful. I remember that American Thread brought in a lot of cheap, cheap help from up in Maine, they were only young girls. Scabs we used to call them.

The day I joined the pickets, I cheered and cheered, I had a great time. I went back to school the next day and the Principal called me into his office. He asked me if I'd seen the *Hartford Courant* that day. I said no, and he showed me the front page and said I would be interested in seeing it. And there was a full picture of me! You couldn't miss it. It was entitled, "A Typical Striker at American Thread." I thought my education was done! I wanted to be a teacher.

I graduated in 1926 and taught in local schools for three years. I taught everything to fourth graders, reading, writing and arithmetic, physical education, music, the whole works. But I soon left teaching and went to New York City to live, as I wanted someone to publish the song lyrics I had been writing. This was in 1928 or 1929. I knew that when I went to New York, I was going to stay there, but I did not tell my mother. My first job in New York was at a hotel.

My mother came to visit me. I was supposed to meet her off the train at Grand Central station but the girl who was supposed to relieve me did not show up. I was wild with worry. Fancy my mother turning up in New York City and there was no one there to meet her. Well, one of the guests at the hotel...I think his name was Jack Thompson, he was Mae West's leading man at a show on Broadway. He had a lot of whiskers, a long beard and long hair for the part he was playing. Well he volunteered to meet my mother. I gave him a photograph of her and off he went. When I saw my mother, she was in the doorway of the hotel office with Jack Thompson, both of them killing themselves with laughing. My Mother! Can you imagine. She never forgot it.

I never taught school in New York City. I worked in the hotel business and then with the Police Department. It was strange how I got into that. I used to work in a big hotel up by the Radio City Music Hall, in the front office, but they put me in the tea department which was run by a very harsh guy, but I made good friends with a German girl and a Russian girl. It was a very friendly atmosphere. Then I was offered a job at another big hotel across the road as a luncheon hostess. One day a big tall Yankee guy, from Boston, came into the hotel and asked me what my background was. I told him where I was from, and he said he had a friend in Willimantic, Judge Hinman. And I said, well, I know his son. The next thing I knew I was offered this very, very fine job at the New York Police Department. He had investigated me and they put me on subversive activities, and you know what happened to me, I fell into cahoots with the people I was supposed to be watching and observing. I had to become a member of the Communist Party.

After I was there for a while, I felt sorry for those people. I went to their meetings, I saw what they were suffering. I never knew what a cold water flat was. I liked these people I told my boss, and they transferred me to the Police Department offices. I worked for the Chief, he was grand. He got a beautiful apartment for me uptown, but I was still on subversive activities.

I worked on the Lindbergh baby case for a very long time. You know what I always believed? Lindbergh did it. I went into so many details and all the time

I was thinking that this was a waste of time. It was my inner feeling that he did it, and they accused another man of doing it, and I think they executed him. All in all, I didn't like the subversive duties job. New York has always been full of subversives, and it always will be, but I got paid for watching them! There were other parties I watched, Trotskyites, yes, but they were all poor slobs. They were fighting things they had no business being subjected to. That was my problem, I always saw the other side. I liked most of the people I was watching.

I liked everybody - I used to think. Well, by golly, my own people had to fight like this in Ireland and why should I be...that's why I left. I used to feel like a rat. I never went back and gave them a full story, I used to brush over things. These people had a right to be mad about what was going on in the world. I used to like the people who I was interrogating. They were people who had had a rough time. I got out of it because I knew it wasn't for me.

This happened just before I was married in 1933. I was beginning to be observed. I used to get my pay check from the Police Department at St. Patrick's Cathedral. One of the young policemen told me that I should talk to the boss because there's been the same guy here watching us for the last three times. So I told the boss, and the man I was going with, Barney, said we are going to get married now and get out of town - and we did. Barney was a salesman, based in Virginia. We had a daughter, but the marriage did not last. We separated and I returned to Willimantic in 1937 or 1938.

The job situation was bad, no one was hiring, it was the Depression. There was nothing doing, but I remember going to some kind of meeting up in the Town Hall. Kate Jack was a big wheel in local politics at the time. She sent for me. Someone told her that I was looking for a job, and she told me I start work the next day, but I couldn't work for the Democratic Party, as I was not a registered voter in the City of Willimantic. She swore like a trooper, "To hell with that," she said. But I refused, as it was against the law, even though I needed a job to support myself and my daughter.

I managed to get a job at the University of Connecticut for a while. I liked it up there but I was made redundant after a while. One day I met an old friend from high school on Main Street. Her father was a big boss at American Thread. His name was David Moxon, a very fine man, he was English. She invited me to her house on Windham Road. I had a lovely visit, and Mr. Moxon told me that I had to report to a Mr. George Twist, who had a nice job for me at American Thread. Mr. Twist was a fine man, we had a lot of fun in the office on Main Street.

I was in charge of selling War Bonds to workers at American Thread. I went from one end of the mill to the other, selling and delivering War Bonds, but there was one place where I never went, up in the corner where the men did not wear any clothes because it was so sweaty. It was the finishing department or something. I never used to deliver bonds up there. It used to be a standing joke

- when it gets to the point where she's delivering bonds upstairs! So I knew all of those foremen and their jobs. I used to stop off and talk to everybody. I enjoyed it. I used to visit the lab a lot, it was situated in the dye house, and got a job there eventually when the bond job wore down. I had a great time there.

After American Thread, I worked at Pratt and Whitney in their new works in Willimantic. I hated it. I had a good job in the office there, but I got tired of it. They were making munitions. After that I worked for the State employment service. I helped to get work for all the GIs who were returning to Willimantic and civilian life after the war. It was very satisfying. I really enjoyed it. From there I worked at the screw company who took over Pratt and Whitney. I was in charge of all the employment there. I did all the hiring for the plant. I loved it. I was there for two or three years, but the job was winding down, I saw the writing on the wall, and left. I then worked as a social worker for the state, I was a child welfare officer. I loved it. I was working with children all around this area. I had some nice experiences with kids. I felt needed; it was a very nice feeling. I couldn't bear to see kids mistreated.

I've had a lot of jobs. My mother used to say, "what are you doing now, why don't you stay with one thing?" But I wanted experiences, because I wanted to write songs. I've been very lucky. I've just fallen into things, but my mother used to say that, "they saw me coming."

There were several different nationalities in Willimantic in those days. I remember the Irish first, of course, and there were the French Canadians. We used to taunt and torment each other when we were kids. They used to chant to us Irish kids, "Corn beef and cabbage make the Irish savage." We replied, "Pea soup and Johnny cake makes a Frenchman's belly ache." This was at school. There was just a fence dividing their school and ours. When school was over we played together, and they continued speaking French, naturally! This was the way they'd been brought up. They spoke French in the mill. The girls who didn't speak French used to get mad. They'd say to the French, "What are you talking about, are you talking about us?" The French stayed together. They still do. They have the French Club and they have their dances down there, but everyone is welcome. But it is a place for them to go. They have their own literature down there. They are Americanized completely, but they go back to their own culture and language. Well, even the Irish rent the place from them when they want to organize anything. In those days in Willimantic, we had the Ancient Order of Hibernians - which was strictly Irish.

My brother married a Pole. We used to have Polish girls in school. They went to St. Joseph's. We integrated with the Poles very nicely because they spoke our language, whereas the French did not, but I was not too familiar with too many Polish people.

When I was very young, there was a strike at American Thread run by people called the "Wobblies." We used to make fun of the Wobblies, we didn't know what they were. We never saw them, but we liked the sound of the word. I think it was mainly French and Irish at American Thread. I told you about the girl who went in to break the strike. Well, Russian and Polish to us were the same thing! And we had many Polish kids at school with us at St Joseph's, where all the teachers were Irish, but we also were taught by Dutch nuns. Sister - what was her name, when I was in the third grade, she was my teacher. I had to sing a song at school, but I shamed my family, I sang, " Over de river an' on troo de voods to grandfather's hoose ve go..." That was the way the Sister taught it! She was Holland Dutch and there were Dutch nurses in St Joseph's Hospital. Father De Bruycker, the St. Joseph Parish Priest, was also Dutch, or Belgium. He's famous. Everyone knew him. He's the one that talked about the people in Sodom in a talk from the pulpit - the people in the east end were like the people from Sodom and Gommorah!

There were also some Italians in town. I don't think many of them worked at the mill. They had fruit and vegetable stores, and there was a fruit man who came around with the wagon and delivered. We also had quite a few Syrians. The main Syrian family were the Haddads, they had their own little stores.

There were also some Greeks. They had a candy store on Main Street and an ice cream store, the "palace of sweets." They lived over the river in a very big house. They were very nice people. We also had Swedish people in town. Some of them worked in the office at American Thread. There is a Swedish church up on the corner. It is one of the older churches in town.

Willimantic has changed in recent years. Take the railroad station. It was lovely. It was a big, big station down there. The trains came from everywhere. Yes, I loved trains. My brother was a railroad engineer. I came home regularly from New York, and took the train. It was often busy down there at the station. Sometimes, especially on a Sunday night, it was difficult to get a seat on the train to New York. We also had the roundhouse here. The train went to Providence too, several lines came through the town. You could also get to Hartford quite easily. It's a shame that it all had to fall apart. It was a busy area down there. It was a lot better then. How do you get anywhere if you do not have a car? But I remember the station building was a big beautiful building. A friend of mine used to run the cafeteria inside the station. It's a shame they had to knock it down. It's a parking lot now.

The old town has changed a lot. Take Railroad Street for example. It went down to the railroad from Main Street. There was a lot of old buildings down there. There was a pool hall and a little restaurant. It was a very lively place. There was the footbridge, but they have not taken that down - yet! An old girlfriend of mine, her father drew all the plans for that, his name was Harry Mitchell. It was exciting when you were a small child to walk over the footbridge and look down at the river and the railroad. We also had the building across the river, the armory, that was beautiful, that's gone to pot now, I guess. They held big dances there. When there was a big ball, it was held at the armory because it was so large. I went to several of them, but we preferred the "Tab" on Valley Street. That was the place to go on a Saturday night.

We also had several movie houses, the *Gem* theater on Main Street, the *Scenic*, near the firehouse, and there was the *Capital*. Where the new movie house is, there were houses there, they only pulled them down a few years ago. They ripped all the buildings out of lower Jackson Street. They ruined the town. That space is still empty down there.

I remember the trolley cars. My mother used to go on them to visit her friend in Taftville, but she often got carsick, and I had to go with her. The trolley went on down to Norwich, and from there to New London. A lot of people used the trolley, especially to Coventry. There was a separation where the railroad went across. It was a good time to be young. Everybody hopped onto the trolley on Saturday nights to go to dances there, and boys used to jump on the sides and sway it about. The old man who drove the trolley cursed them, and the young girls screamed. You thought they were going to tip it over. It was our idea of a good time, there was not much drinking in those days. If there was, we didn't know much about it. We also had good times up at Coventry Lake on a Sunday, where everybody used to go swimming. Willimantic was a nice place to live.

CHAPTER 9

I Liked Getting My Hands into the Machinery

Mitchell M. Rosenstein, interviewed May 3, 1991

Tom Beardsley

I was born in the lower east side of New York City in 1909. That's where my mother's folks came to when they arrived here from Europe. My mother was two-years-old. They came to America some time around 1885, so that their sons, my mother's brothers, would escape military conscription in Russia and Poland, and also to get away from religious and political unrest. They were farmers in the old country. I'm not sure what jobs they did when they arrived in New York, but my mother met my father in New York. He was a foreman in a narrow fabric business which made braid. Braiding was a big trim item years ago. That business was located in the lower east side, and in 1921, my father, Isadore Rosenstein, formed a company with my mother's brother. They bought some new and used braiding machines. Different widths of braiding could only be produced by different sized machines. The wider the braid, the bigger the machine was. My uncle, my father's partner, was named Lintz, and that's where the name Roselin came from, a combination of Rosenstein and Lintz.

My folks moved up to the Riverdale section of the West Bronx when I was about 14. I attended public schools in New York, but I did not graduate from high school. I think my father expected me to come into the trade. I suppose he might have wanted me to go to college, but I was not a first class student. I left school to go and work with my father at his factory on Bleeker Street, a little above Greenwich Village. That was sometime around 1927. My father employed between 20 and 30 people in a typical loft building. Nearly all lower Manhattan was built up in that fashion. The clothing industry gradually moved out of that area and moved uptown. Our workforce was mostly female. We employed around three women to every man. The men were usually the machine fixers, but a few were sometimes operators. I guess a lot of them were Italian and Jewish. A typical mix of the sons and daughters of immigrants.

We came to Willimantic in 1935. We had a relation in Willimantic who we used to come and visit, and he suggested that we should relocate here. It seemed to be a good idea, because in our loft workshop in Manhattan, we paid rent, and we discovered a building for sale here in Willimantic at a very reasonable price, and Willimantic's Chamber of Commerce gave us $5,000 to pay for our moving expenses, and that decided it for us to move to Connecticut. This was in the middle of the Depression, and times were hard and we had to cut costs, so owning our own building helped us to cut overheads.

We had employed between 20 and 30 workers in New York. That figure varied of course, it depended upon our orders. The braid and ribbon producing industry was cyclical. The foreman fixers moved out here to help us get started. You had to have fixers. Of course, the reason for asking us to come to Willimantic was that we would employ local people. We hired about 20 local people. We didn't have to advertise for workers, because there was such a shortage of work at the time, and everyone knew that we were coming to town because it was in the papers at the time.

There was a plant in Willimantic which braided fish line, and eventually they did commission work for us. Their fish lines were made on a tubular braider, and decorative braids on a flat braider, and they had some flat braiders and they were commissioned to do braiding for us. We bought braiding from them when we were busy. This company had originally been owned by the Chaffees, and it was located on Church Street.

Braid is produced on a braiding machine. We did not do any weaving in New York City. We didn't weave until we moved to Willimantic. We were supplied with the yarn and we would put it on a bobbin on the braiding machine, on which there is no warp in the real sense. Braid warp crisscrosses diagonally and creates the filling which binds it up. There is no cross filling to hold it together. The braiding machines were of varying sizes, so as to produce the different widths of braid. Each bobbin was on a carrier which went across a track, and crossed each other. Just like a hair braid you might say. One person can run about 20 of those machines, depending upon the width being braided, and when the yarn would run out from the bobbins. A wide braiding machine would have a lot more bobbins than a narrow machine, so they would run longer.

There was a lot of work to do when we relocated. Setting up was time consuming and expensive. Our new building had belonged to the Windham National Bank, and before that it belonged to the Willimantic Machine Company, who had gone out of business. They used to manufacture a winding machine for the textile industry. I can't remember the name of the machine.

It was not that much of a shock to us when we first arrived in Willimantic. Of course, the pace of life was a little steadier than in New York. We had been visiting mother's relations, and we had also been here to do some negotiating with the Willimantic Chamber of Commerce before we moved in. We didn't just walk in here without knowing what we were to get. Our new workers were from this area. They were people of French descent, Polish descent and "swamp Yankees," old natives who had been here long before the immigrants came. They were good people of farming stock, but they were not that reliable when the fishing or hunting season began! They were apt to be absent, but we made provision for that because you could count on them not being there. You are not going to change the habits of generations. They preferred hunting and fishing to working. We had a core of regular workers and we would increase the numbers when orders demanded it.

Clothing firms made up the biggest market for our braid products. We made a certain narrow braid for washable garments, and we had to make sure that the dyes would not run. When you made a braid for a garment that had to be dry cleaned, you had to use a different yarn of wool or worsted, and, of course, you had to have a good dye job then, but we did not do the dying. We used cotton, rayon, mohair and some worsteds for the dress trade, and we'd obtain that from yarn jobbers - the selling agent for the yarn mills, most of which were in the

South. We'd tell them what size, kind and dyed yarn we needed and what the put up was, whether it was on cones or tubes.

Our business slowly improved, but we had a hurricane to contend with. That was in 1938. We were working in the building that day, and the walls of our building in Milk Street came tumbling down. It was around four in the afternoon. We had a second floor and the wind picked the roof up and took it a half a block away and dropped it down on the street, then the walls blew in, some walls blew out, some blew in. We had a lot of damage, and we were just beginning to settle in, but fortunately we were insured. If we had known we were to have a hurricane we would have been insured better! We didn't have to replace any of the machinery that was damaged. We managed to fix it up, and we then purchased some good used machinery.

We were also lucky that no one was hurt. We had no idea that there was a hurricane coming. All we knew was that we had a lot of rain that day, but nobody said anything about a windstorm. We realized it was more than a rainstorm when we saw the roofs lifting off other buildings. We could see sheet metal and girders flying through the air. We knew by three o' clock that it was much more than a bad rainstorm. There was a terrific amount of noise in the factory, a lot of roaring, and our workers began to get excited when the roof began to lift off one end of the building. The girls got down on their knees and started to pray. The finished braid was being blown out of the holding cans, all over the floor and all over the ceiling. We had streamers all over the place! Then the wind hit us with a broadside, and bricks came tumbling down the stairs. It was a big rebuilding job for us, and we bought another building, alongside of ours, which was on Moulton Court. That building had lost its second story in the hurricane.

I lived with my parents at 337 Jackson Street when we first arrived. It was a two-family house. It wasn't our's, my father paid rent for it. I also lived with them after I was married. We had a good view from there, because the circus used to set up on the field behind us on a ballfield. My father bought that ballfield and after the war he sold it so it could be used for a housing development for soldiers returning after the war.

In those days I worked as a machine fixer for my father, and also as a shipper and packer. I did a little bit of everything. I learned the trade on the commercial and industrial sides. I was happy in my work. It was the only job I knew. I worked for my father right up to the time he died. I got married in 1937 to a Willimantic girl. My wife's grandfather, Hyman Israel, was the first Jewish person to live in Willimantic. He ran a lunch wagon on Railroad Street, near to the footbridge, where the trains came in to town. He'd hitch the wagon to the horses at five in the morning and ride it down to near the railroad station, and the rail crews would come in and get breakfast, then at the end of the day he used to drive the wagon home to Natchaug Street down near the river. My wife worked next door to our factory in the building we eventually purchased. It had belonged to the New England Pants Company.

Business improved when the War began, but in the beginning we lost some good men, foremen and fixers, who left to go and work for better money at Pratt & Whitney. We obtained some government contracts, and we eventually got the men back, because government work gave the company a classification which meant that the workers employed by firms who did essential war work were exempt from the draft. We got plenty of work from the airforce, producing parachute cord for cargo and bomb chutes which were made out of rayon, a synthetic fiber. I think it was invented in the 1920s by an English company called Courtaulds. We had bought some looms and started weaving ribbon back in 1936. We found that the customers who we sold braid to were beginning to ask for ribbon, so we installed the looms and produced our own. There was a demand for rayon and cotton ribbon in clothes and hat trimmings, so we developed an expertise in weaving rayon, and the parachute tape was made out of rayon. It was a sizable order and kept several machines running.

The tape made the shroud lines. On a parachute you have a canopy which blows up, and the shroud lines come down around the canopy and connect it to the harness. These shroud lines consisted of tapes and webbings which were braided and woven. The lines for the cargo chutes were flat, but the line for chutes for humans was round and made of nylon yarn, to ensure ultimate strength. The cargo and bomb chutes were dispensable, but you had to make sure with humans.

We also did cotton tape for the army. The soldiers used all kinds of webbing. A common type was a lightweight webbing used for seam binding for tents and backpacks, which we could make on our looms which were not webbing looms. They were designed to weave a four inch width of lightweight fabrics. There are all kinds of sizes and varieties. You go from webbing to tape to ribbon. The webbing is made up of a heavier yarn. We used a lot of cotton yarn which we bought already dyed. On occasion we would buy some from the American Thread Company. It was hard to get hold of and you got it from wherever you could. You'd think that the American Thread Company, being so near, would have been a good source for us, but what we did get from them, came from down South. We were not particularly a big customer of American Thread, as they specialized in sewing threads; and yarn for fabrics was not really one of their fields. That market was very competitive and American Thread did not get in to it too much. We had to run two or three shifts, no less than two. We still run two shifts. We never run less than two shifts if we can help it. If we didn't run two, we'd run for four days instead of five. One shift doesn't pay, really. We almost doubled our workforce and employed about 50 people.

Maybe we paid a little less than other firms in town. There was a competitive wage rate and we were near that. I remember that after we had been here about a year, we got a visit from the President of American Thread. He discussed aspects of the textile business with us, and asked how our business was going. We said, "Fair," and he said, "Can you use some money?" and we said, "Of course!" And he wrote us out a check for $500! I guess he wanted to show us some generosity. We didn't ask for it, but we could use it. I thought that this was a nice gesture and I took a copy of the check. I can't bring his name to memory, though, but he was the President of the American Thread Company, and he came up here from New Jersey.

We didn't have a union in our works in New York, but after we came here we had one lady who found a lot of things wrong with us and brought the union in. American Thread had a union at this time, but we didn't. The unions did not want us. We were too small, too much of a nuisance to them - until this lady went to them and told them that they should organize our workers. This was sometime during the war, and she bought in the Textile Workers' Union. The union didn't offer the manufacturer any advantages. They were strictly looking for higher wages and better benefits and more holidays. They were only interested in getting their "dues." Our workers were hourly paid. They were not on piece work, so we didn't have to agree on any quotas.

We had a strike once, sometime after the war. It lasted a couple of weeks. It was over pay rates. The union organized it and I guess they won as they got the pay rise. The strikers were picketing outside the factory and my father told them to, "Come on in, it's raining!" There was not much bitterness, it was a good natured strike. My father asked them to come in and get some coffee. There was also one or two single day strikes, but nothing serious. My father was good to those he employed. He loved throwing parties for them, especially at Christmas, and he always gave each employee a turkey and a cash bonus every year. The foremen dressed up as Santa Claus. It was a close knit group, and it still is. We've employed, on average, between 20 and 30 people since the war.

We stopped making the braid after the war, and concentrated on ribbon manufacturing. Ribbon is used for apparel trimming in such things as ladies' suit coats, and it's now made from acetate which is a kind of rayon. There's also a viscose and coopermonium rayon. We make a variety of multi-colored ribbon and the yarns in them are made from solution dye. These yarns are not dyed, the color is in them when they are extruded. The Rayon is viscose in an acetone solution, and acetone evaporates, and the solution is cellulose from wood pulp in acetone, and it is pumped through a die the size of a 10 cent piece, full of little holes, and the acetone evaporates, leaving the solid which is the wood pulp. Ribbon sold easier. Ribbon was in demand, and braiding was a tough thing to produce, so we sold our braiding machines and invested that money into the looms. Trimmings on clothing used ribbon more than braid.

I liked getting my hands into the machinery, and worked for a long time as a machine fixer. I did not get fully into administration until the 1960s when my father died. He passed away in 1963. He was 75 and it was then I took over, and

I ran the business for 26 years. We had offices on site, and also a New York office, which we kept going after we left. I still used to get my hands dirty, though, if it was necessary. My son runs the firm now. I'm retired.

We manufacture a high quality product. That's the first thing you have to do. You soon hear about it if the quality is poor. We still run two shifts, from seven in the morning until three in the afternoon, and then from three in the afternoon until eleven at night. We have a loyal and capable workforce. We have some Vietnamese women with us now, and they're good workers. We also diversified. To broaden and spread sales and production we expanded in "tricot" knitting. We built another building on Milk Street, next to ours, in 1949. Tricot is flat, and from it we produced knitted fabrics which were 168 inches wide. That was used mostly for lingerie, but you could make t - shirts from it. We used new, high speed knitting machines, and we hired a foreman and helper from Pennsylvania to run them, as that was the center for tricot knitting in this country. No one knew tricot knitting in this area.

I attempted to hire an Englishman who had a lot of expertise in this field. I finally tracked him down to South America, but I could not tempt him to come to Willimantic. I advertised in English newspapers after this, as the English were the leaders in this field. I got a few replies, and I went over to London and interviewed one of the applicants who sounded very promising. Anyway, we sold the whole building, and the knitting machines in the 1950s, to a firm called Textron. We had problems in obtaining yarn to run the machines, and Textron carried on. We only produce ribbon today, but we run 24 ribbon looms, which make anywhere between 20 to 72 ribbons on each machine.

I enjoyed it right up until I retired a couple of years ago when I suffered a stroke. My son Stanley is in charge now. He came into the business in 1964, but I don't know if his son will take over after him. My grandson is at the University of Vermont and is interested in geology and the environment. But my son Stanley wasn't interested when he was younger. He was a teacher.

CHAPTER 10

We Have No Regrets About Coming Here.
It's a Great Country.
It's the Best Place in the World

Victoria Uskurs, interviewed April 26, 1991

Tom Beardsley

I was born in 1912 near a small town called Skaunes, in Latvia. My family were farmers who worked about five hectares, and I was one of four sisters. I remember the First World War, when Polish and Russian soldiers passed through our land and took away my father and some horses to carry their weapons. These soldiers also ate everything we had! There were also a lot of deaths in the area from an outbreak of typhus.

Latvia is one of the Baltic states, south of Finland and Estonia and across the Baltic Sea from Sweden. When I was a child, Latvia was partly under German rule and partly under Russian rule. It was also partly controlled by Poland and Sweden. The Latvian language is similar to Russian. Lots of words mean the same thing in both languages.

I started out taking lessons from the house, and then I attended three different schools before going to teacher's college for five years. I was 19 when I finished school, and I started work as a teacher in 1932. I taught everything. Reading, writing, singing - everything! There were 80 children in five grades, and later I went to work in a sixth grade school. I worked as a teacher for 12 years, from 1932 to 1944.

I met my husband, Martin, in Skaunes on Forest Day in 1933. That was a traditional Latvian celebration in May, when we plant trees and hold celebrations for the coming of spring. He worked near Skaunes. He was a border guard in the Latvian army, doing his two year duty. We were married in 1936 and lived in Skaunes.

The Russians invaded us in 1940. They drove their tanks into the capital city, Riga. On one night during the following year the Russians took 36,000 educated people away. (Martin, Victoria's husband intercedes at this point and says, in Latvian, that there have been two very unhappy days in his life. The 14th of June when the Russians took away and imprisoned or killed all those people, and the 16th of June when he got married!) They took away everybody who they thought posed a threat to the Soviet Union. The Germans arrived soon after when they invaded Russia, and drove the Russian army out of Latvia. Then, in 1944, the Russians re-invaded and drove the Germans out. But before that, in 1943, Russian partisans invaded Skaunes and burnt churches and buildings. Also, when they came back in 1944, they took away more Latvian people.

The Russians took away the bells from the churches. Everything was changed into Russian. We were all converted into communists. We couldn't go to church, we had to go to communist meetings, as teachers we were told to teach the communist doctrine to the children in school. We were given many books and had to read all about the communist ideology. We were on a list to be taken away by the Russians, but when they came for us, I took my son and went to hide in a rye field. We slept there overnight until the Russians had gone. Martin was away working in the forest brickmaking. They always took people away during the night. Never in the daytime. When the Russians returned in 1944, we left Latvia and went to Germany to escape them. We remembered also how the Latvian army border guards had been liquidated by the Russians in 1940. We didn't want to live under the Russians again!

We lived in Hamburg. I got a job in a Latvian school in Hamburg and taught there for six years. There were lots of Latvian refugees living in Germany. We were known as displaced persons, or DPs. My husband worked as a warden/guard for the British Army on the border between Holland and the British sector of West Germany. He guarded an ammunition dump. We were separated for two years. (At this point, Martin Uskurs handed me a British Army certificate, dated July 1, 1950, which stated that Martin Uskurs had been employed by the British Army since 16 May, 1948. Martin was considered to be "industrious, honest, of high intelligence and integrity." It was signed by a Major T. B. Tighe.)

There were not many opportunities in Germany at this time, and we heard that America was looking for people who could work on farms. The Pastors and Ministers of Latvian Lutheran and Baptist Churches in America helped to bring many of our people over. The Churches organized it for us to the United States. We didn't have any relations here, but Martin had a friend who was already here, and he became our sponsor, so we came through friends and not directly through the Latvian Church. Nevertheless, the Church did help with the organizing of documents and such things. I am a Catholic, but Martin is a Lutheran, so when we started to look into ways to come here, we asked a Lutheran minister to help us, but he said, "No! You are a Catholic so we cannot help." So we went to the Catholic Church for help, and they told us to go to the Lutheran Church for help, because Martin was not a Catholic, but things were eventually worked out.

We came on a big ship, the "Sturgis," and sailed from Bremen to New York City. We did not come through Ellis Island as everything had been worked out before. We came in one big group. We came straight to Willimantic with our two children and stayed in the Ukranian Club House. There were seven Latvian families, and we all lived in the same area, divided only by blankets.

We arrived here on December 20, 1950, and after Christmas I went to look for a job. I went to the Electro Motive factory, but every day they said "No, job, no job. Come tomorrow." But everyday it's the same. There was no work. Then one day I stopped in at the American Thread office, and they said I could start. They took me, but it wasn't easy as we did not speak any English. We communicated through interpreters. There were some at American Thread who could speak Latvian. I worked in Number Two Mill, twisting and spinning spools. I would have liked to have taught of course, but I could not speak English. I was surprised, when I learned of the schoolwork my children were doing, at its easiness when compared to schools in Latvia and Germany. For example, I was surprised at how little algebra was taught compared with that taught to children of a similar age in Europe. I think it's easier being a teacher in this country than in Europe!

My children were 14 and 13 when we arrived here. One went to St. Joseph's the other to St. Mary's, then they went to high school. They had already learned to speak English at school in Germany. We soon moved into a rented apartment, as we could not afford to buy a house. I was only earning $1. 34 a hour at American Thread. We lived in Chapman Street, Elm Street, Pleasant Street and we now live on Ash Street.

I think I adapted quickly to the American way of life. Martin felt it more than I. But we were homesick. In fact, we still get homesick for Latvia after all these years, but we're very happy that we came here. We learned a lot from our children. This is the best place in the world for people to get back on their feet again. Where else could you do that?

I went back to Latvia for three weeks just after I retired, but you cannot go back home to live if you own foreign capital, and there is also a rule which forbids you to visit anywhere that is beyond a 50 kilometer radius of the capital city, Riga, so I could not go back to Skaunes. Now they say the rules have changed and you can go all around the country. I went alone, as Martin dare not go back because of the communists. He says that he'll never go back until it's a free democratic country. He is still bitter that the Russians stole all his money. Martin worked 10 years for the Latvian government before the Russians invaded, and he lost all his savings. The Russians stole their horses, weapons and all their food to supply themselves. They stripped Latvia clean.

Martin also worked at American Thread from 1951 to 1974. There were problems because we didn't speak English, but nothing serious. They didn't speak our language and we didn't speak their language so we kept to ourselves somewhat. I do remember that the job itself was very difficult. You had to work so fast. There was no time to stop and have a drink or something to eat. After three years I changed jobs and left Number Two Mill to work in Number Five Mill on shuttle bobbins, which was a sitting down job. Martin worked in Number Four Mill, doffer spinning for the first five years, and he left after a disagreement with his boss over which shift and which job he worked on, so he left and a got a job with Leiss Velvet. It was in the place now used by Roy's Autoparts. Leiss Velvet went into liquidation soon after, and Martin got a job back at American Thread in Number Six Mill. Sometimes he worked for 16 hours a day, seven days a week. Martin retired in 1974, and I retired soon after when I was 62. The job was becoming a little too hard for me. The working conditions were not too bad, but I didn't like piece work. I couldn't take it. Some girls were very fast and often earned a lot of money, but I could not. I was not as fast. Also, I was very quiet, and a little scared. There were some girls who were smart, and nice to the boss, so they got bigger and better jobs and a lot of money. At times it was a very hot place to work, especially in the summer. It was an ideal place for many displaced persons to get a start in America. It was easy to get a job there. We stayed there, but many of our friends moved onto different jobs

I was a member of the union. We had to join. The union was a good thing. They were on our side. I had no grumbles about the union. Every now and then we would get a raise when the union negotiated a new contract, but other firms in Willimantic paid a lot better wages than American Thread.

There were many different nationalities at American Thread: Polish, French from Canada, Germans, Ukranians, Cubans, Puerto Ricans. One Puerto Rican was sent back home by American Thread to recruit more workers, and he got $50 for every one who signed up to work. He brought back 20 workers. We got on well with everyone. I remember that there was a shortage of labor at American Thread in the early 1950s. I think that this had something to do with the Korean War. There were quite a few black workers who came, but many of them only worked there for two or three weeks before leaving.

I'm still a Latvian citizen. American Thread never required of you that you became a citizen, but other Latvians who came here had to change their nationality because the firms they worked for demanded it. I don't have a passport, just a small identification card. (Martin Uskurs announced at this point that he had pledged his allegiance to the Latvian flag in 1929, and that he had no intention of pledging allegiance to two flags.)

We are very proud of our Latvian heritage, very much. We're very proud that Latvia is trying to become independent of the Soviet Union, and we help them where we can, although we do not send money as the exchange rates are so false. We do not want to help the communists. The Russian people are alright, its the party members who are no good. We keep the Latvian culture alive through the church on Route 32, and we also have a Latvian choir group. We also receive Latvian newspapers, and there's a Latvian movie on at the church this weekend. Over 400 Latvians came originally. Even so, we have no regrets about coming here. It's a great country. It's the best place in the world.

I have a son in Seattle, Washington. He's now 55, and works for a transportation company that has branches all around the world. My daughter died of cancer when she was 47. We have four grandchildren and four great grandchildren. We kept our Latvian name because it is easy to spell and easy to pronounce in English, and it's not a very long name.

CHAPTER 11

I Was Just a Millhand. It Was in My Blood

Irene Monroe, interviewed March 1, 1991

Tom Beardsley

I was born on September 19, 1919, on High Street in Willimantic. My father, Exauriause Ducharme, was French Canadian. My mother, Elsie Cardin, was born in Norwichtown of Irish and French Canadian parents, but they died young and my mother was adopted by her aunt who lived in Baltic. My father, who was a blacksmith, came down to Baltic, Connecticut when he was about 18 or 19. He met my mother in Baltic, which in those days was known as "Swing City" because every house had a swing chair in the front yard.

I don't know too much about their eventual marriage, but in those days a lot of the marriages were arranged. They had five children but I had a brother and sister who died when they were very young. I didn't know them. I'm the only one left as my elder brother died about 16 years ago and my sister died in Arizona about 21 years ago. My father only worked about one year, sometime during the 1950s, at American Thread because he couldn't take working inside. He was from the wide open spaces in Quebec. In fact it was so wild up there that my grandmother used to see bears when she went to the well to draw water!

My whole family worked at American Thread as a matter of fact. My mother worked in Mill Number Four in the card room. She began there after I was born, somewhere around 1921 or 1922. My brother worked there too, in the warehouse and my sister worked in the yarn twisting department.

We went through the Depression like everybody else. My father worked most of his life as a blacksmith, shoeing horses in Willimantic, but gradually machinery came in and there wasn't much call for shoeing horses, so he had to chop wood for a living. My mother worked at American Thread, and my sister worked at the Holland silk mill on Valley Street. We lived up on High Street, way atop of the hill at first, then we moved to the bottom. I went to St. Mary's school. I can remember walking to school and back from High Street every day. We went for eight in the morning and walked back for lunch. We returned in the afternoon, and left at a quarter to four in the afternoon. After graduating from there I did part time housework for a couple of years, then I went to American Thread in 1938.

Willimantic was a very busy town in those days. I remember taking the trolley car from Willimantic to Baltic to visit my mother's aunt who lived in a company house in Baltic. My mother had worked at the mills in Baltic before she met my father. We used to board the trolley outside the town hall on Main Street, every Sunday morning after we'd been to church, and we'd come back from Baltic about seven at night. That was a treat! I really liked that. We also used to visit Ocean Beach on the trolley once in a while, but we never went in the water. My mother would not wear a bathing suit in those days! I'd play in the sand and my parents walked on the boardwalk. But Ocean Beach was completely wiped out by the hurricane of 1938. It wiped out everything on the shoreline around here. It also hit Willimantic. The bridge next to American Thread was under water! That was just before I started working there, but I was there in 1978 when Ella

Grasso shut down the state because of the blizzards. American Thread rarely closed down, except for what they call "Acts of God." Sometimes, when it was really hot and humid they closed. Through the years, I preferred working on the third shift, because at night it was cooler in the summer, and you did not have all the bosses walking about.

I remember that my mother worked at American Thread at the time of the 1925 strike, but she stayed out for its duration. She wouldn't return to work. American Thread brought in people from New Bedford and Fall River in trucks. They lived in tents in Recreation Park until houses could be found for them. The strike was never settled. My mother eventually went back to work. I don't remember much about it, I'm only going by what my mother told me. She worked there in Mill Number Four until she had to retire because of illness. There was no social security in those days so you had to work.

When I was older, my family moved to Mansfield Center. My father went out there to continue his business as a blacksmith. It was very rural and there was more of a call for horse shoeing as a lot of the farm machinery was still pulled by horses. In Willimantic, his workshop was on Meadow Street. I remember going there with my mother really early in the morning. He used to shoe I don't know how many horses just in one day. He was always very busy. We still have his anvil and all the tools he used. My sister-in-law kept them because my brother took over the business when my father retired. A lot of collectors wanted to buy them, but my nieces and nephews don't want to sell them. They are very old and my father made them all.

When demand dropped off in Willimantic for horse shoeing, my father used to go up to the Veterinarian College in Storrs to shoe the horses. Horses did all the work when I was young. I remember that they used to pull the ice wagon. The fruit man's wagon was also pulled by a horse, and when we lived in Mansfield we used to go to church in a horse and buggy.

My mother returned to Willimantic to live. There was a bus service, but it was hard to travel back and forth every day to and from American Thread. My father stayed at Mansfield Center because he had a very good business. My brother went into the army, into the cavalry, and learned how to shoe horses, and came back to work with my father. When we lived in Mansfield I went to another school, it had four grades on one side and four grades on the other side. It was only a small school. I wasn't there very long and I returned to St. Mary's in Willimantic when the bus service started.

I got my job at American Thread through my mother. She got me an interview with David Moxon, the agent, and I got the job. I worked in Mill Number Six, in the finishing department from 1938 through until 1985 when American Thread closed. I was not there all the time though. I went into the forces during the war and had time off to have my children.

We had everything in that department. All the packers and winders were there until the cotton was transferred out. I was then transferred downstairs to work in the nylon department. I was supervisor and taught several jobs such as cones, tubes, winding and splicing - just about every kind of operation. My very first job was working on eight ounce cones, even though they only carried four ounces of thread. I learned how to work on the cone machine. I spliced and eventually ran 45 winders. I worked on glacé and plastic tube winders. I also ran a tube spool machine just like the one in the Museum in Willimantic. All the wooden tube spools you see at the Museum were eventually replaced by plastic spools.

I joined the forces about 1944 and stayed in for two years. I was posted to Fort Oglethorpe, Georgia for eight weeks of basic training. From there I was transferred to Louisiana, and after there I went to Mississippi and finished in Trenton, New Jersey. I worked in the hospital, and was a French interpreter, but I didn't go abroad. I helped to translate for the blacks who came from Martinique and Guadalupe who came to join up. They couldn't understand a word of English, they could only speak in French. They worked with me in the wards of the hospital, so I used to interpret. When I was through, I came back to work at American Thread as my job was kept open for me.

There was not a union at American Thread, not at first, but they started soon after, but we didn't have to join. The closed shop did not come in until later. Everyone had to join the union after the war. We had the same union as Brand Rex, and other textile mills in the area, such as Fall River. When they got a raise, we got a raise, and those down South would get a raise, even though they didn't have a union down there.

I was never really involved in the union, but I used to go to meetings. I could have been involved, but I wasn't the type to fight for things. We were never involved in strikes, although at one time it looked as if we would strike but it was quickly resolved. I never had any complaints at American Thread. If they were still in town I would have stayed there, I would not have retired. I liked it. I was just a millhand. It was in my blood. I liked anything to do with thread. I remember that when I was in grade school, I used to go and have lunch with my sister who worked in the Holland silk mill, which was near to St. Mary's. I used to help her set up the machines. Silk was phased out after the Second World War, and that's how she came to work at American Thread. The Holland silk mill closed just before the War as nylon was just coming in.

As far as the union was concerned, we had Betty Tianti. She started work in the shuttle bobbins, became president of the union and ended up as president of the whole union in Washington. I knew her, she was a fixer soon after she started. Andy Sabo, the last agent, was another who worked up from the bottom. He started in the dye house. The agent before him, Bert Shaw from England, also started at the bottom. He was a fixer in Number Four when my mother worked there. He ended up by being the head of the whole company. His son,

Ted Shaw, was a superintendent in our department.

I was married when I was 26 or 27. My husband worked at Electro Motive. We separated about 26 years ago. My daughter Judy worked at American Thread. She worked in the wool department for ten years. I managed to get her an interview. I remember that I worked for a while in the wool department at the time we were working a four day week. A few of us had seniority and we were sent over to the wool department where there was some work, on packing.

It was all cotton when I first started there. It gradually changed to synthetics some time after the war, although I think cotton was produced on a smaller scale through the 1950s and 1960s. Glacé was originally cotton, but we called it intrinsic. It was dressed by a certain wax formula which made it shiny in appearance. It was used to make seat covers and anything that was heavy. Shoe thread was also dressed and used for insulation in electrics. Before dressing, the glacé was very fuzzy in appearance.

I worked with French, Polish, DPs (displaced persons) and Hispanics. I saw a lot of different nationalities over the years. There were a few black people in there, and towards the end we had some Vietnamese people and Koreans. They also used to employ some people who were a little retarded or handicapped. American Thread was very good about that sort of thing.

When I was young the area down past the mill was known as Sodom, and a lot of Polish people lived down there in the apartments. It was mostly French people who lived in the company housing down there on lower Main Street. The Irish used to live down there too, but that was before my time. I don't remember many Irish people. There were a few English people, Edith Blackburn for example, but most of the English people were "big shots." When we knew they were coming through, everything had to be spotless, and they would walk right through and not even look at anything! The overseers would say to us, "Hurry up and clean your alley," but we would say that if the bosses saw everything clean, they would think that we were doing no work! There's nothing on the floor! But we would have to sweep everything up every five minutes! The overseers were going crazy. You even had to shove it into your pocket, because they wanted everything to be so clean. It was really ridiculous. When we knew they were coming to go through the plant we used to say, "The Limeys are coming!"

A family of displaced persons moved in next to us on High Street. I think their name was Jacoby, or something like that. They were Lithuanians. They all worked at the American Thread. When their women had babies, they didn't go to the hospital, they had them at home. One day I got a knock at the door at two in the morning. It was the husband. His wife was having the baby. They didn't have a telephone. So I called their doctor, and I asked him if there was anything I could do to help, even though I'd never seen a baby delivered. They did everything so different, although everything was clean, it was nothing like

This photograph was taken outside Mill Number Four in 1931 by Willimantic's Dinneen Studios. It features approximately 66 workers and management employed in American Thread's Mill Number Four carding room. Irene Monroe's mother, Elsie Ducharme, can be seen standing on the platform, the second person to the right of the lady in the dark smock leaning on the railing.

The photograph was reprinted in the Willimantic *Chronicle* in November, 1992 along with an appeal for information. Thirty-six people in the photograph were subsequently identified. I would like to thank those who furnished information: Elizabeth Adamcik, Sophia S. Andrychowski, Stella Anthony, Doris G. Bednarz, A. Cote, Dominic Di'Ange, Mrs. LaBrie, John Love, Debra D. Merritt, Irene Monroe, Mrs. George Oulton, Mary T. Prescott, Alma Proulx, Eva Valliere, Denise M. Valliere-Peay, Dorothy Cartier Verteufeille, and Donna Young.

The vast majority of those in the photograph were of French Canadian and Polish extract, with a sprinkling of British and Italian. This picture is on display at the Windham Textile & History Museum, and includes the names of the 36 individuals identified.

being in the hospital. All they had was this big tub of warm water, and they
dipped this new born baby into the tub of water and then wrapped the baby up.
When the doctor was through, the man brought out a bottle of wine he had
made and he poured out a glass for me and the doctor. It knocked the hair right
off your head! This was between 11 at night and six in the morning.

They were great people. They couldn't do enough for you. They were so
thankful for everything you did for them. My husband put a fence up around
the house, and this man came over and worked hard to help my husband, and
wouldn't take anything for all his hard work. Today, their children are very well
educated. The DPs strongly believed in education. All of them I knew worked
in the mill. I worked with this woman who didn't speak a word of English, and
I communicated with her through sign language, but she picked up English
really quickly from this. They learned well because they wanted to work. There
were quite a few of them. They built churches and clubs in town. There were
a lot of Ukranians who worked in the American Thread.

One lady I worked with on cones, Mrs. Kadilka, was German. She was very
nice. Their children used to play with my children. When she was made into a
citizen in Putnam, I went with her and her husband to be a witness. He changed
their name to Teagarden. They were starting fresh, so they changed their name.
So the DPs were all kinds of nationalities. I remember there was also one Jewish
woman. There were very few negro people until the Spanish came in, but the
DPs were the best workers. They wanted to get ahead and what they have today,
they earned.

Some of the Hispanics were very lazy. I don't want to say anything about
nationalities, but they had an attitude like you owed them, but most of them
were OK, and I got along with them. A lot of the Spanish women in my
department were on piece-work, some of them were thread carriers and some
of them were fixers. There were all kinds of people working there. Have you
heard of the pop group the Monkees? Well, one of them worked in my
department. His name was Peter Tork. He was going through college and he
worked part-time one summer at American Thread. He was a tall thin fellow.
His father was a professor at the University of Connecticut. We also had this guy
in my department who was learning to be a psychiatrist. A lot of college kids
came in on second shift to earn some money to get through school.

I think American Thread invited the Spanish to work there. There was a
shortage of labor in the 1960s and they sent for them. There was a lot of jobs
then, but some people were not satisfied to work there, even though with piece-
work you could earn up to $300 a week.

I saw things change a lot. My first wage was $8 a week. When I started there,
I used to run only two machines, but after piece-work was introduced, a lot of
people used to run 14 machines. This all started by a few who were very fast, so
they kept adding machines. The wages kept going up through the years, but

American Thread didn't like it if you made too much money, and a few, who were very fast, made a lot. I remember when I was first earned $25 a week. I thought it was heaven. And after the union entered you would get regular raises, and this was passed through by raising the price of the thread to the customer. At one time, it was quality and quantity which American Thread wanted, but towards the end it was all quantity and the quality was not so good. For example, the glacé thread would get a lot of knots in it.

I worked on several different types of thread; mercerize, philco, soft shoe thread, glacé shoe thread, glacé intrinsic, nylon and wool, and a type of thread used in medical operations to sew people up. This thread went through a lot of different phases to get it just right. It had to be spotless, and the machines had to be spotless to run it, and it was made in different thicknesses from coarse to very fine. The finest type of that special thread was also used in the furrier trade. And there was also different sizes of shoe thread. Some of it was used to sew upholstery. There were also a lot of different colors produced on the tube spools where the girls had to work with a clipper and a knife to notch the tube so the thread would not unravel.

The working day was a basic eight hours, and anything over that was overtime. During the war I would work between 50 and 60 hours a week. When I first started in 1938, there was only one shift, seven in the morning until three in the afternoon. When the war started, we were put onto three shifts because there was so much going out because of the war. I remember working on a special khaki thread they used in the army. There was also a thread which was soaked in formaldehyde which was used to preserve corpses! This preserved the thread which held the uniforms together, so they wouldn't rot in the hot climates in the jungle. It smelled awful. Of course, these government orders were priority and we had plenty of overtime. I often worked 16 hour shifts during the war. Even right up to the end, in 1984 and 1985, I was working 12 hours a day to get certain orders out for the customers.

I think we were told about two years before they closed. We had an inkling that something was going off when they started moving machinery out of different departments. I was one of the last there as they worked on seniority. Right at the end, there were only three of us there. I was finished in October, 1985 and they closed down in December, 1985. One girl would be laid off, and I would have to learn how to do her job. Another girl would be laid of, and I would go do her job. I worked everywhere. When I got through, I was doing inspecting. They knew nothing about splicing down South, and they took photographs of my hands doing splicing. The bosses from down South came around and checked the different jobs to see how they were worked. I was sorry to see it close. That's why I enjoy going over to the Museum to work, because I can sit there and look over the road at the buildings I used to work in.

The Museum building was American Thread's main office, where the agent and his assistant had their offices, and where the telephone operator was. When I was a kid I often went to the Dunham Hall Library, but later that place, on the top, was used as a projection room and we would also have union meetings there. Where I work now, at the Museum, that building was originally a firehouse and then warehouses, and upstairs was a hall which people could rent if they wanted baby showers or birthday parties, and union meetings were held there sometimes. But in later years we held our union meetings in the union hall up Jackson Street.

The meetings for the signing of the contracts were every three years, and then we'd have to meet in the Polish Club or up at the high school. And we also received service bonuses and perfect attendance records. After 25 years service, American Thread held a party and a dinner for you at the Elks Club on Pleasant Street. They were good to their workers, but we got more holidays after the union came in. We got the day off after Thanksgiving and the day off before Christmas. Towards the end we got two extra holidays in our contract. One was Washington's birthday, I remember, and you got paid for the odd day when you couldn't make it to work. One day my car broke down and I couldn't make it in, so I called my boss and I got paid. Also, you qualified for extra holiday pay depending upon how many years you had worked there. The union also introduced the seniority system which was much fairer for those who had worked there the longest. Yes, the union introduced a lot of improvements over the years. The union was a good thing for the working person.

I really enjoyed it at American Thread. I enjoyed working on thread and I enjoyed every job I did. I had no problems with the bosses. Some people had problems with the bosses, but you went to work to work, and if you want to laze around, you should stay home. We took breaks. I smoked at one time, and we could make a system where you could take a few breaks and go for a smoke. Towards the end there were no official breaks so you had to work out your own breaks. When I first went to work there we had an hour off for lunch at noon. Everything shut down. It would start up again at one in the afternoon, and you worked through to four o'clock.

I liked it there, the working conditions were not bad. It was quite noisy. That's why I speak loudly nowadays! It was terrible where the carding machines were, and it was hard to hear anyone talk where the twisters were running. They wore earplugs in that department. But it was not that noisy in the glacé department. The only thing was that it was very, very hot and the guys used to work in their shorts up there.

There were other textile companies in Willimantic. There was a mill on Bridge Street which was a silk mill. Those mills were taken down sometime after the war. They were empty for a while. There was also a big plant on Valley Street which was some kind of thread mill. We had a lot of mills in Willimantic at one time. Electro Motive was one of the last to move in here. They made parts for televisions and radios. My husband worked there. There was also a pants factory and a braid shop. I worked there when things were slack at American Thread. The braid shop is still in town, on Milk Street. I was there for six months and I went to work at the pants factory for a couple of weeks, but I packed it in. I couldn't stand working on sewing machines, sitting down. I've always worked standing up, and I preferred that to sitting down. To this day I don't like to work at a sewing machine. The pants factory used to be on Valley Street extension, behind the braid shop. They made men's pants there. They were both Jewish concerns. And of course, there was the Holland silk mill, but that was not built on the river like the other mills.

There was not a lot to do in Willimantic. We had the movies, though. We'd pay 10 cents to go in and we'd buy a bag of candy for a nickel. The movies we saw in those days were nothing like the movies you see today! Thanksgiving and Christmas were special occasions when we were kids. You can get turkey all the time nowadays, but not then. We only had it when it was the holidays. I can remember my mother making the French meat pies. Real old fashioned meat pies. I miss them so much. I can't make them, but I remember walking in the house when I was a child and smelling the aroma of that meat cooking. She used to make seven or eight pies every time she cooked.

We had wood stoves where we lived, and we would have frost on the inside of the windows from the beginning of winter until the end, and we had a pantry which was so cold that my mother could make jello in it! It was wonderful and a good atmosphere to grow up in. All we had in the house was a wood stove and a pot bellied stove, and they supplied all the heat. In the summer we used the old ice boxes where you had to empty the trays which were full of water.

I remember our first radio. It was the main event of the evening when we sat down and listened to it, but we were up in bed by half past eight at night because my father was up at the crack of dawn. All the family was. He would light the wood stove at four in the morning, because he was at work at the first daylight to go and shoe horses.

We could never go into a dance hall. God forbid. We were a church-going family, but towards the end my father was not that religious. He always used to say that the Pope had a lot more money than us. I'm still religious to a certain extent. I'm Catholic and still keep up my religion. My brother was into his 20s before he ever went out with a girl. It was not allowed. As far as dancing was concerned, we were Catholic and belonged to societies which prohibited it. Missionaries used to look out and check that you weren't in dance halls, and if you were at a dance you would go to hell, fire and brimstone. That was it. We were brainwashed then! We believed in all this, but my mother was a broad minded person to an extent.

We always had a good time at New Years which was a very French holiday. I always used to hide because all the people would gather at the house and they would want to kiss you. I didn't like that and I used to go and hide. The Fourth of July was a good holiday to a certain extent. We had the firecrackers, and watermelon at the picnics. As I grew older, I rode horses. I grew up with horses of course. But my favorite social pastime was going to Baltic on the trolley every Sunday.

Willimantic is just not the same nowadays. We have all these malls on the outskirts and downtown is deserted. The only time I go into Willimantic itself is when I go to the bank, to the Museum or on a Sunday morning when a few of us gather at the donut shop before going to church. When I was younger you could walk down Main Street and you were not afraid of being attacked. I wouldn't walk down Main Street now at nine or ten at night. It's not safe at all. Things have changed. When I was a kid you could go to the gas station and pump the gas, and if the attendant was not there you left the money in a can. You couldn't do that today. People would drive away with the can and everything! It's probably not as bad as the big city, but it's like anyplace else now, what with the drugs.

CHAPTER 12

The 1925 Strike Ruined Willimantic.
We Lost All the Good People
Who Had Lived Here

Valentine Allaire, interviewed June 13, 1990

Tom Beardsley

I was born in Willimantic on February 6, 1908. My father, Stanislas Aubin, came from St. Valentine, Canada. My mother came from Quebec, both were French Canadians, and they met in Lowell, Massachusetts, where they made shirts. My mother used to press collars and cuffs on shirts - and my father often passed her notes as he went through the mill. That's how they met. My parents came here about 1904 or 1905, the year they built St. Mary's Church. My father got out of the mill in Lowell, and became a furniture dealer. He learned how to polish damaged furniture. He left Massachusetts to come and work for a furniture store in Willimantic, and we lived right around the corner from the store. He had a job there for a long time. Most furniture stores in those days were also undertakers. The two businesses ran together. He then opened a little second hand store across the street from American Thread. Some time after 1914, he went and worked for American Thread.

Before my father worked at American Thread, my oldest sister, Antonia, went to work there. I can't remember what her job was. The next one in our family to work there was Eva. She packed "Philippine balls" which used to go to the Philippines for the embroidery on babies' clothes. That was quite a thing years ago. The embroidered clothes were expensive. My other sister, Albertine, who will be 91 this year, worked there. I had a brother who worked there also. He'll be 87 on the 29th of August. And another sister who worked on ticketers first, before graduating onto winders when there was an opening. She's 85 now. Then I'm the next in the family. I'll be 83 on my next birthday. I have a brother who will be 81 this year, my youngest brother is 79 - we're all 80 except him. There's six of us still living. The oldest brother died in World War One, he worked in the box shop at American Thread. He was 18 when he was killed.

The building next door to the Museum was the employment office, run by a Mr. Webber, the employment manager. I remember getting my papers from a Mr. Smith at the employment office to get permission to work at age 14. I went to St. Mary's School, the present one is the third one. The first one burnt. The second one burnt, this is the third one. I went to the first one. I was going into the eighth grade, but I didn't want to go to school any more; I didn't like school. I told my father, and he said if you want to go to work, go down and see Mr. Smith at the employment office. Well, everyone knew my family, we were all good workers, and I was set on.

Mr. Smith took me up to the town hall to get my papers. I started work at American Thread in 1922 on the shuttle bobbins. But we were not allowed to work many hours, we had to go home at eleven in the morning. We started at six in the morning. The others got out at four in the afternoon. I had several jobs there, at American Thread. I started on shuttle bobbins, then cone winders and two pound tubes for the shoe thread. I also used to wind thread which was heavily coated to cover underground wires. It was very sticky.

Well, you get married and have babies, and you have to leave work, then you go back. When I went back I worked in the box shop just closing boxes for the Phillipine balls - as I told you, that's the job my sister did. She worked on a big machine which had about 15 ends of thread. Fifteen balls of thread would be formed at the same time, then it would stop, but she had these to keep filling little cups with the tickets which used to be mechanically fixed onto the Philippine balls.

It was years and years and years before they ever got a union in there, and when they started it, oh my God, that was an uproar. When they got the union in, that's when the trouble started. We all came out on strike, that was in 1925. My father-in-law was involved with the union. Many years before that strike, he started a union at American Thread but they didn't want a union in there, so my father-in-law, Philias Allaire, a French Canadian, had to hide the union charter in the back of a picture frame so no one would know about it. He had to keep things quiet, so no one must know where the charter was! My mother-in-law was the one who gave me the picture frame. She told me this story, I never knew her husband, he was dead before I got married. She said never throw this away, there is something valuable in the back of this picture, so I kept it and never opened it, but I was curious and opened it after all those years, and there it was, but I was frightened to damage it so I gave it to the Museum. [*The charter, dated January 14, 1902, is from the United Textile Workers of America, and announces the fact that a loomfixers local, no. 307, had been initiated in "Williamantic" Connecticut.*] My father-in-law was a loomfixer, a skilled man. He then went to work for that cotton mill on Bridge Street. He and his wife moved 11 times in one year, because he had to go where the work was.

There was no union when I started, but they did get a union. That's when they went on strike in 1925. Oh! And how I remember the strike. They had police in the Elms home down here. They had guns and ammunition in that little stone house, and the police used to take people into the mills in cars to protect them. They wanted me to go into work at that time on shuttle bobbins, but I was looking after my baby. We figured that when they were ready to settle we would go back to work. We never came down to picket; we were not that kind of people. Some people picketed until they almost died. That strike was never settled, so what was the use of going down there everyday to watch people walk in.

The strike started in March, and my dad went back to work in September. He thought it was long enough. He figured he was not getting any younger and the strike would never get settled anyway, and the worst was over. They no longer needed the police and the ammunition they had. They had to protect the help. That's what ruined Willimantic. It never came back to where it had been before the strike.

The American Thread brought replacement workers in from Lowell and Fall River. They were all cotton workers. They came because they needed the work, like anyone else. You can't blame them, but I never held it against them. I worked with them after the strike. What can you do? But some people would never take it, never, but when I see people going out on strike, I think, poor people, if they only knew, what's lost is lost is never gained, they never get it back, never. I don't know what the strike was about, because at that time they were making fairly good wages. My dad was satisfied, but I really don't know what they wanted, because I was only young and I didn't go into it too much.

My dad stayed home all summer long during the strike, he worked in his garden, he was a hard worker. We got by the best way we could, we didn't live high, and when it came to the mortgage, the woman told him not to ever worry about the mortgage and that she was satisfied if he only paid the interest until the strike was over. Everybody came out on strike, and American Thread said that everybody had to leave, but if anyone wanted to go back, they could go back, so the whole mill walked out. But they had taken chances on account of the pickets and the strikebreakers.

They had a tent city on the other side of the Natchaug River here, on the other side of where the Windham Heights apartments are today. People put up tents to live because they had lived in the American Thread Company's houses and they could not live there anymore because they were not working. The people who did live in the company houses paid their rent by the oldest millworker in that house having it deducted from their wages each week. I worked with one of the girls who lived their, and I asked her, "How come they take money out of your pay?" "Oh," she says, "that's because I'm the oldest in the house to work at the mill, so they take it out of my pay." I lived way up on Carey Street in those days.

After the strike, my dad got his old job back. He was a packer. He would pack cases, and seal them. They knew he was a good worker. He wouldn't go into work before then, because he wanted to avoid any trouble. People used to stand at the gate and poke you with umbrellas, and you can't take a chance on your life when you have a family.

Everybody started going back gradually. Everybody dwindled back, first this one and that one would come back in, and most of those who wanted their jobs back, went back. Most of the danger was over, you see, it was the danger they were afraid of. Some of the people were really mean, but we were not that type of people. I only came down once to see what was going off. I stood on the hill to look to see what was happening, and oh my goodness, I went back fast, we were not brought up that way, we were brought up quiet living people.

The 1925 strike ruined Willimantic. We lost all the good people who had lived here. The good living people were gone. There was one man who had a grocery store and a bakery, who trusted these people who paid up every week when they got paid, and during the strike he told them that they could come in his shop and get groceries as long as they paid him when they could. You know, they drained him. He had to sell the store. He was good to them, but these people disappeared. They went out of town to get other jobs. The good honest people went. But some of the people who came were also good honest people - when you got to know them. But this took time. It takes time to get to know people.

Some of the replacement workers were French Canadians, like us. There were people from all over. There used to be some very nice Italian people. Polish people were "A" number one. They used to work down there in Mills Number One and Two. They were hard-working people, very hard working. The French and Polish used to work in the finishing department. There were some who were Yankee, and a lot of the bosses were English. There were several languages being spoken.

I can still speak French. Parlez vous *français!* Parlez vous *anglais!* My mother made us talk French. She'd say, "Talk French in the house, so you will not lose your French, because when you go out to school and talk with your friends, you will always talk English, and you'll lose your French." It's nice to be able to speak two languages. One of my sisters would only speak English - but she married a Frenchman and went to live in France, and when she came back to America, she spoke the best of French. My mother could not believe it.

After I finished work at American Thread, I got a job at the New England Pants Factory in town, where they made men's trousers. I used to work on over 500 pairs a day, running the seams up the legs. I was there nine years, and during that time the displaced people came to town, they called them DPs, the Lithuanians, the Estonians, the Ukranians. So many of them worked at the pants factory that we renamed it the "port of embarkation." Some of them were very well-educated people. There was a woman who lived across the street from me. Her husband was a professor and she was a teacher and they had to come and work in American Thread. That was very degrading for someone who had such a good education in their own country, but the Germans had put them out. They were nice people, very, very nice.

The New England Pants Factory was on Milk Street, next to Rosenstein's braid shop. It had its roof blown off in the 1938 hurricane. It was a Jewish concern, owned by Abraham Cooperman. Mr. Cooperman had originally operated out of the old Holland silk mill. He then moved to the Windham silk mill on North Street, before moving to Milk Street. He moved after the War, and built that factory on Ash Street, which is now Akim Engineering.

I never had occasion to join a union, anywhere - except when I worked in the New England Pants Factory on Ash Street. We had to join the union there. I felt real bad, because we had all those DPs, and they didn't want to join the union. They said that the union was bad, but they gave them no choice. The union was the United Garment Workers. I worked there after the war, from about 1946 to 1955. I liked it very much because I liked sewing anyway. I didn't work during the War. I was looking after young babies, but my husband worked at Electric Boat on submarines.

I worked off and on for years at American Thread. Like I said, I worked on shuttle bobbins, tube winding, cone winding, shoe thread winding. They gave me different jobs every time I went back after having children. I was three years on shuttle bobbins, and in the box shop. It's hard to tell, but I worked from 1922 until around the time of the War. Sometime they ran out of work, and they laid you off. What could you do? I also worked for a spell in the silk mill up near Bridge Street, I worked there free for two weeks, just so I could learn to handle the raw silk. The other silk mills would not hire you unless you were experienced with silk, so how are you going to get experience if no one will give you a job?

I remember that my sister worked for about 10 years on Philippine balls, and that my father worked for about 15 years there. We were an American Thread family. My father worked there until he was 73. He used to walk to and from work, everyday. It kept him fit. He was wiry, thin and very active. I lived with my parents when I was first married, then I lived on West Park Street, then on Park Street.

I also worked at the Depot Restaurant, which was on Railroad Street. We didn't have an electric stove, it was all coal, but it kept the mashed potato and the peas warm and all the food that was there. We used to feed all the people who came off the trains. I worked there about a year or so, and went back to American Thread. I also worked in a florist shop, I started when I was about 55, the year I got my drivers' license. I worked until I was 65.

You always had to work hard, but I enjoy hard work, whether it was at the Pants Factory or at American Thread. I'm not bragging, but I was a workaholic, I loved work. I used to earn piece-work even when I was not supposed to - that was on tube winding at American Thread. We were all good workers, we always gave a good day's work for our pay. No one ever came out and timed us, the only ones who came around were those who were chasing after an order that had to be filled. Order chasers we used to call them.

There wasn't too much social life around years ago. There was a roller skate rink in Coventry, and we went up there on the trolley for five cents. They also had roller skating and dancing in the French Club, which was demolished. It was on Center Street. Then there used to be pinochle parties and whist parties. We used to go to those sorts of things. There were also a lot of theaters in town in those days. They had the *Gem* and the *Strand*, and years before then they had the *Bijou* on Main Street and the *Scenic* on Bank Street. Things were different in those days. Take the boys, for example. They weren't fresh then like they are today. They would never talk out of the way. They'd flirt with you and say "Hi babe" or something like that. It was a different life and this generation today is altogether different from us.

I'll never know why they ever tore down some of those houses on Center

Street. I'll never know. They were some of the best kept houses in town. It was really sad when they demolished them. I couldn't believe it. I remember that a lot of the people who lived there were millworkers. They were all good living people who raised their families. There was a lot of stores on those streets. There was a very well kept pool room on the corner of Center Street. There were never any police there nor rowdiness of any kind. Things were really different. There's a cinema complex there now. I only went there once, that was to see "On Golden Pond." It was a very good movie. If I had known they were going to show it on TV, I would have waited! But it was a wonderful story with some marvelous actors.

Willimantic was a busy railroad center when I was young. There were plenty of trains which came into Willimantic, plenty of them - the New York Central and the Vermont and Canadian trains came through, and the trains used to bring coal and lumber into town. You could go to Hartford for a dollar and a quarter! A lot of people used to travel on the railroad during the strikes. They got jobs in Hartford and traveled in every day.

I've always lived in Willimantic. I was born on Walnut Street. That's where my parents first lived when my father came to town to work in the furniture store. Then we moved to Windham Road because the family was getting bigger. But that house, which was made of cement blocks was not insulated, and the walls were damp in winter. We later took a rent on Jackson Street for a while, then my father bought a house on Carey Street. Today, the people will not believe you, but in those days you could build a house for $500. You'd buy the lumber and do all the work, and get a nice bit of land as well. The house on Carey Street cost my father $1,500. I don't know how much it's worth today.

CHAPTER 13

I Would Not Dare Walk Down
Main Street Nowadays

Clair Giordano, interviewed September 18, 1990

Tom Beardsley

I was born in 1922 on Card Street in Willimantic, and I have lived most of my life here in Willimantic, other than for two brief periods. When I was five-years-old my family moved up to Montpelier, Vermont. I think my father was looking for work at the time, but we didn't stop for long and we were back in Willimantic when I was seven. My parents were like gypsies, they moved around all over the place, I suppose they went where the work was. For example, my eldest brother and sister were born in Baltic, Connecticut, and I have a sister who was born in Taftville, Connecticut, and I have two brothers who were born in Vermont.

My father worked in the boiler room at the American Thread mills, stoking the fires, working nights. In those days we had moved down into the part of Willimantic called Sodom. Soon after, we moved up to live on Main Street when my father began janitorial work at the mill. My brother, who has passed away now, used to work at American Thread, but I can't remember what he did. My three sisters also worked there at various times, so all my family worked there. My husband's folks also worked there, my mother-in-law, brother-in-law and sister-in-law all worked there in different departments, and I worked in the testing department.

I was from a large family. I was one of 10, but one sister was only a baby when she died. My parents were French Canadian. My maiden name was Boisvert, which translated means Greenwood. We pronounce it "Boysvert." My father was born in Sherbrook, Quebec, but I'm not sure where my mother was born, I'd have to look it up. Her maiden name was Martel. I can read and write in French. My youngest daughter teaches French and Spanish at the middle school in the Windham system. I remember that years ago, some French parents in Willimantic would not allow their children to speak in any other language than French in the home. But it was different for us. We had Irish friends and Polish friends, and we picked English up when we went to school.

My husband was born in Connecticut, but his parents came over from Sicily. They went through Ellis Island. My father-in-law worked in construction and my mother-in-law worked at American Thread for many years. They worked very hard and gave their children an education. There were quite a few Italian families in Willimantic in those days. The Italians lived on Windham Road and up West Main Street, the Ferrignos, Ternellos, Insalacos and Melos, and of course my husband's family, the Giordanos.

When my husband went to school, some of the teachers would change his name and pronounce it Jordan. The immigration officers at Ellis Island used to do that sort of thing. They made the difficult names pronounceable, but my husband returned to the original Italian way of spelling his name after school.

A lot of the French Canadians lived down in Sodom in company housing, I could still name all the families who lived there. We rented our house from American Thread. It was near Recreation Park, but was knocked down years ago. It was great for us kids because we used to play in that park. There's a gas station there now. We walked everywhere in those days. I walked all the way up to St. Mary's School on Valley Street. I had a friend who lived on Union Street. I'd call for her on the way to school. I remember, very vividly, that on the way back from school we often stopped in at the American Thread library, to borrow books. I've always read a lot. I like to read.

We had a lot of fun in those days. All the kids in the neighborhood used to play games, like hide and seek. One of my brothers had a bike and charged us a nickel to ride on it. The other girls did the same thing to get their brothers' bikes and we rode around the streets. When we were a little older we started to find the boys. We never went on dates, but we liked boys. I was 16, going on 17 when I met my husband. We went steady for a while and used to go to a dance hall in Willimantic, on Valley Street, called the "Tab." Everybody used to go there. Sometimes I used to go there with friends and with my sisters. Naturally we'd dance with boys - but there was a curfew. Our parents made sure we were home for a certain time! Sometimes we went to a see a show in one of the theaters in town, and of course we went to see the movies. When I was older, my parents moved further up Main Street. That house is still there. It's on the corner next to "Jasper's."

We never visited any of the saloons in town, but my father liked his beer. The French Canadians used to make their own. My brothers also made their own beer, and the Italians used to make wine. It was always on the table in an Italian house but they never got drunk on it. They drank wine with their meals. For us it was beer, but I personally do not care for beer. There were several saloons on Jackson Street and down Railroad Street in those days.

As kids, we spent a lot of time down at the train station. We walked down Railroad Street and went into the five and ten. It was a big thing in those days to hang around the railroad station. It was a big event for us when the trains came in, but we never stayed too long. Thursday night was a very important night because the stores were open until nine in the evening. That was great, particularly when we were working and had some money to spend, but in those days we turned our wages over to our parents and they would give us spending money - about $10, but that was a lot of money then. Main Street was full of people walking back and forth and in and out of the stores. Thursday night was a big event in Willimantic.

I did not graduate from high school. My mother was sick and someone had to be around to look after her. My dad was already working at American Thread and we knew lots of people who worked there. I first worked in the Elm Hotel, American Thread's boarding house for single people. My dad was a janitor at American Thread, and if they ever had a banquet or meetings at holiday time in the big room there, at weekends, my dad went in and helped to prepare the food - he wasn't the chef though, just a helper. He invited me to work there and

This picture was taken in 1909 from atop the Windham Company's chimney, looking east. In the foreground are the granite mills of the Smithville Company, subsequently demolished in 1939. Clair's husband, Richard Giordano, was employed in their demolition, and he recalls how solidly they were built - with no expense spared. The granite was sold to local builders, and Mr. Giordano believes it was used to build houses on Gurleyville Road in nearby Storrs. *Francois Gamache.*

I helped him to peel potatoes. I earned a few dollars. I suppose that's how they got to know about me. I also had sisters who worked there, and they told me to go for a job. I had an interview and they asked me if I wanted to work in the testing department, and I said "sure." That would have been in about 1938. It was a nice department, very small with eight or nine girls and a woman boss. The boss's name was Jenny Peterson. She was the nicest person to work for.

We worked on a little machine and tested the strength of the thread. When the thread broke we wrote the number down on a pad and added the numbers up on an adding machine. We did so many per hour, but it wasn't piece-work. I was the last one in there, and the youngest, so I was their errand girl. I used to walk all over Number Five and Six Mills. It was an enjoyable job.

We went in at seven in the morning, and I would walk home for lunch with my sisters. We had an hour for lunch at midday and then worked until four in the afternoon. I can't remember exactly how much we were paid, but as I've said, my sisters and I handed our pay packets over to my mother, but she was fair with us. She gave us spending money and bought all our shoes and clothes. We were poor, but we weren't dirt poor. I probably realized we were relatively poor at school when we began to mix with the children whose parents were lawyers and doctors.

There was no union that I was aware of, not while I worked there. There may have been a union later, but I don't remember my sisters or my father being in a union. There had been a big strike at the mills when I was a very young girl. A lot of the workers who came to Willimantic to replace the strikers were French, and I recall that a lot of people here thought my family were scabs because we were French, but we were not here when the strike started, and we came back when it was over.

I met my husband at a party on Windham Road. It was at a hot dog roast at a place called the "rock" which was near the turn off for the Immaculata Retreat House. He was going to the Natchaug School and I was going to St. Mary's. My sister and I would go up to the "rock" on the trolley car and my future husband would walk us back to the trolley. There were some families who would not have approved of their daughter marrying an Italian, but my mother was very good, maybe because we lived in a neighborhood with so many different nationalities. My family and my husband's family got along well. My mother always told us to respect other people and other religions. We were all well-integrated. There were quite a few Irish families on Jackson Street and I had some good Irish friends. The Irish were here well before the French, and they had a lot of political clout in town. But there were no problems I know of regarding intermarriage. I was married in February, 1943 at St. Mary's Church, and my husband and I were both 21. My husband's church was St. Joseph's. We were both practicing Catholics.

My husband tried the American Thread and lasted a couple of days! He was the kind who liked the outdoors. He worked in construction for a long time, and liked to take things apart and put them back together. He went to work as a mechanic for the Ford garage on Valley Street, and after a while he tried selling cars, and he's been doing that since about 1953. He now works for "Gem Chevrolet" on Route 195. Just after we were married, we decided to move out to Florida to a nicer climate because my husband had had an accident at work and hurt his legs. The doctor thought that the warmer climate down there would be good for him. We were there less than a year and decided to come back to Willimantic. I then went to work for the Electro Motive Company for a couple of years, and I quit when the children began to arrive. I didn't work for years, then I got a job in the E. O. Smith High School and for 12 years after that I was a cook at the University of Connecticut.

I like Willimantic and Connecticut, although years ago Willimantic was a safer place to live. I would not dare walk down Main Street nowadays. We never used to lock our doors back then. We had a front door and a back door and the kids and friends just came into the house. But now we lock our doors and windows. We walked everywhere in those days, we often walked to church because there was always something happening there - it may seem a bit boring to kids today, but we had fun. We'd also go to the libraries and take out books.

We didn't move about like my parents did. After we returned from Florida, it was hard finding a rent, it was war-time, so we lived with my in-laws for about a year on Windham Road near to the Willimantic Camp Ground, and we then found a rent in a house near to where the IGA market is today. In those days it was called "Bergerons." And then we moved to Puddin Lane and we've been there for going on 34 years. We really like it there. It's like living out in the country, but actually, it is not that far from Willimantic. It's near to the schools and to my husband's work. Yes, I still like Willimantic despite the changes.

CHAPTER 14

I Was the Youngest in the Office so I Called Every-one 'Mister'

Joseph R. Lariviere, interviewed March 5, 1991

Joe Lariviere

I was born April 12, 1916 in Willimantic. My grandparents came to the United States in the 1890s from Drummondville, Quebec, and originally settled in Baltic, Connecticut, before coming to Willimantic. My grandfather worked at the Windham Silk Company on North Street right up until 1927 or 1928. My grandparents didn't speak any English. They only spoke French - they knew a little English, but they would never use it.

My father, Joseph Dominic Lariviere was born in Willimantic in 1896. He met my mother in Willimantic. She too was of French descent, her maiden name was Evonne LaChance, but she never worked in the textile industry. I had a sister, but she died during the flu epidemic of 1917. My father went to work for American Thread sometime around 1921, but left and began work on the railroad around the time of the 1925 strike. He worked there for about four years, in the dye house. He worked on the railroad until he retired in 1959. I lived with my parents on Meadow Street. There was a blacksmith shop nearby, owned by a man called Johnson, and they were shoeing horses almost all day long. That was in the rear of the Capital Motor Garage on Bank Street. On North Street, a large three or four-story building, the Hills building, burnt down. I was about eight-years-old. That was next to the barn where you could hire a team of horses, or a horse to go riding on a Sunday - and that was right next to the Windham Silk Company mill. The horses were used for plowing the snow from the road, and they used to leave a big pile of snow right in the middle of the road. It didn't matter then, because there weren't any cars on the road in winter. They were off the road because the batteries wouldn't work in the cold weather. I remember the trolley cars which ran down the middle of the street. In one direction they went to Coventry, and in the other direction, they went through to Baltic and New London. I think it was 10 cents a ride. They stopped running sometime around 1939.

Willimantic was mainly a French Canadian town in those days. I was a pupil at St. Mary's, the French school, and at Windham High. There were also quite a few Polish people in town, but it seemed at that time, that the Polish were a poor class of people. They were immigrants just coming in. Some of them could hardly speak English. There were also a few Italians in our part of town.

There were old stone mills on Bridge Street. They were run by the Corn Brothers. There's a shopping plaza there now. There was also the Holland silk mill which was on the corner of Church Street and ran right down to St. Mary's Church. On the opposite corner was the Masonic Temple and on the first floor were the funeral directors Avery and Van Zandt. The Willimantic Velvet Company was over on South Park Street. They closed down sometime around 1933 and Electro Motive took that building over.

There was a serious strike in town. I remember my grandparents talking about it. There were a lot of people in town on strike. I used to walk down to Main Street when I was a kid to watch the strikers. It seemed like a long way from home. They marched up and down in the rain and all. There was some trouble, the police were there, about half of the state's police force were here at that time. Frank McLean was the Captain and Leahy was the Lieutenant of Willimantic's police.

I went to Storrs College, which is UConn today. I started there with calculus and English and a little bit of science. School was different then, not like today where you take a lot of courses and get credits. I had to stop because it was too expensive. At that time I was working for the Hartford *Courant* delivering papers, and from around 1930 I worked part time in Heller's bicycle and tire shop next to the old post office on Main Street. My father was away on the railroad, and my grandmother had died, so I was raised by my grandparents, and there was just the two of us, my grandfather and I.

I also worked for a package store, from 1937, and then after about two years I went to the First National Store on the corner of Main and Walnut Street, which was a large grocery store. I was there for about a year, and then I went to work for American Thread. A man called George Twist used to stop in the First National, he was the employment man at American Thread. The employment office was in the Museum building next door (Dugan Mill). Twist said to me, ". . . come on down, I'll get you fixed up." So I went and began work in this building, which is today the home of the Windham Textile & History Museum, early in 1940. I started as a cost accountant in manufacturing, under George Wilcox. I then learned how to do payroll, and once in a while I went down to Mill Number Four to pay the paychecks for the third shift when the regular guy was on vacation or out sick. I was there for about seven weeks at one time and learned all the operations from carding right up to the dye house, so I could cost the operations. One guy used to operate about 30 of those carding machines at once. There were about 120 carding machines in Mill Number Four.

I worked on adding machines. My first wage at American Thread was about $24 a week, which was a pretty good wage in those days. It got me by. I was only earning $17 a week at the First National store. I was also still delivering newspapers for the Hartford *Courant*. I did that job for about 12 years. I got good tips at Christmas.

I started at eight in the morning and worked until about five in the afternoon. The agent was David Moxon, and his office was on the second floor. Outside of his office were six desks and I worked with Messrs. Wells, Wilcox, Albert Sorten and Bud Anderson. Wilcox and Sorten were of English descent. The four of us worked next to the window, which is now in the Museum's office. Many of the others were of Irish and French Canadian descent. On the left of us was the office manager's office. We worked on payroll, cost accounting and the prices of manufacturing.

Things were much more formal in those days and we called each other "Mister" - not just the managers, but your fellow workers were referred to as Mr.

Sorten or Mr. Wilcox. I was the youngest in the office so I called everyone "Mister." The agent, Moxon was English, and so was his assistant, Bert Shaw. Eventually all the managers moved down to Carolina.

It was a relaxed atmosphere, but we had to be in that office in the morning at eight. We worked through till noon and had an hour off for lunch, and came back and worked till five in the afternoon. It was strict inasmuch as you had to get your work done. We never talked to each other much unless it was business. We had a coffee break in the morning for about five minutes. We worked some overtime, especially at the end of the financial year, closing up the costs. On warm days we went out for lunch. There were quite a few restaurants around and we regularly went to "Liberty's."

I don't recall many social functions organized by the American Thread Company. I went on picnics once in a while, but I didn't go much anywhere as things were rather expensive. I couldn't afford to drive a car. The insurance in those days was very high. Sometimes I went down to Norwich and watched a movie, and sometimes down to Watch Hill in New London. That's about all. There were a few activities down at Recreation Park. There used to be trotting and car racing, although in those days you were racing if you drove over 35 mph! I never went in bars as I never drank much. Willimantic was a busy railroad town, although I never went much anywhere on the train, but I did use it to go down to New Haven for the draft, although that was after I left here. I was working at Pratt & Whitney then.

I liked the job at American Thread. It had its boring times but it was a good job as you had to use your head a bit. I worked on calculators and adding machines, and when I left Willimantic I had some training on machinery in Hartford before actually starting at Pratt & Whitney. I started in Willimantic as a machine operator. From Willimantic I went to Southington, and from there to East Hartford. In Southington I worked on the cylinder heads. I worked on a Bullard vertical turret lathe and worked on crankcases which went into the nose of the aircraft, working on the small engines with one propeller. Towards the end of the war we worked on the hydraulics on the jets, which was experimental work. I left right after VE Day. The working conditions were hot, there was no ventilation. It was hotter than in Mill Number Four.

The wages were very high. I made $100 a week at Pratt & Whitney, and the department bonus was 20% so I made $120 a week, and sometimes it was 50% so I made $150 a week. Other firms were also paying good bonuses. Royal and Underwood Typewriters were making bomb sights, and they paid good wages. Colt firearms also paid good bonuses if the production was up. My last wage at American Thread was about $25 a week and my first wage at Pratt & Whitney was $92 a week!

After Pratt & Whitney, I worked for Sealtest Dairy which was a branch of Kraft Foods, and I worked in the dairy business from 1946 to 1972. When they closed down I went to Borden's at Wethersfield until 1981, and then they closed up. I was just about ready for social security anyhow. But in 1982 I started work for the Shwartz Company as a parking garage and lot attendant at Traveler's in Hartford. I live in East Hartford, but I visit Willimantic regularly, and subscribe to the *Chronicle* to keep in touch.

EPILOGUE

A Future of Potential

This book features an industrial urban community that has, for all purposes, disappeared. However, memories and research have brought 'Thread City' back to life. The reader can dance and listen to the big bands at the "Tab" on Valley Street, take the trolley to Coventry Lake on a hot Sunday afternoon, sit in the *Scenic* and the *Gem* and watch the silver screen, hear the "steam gong" which called the workers to American Thread, walk along Valley Street and note its many silk mills, stand on the footbridge, or at the railroad depot, and smell the steam locomotives which snarled the traffic on Union Street, Main Street and Bridge Street. The reader can also walk down Center Street, Broad Street and Temple Street, and admire the fine buildings which once stood in this old historic center of town, or visit the old town's numerous saloons which slaked the thirst of millworkers, walk along Main Street's packed sidewalks and be bustled by the Thursday night shoppers.

The downtown area is relatively quiet today. Almost everyone interviewed declared they would never dream of walking down Main Street after dark. This look back at Willimantic has not lingered upon the city's historical problems regarding racism and poverty, but modern-day social and economic inner-city decay is evident, as it is in every other city across the nation. Today, Main Street is easy-on-the-eye. The hill section is beautiful, but this pleasant community has been in a steady decline since the end of the Second World War. Urban redevelopment in the early and mid 1970s merely beautified the area. For many, the demolition of the old core of the town was an heartbreaking experience. Was it progress? Probably not. A new brush does not always sweep clean. But one has to consider the mind-set which ruled urban planners in the 1950s and 1960s. Thankfully, the "tear it down, and start again" attitude is disappearing. Old, decaying buildings have been renovated in numerous urban areas across the United States, helping to rejuvenate many abandoned downtown sections. The money used to demolish the old Center Street area might have been better employed in renovating buildings which dated back to the 1860s and 1870s - but we're all wiser after the event.

Can the decline be reversed? The key lies in the plans to redevelop the vast, vacant American Thread mill site. The introduction of small industries and shops could provide badly needed jobs, and fit into a "history park." The Windham Textile and History Museum can be a catalyst in the revival of the old city, and develop sections within the mills to remind the world of their historical importance. For example, here are the sites of the world's first experiments in electrical illumination for industry. A revival could also be encouraged by new railroad and improved highway links with Hartford and

Providence. It is no coincidence that Willimantic's decline began once the rail route to Hartford disappeared during the 1950s, and was speeded by the flight of the American Thread Company in 1985. We often have to look back to look forward. What was at the heart of Willimantic's nineteenth-century growth and prosperity? One does not have to look far to find the answer: the complex rail links which connected Willimantic to Hartford, New York, Boston and Providence. Without doubt, this old industrial city has great potential. With luck, enough investors and planners will note the fact. I hope this book will inspire them.

NOTES

INTRODUCTION

1. Willimantic *Chronicle*, February 7, 1910. Also see Chapter 6, "Silk City 1900-1940."
2. See David K. Dunaway, Willa K. Baum (eds), *Oral History: An interdisciplinary Anthology* (AASLH & OHA 1984).
3. Paul Thompson, *The Voice of the Past: Oral History* (Oxford, 1978).
4. Ibid., 211.

PROLOGUE

1. Willimantic *Public Medium*, November 24, 1849.
2. *Connecticut State Register and Manual*, 1983.
3. Willimantic *Chronicle*, June 1, 1881.

INDUSTRY

Chapter 1

1. Willimantic *Chronicle*, January 14, 1882.
2. Ellen D. Larned, *History of Windham County, Connecticut.* (2 Vols.; Worcester, Mass., 1880), II, 512, 513.
3. Willimantic *Journal*, March 30, 1877.
4. Willimantic *Journal*, July 26, 1866.
5. Larned, Op. Cit., 512; Willimantic *Chronicle*, April 5, 1881.
6. *Seventh Census of Connecticut Industry* (1850).
7. Lloyd Baldwin, *Willimantic Before 1850* (1895), 10.
8. Willimantic *Journal*, November 2, 1865. Charles Lee was a founder, and the first deacon of Willimantic's Congregational Church in 1828. His obituary refers to him as a "pioneer of cotton manufacture in this place."
9. Horace Winslow, *A Centennial Discourse Delivered in the Congregational Church, Willimantic* (1877), 5.

10. Lloyd Baldwin, Op. Cit., 9.

11. Willimantic *Chronicle*, January 6, 1909.

12. *Seventh Census of Connecticut Industry* (1850).

13. Allen B. Lincoln, *A History of all the Fire Companies ever formed in Windham Connecticut, Together with a Sketch of the Willimantic Water Works* (1885), 25.

14. H. F. Donlan, *Willimantic Journal Souvenir Edition* (1894), 37.

15. Willimantic *Journal*, June 14, 21, 1861.

16. Willimantic *Journal*, May 2, 1862; February 14, 1867; Willimantic *Chronicle*, May 5, 1892.

17. Bruce Clouette and Matthew Roth, *Connecticut's Historic Highway Bridges* (CT Dept. of Transport 1991). Today, Connecticut's second largest stone arch bridge spans the Connecticut River at Hartford. Each single arch of the Bulkeley Bridge, built between 1903 and 1908, has a span of 119 feet. The 80 foot span of Willimantic's Bridge Street bridge earns it the title of Connecticut's third largest stone arch bridge.

18. *Willimantic Directory* (1877), 10; Willimantic *Enterprise*, February 15, 1877.

19. Willimantic *Enterprise*, March 18, March 25, May 6, 1879.

20. *Leading Businessmen of Willimantic* (Mercantile Publishing Company, 1890), 27.

21. *Windham Deeds*, Volumes 79, 198, 206; Willimantic *Chronicle*, November 4, 1895; March 28, April 2, 1907.

22. Windham Manufacturing Company's 1825 ledger, held by the Connecticut Historical Society.

23. Larned, Op. Cit., 518.

24. Ibid., 512.

25. Allen B. Lincoln, *A Modern History of Windham County* (Chicago,1920, Volume I, 131 - 133).

26. Willimantic *Journal*, June 20, 1873.

27. Richard Bayles, *History of Windham County, Connecticut* (New York, 1889), 341; *Willimantic Directory* (1877), 8, 9.

28. Willimantic *Journal*, January 4, 1881.

29. Willimantic *Chronicle*, February 2, 1881; September 20, October 18, 1882; Willimantic *Journal*, November 17, 1882.

30. *The Willimantic Annual* (1888). "Summary of Leading Local Events During 1887."

31. Willimantic *Chronicle*, January 5, 1887; Donlan, Op. Cit., 17. The Normal School building burnt to the ground on August 21, 1943, but a new state teacher's college was built on the site and opened in 1947.

32. Willimantic *Chronicle*, May 17, 1899, February 1, August 4, 1910.

33. Willimantic *Chronicle*, May 21, July 26, October 26, 1926.

34. Willimantic *Chronicle*, July 18, 1888.

35. William R. Bagnall. *Record of American Textile Manufacturers* (1908), 1723-1724. This vast, unpublished work contains a mass of detail regarding America's textile manufacturers during the 19th century. Bagnall (1819 - 1892) spent ten years, 1882-1892, collecting the information. It was documented 16 years after his death. A microfilmed typescript is held by the Connecticut Historical Society. The Willimantic *Journal* of August 12, 1892, reported Bagnall's death, which

occurred on August 3, 1892. The brief obituary states that Bagnall, a graduate of Wesleyan University, class of 1840, had been engaged for 12 years upon a "History of the Textile Industries of the United States." It was intended to publish the work in three volumes in the near future.

Chapter 2

1. Hartford *Courant,* July 2, 1867.
2. Willimantic *Enterprise,* March 23, 1877.
3. *The Windham County Business Directory* (1861).
4. *Ninth Census of Connecticut Industry* (1870).
5. Willimantic *Journal,* March 2, 23, 1877.
6. Bayles, Op. Cit., 342.
7. *History of the Willimantic Linen Company* (New York, 1868), 9.
8. Allen Bennet Lincoln, *A Memorial Volume of the Bi-Centennial Celebration of the Town of Windham, Connecticut* (Hartford, 1893), 75.
9. Willimantic *Journal,* April 19, May 24, 1866.
10. Willimantic *Chronicle,* January 6, 1909.
11. Hartford *Courant,* August 17, 24, 1857.
12. Willimantic *Journal,* October 7, 1879; Willimantic *Chronicle,* February 11, 1880.
13. Bagnall, Op. Cit., 1724 - 1735.
14. Willimantic *Journal,* June 6, 1861.
15. Willimantic *Journal,* January 17, November 7, 1862.
16. Willimantic *Journal,* June 5, 1863.
17. Willimantic *Journal,* September 25, 1863.
18. Willimantic *Journal,* December 29, 1864.
19. Willimantic *Journal,* December 27, 1866.
20. Willimantic *Journal,* May 11, 1865.
21. *History of the Willimantic Linen Company* (1868), 16.
22. Willimantic *Journal,* August 10, 1865.
23. Willimantic *Journal,* January 31, 1867.
24. Willimantic *Journal,* September 18, 1863.
25. Willimantic *Journal,* April 1, 29, December 15, 1864.
26. *Scientific American,* November 26, 1864.

Chapter 3

1. *Appleton's Cyclopaedia of American Biography* (1888) Volume I, 179; *National Cyclopaedia of American Biography* (1909) Volume X, 102-103.

2. Copies of William Barrows' Civil War letters were donated to the Windham Textile & History Museum by his granddaughter, Molly Fultz, in 1990. They consist of 47 letters to his mother, father, brothers and sisters dated between October, 1861 and June 1865. The collection also includes a letter from General George Meade to a Mr. Russell at the Boston Custom House, recommending that Barrows be appointed to a position there, and an undated letter from General Alexander Webb to General Raymond Lee at West Point, recommending Barrows for a temporary position after his training period at the Lowell Machine Shop had been completed. There is also a letter from Colonel Norman Hall to Barrows, inquiring about Barrows role in the Battle of Gettysburg, and a reply from Barrows to Hall.

3. Major General George G. Meade to Judge Russell of Boston, Massachusetts, August 25, 1868.

4. Major General Alexander Webb to General Raymond Lee of West Point, August 28, 1871.

5. Daniel Pidgeon, *Old World Questions, New World Answers* (1884), v.

6. Ibid., 221.

7. Willimantic *Journal,* February 23, 1877.

8. Willimantic *Enterprise,* February 11, 1879.

9. Hartford *Courant,* March 14, 1878.

10. Willimantic *Chronicle,* February 28, 1883.

11. Willimantic *Chronicle,* May 31, 1882.

12. Willimantic *Journal,* April 14, 1882; Willimantic *Chronicle,* April 12, May 31, 1882.

13. Willimantic *Chronicle,* November 28, 1883, January 28, March 25, April 15, 1885; May 1, 1889; July 25, 1892.

14. Willimantic *Journal,* March 3, 1893.

15. New Haven *Evening Register,* February 22, 1883.

16. Hartford *Courant,* March 14, 1878; *Willimantic Directory* (1881), 30.

17. Willimantic *Enterprise,* February 11, 1879; Bayles, Op. Cit., 343; Lincoln, *History of Windham County,* Op. Cit., 126.

18. Willimantic *Journal,* June 25, 1880.

19. Willimantic *Journal,* October 7, 1904.

20. The Loomer Opera House theater, shop and office block was built on Main Street by Samuel Loomer in 1879. It was considered to be the finest variety theater between Hartford and Providence. The most famous names in American vaudeville played there. Silent and talking movies were shown in the 20th century. It was demolished in 1940.

21. Willimantic *Enterprise,* December 31, 1878; Willimantic *Chronicle,* April 12, 19, 26, 1882.

22. Willimantic *Journal,* October 6, 1882.

23. Willimantic *Chronicle,* August 18, 1882.
24. Pidgeon, Op. Cit., 222.
25. Willimantic *Chronicle,* December 20, 1882; July 18, 1883; Willimantic *Journal,* December 22, 1882.
26. Willimantic *Chronicle,* August 25, 1886.
27. *Atco Star,* Vol. 2, No 11, January 1925, 9.
28. Willimantic *Chronicle,* January 15, 1942.
29. Kenneth Jackson, *Crabgrass Frontier* (New York, 1984), 74.
30. Ibid., 80.
31. Willimantic *Chronicle,* October 20, November 10, 1880; August 10, 1881.
32. Pidgeon, Op. Cit., 224.
33. For a more detailed account of the development of the "Oaks" and the dance pavilion, see *A Tour of The Oaks* (WTHM 1992), on sale at the Windham Textile and History Museum.
34. Willimantic *Journal,* May 14, 1880; Willimantic *Chronicle,* May 19, 1880.
35. Willimantic *Chronicle,* March 3, 1880.
36. Willimantic *Journal,* April 2, 1880.
37. Willimantic *Chronicle,* December 15, 1880.
38. Willimantic *Chronicle,* November 28, 1883.
39. Willimantic *Chronicle,* October 3, 1883.
40. *Harpers New Monthly Magazine,* vol. LXX, February 1885, 452-466.
41. Ibid., 463, 464, 465.
42. Stanley Buder, *Pullman: An Experiment in Industrial Order and Community Planning,* 1880 - 1930 (1967), 102. Buder mistakenly refers to the disgruntled employee as "Walter" Barrows. He used a letter from Barrows to Ely as his source, which suggests that William Eliot Barrows may have been the disgruntled employee.
43. *Harper's,* Op. Cit., 462.
44. William Eliot Barrows to Richard Theodore Ely, March 8, 1885. This letter was referred to by Stanley Buder (see Note 42)
45. Willimantic *Chronicle,* February 14, 21, 28; March 7, 14, 1883.

Chapter 4

1. Willimantic *Enterprise,* January 28, 1879.
2. Willimantic *Enterprise,* February 11, 1879.
3. Willimantic *Enterprise,* October 29, 1878.
4. Willimantic *Enterprise,* September 9, 1879; Hartford *Courant,* September 18, 1879.
5. Willimantic *Chronicle,* December 10, December 24, 1879.
6. Willimantic *Journal,* April 23, 1880.
7. Edward C. Lavelle, *Adventure in Partnership The Story of Electricity in Hartford* (1964), 38.
8. Glenn Weaver, *The Hartford Electric Light Company* (1969), 4, 5, 21.
9. Willimantic *Journal,* September 10, 1880.
10. Willimantic *Chronicle,* September 22, 1880.

11. Willimantic *Journal,* September 24, 1880.
12. Willimantic *Journal,* May, 27, 1881.
13. Willimantic *Chronicle,* June 29, 1881.
14. Willimantic *Journal,* September 22, 1882.
15. Willimantic *Chronicle,* July 11, August 15, 1883.
16. Willimantic *Chronicle,* August 29, 1883.
17. Willimantic *Chronicle,* October 3, 10, 1883.
18. Willimantic *Chronicle,* October 29, 1884.
19. William T. O'Dea, *The Social History of Lighting,* (London, 1958), 117.
20. Willimantic *Chronicle,* April 3, 1889.
21. Willimantic *Chronicle,* April 17, 1889.

Chapter 5

1. *Chronology of Mansfield* (1974), 78. Mansfield Historical Society (MHS),
2. Samuel Slater was an English mechanic who is credited with introducing the industrial revolution to the United States. British technology led the world in the late 18th century, and Parliament, wishing to preserve Britain's advantage, banned the exportation of machines to other countries. In 1789, Samuel Slater, a mechanic with a good memory, came to America and reproduced a cotton-spinning machine for Almy and Brown, two merchants of Providence, Rhode Island. Almy & Brown built a cotton factory at Pawtucket, Rhode Island, and put Slater in charge.
3. MHS, Op. Cit., 68.
4. L. P. Brockett, *The Silk Industry in America* (1876), 52.
5. They included Zalman Storrs in 1833, Messrs. Rixford and Dimock at Mansfield Hollow in 1839, James Royce and Lewis Brown at Gurleyville in 1848, Messrs. Atwood and Crane at Atwoodville in 1850, Phineas Turner and Ebenezer Gurley at Mansfield Hollow in 1850, and Emory B. Smith at Gurleyville in 1870. In 1854 Philo and John Hanks built a new mill at Hanks Hill near the original 1810 mill which remained on the site until it was removed to Greenfield Village Henry Ford's Dearborn, Michigan museum, "Greenfield Village," in 1930. MHS, Op. Cit., 75, 79, 81, 82, 94.
6. Ibid., 83.
7. Brockett, Op. Cit., 58, 76.
8. Willimantic *Chronicle,* November 22, December 27, 1882.
9. Willimantic *Journal,* May 13, 1892.
10. Hartford *Courant,* July 14, 1870.
11. Hartford *Courant,* August 11, 1870.
12. Lincoln, *A Memorial Volume,* Op. Cit., 146.
13. *Ninth Census of Connecticut Industry* (1870).
14. Willimantic *Journal,* October 4, 1866.
15. Horace Winslow, Op. Cit., 11.
16. MHS, Op. Cit., 90.
17. Willimantic *Journal,* April 27, September 21, October 5,1865.
18. Bayles, Op. Cit., 344.

19. Willimantic *Chronicle*, October 10, 1888.
20. Willimantic *Chronicle*, February 2, 1929.
21. Willimantic *Chronicle*, October 20, 21, 1932; August 29, 1933.
22. Hartford *Courant*, July 14, 1870.
23. Willimantic *Journal*, October 17, 1873.
24. Winslow, Op. Cit., 11.
25. Willimantic *Chronicle*, January 7, 1880.
26. Willimantic *Chronicle*, July 12, August 16, 1882.
27. Willimantic *Chronicle*, July 27, 1887.
28. A detailed biography of Charles Fenton appears in Allen Lincoln's *Modern History of Windham County* (1920), Volume II, 1226. Fenton was a central figure of the development of the silk industry in New England after the Civil War.
29. Willimantic *Chronicle*, August 29, 1888.
30. Willimantic *Chronicle*, January 9, 1889.
31. Donlan, Op. Cit., 11.
32. Willimantic *Journal*, March 11, April 6, October 14, November 18, 1892; January 6, March 10, May 5, November 10, 17, 1893.
33. Willimantic *Journal*, August 11, November 10, 1893; Willimantic *Chronicle*, October 10, 1894.
34. Willimantic *Journal*, May 4, 1894; Willimantic *Chronicle*, October 10, 1894.
35. Willimantic *Chronicle*, April 13, 22, 26, 30, 1895.
36. Willimantic *Chronicle*, May, 6, 7, 9, June 11, 12, 1895.
37. Willimantic *Chronicle*, September 14, 1895.
38. Joseph Dwight Chaffee and Frederick Barrows, his treasurer at the Natchaug Company, were arrested on April 19,1899, and charged with embezzlement and making false entries in the Company's books. For those interested, the details of the arrest, and the ensuing long and complex trial, can be found in the issues of the Willimantic *Chronicle* dated April 19, June 27, 28, 29, 1899. Chaffee eventually retired from the silk business on August 31, 1927. He died in the Windham Community Memorial Hospital on December 14,1938, aged 92.
39. Willimantic *Chronicle*, December 11, 18 20, 24, 1895; April 22, 1899.
40. *Tenth Census of Connecticut Industry* (1880).
41. Willimantic *Chronicle*, February 9, 1881.
42. Willimantic *Chronicle*, March 29, 1882.
43. Willimantic *Chronicle*, March 28, 1883.
44. Willimantic *Chronicle*, May 23, 1888.
45. Willimantic *Chronicle*, June 6, 1888.
46. There are several excellent accounts of the Coxey movement in print. I would recommend Nell Irving Painter's summary in her, *Standing at Armageddon: The United States, 1877-1919* (1987),117-121, which draws on and includes a wide bibliography of the subject.
47. Willimantic *Chronicle*, April 28, 1894.
48. Willimantic *Journal*, December 22, 1893.
49. Willimantic *Journal*, June 27, 1873.
50. Willimantic *Journal*, March 3, 1876.

51. Pliny LeRoy Harwood, *History of Eastern Connecticut* (3 Vols, 1931), III, 20-23; New York *Times*, June 4, 1926.
52. Bayles, Op. Cit., 347.
53. Willimantic *Chronicle*, April 28, December 15, 1886.
54. Donlan, Op. Cit., 47-48.
55. Willimantic *Chronicle*, May 26, 1886.
56. Willimantic *Chronicle*, October 12, 1887.
57. Willimantic *Chronicle*, July 18, 1888.
58. Willimantic *Chronicle*, September 8, 1892.
59. Willimantic *Chronicle*, May 8, 1917.

Chapter 6

1. Willimantic *Chronicle*, November 30, 1910.
2. Willimantic *Chronicle*, February 25, July 13, 1905.
3. The Willimantic Board of Trade, *Why Don't You Locate in Willimantic? This Means You.* (1906).
4. Willimantic *Chronicle*, January 10, 12, 18; May 3, 1910.
5. Willimantic *Chronicle*, April 12, 1916.
6. See interview with Mitchell Rosenstein in "Community," Chapter 9.
7. Willimantic *Chronicle*, August 20, 1910; January 10, 1911; January 17, April 15, May 12, 1938.
8. Willimantic *Chronicle*, February 2, 1929.
9. Willimantic *Chronicle*, June 7, 1929.
10. Interview with Arthur Garneau, March 21st, 1992.
11. Willimantic *Chronicle*, November 5, 11, 21, 1932.
12. Willimantic *Chronicle*, July 17, 20, 26, September 15, 1933.
13. Willimantic *Chronicle*, April 1, October 15, 17, 1938.
14. *Willimantic City Directories* (1938-1942); Willimantic *Chronicle*, February 6, 11, March 16, 1939.
15. Willimantic *Chronicle*, February 8, 1938.

COMMUNITY

Chapter 1

1. When he died in 1919, Hugh Clark Murray was considered to be one of the richest men in Willimantic. He was born in Catrine, Ayrshire, in 1849, and emigrated to the U.S. in 1871. Murray worked in dry good stores in Boston and Providence before arriving in Willimantic in 1879. He opened a store in the Loomer Opera house in 1880. In 1893, Murray erected the fine brick building which still stands on the western corner of Main and Church Streets. The "Boston Store" opened for business the following year, attracting custom from across New England .
2. See the interview with John Love in Chapter 2 of "Community."

BIBLIOGRAPHY

1. SOURCE MATERIALS

A. Unpublished Sources

Adventure in Partnership: The Story of Electricity in Hartford, by Edward C. Lavelle. A typed manuscript held in the library of the Hartford Electric Light Company.

Ledger of the Windham Manufacturing Company for 1825. Connecticut Historical Society (CHS).

Record of American Textile Manufacturers (1908), compiled by the Reverend William Bagnall and held on microfiche by the CHS.

Windham Deeds. Various volumes, held at the Windham Town Hall.

William Eliot Barrows' Civil War correspondence. Unless stated, letters below are reproduced by permission of his grand-daughter, Molly Fultz.

William Eliot Barrows to Sara Maria (Lee) Barrows, his mother, October 16, 1861; Elijah Porter Barrows, his father, December 23, 1861; Sara Maria, his sister, January 3, 1862; his father, January 5, 1862; his father, February 21, 1862; his mother, February 28, 1862; his father, March 23, 1862; his father, Spring, 1862; his mother, May 13, 1862; his father, May 23, 1862; his mother, June 2, 1862; his father, June 7, 1862; his father, June 12, 1862; his father, June 26, 1862; his sister, Sara Maria, July 14, 1862; his mother, July 19, 1862; his father, July 22, 1862; his mother, September 29, 1862; his father, December 9, 1862; his mother, December 12, 1862; his father, March 13, 1863; his father, April 20, 1863; his father, June 5, 1863; his brother, Franklin Lee, June 12, 1863; his father, June 18, 1863; his mother, June 22, 1863; his mother, June 30, 1863; his father, July 17, 1863; his father, August 3, 1863; his father, August 14, 1863; his father, August 26, 1863; his father, September 5, 1863; his mother, October 19, 1863; his father, October 29, 1863; his father, December 10, 1863; his father, December 11, 1863; his father, December 16, 1863; his mother, March 9, 1864; his sister, Charlotte Malvina, April 24, 1864; his father, June 5, 1864; his brother, Nathan, July 18, 1864; his father, October 18, 1864; his sister, Sara Maria, December 11, 1864; his father, December 31, 1864; his mother, May 3, 1865; his father, June 21, 1865.

Adjutant General George W. Ruggles to Professor Elijah Porter Barrows, June 15, 1865.
Major General Alexander S. Webb to William Eliot Barrows, September 17, 1865.
Colonel Norman Hall to William Eliot Barrows, August 18, 1866.
Major General George G. Meade to Judge Russell of Boston, Massachusetts, August 25, 1868.
Major General Alexander S. Webb to General Raymond Lee of West Point, August 28, 1871.
William Eliot Barrows to Richard Theodore Ely, March 8, 1885: Courtesy of archivist Harold L. Miller, of the State Historical Society of Wisconsin.

B. Published Sources

PUBLIC DOCUMENTS

U. S. Bureau of the Census:

Seventh Census of Connecticut Industry, 1850. Microfilm, Connecticut State Library (CSL).
Ninth Census of Connecticut Industry, 1870. (CSL).
Tenth Census of Connecticut Industry, 1880. (CSL).
Tenth Manufacturing Census of United States Industry, 1883. Homer Babbidge Library, University of Connecticut.
Manuscript Population Census, Windham - Willimantic 1860, 1870, 1880. Microfilm, Eastern Connecticut State University (ECSU).

State of Connecticut:

Bureau of Labor Statistics, 1879-1890. ECSU.

NEWSPAPERS

Willimantic:

Weekly Chronicle. 1877-1891.
Daily Chronicle, 1891-1992.
Weekly Enterprise, 1877-1879.
Journal, 1861-1866, 1872-1911.
Public Medium, 1847.

Various holdings, microfilm, bound volumes and loose single issues held at CSL, ECSU, CHS, the Windham Historical Society and the offices of the Willimantic *Chronicle.*

Hartford: *Courant,* 1857, 1879. ECSU.
New Haven: *Evening Register,* 1883. CSL.
New York: *Daily Graphic,* 1877. New York Historical Society.

MAGAZINES

The ATCO Star, 1924, 1925.
Scientific American, 1864, 1879.
Scribners' Monthly, 1878.

PAMPHLETS - DIRECTORIES

Baldwin, Lloyd E. *Willimantic Before 1850.* Willimantic: Willimantic Journal, 1895.
Beardsley, T. R. *Willimantic Women: Their Lives and Labors.* Willimantic: Windham Textile and History Museum, 1990.
_____ *A Tour of the Oaks.* Willimantic: Windham Textile and History Museum, 1992.
Borough of Willimantic, Connecticut. Its Advantages as a Manufacturing Point. Willimantic: Willimantic Board of Trade, 1887.
History of the Willimantic Linen Company of Willimantic, Conn. New York: Willimantic Linen Company, 1868.
Illustrated Review of Northeastern Connecticut. New York: Sovereign Publishing and Engraving Company, 1891.
Leading Businessmen of Willimantic and Colchester. Boston: Mercantile Publishing Company, 1890.
Lincoln, Allen Bennet. *A History of all the Fire Companies ever formed in Windham, Connecticut, Together with a Sketch of the Willimantic Water Works.* Willimantic: Willimantic Journal, 1885.
_____ *The 1888 Willimantic Annual.* Willimantic: The Connecticut Home Printing House, 1887.
National Cyclopaedia of American Biography. New York: J. T. White Company, 1909.
Why Don't You Locate in Willimantic? This Means You. Willimantic: Willimantic Board of Trade, 1906.
Willimantic Directory. New Haven: Price and Lee, 1880-1900.
Windham County, Connecticut Business Directory. West Killingley: Windham Transcript, 1861.

Winslow, Horace. *A Centennial Discourse Delivered in the Congregational Church, Willimantic.* Willimantic: Willimantic Journal Book and Job Print, 1877.

Wilson, James Grant. & Fiske, John. eds. *Appleton's Cyclopaedia of American Biography.* New York: D. Appleton & Company, 1888.

2. SECONDARY MATERIAL

BOOKS

Barber, John Warner. *History and Antiquities of Every Town in Connecticut.* Hartford: A. Willard, 1836.

Bayles, Richard Mather. *History of Windham County, Connecticut.* New York: W. W. Preston & Company, 1889.

Brockett, L. P. *The Silk Industry in America: A History Prepared for the Centennial Exposition of America.* New York: The Silk Association of America, 1876.

Buder, Stanley. Pullman: *An Experiment in Industrial Order and Community Planning, 1880-1930.* New York: Oxford University Press, 1967.

Clouette, Bruce. and Roth, Matthew. *Connecticut's Historic Highway Bridges.* Hartford, CT: State Department of Transportation and the Federal Highways Authority, 1991.

Cole, J. R. *History of Tolland County, Connecticut.* New York: W. W. Preston & Company, 1888.

Donlan, H. F. ed. *Willimantic Journal Souvenir Edition,* Willimantic: Willimantic Journal, 1894.

Dunaway, David K. and Baum, Willa K. eds. *Oral History: An Interdisciplinary Anthology.* Nashville, Tennessee: American Association for State and Local History & the Oral History Association, 1984.

Haraven, Tamara K. and Langenbach, Randolph. *Amoskeag: Life and Work in an American Factory-City.* New York: Pantheon Books, 1978.

Harwood, Pliny Leroy. *History of Eastern Connecticut.* Chicago and New Haven: The Pioneer Historical Publishing Company, 1931-1932. Three Volumes.

Jackson, Kenneth T. *Crabgrass Frontier: The Suburbanization of the United States.* New York and Oxford: Oxford University Press, 1985.

Larned, Ellen Douglas. *History of Windham County, Connecticut.* Worcester, Mass., Published by author, 1874 -1880. Two Volumes.

Lincoln, Allen Bennet. *A Memorial Volume of the Bi-Centennial Celebration of the Town of Windham, Connecticut.* Hartford: 1893.

_____ *A Modern History of Windham County: A Windham County Treasure Book.* Chicago: The S. J. Clarke Publishing Company, 1920. Two Volumes.

Mansfield Historical Society, History Workshop. *Chronology of Mansfield, Connecticut, 1702 - 1972.* Mansfield, 1974.

O'Dea, William T. *The Social History of Lighting.* London: Routledge & Paul, 1958.

Pidgeon, Daniel. *Old World Questions and New World Answers.* London: Kegan, Paul, Trench & Company, 1884.

Stave, Bruce M. and Palmer, Michelle. *Mills And Meadows: A Pictorial History of Northeast Connecticut.* Virginia Beach: The Donning Company, 1991.

Thompson, Paul. *The Voice of the Past: Oral History.* Oxford and New York: Oxford University Press, 1978.

Weaver, Glen. *The Hartford Electric Light Company.* Hartford: The Hartford Electric Light Company, 1969.

Finders' Guide to the
Windham Textile & History Museum's
Oral History Collection

May, 1993

The Windham Textile & History Museum's oral history collection currently consists of audio tapes and transcriptions of 35 interviews conducted in two time periods. Bruce Stave conducted an oral history project during the fall semester of 1979 in the History Department at the University of Connecticut, entitled, "The Millworkers of Willimantic." He supervised a class of under-graduate students who came into Willimantic and sought out individuals who had labored in the city's textile mills. One of the students, Daniel Schwartz, continued the interviewing through 1980. The typed and handwritten tran-scriptions, which Dr. Stave donated to the Museum, contain a great deal of important raw, historical information.

The essay in Chapter 1 of 'Community' in *Willimantic Industry and Community*, is based upon those transcriptions. The rest of the collection consists of tapes and transcriptions generated by the Windham Textile and History Museum's Oral History Institute since its March, 1990 inception. Tom Beardsley was the interviewer in each case, except for the interview with Grace James which was conducted by student intern Tracie Molinaro from Connecti-cut College. Dr. David Shuldiner, of Connecticut's Department of Aging, assisted in the interview with Robert Mathieu. Various student interns were present at other times to witness the interview process. The oral histories are listed in alphabetical order by surname. Those conducted by UConn in 1979 are depicted as OHP. Those conducted by the WTHM Oral History Institute are depicted as MOHI. This Guide will be circulated to libraries, schools, colleges and universities.

Valentine Allaire

Valentine Allaire was named after her father's hometown in Canada, St. Valentine. She was born in Willimantic in 1908. Her parents settled here in 1904. Valentine's father-in-law, Philias Allaire, secretly organized a local of the UTWA at American Thread in 1902. She started work at American Thread in 1922 and has vivid recollections of the 1925 strike. She recalls Willimantic's various ethnic groups, the railroad depot, the New England Pants Factory, and Willimantic before urban redevelopment. MOHI

Robert Beaudreault

Bob Beaudreault is the manager of the vacant American Thread complex in Willimantic. This is an account of his early life in Putnam, Connecticut, the U.S. Marines, the Mansfield Training School, skyjacking in the Big Apple, and his eventual career as a plumber and boiler engineer, plus a job description of his mill duties. He has supervised the site since 1985, and gives an insight into the massive complex. MOHI

Romeo and Mary Benoit

Romeo Benoit was the first president of the CIO Textile Workers Union at American Thread in Willimantic, circa 1939. Mary Benoit's contribution exceeds that of her husband. She took part in the 1925 strike and is highly critical of the AFL leadership in the dispute. There are accounts of where dismissed strikers found employment. Mrs. Benoit died in 1981, aged 83. OHP (Interviewed by Daniel Schwartz).

Richard Benoit

In 1979, Richard Benoit was a 29-year-old machine fixer in American Thread's Number Four Mill in Willimantic. He was born in Quebec and came to the U.S. in 1963. A useful account of shopfloor attitudes to union and management, the duties of a box maker, yarn-steamer, machine fixer and an assessment of the ethnic make-up of the mill workforce at the time. French speaking Benoit taught himself English by watching movies on TV. OHP (Interviewed by Daniel Schwartz).

Edith Blackburn

Edith Blackburn was born in Lancashire, England in 1908. She emigrated to America twice. She recalls her youth in a Lancashire milltown. These experiences prepared her for Willimantic - but not for American weather. She began work at American Thread in 1923 and worked in Rhode Island for the duration of the 1925 strike. She returned to Willimantic in 1927 and worked as a spooler at American Thread for the next 27 years. There are recollections and opinions about the Depression, mill work, unions, Puerto Ricans and old time Willimantic. MOHI

Gladys Bowman

Gladys Bowman is a descendant of an English tailor who arrived in Willimantic shortly after the Civil War. She never worked at American Thread. Gladys was a teacher, one of the first degree recipients from the new Willimantic State Teachers' College. She possesses a deep knowledge of local history, and gives insights into the various districts of Willimantic, its various ethnic make up. Her French Canadian mother lived in "Cork Alley." She recalls the "Tab," and the famous dance bands who performed there. MOHI

Vera Brobek

Vera Brobek was born in the part of Europe once known as Yugoslavia. She came to the U. S. in 1966, aged 15, and began work at American Thread in 1970. Vera became part of the city's Ukrainian community. She recounts the problems of being a recent immigrant and describes her job on the second shift in American Thread's Mill Number Four. OHP (Interviewed by Daniel Schwartz).

Celeste Roy Bucko

Celeste Roy Bucko was born in Willimantic in 1909. She started work at American Thread in 1923 and recalls the 1925 strike. She was also employed by Electro Motive. Ms Bucko is staunchly anti-union. There is an account of the local political influence held by American Thread, and some colorful recollections of life in Willimantic, plus references to social class and an example of working class feminism. She recalls a social occasion caused by the strike: "The striking families held 'kitchen dances,' attended by other strikers and sympathizers, designed to raise funds." She also recalls the housing; "Those old mill-houses all looked the same...if anyone came home a little tipsy, they never knew which door to go in." OHP (Interviewed by Daniel Schwartz and Barbara Klein).

Henry Costello

Henry Costello was hired by American Thread in 1910 because of his baseball expertise. He began work as a clerical assistant and rose to office manager. He also worked in the Company's New York City offices. He left in 1938. He was 87 in 1979. The interviewer allowed Costello to wander into reflective and philosophical realms, and the results are not as informative as they should have been. Costello knew Charles Hill (see "Community" chapter 1) well and still visited him: "He was a good man for American Thread...he's not much to look at, he's a homely fellow, but he's broad minded." OHP (Interviewed by Daniel Schwartz).

Leona Delude

Leona Delude is very critical of the American Thread Company. This is a good example of a worker who did not fit in with the rigors and stresses of shopfloor, industrial production. Q. How did one gain advancement at American Thread? A. Join the ten pin bowling team. She worked in the mills for 26 years until being unceremoniously laid off in 1972, but she later found job satisfaction in a meals-on-wheels program for the elderly. OHP (Interviewed by Nancy Leonard and Lynn MacDonald).

Rose Deshaies

Rose Deshaies was born in Quebec in 1916. Her parents were recruited by American Thread as replacement workers during the 1925 strike. She recalls being insulted by local kids whose parents were on strike. She began work at American Thread in 1932, and was put to work as a waitress for the State Police lodged in the Company's "Elms" boarding house during the duration of the national textile strike in 1934. Rose was a staunch trade unionist and worked as a winder. She retired in 1980. MOHI

Lil Despathy

This interview stands in strict comparison to Ms. Delude's. Lil Despathy worked as a winder at American Thread between 1916 and 1967 - and loved every minute of it. This interview, and the one above, demonstrate that each account must not be examined in isolation. OHP (Interviewed by Dan Krause).

Rose Dunham

This is an account of a woman who considers herself to be "extremely Irish" despite the fact that she was born in Willimantic in 1906. Rose trained to be a teacher but worked summers at American Thread packing spools. She vividly recalls the 1925 strike, recalling the marches, police, guns and the dispute's subsequent impact upon the community. Rose worked in New York City during the Depression, but returned to her home town. This is an informative interview covering many topics. MOHI

Margaret Dubina and Mr. Dubina

This is an excellent account of the bitter 1925 strike at American Thread. Margaret Dubina worked for the union as a translator for the large number of Polish strikers. There is also a brief account of life in one of Willimantic's many silk mills before the First World War, and an example of ethnic discrimination. It is the best of the 1979 histories. OHP (Interviewed by Daniel Schwartz).

Daniel Gallagher

Daniel Gallagher was Joint Board Manager of all local Willimantic textile unions from 1943 until 1965. This interview provides a useful account of the duties of a high union official. He talks about the legacy of the 1925 strike, the Taft-Hartley Act, advances for female employees, seniority rules and the early history of the CIO in Willimantic. OHP (Interviewed by William Knox).

Arthur Garneau

Arthur Garneau was born in Barford, Quebec in 1907. After a varied adventurous life, and a momentous cross country drive, he arrived in Willimantic in 1930. There is a graphic account of working conditions in Willimantic's Corn Spinning Company Plant on Bridge Street. "You knew you had to work under those conditions, because there were four or five people waiting for your job." The interview also contains some interesting accounts of life and characters in Willimantic. MOHI

Clair Giordano

Clair Giordano was born in Willimantic in 1922. She recalls her youth in Willimantic. Clair started work at American Thread in 1938, testing the tensile strength of the thread. This account provides a starting point to further investigate the history of the local Italian-American community. Clair Boisvert married Richard Giordano, a man of Sicilian descent. Mr. Giordano's school teachers attempted to change his name to "Jordan." MOHI

Charles Hill

Charlie Hill was probably one of the most well known personalities in Willimantic. He was 92 when interviewed. Hill was involved in a wide ranging number of local social and civic activities. He provides a "management" point of view of the 1925 strike. There is a good account of the strikers' attempt to sequester the funds of American Thread's Athletic Association to support their industrial action. Regarding Willimantic's ethnicity, Hill was a staunch melting pot supporter. OHP (interviewed by Nancy Leonard and Lynn MacDonald).

Frances Hoxie

Frances Hoxie was born in Willimantic in 1917, a product of old Yankee stock. Her mother worked in the M. M. Johnson thread mill in Mansfield Hollow which, after 1902, began the manufacture of optical accessories and jewelry. Today, it is commonly known as the Kirby Mill. Her father worked as a thread carrier at American Thread in Willimantic. Her cousins, Jenny Ford and Hattie Gates served for many years as librarians in the Dunham Hall Library. Although she moved from Willimantic as a child, Frances has clear recollections of the town. She also recalls industries in Manchester, Connecticut. Frances has worked at the Connecticut Historical Society for 53 years. MOHI

Grace James

Grace James was born in Willimantic in 1899. Her father was Scottish, her mother English. Her father was the boss dyer at American Thread and a friend of the English-born manager of American Thread, David Moxon. Thanks to this family connection, Moxon gave Grace a job as a clerk in 1917. When work was slack she wound samples of colored cotton onto cards. Grace worked at American Thread until she was married. Grace's husband refused to let her work, and she did not work again until after he died. She knew Willimantic intimately, not being away from the town for more than four of her 91 years. MOHI (Interviewed by Tracie Molinaro).

Charles Johnson

Brook Johnson made news in Connecticut in 1992 when he challenged incumbent Senator Chris Dodd. Brook's father, Charles, arrived in Willimantic in the late 1930s when his father was appointed pastor at the old Methodist Church on Church Street, Willimantic. Charles Johnson joined the ranks at American Thread as a young man. He joined the USAF during the war, and rose to the rank of captain. He returned to Willimantic after the war and made another rapid rise through the ranks. He eventually become general manager of all American Thread's plants. This interview gives an insight into the textile trade in the South, the management structure at American Thread, and the many mergers from which the current Coats-American Company has evolved. MOHI

Sophie Kaminski

Sophie (Racho) Kaminski was the daughter of Polish immigrants. She was born in Willimantic in 1906 and has excellent recollections of Willimantic before World War One. She started work for American Thread in 1921, packing shoe thread. Sophie recalls the 1925 strike and Willimantic's various ethnic groups. She was divorced in 1946 and brought up two sons single handedly, by working around the clock hours at the mill. She retired in 1982, aged 76, piling up 50 years of service. MOHI

Frank Klosowski

Frank Klosowski was born in Poland in 1904. He came to the United States through Ellis Island in 1913. He was a well known tailor in town and a pillar of Willimantic's Polish community. Frank was a keen local historian and had researched the history of the town's Polish community. He often wrote in the local newspaper about the old days in Willimantic. Frank was a paper boy for the town's legendary Irish-American mayor, Danny Dunn. This is a very informative interview and supplies a great deal of background for those interested in the history of Willimantic. MOHI

Joseph Lariviere

Joseph Lariviere was born in Willimantic in 1916. He lived on Meadow Street as a boy and held a wide variety of jobs in town before being employed by American Thread as a cost accountant and payroll clerk in 1940. This interview provides insights into office work. Joseph recalls his workmates and the section of the building which now houses the Windham Textile and History Museum. He left American Thread in 1943, and tripled his weekly wage at Pratt & Whitney. MOHI

John Love

John Love was the first ever university trained management employee at American Thread. He started work in Willimantic in 1947 as a management trainee, and became General Manager of the Willimantic plant in 1961 at the age of 36. In 1963 he moved to New York to take charge of American Thread's research, personnel and purchasing, and remained with the Company until 1979. This is an inside view of the top echelons of one of America's leading textile manufacturers. MOHI

Robert Mathieu

"Bobby" Mathieu was born in Columbia, Connecticut in 1920, and began working at American Thread in 1940, after working on a farm. He started with general yard duties and briefly worked in Mill Number Four's carding room, before taking an "apprenticeship" as a pipe fixer. This gave Bobby the run of the works as a maintenance man. He discusses the old water wheels and water turbines, and other intricacies of his trade, which enabled the plant to continually produce its textiles. He possesses an intimate knowledge of the vast American Thread site. MOHI

Irene Monroe

Irene Monroe spent over 30 years at American Thread save some wartime service and family leave - and she enjoyed every minute of it. She was born in Willimantic in 1919. Her father was a blacksmith. Irene worked in the finishing department in Mill Number Six. She witnessed the gradual change from cotton to synthetic textiles. Irene recalls the various ethnic groups, management and a member of the 1960s pop group, the Monkees, who spent his summers working at American Thread. MOHI

Isabelle Moran

This is an excellent account of the Irish community which dominated Willimantic between 1890 - 1920. For example, discover "Cork Alley." It demonstrates social mobility, and changing ethnicity patterns. It is also an entertaining account of life in Willimantic in the early years of this century. Miss Moran was an office worker at American Thread between 1909-1955. There are references to Willimantic's social classes and the areas which constituted the better parts of town. OHP (Interviewed by Daniel Schwartz).

Corrine Pender

Corrine (Krombie) Pender was born in South Coventry, Connecticut in 1903. She recalls her early childhood in New York City and New London. Her family eventually resettled in Coventry. Corrine started work as a teenager in Willimantic's telephone exchange. She later worked in the Holland silk mill and was briefly employed as a nurse. She returned to the silk industry, and worked at Cortizelli's in Putnam, Connecticut. From there to the Washburn silk mill in Coventry and on to Pratt & Whitney. MOHI

Morris Rosenstein

This is of particular interest as it tells the story of Willimantic's surviving textile producer. The Roselin factory has been producing braid and ribbon on Milk Street since 1935. The company was started by Morris' father in New York City in 1921. Morris took over the business when his father died in 1963. The interview reveals details about the company's various products, its workforce, a strike and the devastating 1938 hurricane. MOHI

Gail Smith

Smith's family has lived in Windham since colonial days. Gail is quite knowledgeable about local history. He was born in Willimantic in 1915, and recalls life in Willimantic including its class and race differences, the 1925 strike and American Thread's domination of the local economy. Smith holds an interesting view of the scab workers. In his opinion they were, "a different kind of French people...less genteel...but the nuns at the Catholic school straightened out their kids...and the French people in the 1940s were just as good as those in the 1920s." OHP (Interviewed by William Knox).

Alice Stabile

This oral history is not too informative. However, the information and humor contained in Ms. Stabile's autobiographical essay, which accompanies the interview, makes up for its lack of content. Alice was of French descent. She was born in 1911 and worked at American Thread between 1927 and 1935. She discusses the ethnicity of the workforce and relations with management. OHP (Interviewed by Nancy Leonard and Lynn MacDonald).

Dorothy Stygar

Dorothy was born in Stafford Springs, Connecticut in 1929, of French Canadian and Czechoslovakian parents. Her childhood was spent on Center Street, Willimantic. She vividly recalls the area of Willimantic which no longer exists. She started work at American Thread in 1941, in the Packing Department, and then moved onto spring and cone winding. Dorothy worked for a short time in a "tedious" job at Electro Motive, but returned to American Thread. She recalls the various ethnic groups at the mill, and asserts that "Willimantic has changed a lot - but not for the better." MOHI

Betty Tianti

American Thread can claim that it launched the career of a future State Commissioner of Labor - albeit unwittingly. Betty (Mathieu) Tianti was born in Plainfield, Connecticut in 1929. She recalls the tough times of the Depression. She was the first in her family to complete high school. She found her way into textile mills and a job in New York City. Betty arrived in Willimantic in 1956 to work at American Thread. By 1962 she was a union organizer in the South. By 1965 she was president of the local. In 1970 she began work in the State Labor Department. In 1988, Betty Tianti was appointed State Commissioner of Labor by Governor of Connecticut William O'Neill. MOHI

Ken Tyler

Ken Tyler was a foreman in the dye shop at American Thread. He was born in Sterling, Connecticut in 1926. His working life began at the U.S. Finishing plant in Sterling, where he was employed as a jig dyer. He did service in the navy for three years, and worked several jobs before landing in Willimantic in 1955, to begin work in the printing department at American Thread. He quickly progressed and became assistant foreman in the dye house. This interview includes views on ethnicity and gives detailed accounts of the dyeing process involved in textiles. MOHI

Victoria Uskurs

Willimantic has a large population of "DPs", or displaced persons, political and economic refugees from Europe who came to these shores after the Second World War. This subject, plus the Latino immigration into the city, deserves a volume of its own. Victoria's story is moving and eventful. She arrived in Willimantic at Christmas, 1950. It bore little resemblance to Latvia. MOHI

The tapes and transcriptions of the oral histories included above may be used for research and/or inclusion in publications, academic work, and school or local history association projects. Written permission must be obtained from the Windham Textile and History Museum Oral History Institute. Phone: (203) 456 - 2178. The source must be quoted in any subsequent written or published work. If more information is needed about individual histories, also refer to *Willimantic Industry & Community* (WTHM, 1993).